THE KOREAN LANGUAGE

SUNY Series in Korean Studies
Sung Bae Park, editor

THE KOREAN LANGUAGE

Iksop Lee and S. Robert Ramsey

State University of New York Press

Published by
State University of New York Press, Albany

© 2000 State University of New York

All rights reserved

Printed in the United States of America

For information, contact State University of New York Press, Albany, NY
www.sunypress.edu

Production by Dana Foote
Marketing by Anne Valentine

Library of Congress Cataloging-in-Publication Data

Lee, Iksop.
The Korean language
p. cm.— (SUNY series in Korean Studies)
Includes bibliographical references and index.
ISBN 0-7914-4831-2 (alk. paper)—ISBN 0-7914-4832-0 (pbk.: alk. paper)
1. Korean language. I. Ramsey, S. Robert, 1941- II. Title. III. Series.

PL908.Y524 000
495.7—dc21   00-047035

10 9 8 7 6 5 4 3 2

CONTENTS

Contents

PREFACE

The project to produce a book on Korean began for me in the summer of
1993. The State University of New York at Stony Brook had just initiated a
large-scale project to produce a series of publications on Korean culture,
and a general work on the language was to be one of the first volumes in the
series. At the time, I was a visiting scholar at Seoul National University. One
day, around the middle of my stay on campus, my old friend and colleague
Professor Lee Iksop approached me about the possibility of working with
him and some other SNU scholars to create a work, in English, on the Korean language. I was immediately interested. For a number of years I had
been planning to write a book on Korean, and this project seemed like a
good opportunity to finally get that done. I had worked with Professor Lee
before and looked forward to doing so again.

As it happened, I was living in the Hoam Residence of the university,
and the general project supervisor from Stony Brook, Professor Park Sung
Bae, was staying just a floor below me. It was a simple matter to get together
and discuss the project. Professor Park and I had a pleasant meeting and in
short order worked out an informal agreement. The idea was that Professor
Lee and his Seoul National colleagues were to write a Korean-language
manuscript describing the Korean language, and I was to translate and edit
the work, doing what was necessary to make it into a book for the English-
speaking world.

In less than a year, in the spring of 1994, I received a manuscript in the
mail from Professor Lee. According to the explanation that arrived with it,
the text had been produced by Professor Lee together with two other colleagues, Lee Sang Oak, a phonologist and linguistic historian, and Ch'ae
Wan, a younger scholar specializing in morphology and syntax. It consisted
of eight chapters. Chapters 1, 2, 6, and 8 had originally been written by Lee
Iksop himself, while Lee Sang Oak had contributed drafts of chapters 3 and
7, and Ch'ae Wan drafts for chapters 4 and 5. Lee Iksop had then rewritten
the entire text, aided by Ch'ae Wan's editorial help. The result was a manuscript with the cohesion of a work by a single author. The arrival of that
manuscript marked the beginning of my active participation in the SNU-
Stony Brook translation project and my own work on this book.

From the beginning, I saw my job as twofold. On the one hand, I was
to produce an English-language source of information about the Korean
language that was both informative and readable. But, on the other hand, I
needed to present, in as faithful a way as I could, my Korean colleagues'

views about their language and society to this same English-speaking audience. Those two tasks were not always easy to reconcile. By saying this, I do not mean there was anything about those views that I necessarily disagreed with, or that they were linguistically inaccurate; on the contrary, I felt that the views of Korean scholars were often refreshingly independent of the hegemony of American-style linguistics. Korean ideas and approaches were certainly worth presenting to the English-speaking world. Rather, the challenge for me was one of intercultural communication. Emphases are often different. Discourse styles are certainly different. As a result, my procedure has all along been first to read and assimilate ideas and arguments, then, based upon those views, to write a new text in English. At times I have perhaps exercised editorial license to its outer limits, adding thoughts and materials from a variety of sources, rewriting sections—in one case a whole chapter—whenever I thought the changes would clarify or add interest. In this enterprise, I am grateful to Professor Lee and his colleagues for their trust and patient understanding. Still, in the end, I feel that I have presented their ideas sympathetically and without serious distortion. Both organizational structure and basic content remain Professor Lee's.

Let me give a simple example. On the first page of the introduction, under the heading of "Korean Writing," two sentences of the original Korean text were devoted to Hangŭl. The text stated simply that Hangŭl had been invented in 1443 and that since that time there had been rich records of phonemic writing in Korea. The remaining two pages of the section were given over to other matters, mainly a description of pre-alphabetic writing, covering points most ordinary Koreans do not know. My feeling was that, if anything about writing belonged in an introduction intended for Westerners, it was some mention of the cultural significance of Hangŭl. Of course, what I had to say was patently obvious to anyone native to Korean culture. Besides, a wonderfully detailed and rich analysis of Hangŭl followed, in the same text, in Chapter 2. Still, before plunging into details about history and orthographic practice, the English-speaking reader would, in my judgment, find a brief overview of Hangŭl in the introduction both useful and interesting. The change amounted to a difference in presentation, not basic facts.

A somewhat more serious change was what I ended up writing about Japanese loanwords. The Korean relationship with Japan is not an easy one to deal with for Koreans, but it becomes difficult for others to understand many things about the modern language without knowing something of what happened earlier in this century. We Americans, with our laissez-faire attitude about language, have great difficulty understanding why Koreans would care so much about word origins. Why on earth would they want to purge perfectly good words from their language just because the words happen to come from Japanese? (I suspect all Westerners with any knowledge of the two languages have thought about this matter.) In a discussion Professor Lee and I had about the subject one day, I remember vividly a poignant story he told me about how, as a first grader in a country school, he was given strict orders to stop using his Korean name. Cultural and linguistic identity becomes more important to a people who have had theirs threatened.

I have not made many changes in the chapters on grammatical structure. However, on occasion I decided that certain additional information was necessary to clarify or round out the discussion. I supplemented chapter 3, "Phonology," for example, with some remarks about the morphophonemic processes detailed in Martin 1954, as well as basic information about certain classes of irregular verb stems. These irregular verbs are touched on in the text somewhat later, in the chapter on dialects, but it seemed particularly important to me that the non-Korean reader at least be exposed to these irregularities as part of an introduction to the phonology of the standard language. Elsewhere, in chapters 4, 5, and 6, I have added information from other sources, principally Martin 1992.

In the fall of 1995 Professor Lee came to the University of Maryland as a visiting scholar, and during the seven months he was here, he rewrote, among other things, much of what had been chapter 5. In the process, he separated that part of the text into two separate chapters; these are now chapters 5 and 6. Professor Lee also made changes in the text, deciding, for example, to present the copula as a type of inflecting stem alongside verbs and adjectives rather than as a unique type of nominal particle, which is how the copula is usually analyzed in traditional Korean grammars. For some of these decisions, I have added brief background remarks in the body of the text or in endnotes.

We also agreed that the chapter on history, chapter 8, needed to be expanded and rewritten, and that part of the editorial task fell to me. As a result of that decision, I wrote a new chapter organized along lines very much like those of the original draft but with greater illustrative detail and more background information. The views of Korean linguistic history presented there are largely those of Lee Ki-Moon 1972a, with supplementary information taken from a variety of other sources, but especially Martin 1992. In the section on Middle Korean grammar, I relied heavily on An and Yi 1990.

As a general introductory work, this book has two unusual chapters. Chapter 7, "Honorifics and Speech Styles," is a long but readable essay on how the Korean language reflects the structure of Korean society. Chapter 2, "Korean Writing," presents a great deal of information about writing practices in Korea that is otherwise not available in English.

My own orthographic choices are ones that have by now become common practice among Western Koreanists. In the body of the text, Korean words are transcribed in McCune-Reischauer Romanization. But there are two exceptions. One is that, when known, Korean personal names are written according to individual preferences; for example, I write "Lee Iksop" (in the Korean order of family name first) instead of "Yi Iksŏp." For bibliographic purposes, however, I revert to McCune. The other exception is very minor: the name of the Korean alphabet is written as *Hangŭl* instead of as *han'gŭl*, without the apostrophe used in McCune to show syllable boundary.

As all Koreanists know, the McCune-Reischauer system is an attempt to represent Korean sounds as heard by Westerners (read 'English speakers'), and its spellings are relatively independent of how the same words are written in Hangŭl. Yale Romanization, on the other hand, is the romanization of choice for linguists, because it is constructed to reflect linguistic structure. In addition, Hangŭl can be mapped fairly easily into Yale using the rules given in Martin 1992:9-12. For these reasons, I transcribe linguistic examples in a slightly modified version of Yale Romanization.

In the Yale system, word spacing is used much more liberally than in Hangŭl, and in a few cases I have altered Yale word spacing to reflect the Korean spellings more directly. For example, I write 'be clean' as *kkaykkus-hata* with a hyphen. Writing the form as two words, with a space, as is done in Yale Romanization *(kkaykkus hata)*, would call into question the structural analysis described in chapter 4 (4.1). And, because of this choice, I also write other cases of noun plus *hata* with a hyphen, as in *salang-hata* 'to love'. Here *salang* 'love' is clearly an independent, separable noun, but Korean orthographic practice indicates that *salang-ha-* is a verb stem. I also write verbal forms such as 'gape' as *pel.ecita* instead of *pel.e cita*; I write *mek.eto* 'though one eats' instead of *mek.e to*. I generally follow Yale in setting off particles by spaces, but the compound particle *eyse*, for example, is written solid instead of as *ey se*. These are all rather minor changes, but they seemed to me to better fit the spirit of the Korean text. In any case, for comparative purposes and for the convenience of readers who prefer it, I have also transcribed the examples in Hangŭl in all the chapters following the introduction.

In accordance with usual linguistic practice, a form enclosed in angled brackets, for example, /sewul/, represents a phonemic analysis. Forms in square brackets, [səul], are phonetic transcriptions of the sounds. An asterisk is used whenever a phoneme, morpheme, or word is historically unattested and has been reconstructed. A raised ˣ indicates that the phrase or sentence is ungrammatical, while a raised question mark, ?, shows that the expression is borderline grammatical or not quite idiomatic.

The phonetic symbols used in this work for vowels generally follow international standards (IPA), but some symbols have been altered to better fit an English-speaking audience. The consonant [j] for example, is used to represent a voiced palatal affricate (as in [kaji] 'eggplant'), while [y] is used for the palatal glide (as in [kyəul] 'winter'). A raised glottal stop is used to indicate a fortis, or reinforced, pronunciation: [tʔal] 'daughter', while a raised *h* is used for aspiration: [tʰal] 'mask'.

A final remark about the nature of this work. In producing this volume, our intent has been to provide a general introduction to the Korean language that does not require specialized linguistic knowledge to read. That is the kind of work that has long been missing in the Western-language literature on Korea. But, at the same time, we have tried to avoid writing down or oversimplifying. In places, the discussion can be demanding, and the casual reader should feel free to skip over parts containing more detail than is needed. The text can be read on different levels, and the chapters in any order, and we encourage readers to approach it in that spirit or in any other way they find useful or interesting. My rule of thumb has been to assume, in all chapters after the introduction, that the reader has some familiarity with the Korean language, but not necessarily an understanding of its structure. To assume less would have been patronizing, to assume more would not have been in keeping with the goals of this book.

—S. Robert Ramsey
College Park, Maryland

1
Introduction

1.1 The Distribution of Korean

Korean is the language of all native-born inhabitants of the Korean peninsula. There are no varieties or dialects of this language so different they cannot be understood by all. The Korean people are fond of saying that they are a unified nation speaking one language, and linguistically it is clearly true. Korea itself may still be politically divided, but the people on both sides of the border speak one and the same language.

The Korean language has a relatively large number of speakers. Counting the 46.4 million people in South Korea and the 21.4 million in North Korea, the population of Korea today is almost 70 million, a number greater than the population of England or France. About the same number of people speak Korean as Italian. The size of the territory on which Korean is spoken may not be large, but in terms of the number of speakers, it ranks twelfth in the world.[1]

Korean is also spoken in overseas Korean communities, especially in China, North America, Japan, and the former Soviet Union. Today there are 1,460,000 people of Korean extraction in the United States, and another 730,000 in Japan. There are about 1,760,000 people belonging to the Korean nationality in China, and 500,000 in Russia and the former Soviet Union. In the larger communities in all of these places the Korean language maintains an existence. Korean-speaking populations are conspicuously active in New York and Los Angeles, where, among other things, Korean signs line the streets of "Korea Town," often as far as the eye can see. Korean-language newspapers, many of them printed locally, circulate widely. But even in smaller metropolitan areas across the length and breadth of the United States, Korean writing on signs, especially church signs, has become commonplace. In the former Soviet Union, language maintenance in Korean communities is reported to be higher than is the case with almost all other ethnic minorities.

Koreans in Japan, with large concentrations in the area around Osaka, are the only significant minority in that country; although 75 percent are Japanese-born, most remain legally aliens, a status that keeps them apart from the mainstream of Japanese society and fosters the maintenance of the Korean language. But the largest and most vigorous Korean-speaking population anywhere in the world outside of Korea can be found in China. In the northeast, in the area centered around the Yanbian Autonomous Region, complete Korean institutions remain in place, including Korean-language schools up to the university level. In China, Korean is officially classified as a "major" minority language.

Elsewhere, outside of these larger concentrations of overseas Koreans, Korean-speaking communities are distributed worldwide, especially in South America. With the growing economic and political importance of Korea on the world scene, Korean has also become widely taught as a second language.

1.2 Korean Writing

The Korean alphabet is used by Koreans only, and only for writing the Korean language. As will be explained in chapter 2, it is unlike any other writing system in the world. It is also the only alphabet of any kind completely native to East Asia.

In South Korea, this national alphabet is called Hangŭl, which in popular usage can also mean 'the Korean language'. As a result, in overseas Korean communities settled by South Koreans, Korean schools are popularly referred to "Hangŭl schools." In North Korea, however, the name of the language, *Chosŏn-mal,* can in informal, unguarded speech serve as the name of the alphabet. The two usages may seem to be mirror images of each other, but they share the perception that the national writing system is the Korean language itself.

For Koreans, especially in the South, the alphabet is a powerful cultural icon. It is the very symbol of nation and national culture. Each year, 9 October is celebrated as "Alphabet Day," and King Sejong, the inventor of the alphabet, is honored in countless ways—his likeness appears on money and stamps; institutions, societies, streets, and the like carry his name. Much as American schoolchildren read Lincoln's Gettysburg Address, Korean schoolchildren read Sejong's essay on the alphabet. That this writing system is completely and uniquely Korean is enough to swell the pride of the nation. But that it is also one of the most remarkable writing systems ever invented[2] makes it fully deserving of attention in the wider world.

Thus, the Korean alphabet has unchallenged respect among Koreans as their native writing system. From the time they enter elementary school until they graduate college, Koreans study from books written in Hangŭl. Newspapers and magazines, fiction and poetry, books and journals in every professional field, government documents and legal codes—all are written in Hangŭl.

And yet, Koreans still sometimes write their language by mixing Chinese characters into the Hangŭl text. This mixed style of writing may seem curious, considering the pride that Koreans take in their alphabet. But the use of Chinese characters follows a long and earlier tradition. Even after the invention of the alphabet, and until the end of the nineteenth century, most government documents and professional writings continued to be written entirely in Literary Chinese. Then, around the beginning of the twentieth century, writing reforms inspired by modernization and nationalism produced a true written Korean, and the form this style of writing took was one in which the alphabet was mixed with Chinese characters. The reasons for preserving this mixture were largely cultural because knowledge of Chinese writing was still seen as a measure of intellectual achievement and level of education. But the rationale given was often different. An enormous number of Sinitic morphemes had been borrowed into the Korean vocabulary, and writing them in Chinese rather than Hangŭl was believed to show meanings and etymologies more clearly.

Over the years, the arguments for and against Chinese characters have been repeated, attacked, and defended countless times, often with great passion. But, with the passing of time, the issue has become largely academic. For the use of Chinese characters, in mixed script or otherwise, has slowly, and naturally, waned. In North Korea, Chinese characters have been banned from use since 1949. In South Korea, too, the frequency with which Chinese characters appear has decreased dramatically in recent years. Newspapers and most professional writings still contain a mixture of Chinese characters, but the relative number of magazines and educational materials (even at the college level) that contain almost no Chinese characters has grown considerably. The proportion of books using Chinese characters is far smaller than that of books using only Hangŭl. Signs in Chinese, once common on stores almost everywhere in Seoul, are now largely restricted to Chinese restaurants and herbal medicine shops. This trend away from the use of Chinese characters is probably an indication that the number of people familiar with them has become smaller. It might also be part of the cause. In any case, Chinese characters are rapidly becoming as unfamiliar to Koreans as Greek letters are now to Americans.

In contrast, the use of Roman letters in Korea has increased in recent years. Such abbreviations and acronyms as FM, CD, VTR (Video Tape Recorder), KBS (Korean Broadcasting System), and MBC (Munhwa Broadcasting Corporation) have become commonplace in Korean publications. Koreans give only the Roman letters for these forms, which has resulted in a new kind of mixed script. English and pseudo-English can be found liberally sprinkled on shop signs (Donky Chicken) and billboards (Galloper Life, Wide Bongo) throughout Seoul and even smaller cities. But this trend, though driven by the movements of a larger world culture, in no way threatens the native writing system. No one would seriously advocate replacing Hangŭl with romanization.

The written history of Korean, in the most literal sense, is five and a half centuries old. The Korean alphabet, which has been in existence since

1443,[3] is the medium for unusually extensive and detailed phonological records of the language.

But even before the invention of the alphabet, Korea was a literate society. Chinese characters and Chinese writing had been imported from China at least by the early centuries of the Christian era, and Koreans very early on learned to write in Literary Chinese. At first, such things as record keeping may well have required the assistance of Chinese immigrants, but native specialists soon mastered the art. Literary Chinese may have been far removed from any variety of spoken Korean, but Koreans lived active and literate lives for many centuries with it as the written medium.

Koreans were more than simply users of this language. They were innovative and creative in what they did with it. It is known, for example, that Koreans were the first people in the world to use metal movable type. Records show that Koreans were using metal type to print books by A.D. 1234, and a copy of such a text from 1377 is preserved today in the Bibliothéque Nationale in Paris. Both dates are much earlier than Gutenberg's famous "invention" of around 1440. But the kind of East Asian printing that parallels what Gutenberg did is far older still. Xylography, the printing of a written text by means of wood blocks, was developed at least by the eighth century and became the common means of producing books in the tenth and eleventh centuries. The result was an expansion of knowledge in East Asia much like that caused by the European innovation—except that it occurred about half a millennium earlier. The oldest known sample of printing in the world, dating back at least to 751, has been found in Korea.

Literary activity on so many levels, even through the medium of Chinese characters, naturally involved the recording of the native, spoken language. In the Three Kingdoms period, Koreans developed the device of borrowing either the reading or the meaning of Chinese characters to record the names of local people and places. And in the Silla period, complete poems known as *hyangga* were written down using this method (cf. chapter 2). If these kinds of transcriptions are taken into consideration, Korean can be said to have been transcribed perhaps as early as the fifth century.

Transcriptions of Korean from this early period are rare, however. As time passed, Koreans must have begun to compose with more confidence in Literary Chinese, and attempts to represent the local language in writing occurred with less and less frequency. Only twenty-five *hyangga* still exist, and they are all extremely difficult to interpret. Other early attempts to write Korean are little more than fragments. The transcriptions in Chinese characters hint and tantalize, but they do not provide much concrete information about the sounds of earlier Korean. The first systematic records of the Korean language come only with the invention of the alphabet in the middle of the fifteenth century. It is from the texts of that period that the history of the Korean language, in its truest sense, begins.

1.3 The Origins of Korean

Where does the Korean language come from? Like the ancestry of the Korean people themselves, the origins of the Korean language have never been definitively established. But there are two widely accepted and interconnected theories about its genetic affinities. The first is that Korean is related to Japanese. The second, which perhaps subsumes the first, is that Korean is related to Altaic—Turkic, Mongolian, and Manchu-Tungus.

For a long time now—at least since their liberation from Japan—most Koreans have preferred to consider the latter relationship. Western writers have tended to compare Korean first with Japanese, but Korean scholars have tended to play down that possible relationship. In any case, consideration of the Japanese connection is unavoidable since in its larger formulation— "Macro-Altaic"—the Altaic family would include both Japanese and Korean.

The hypothesis that Korean is related to Altaic reinforces, and for the most part underlies, the widespread belief that the Korean people originated in central Asia. Many writers have described the ancestors of the Koreans as nomads living somewhere around Mongolia who subsequently migrated east and south into their final homeland on the Korean peninsula. Partly based on earlier linguistic scholarship and partly based on imagination, this version of Korean prehistory has given Koreans a feeling of kinship with horse-riding peoples of central Asia such as the Mongols.

Doubts about the relationship between Korean and Altaic seem to have grown recently in the West, to the point where many linguistic dictionaries and introductory texts now describe Korean as "a language whose genetic affinity is unknown." In his best-selling book *The Mother Tongue* (1990), Bill Bryson states this negative view even more strongly. In a general discussion of language origins, he asserts bluntly that, like Basque, Korean is "quite unrelated to any other known language" (p. 24). In Korea itself, however, the situation is completely different. There, most experts continue to believe strongly in an Altaic connection. It is obvious that Korean is similar in structure to Manchu, Mongolian, and other such northern languages, and when the great comparativist G. J. Ramstedt put forward the hypothesis that Korean had sprung from the same source as these other, Altaic languages, he found a sympathetic and responsive audience in Korea.[4] Even today, his publications (especially 1928, 1952, 1957) are among the works most frequently cited by Korean linguists.

The picture of this relationship painted by Koreans follows fairly closely that sketched by Ramstedt and, later, Poppe (1960). They reason that, although not as closely related to Turkic, Mongol, and (Manchu-)Tungus as these three branches are to each other, Korean nevertheless forms a larger language family with them and that, of the three, Korean has the closest relationship to the Tungusic branch of the family.

It has often been pointed out—by observers even before Ramstedt—

that the many resemblances between Korean and Altaic could hardly be accidental. There is first of all the overall, general structure. Like the Altaic languages, Korean is agglutinative, forming words by adding inflectional endings to the end of a stem. Then there is the matter of "vowel harmony"; Korean, especially in its older recorded stages, shows in the vocalism of endings combining with stems the kind of vowel concord typical of Altaic. Just as is true in Altaic, the liquid *l* (including [r]) cannot begin a word. There are no relative pronouns or conjunctions, verb endings performing the functions that those words usually do in Indo-European languages. All of these grammatical features characterize both Korean and Altaic.

But what is more important are the results obtained by comparing concrete lexical items and grammatical forms.[5] For example, it can be seen in comparisons such as that shown in (1) that Old Korean **a* corresponds to proto-Altaic **a:*

(1) Middle Korean *alay* 'below' (< ** al*), Evenki *alas* 'foot', Mongolian *ala* 'crotch', Old Turkic *al* 'downward', Middle Turkic *altïn* 'below'

In the lexical items shown in (2), Korean *p* corresponds to proto-Altaic **p* or **b.*[6]

(2) Middle Korean *puz-* 'pour', Manchu *fusu-* 'sprinkle water', Mongolian *üsür-* 'sprinkle, spill', Monguor *fusuru-* 'pour', Turkic *üskür-* 'spray with the mouth'.

In grammatical forms as well, some extremely suggestive correspondences have been found. For example, the Korean locative particle *lo*, which indicates directionality, can be compared to Old Turkic *rü* and Mongolian *ru*, for which proto-Altaic **ru/rü* has been reconstructed. More striking still are the correspondences of the verbal noun endings *-*r, -*m,* and *-*n* with virtually identical endings in Korean. These point strongly to a genetic affinity between Korean and the Altaic languages.

In general, Korean scholars attribute more significance to these resemblances than do their Western colleagues. Even though Korean researchers are fully aware of the limitations caused by the lack of ancient records, they nevertheless believe strongly that, in all probability, Korean belongs to the Altaic family. They tend not to consider the possibility that it is related to some other language family besides Altaic. The conclusion reached by Lee Ki-Moon (1972a) is that, if Korean did not branch off from proto-Altaic, then, at the very least, both Korean and Altaic sprang from some common source. In Korean scholarly circles, it is this view that has prevailed.

In considering the relationships between the languages of East Asia, it is important to remember that Korean is not genetically related to Chinese. From very early on, Koreans used Chinese writing and consequently borrowed an enormous amount of vocabulary from Literary Chinese (cf. chapter 4), but this borrowing did not change where the language had come from. From the point of view of linguistic origin and genetic affinity, Korean is completely separate from Chinese. Chinese is believed to form a branch of what is known as the Sino-Tibetan family of languages, and no one has ever seriously proposed that Korean could belong to that particular family.

With Japanese, however, the situation is different. As was mentioned above, the general structural characteristics of Japanese are almost identical to those of Korean. Concrete lexical and grammatical correspondences may be thin compared to this strikingly close structural resemblance, but there continues to be optimism about the possibility that the two languages might share a common genetic origin. Of course, it is considered even more difficult to establish the genealogy of Japanese than that of Korean. The probability that Japanese belongs to the Altaic family is believed to be somewhat less than that of Korean. Even G. J. Ramstedt and N. Poppe, who were enthusiastic advocates of a genetic relationship between Korean and Altaic, hesitated when it came to placing Japanese in the Altaic family. Moreover, there are also those who advocate a relationship with Austronesian for Japanese—a "southern hypothesis" as it were. However, it is still true that, among Japanese scholars, support is greatest for the hypothesis that Japanese belongs to the Altaic family and, at the same time, that it is most closely related to Korean.

1.4 The Structural Characteristics of Korean

Korean contrasts structurally with European languages such as English in a number of ways. First of all, in languages like English, the basic syntactic structure is SVO (subject-verb-object), while in Korean it is SOV (subject-object-verb). In other words, Korean is a verb-final language, a language in which the verb always comes at the end of the sentence.

As has already been mentioned, Korean is an agglutinative language. The function a noun has in a sentence is made overt by attaching one or more particles to it, as illustrated in (1), below. Since Korean particles are attached at the end of the noun, these grammatical elements are also known as "postpositions"; their functions often mirror those of English prepositions.

(1) a. Kangaci *ka* kwiyepta.
   puppy SUBJ. cute
   "The puppy is cute."
 b. Kangaci *lul* cal tolpoala.
   puppy OBJECT well look after
   "Look after the puppy carefully."
 c. Kangaci *eykey* mul *ul* cwuela.
   puppy to water OBJ. give
   "Give (to) the puppy (some) water."

Verbs, too, are formed through agglutination—that is, by attaching various

endings to the stem. For example, endings such as those in (2) show the
tense of the verb. In (3), the endings show whether the sentence is a question, a statement, or a command. Other endings, as will be discussed later,
are indicators of the style chosen to fit the situation and the person being addressed—in other words, they determine the speech level in the so-called
honorific system. To a nonnative speaker the sheer number of verb endings
can seem astonishing, and their functional load is great. It is sometimes said
that what is important in English is expressed near the beginning of the sentence, while what is important in Korean is expressed at the end. Though
somewhat of an oversimplification, there is still a measure of truth in that
characterization. The complexity of the verb phrase gives Korean much of
its expressive power.

(2) a. Kkoch i encey phi-*ni*?
        flower SUBJ. when bloom?
        "When do the flowers bloom?"
     b. Kkoch i encey phi-*ess*-ni?
        PAST?
        "When did the flowers bloom?"

(3) a. Minho ka chayk ul ilk-*nunta*.
        Minho SUBJ. book OBJ. read ing.
        "Minho is reading a book."
     b. Minho ka chayk ul ilk-*ni*?
                         ?
        "Is Minho reading a book?"
     c. Minho ya chayk ul ilk-*ela*.
                         !
        "Minho! Read the book!"

In Korean, adjectives are a subcategory of verbs. Sometimes called "descriptive verbs," they are composed of stem plus one or more endings, just
as verbs are. In this way, Korean adjectives are completely different from
English adjectives, which require a form of the verb "to be" to function as
predicates.

(4) a. Matang i nelp-*ta*.
        yard SUBJ. broad.
        "The yard is big."
     b. Matang i nelp-*ess*-ta.
        PAST.
        "The yard was big."
     c. Matang i nelp-*ess*-ni?
        PAST?
        "Was the yard big?"

(5) a. Tongsayng un khi ka khu-*ta.*
       sibling TOPIC height big.
       "The younger sibling is tall."
    b. Apeci nun khi ka khu-*si-ta.*
       father TOPIC HONORIFIC.
       "Father is tall."

There are well over four hundred verb endings in modern Korean,[7] and their functions range far beyond the marking of predication at the end of the sentence. As can be seen in the following simple examples, an ending can be used to express a variety of connective functions.

(6) a. Hanul un phulu-*ko*   kwulum un huy-ta.
       sky   blue AND cloud   white.
       "The sky is blue, and the clouds are white."
    b. Pi ka o-*myen* sophung ul yenki-haca.
       rain come IF picnic put off-let's
       "If it rains, let's put off the picnic."
    c. Kiwun i eps-*uni*   swiese kaca.
       strength isn't BECAUSE resting go-let's
       "Because I'm out of strength, let's rest before we go."

(7) a. nay ka cikum ilk-*nun* chayk
       I   now read ing book
       "the book I'm reading now"
    b. nay ka nayil ilk-*ul* chayk
       tomorrow FUTURE
       "the book I'm going to read tomorrow"
    c. nay ka ecey   ilk-*un* chayk
       yesterday PAST
       "the book I read yesterday"

The topic of the Korean verb ending will be treated in more detail later, in chapter 5; for now, one more example will be given to illustrate some of the functional diversity and complexity of these grammatical elements. In (8), all of the sentences can be translated into English as "How fast is (the speed of) light?" But even within virtually the same context, the sentences all have slightly different nuances of meaning; for in each, the ending placed on the verb indicates a different mood, or a different relationship between speaker and listener in a given social situation. Korean is a language in which the verb ending is extremely complex.

(8) a. Pich un elmana ppalu-*ni?*
       light how-much fast
       "How fast is light?"
       [question to an intimate]

    b. Pich un elmana ppalu-*nya?*
       [didactic question to a subordinate]
    c. Pich un elmana ppalu-*ci?*
       [self-questioning, wondering, to an equal or subordinate]
    d. Pich un elmana ppalu-*lkka?*
       [wondering, marveling, to equal or subordinate, or to oneself]
    e. Pich un elmana ppalu-*nka?*
       [formal, distancing, to equal or subordinate, wondering to oneself]

In Korean, modifiers always precede what they modify. A modifying adjective comes in front of the noun, and an adverb comes before the verb. A modifying clause is put before the head noun.

This kind of syntactic order contrasts with that of languages like Thai or French, where most adjectives follow what they modify (*idée fixe; bête noire;* etc.). In English, some modifiers precede and some follow (*life's* secrets, the secrets *of life*), and the rules governing this syntactic ordering can often be complex. But in Korean the order modifier-modified is invariant. In English, a modifying clause ordinarily follows the head noun ("the book *that I read*"), but in Korean the clause always precedes (*nay ka ilkun chayk*). As mentioned above, the Korean morphemes corresponding to English *pre*positions are *post*positions. Thus, if English can be called a "prepositional language," then Korean is a "postpositional language." English is often said to be "right branching" because modifying clauses follow the head noun ("branching" to the right as they are customarily written); Korean, in contrast, is consistently "left branching."

A well-known and special characteristic of the Korean language is its so-called honorific system, something that has also, and more appropriately, been termed "speech protocol."[8] In Korean, for example, it would be unthinkable to use the same pronoun in the meaning of 'you' when talking to one's friend, parent, or teacher, and the matter is not just one of a choice like that of French *tu/vous* or German *du/Sie.* In Korean, using any pronoun at all to address one's father or teacher is taboo, strictly out of the question; in such cases, an appropriate title is used instead of a pronoun if the deictic cannot be completely omitted. Also, depending on the speaker's relationship to the subject of the sentence, the verb form in the predicate will change, as in (9). Still more basic is the speaker's relationship to the person being addressed, and the verb endings used in the conversation will change to conform with the social protocol. In (10) we see how a simple sentence like 'The bus is coming' can be expressed in four different ways; in other situations, as many as six relationships can be differentiated.

    (9) a. Ai ka ttwi-nta.
        child run ing
        "The child is running."
      b. Apeci ka ttwi-*si*-nta.
        father
        "Father's running."

(10)a. Pesu ka o-*nta.*
    bus come
    "The bus is coming."
    [a college professor to his children, a young person, or an old, close
        friend]
  b. Pesu ka o-*ney.*
    "The bus is coming."
    [a college professor to his graduate students]
  c. Pesu ka *wayo* [= o-*ayo*].
    "The bus is coming."
    [a college professor to his wife or a young stranger]
  d. Pesu ka o-*pnita.*
    "The bus is coming."
    [a college professor to his father, his old teacher, or an older stranger]

Moreover, if it were one's father, a teacher, the company president, or an older person who was coming instead of the bus, the honorific morpheme -si- would have to be inserted after the verb stem: *o-si-nta, o-si-ney,* etc.

In many cases, depending on the level of formality, special polite vocabulary will replace the usual lexical items. For example, what children and friends eat is *pap* '(cooked) rice'; what parents, teachers, and so on eat is *cinci.* The plain way to talk about the act of eating is *(pap ul) meknunta,* while the formal way is *(cinci lul) capswusinta,* replacing both noun and verb.

For anyone not native to the culture, the proper usage of such speech protocol is one of the most difficult aspects of the language to master. It is not simply a matter of choosing "polite" language, or "honorifics," but rather a matter of choosing a style that is appropriate. The style used must certainly be "polite" enough not to give offense, but using language appropriate to someone of a much higher rank than the person being addressed does not make the speaker seem more polite; rather, it might seem bumblingly laughable, or even insulting. At the very least, it would make the listener feel uncomfortable. The style of language chosen must be appropriate to the person spoken to, the person spoken about, and the situation. Koreans themselves worry constantly about such speech protocol, and many books continue to be sold, and lessons given, on the etiquette of speech. The situation is similar to that of Japanese, but of course the systems of the two languages differ from each other because of underlying sociolinguistic and cultural factors.

In the phonology of Korean, too, there are a number of salient characteristics worth noting from the perspective of the English speaker. We will mention a few of them here, and talk about the phonology in more detail in chapter 3. For example, we might quickly note that in the inventory of Korean consonants there are no labio-dentals like *f* or *v* or interdentals such as θ or ð (both written "th" in modern English).

There are no voicing distinctions in the Korean consonants. In other words, there is no contrast between *p* and *b*, *t* and *d*, *k* and *g*, and so on. The uninitiated English speaker can see indirect evidence of that fact in the variant romanized spellings of Korean names. For example, the common surname usually spelled "Park" is sometimes spelled "Bark" instead. The choice of *p* or *b* to write the name is simply a matter of personal choice since there is no difference in Korean pronunciation for it to reflect. Similarly, *Paik* is the same name as *Baik*, *Pang* is the same name as *Bang*, *Kang* is the same as *Gang*, *Ku* is the same name as *Gu*, and so on.

Instead of voicing, Korean has a more unusual manner distinction in its obstruent system, a three-way contrast among lax (or "plain"), fortis (or "reinforced"), and aspirated. Koreans distinguish, for example, the three words *tal* 'moon', *ttal* 'daughter', and *thal* 'mask' by the quality of the initial consonant: The initial consonant of *tal* 'moon' is weakly articulated and released with a slight puff of air; the initial reinforced consonant of *ttal* 'daughter' is pronounced with great muscular tension throughout the vocal tract; and the aspirated initial of *thal* 'mask' is followed by very heavy aspiration before the voicing of the vowel begins. This three-way distinction, which over the past several decades has been the subject of numerous linguistic and acoustic studies, is probably the best-known feature of the Korean phonological system.

The consonants of Korean are never released in final position. For this reason, Koreans sometimes pronounce English words such as "hat" and "help" with a final, minimal vowel, *haythu* and *heylphu*, since it is only when a vowel follows the consonant that the consonant can be released. The extra vowel and syllable is the way to make the very audible, final or postconsonantal English consonant clear when loanwords like *kaymphu* 'camp' and *peylthu* 'belt' are accommodated into Korean.

2
Korean Writing

The Korean writing system is a true alphabet, with a symbol available for each consonant and vowel in the language.[1] It was invented in the fifteenth century by King Sejong, the fourth monarch of the Chosŏn dynasty. The modern name of the Korean alphabet is *Hangŭl*. The word was coined around 1912 by the scholar-patriot Chu Sigyŏng, who found the name then in common use, *Ŏnmun* 'Vernacular (or Vulgar) Writing', distasteful. Chu wanted to give the alphabet and all other aspects of native culture a respect they had not been accorded before, and in proposing the new name, he explained that it was composed of the archaic Korean word *han*, which meant 'big, great', and *kul*, the native word for 'writing'. This literary coinage, 'Great Writing', thus gave the appearance of antiquity, while implying superiority over that other writing system then in use in Korea, Chinese.

But Chu also knew that the name *Hangŭl* would be primarily taken to mean 'Korean Writing' since *Han-* was the name many patriotic Koreans had come to prefer for Korean things. This latter interpretation prevailed, and today, with the exception of a few etymological scholars, the citizenry of South Korea all take *Hangŭl* to mean 'Korean Writing'. In North Korea, however, where any word with the element *Han-* in it suggests South Korea, the name *Hangŭl* is scrupulously avoided. How widely known the word is among the general populace in the North is a question yet to be answered.

In this chapter we will focus on the characteristics of the Korean alphabet, calling it "Hangŭl" in contexts where appropriate. We will examine its origin, the question of who invented it and when, how the letter forms were created, and the orthographic principles with which the letters are used. Finally, we will look briefly at the methods that were used to transcribe Korean before the invention of the alphabet.

2.1 The Letters of the Alphabet

There are twenty-four basic Hangŭl letters in use today, fourteen consonants and ten vowels. Sixteen additional symbols (five consonants and eleven vowels) are made by combining these basic letters.

In the table below, the basic letters are listed in alphabetical order. The order and the names of the consonants are those used in South Korea.

Korean Writing

(In North Korea, different conventions are used.) The names of the vowels are their pronunciations in isolation.

(1) The Hangŭl Letters (Basic Letters)

Consonants

Symbol:	ㄱ	ㄴ	ㄷ	ㄹ	ㅁ	ㅂ	ㅅ
	k	n	t	l	m	p	s
	[k/g]	[n]	[t/d]	[l/r]	[m]	[p/b]	[s]
Name:	기역	니은	디귿	리을	미음	비읍	시옷
	(kiyek)	(niun)	(tikut)	(liul)	(mium)	(piup)	(sios)

Symbol:	ㅇ	ㅈ	ㅊ	ㅋ	ㅌ	ㅍ	ㅎ
	(∅-/-ng)	c	ch	kh	th	ph	h
	[∅/ŋ]	[tʃ/j]	[tʃʰ]	[kʰ]	[tʰ]	[pʰ]	[h]
Name:	이응	지읒	치읓	키읔	티읕	피읖	히읗
	(iung)	(ciuc)	(chiuch)	(khiukh)	(thiuth)	(phiuph)	(hiuh)

Vowels

Symbol:	ㅏ	ㅑ	ㅓ	ㅕ	ㅗ	ㅛ
	a	ya	e	ye	o	yo
	[a]	[ya]	[ə]	[yə]	[o]	[yo]

Symbol:	ㅜ	ㅠ	ㅡ	ㅣ
	wu	yu	u	i
	[u]	[yu]	[ɨ]	[i]

As can be seen from the above chart, the consonant names were made up by using the consonant in question at the beginning and end of the word, as syllable onset and syllable coda. The system by which the names are constructed is regular and predictable, except for the consonants 기역 *(kiyek)*, 디귿 *(tikut)*, and 시옷 *(sios)*.

The modern letter names, as well as their order in the alphabet, are based upon the 1527 Chinese-Korean glossary *Hunmong chahoe* (訓蒙字會, "Collection of Characters for Training the Unenlightened"). This glossary, a pedagogical work compiled by the famous teacher and language scholar, Ch'oe Sejin,[2] is the direct source for the modern names of eight of the consonants, including the three irregular ones. In the introduction to the glossary, Ch'oe arranged the Korean letters in what was to become the standard alphabetical order[3] and illustrated the pronunciation of each letter with one or more Chinese characters. For the eight consonants in question, he used two Chinese characters formulaically; *p*, for example, was illustrated with the two characters 非 *pi* and 邑 *up*. The combined reading of the two characters became the letter's name, *piup*. The same character formula produced the names *niun, liul, mium,* and *iung.* However, the formula could not work for the consonants *k, t,* and *s,* since there were no Chinese characters read in Korean as **uk, *ut,* or **us.* By necessity, these names had to be exceptions. Therefore, Ch'oe illustrated *k* with the character 役 since its reading, *yek,* was a reasonably close approximation of **uk.* For *t* and *s,* however, the situation was somewhat different. There were no Chinese character readings at all that he could use, since (in Korean at least) none ended in *-t* or *-s.* And so, here he instructed that the characters were to be read with native glosses — that is, as Korean words. The Chinese character 末 used to illustrate the pronunciation of *t* was read as the Korean word *kut* [4] 'end'; the character 衣 used to illustrate *s* was read as *os* 'clothing'.

For the consonants *c, ch, kh, th, ph,* and *h,* which were not used at all in those days as syllable codas, Ch'oe changed the formula. These consonants were given readings in the *Hunmong chahoe* as initials with a single vowel, *ci, chi, khi, thi, phi,* and *hi.* It was only later, in the Unification of Hangŭl Orthography of 1933, that these names were regularized to follow the pattern of the other consonants; from then on, these consonants were *ciuc, chiuch,* and so on.

The symbols listed above are the basic Hangŭl letters. Let us now look at the sixteen additional symbols made by combining basic letters. The order of these complex alphabetic symbols is based upon the order of the basic letters. The names of the consonants are made by combining the word *ssang* 'double' with the name of the basic letter. For the complex vowels, the pronunciation serves directly as the name, just as it does for the basic vowel letters.

(2) The Hangŭl Letters (Complex Symbols)

Consonants

Symbol:	ㄲ	ㄸ	ㅃ	ㅆ	ㅉ
	kk	tt	pp	ss	cc
	[kʔ]	[tʔ]	[pʔ]	[sʔ]	[tʃʔ]
Name:	쌍기역	쌍디귿	쌍비읍	쌍시옷	쌍지읏
	(ssang-kiyek)	(ssang-tikut)	(ssang-piup)	(ssang-sios)	(ssang-ciuc)

Vowels

Symbol:	ㅐ	ㅒ	ㅔ	ㅖ	ㅘ	ㅙ
	(ㅏ+ㅣ)	(ㅑ+ㅣ)	(ㅓ+ㅣ)	(ㅕ+ㅣ)	(ㅗ+ㅏ)	(ㅗ+ㅏ+ㅣ)
	ay	yay	ey	yey	wa	way
	[ɛ]	[yɛ]	[e]	[ye]	[wa]	[wɛ]

Symbol:	ㅚ	ㅝ	ㅞ	ㅟ	ㅢ	
	(ㅗ+ㅣ)	(ㅜ+ㅓ)	(ㅜ+ㅓ+ㅣ)	(ㅜ+ㅣ)	(ㅡ+ㅣ)	
	oy	we	wey	wi	uy	
	[ö]	[wə]	[we]	[ü]	[iy]	

It is often said that there are twenty-four letters in the Korean alphabet, a number that only takes into account the basic letters. This view of the alphabet is a traditional one that comes down to us from the earliest record of the invention of the alphabet, an entry in the Annals of King Sejong (世宗實錄) for the year 1443 (or early 1444), where it was noted that the king had created the "28 letters" of the Korean alphabet. Those twenty-eight letters were the original basic symbols. In modern Korean, four of the twenty-eight are no longer used, leaving us with the twenty-four letters said to comprise the alphabet today.

At the time the alphabet was invented, those twenty-eight letters could be taken as basic because of the structural principles laid out for the alphabet. (These principles will be discussed below, in section 2.5.) The treatment reflected well the phonological structure of the language. But for the modern Korean sound system, there is no particular reason why the "basic" letters should be singled out for special treatment. It is true that the complex letters ㄲ, ㄸ, ㅃ, etc. (*kk, tt, pp, . . .*) are written with two symbols, but considering the fact that they represent unitary phonemes just as much as do ㅋ, ㅌ, ㅍ, and so on (*kh, th, ph, . . .*), they are phonologically just as "basic." Moreover, the vowel symbols ㅐ, ㅔ, ㅚ, and ㅟ (*ay, ey, oy,* and *wi*) consist of one of the basic symbols plus ㅣ (*i*) and are therefore considered complex. However, phonetically they represent single vowels [ε, e, ø, ü], while, in contrast, it is the "basic" vowel symbols ㅑ, ㅕ, ㅛ, and ㅠ (*ya, ye, yo,* and *yu*) that represent glide plus vowel combinations. The concept of the basic letter also has no special significance for the typewriter or computer keyboard. On standard Korean keyboards today, the consonants ㄲ, ㄸ, ㅃ, ㅆ, ㅉ (*kk, tt, pp, ss, cc*) and the vowels ㅐ, ㅔ, ㅒ, ㅖ (*ay, ey, yay, yey*) are typed with single, independent keystrokes and are thus treated the same as the "basic letters." It is probably closer to the truth to say that, instead of twenty-four letters, there are actually forty letters in the Korean alphabet.

In the alphabetical order used in most dictionaries, the basic letters and the complex letters are also not distinguished. The order found in the majority of South Korean works is as follows:[5]

(3) Hangŭl Alphabetical Order

Consonants

ㄱ	ㄲ	ㄴ	ㄷ	ㄸ	ㄹ	ㅁ	ㅂ	ㅃ	ㅅ
k	kk	n	t	tt	l	m	p	pp	s
ㅆ	ㅇ	ㅈ	ㅉ	ㅊ	ㅋ	ㅌ	ㅍ	ㅎ	
ss	Ø-/-ng	c	cc	ch	kh	th	ph	h	

Vowels

ㅏ	ㅐ	ㅑ	ㅒ	ㅓ	ㅔ	ㅕ	ㅖ	ㅗ	ㅘ	ㅙ
a	ay	ya	yay	e	ey	ye	yey	o	wa	way
ㅚ	ㅛ	ㅜ	ㅝ	ㅞ	ㅟ	ㅠ	ㅡ	ㅢ	ㅣ	
oy	yo	wu	we	wey	wi	yu	u	uy	i	

The Korean term for this arrangement is "*kanata* order" (가나다順). The term combines each of the first three consonants in the alphabet with the first vowel. In talking about Korean alphabetical order, it might seem more appropriate just to use the names of the first three letters, as Americans do when they say "abc *(ay-bee-cee)* order." But (as will be shown in the next section) although Hangŭl may be a true alphabet, it also has the characteristics of a syllabary. In other words, the letters are not written as separate units, one after the other, but rather are combined to form syllabic units. As Korean alphabetical order is actually used, each of the consonants is combined with each of the vowels in sequence before moving on to the next consonant. By combining each of the first three consonant letters with the first vowel, the name "*kanata* order" provides tacit recognition of the importance of these syllabic units.

2.2 Combining the Hangŭl Letters

Hangŭl orthography is unlike that of most other alphabets. The letters are not written one after the other in a line; rather, they are grouped together into syllables. Here are a few examples:

(1) a. ㄴㅏㅁㅜ → 나 무
     n a m u   na-mu 'tree'
  b. ㅂㅗㄹㅣ → 보 리
     p o l i   po-li 'barley'
  c. ㅁㅣㄴㄷ—ㄹㄹㅔ → 민 들 레
     m i n t u l l ey   min-tul-ley 'dandelion'

This method of writing Hangŭl in syllables is one that has been used ever since the invention of the alphabet. The construction of syllables is based on several well-established principles. The first principle is that the vowels are divided into two types. One type consists of vertically shaped vowels written to the right of the initial consonant. The vowels ㅏ *(a)*, ㅑ *(ya)*, ㅓ *(e)*, ㅕ *(ye)*, and ㅣ *(i)* are in this category. Thus, the syllable *ka*, for example, is written like this: ㄱ *(k)* + ㅏ *(a)* → 가 *(ka)*. The other vowel type consists of horizontal symbols written below the initial consonant. The vowels in this second category include ㅗ *(o)*, ㅛ *(yo)*, ㅜ *(wu)*, ㅠ *(yu)*, and — *(u)*. Thus: ㄱ *(k)* + ㅗ *(o)* → 고 *(ko)*. Here are some additional examples contrasting the two types of vocalism:

Vowel to the right: 냐 *(nya)*, 더 *(te)*, 려 *(lye)*, 시 *(si)*, etc.
Vowel underneath: 뇨 *(nyo)*, 두 *(twu)*, 료 *(lyo)*, 스 *(su)*, etc.

The second orthographic principle used in writing Hangŭl is that every syllable must begin with an initial consonant. In case the actual syllable begins with a vowel, a "zero consonant," ㅇ, is used to preserve the canonical shape, as shown in the examples given in (2), below. This practice is like that of writing an *alif* at the beginning of a word in Arabic (except that the Korean letter also appears in the middle of a word). The letter used as a zero consonant is the same one used to write *-ng*, but since the sound does not appear at the beginning of an orthographic syllable, the symbol can be used there without causing confusion.[6]

(2) a. ㅏ *(a)* + ㅜ *(wu)* → 아우 *awu* 'brother'
     b. ㅠ *(yu)* + ㅓ *(we)* + ㄹ *(l)* → 유월 *yuwel* 'June'

Another orthographic principle is that when a consonant follows the consonant-vowel combination in the syllable, it is written at the bottom. A consonant used in this way has a special name, *patchim,* which means 'support' or 'underpinning'. Complex consonants and consonant clusters are also used in this way to "support" the syllable. In (3c), for example, the double consonant ㄲ *(kk)* forms a *ssang-patchim,* or 'double support', and the consonant cluster ㄺ (lk) in (3d) is a *kyep-patchim* 'joint support'. Consonants written underneath are also called by the letter names; for the words in (3), for example, we find *mium-patchim* '*m*-support', *liul-patchim* '*l*-support', *ssang-kiek patchim* 'double-*k* support', and *liul-kiek patchim* '*lk*-support'.

(3) a. ㅂ *(p)* + ㅗ *(o)* + ㅁ *(m)* → 봄 *pom* 'spring'
     b. ㄱ *(k)* + ㅕ *(ye)* + ㅇ *(Ø)* + ㅜ *(wu)* + ㄹ *(l)* → 겨울 *kyewul* 'winter'
     c. ㅂ *(p)* + ㅏ *(a)* + ㄲ *(kk)* → 밖 *pakk* 'outside'
     d. ㅈ *(c)* + ㅣ *(i)* + ㄴ *(n)* + ㅎ *(h)* + ㅡ *(u)* + ㄹ *(l)* + ㄱ *(k)* → 진흙 *cinhulk* 'mud'

Because Hangŭl is written in syllables this way, it is usual to recognize these clusters of symbols as the basic, individual units of the writing system. Thus, Koreans think of 그림 *kulim* 'picture', for example, as consisting not of five units, but of two units.[7] The length of manuscripts is described in terms of the number of syllables, and when a document requires an answer of a certain length, it is the number of syllables, these groupings of letters, that is counted.

The composition of the syllable will be discussed later in more detail. We should note here, however, that there are more than a few problems arising from the fact that Hangŭl is written in syllables. There are advantages to the system, but there are also aspects that are undeniably troublesome. Perhaps the most serious difficulty arises when deciding on the alphabetical order of the entries in dictionaries. Here, the consonants written underneath the syllables as *patchim* require special treatment. If these consonants were treated as if they appeared in linear order after the vowel, the situation would be fairly straightforward and simple. The word *kaksi* 'bride' would be listed before *kahwun* 'family precepts', for example. But because the letters are grouped into syllables and those syllables used as primary units of order, *ka-hwun* appears before *kak-si*.

(4) a. ㄱ ㅏ ㅎ ㅜ ㄴ (가훈) 'family precepts'
     k a h wu n
  b. ㄱ ㅏ ㄱ ㅅ ㅣ (각시) 'bride'
     k a k s i

This fact shows that the ordering of Hangŭl letters is based upon the syllable as the primary unit of the orthography. A syllable with a final, *patchim* consonant is always ordered after the syllable without one. Accordingly, the ordering of words is determined by the shape of the first syllable, as shown in (5), below:

(5) 가 각 간 갇 갈 감 갑 갓 강 . . . 개 객 갠 . . . 거 격 건 . . .
    ka kak kan kat kal kam kap kas kang. . . kay kayk kayn. . . ke kek ken. . .

Complex consonants fit into the same order. Double consonants, such as those in 밖 *pakk* 'outside' and 있다 *issta* 'exists' follow the basic alphabetical order; for example, 각 *kak* 갂 *kakk* . . . 갓 *kas* 갔 *kass* . . . So do the "joint support" consonants, as shown by the example sequence given in (6):

(6) 달 닭 닮 닯 닳 담 답
    tal talk talm talp talh tam tap

The problems arising out of writing in syllables are not confined to such questions of what to do with *patchim* consonants, however. There is also the difficulty presented by the "zero consonant," ㅇ. That consonant is not the same as the ㅇ that is written underneath the syllable as *patchim*. The zero consonant written in initial position in the syllable has no sound value, which raises the question of how it should be handled when sequencing the letters. For example, the word *aki* 'baby' by rights should be listed after the word *pha* 'scallion' in the dictionary, because the Hangŭl letter for *a* (ㅏ) comes after *ph* (ㅍ) in the alphabetical order. But because the syllabic orthography requires that the zero consonant ㅇ be written before the vowel, the word *aki* is written 아기, and treated as if it began with the same consonant that ends the word 강 *kang* 'river'; and so, just as the syllable 강 *kang* comes before the syllable 갚 *kaph* in the dictionary, the word 아기, *aki* comes before the word 파 *pha*. This inconsistent ordering is the one that is used in Korea today. The syllabic features of the Hangŭl writing system, as found in the so-called *kanata*-order, make Korean alphabetical order much less simple to use than that of the alphabetical order of the English writing system.

However, the grouping of the Hangŭl letters into syllables allows freedom in the direction in which the lines are written. Today, almost all books in Korea are written Western-syle, with the lines running from left to right across the page. However, from the time the Korean alphabet was invented until the middle of the twentieth century, the writing in all texts was vertical, with the lines running from the top to the bottom of the page. Even today, newspapers occasionally preserve this traditional, vertical style of writing (though, in very recent years, far less than before), as do many shop signs and billboards. What gives Korean writing the flexibility to be written in different directions this way is the grouping of the letters into syllabic units. The syllabic units of Hangŭl can, in a natural way, be written horizontally or vertically—just as is the case with the syllabic and logographic writing used in China and Japan.

Today, writing in Korea is usually done horizontally (this contrasts with the situation in Japan, where the traditional vertical style of writing continues). In the future, under the influence of modern technology and the computer, horizontal writing will as a matter of course become even more widespread; still, it is an advantage of the Hangŭl writing system that it affords the freedom to choose which direction one writes in. The sign on a shop, according to the position that is convenient, may be placed horizontally or vertically, whatever is deemed aesthetic or eye-catching. An even more effective place where the two methods of writing are mixed together is on the covers of books. On the front of a book, the title is printed horizontally, while on the spine, the title is almost always written vertically, a practice that affords a convenient way to read the titles when the books are displayed in book stores and libraries. The result of this practice is that, unlike English titles, the title of a Korean book can be read from top to bottom with ease, without twisting the head to the left or right.

2.3 Orthography

Ever since the Korean alphabet was invented, there have been two points of controversy about the syllabic orthography. One is the question of which consonants can be written as *patchim* underneath the syllable. The other is the question of how to write a consonant found at the end of a noun or verb stem when it appears before a grammatical element beginning with a vowel; since the stem-final consonant in such cases is pronounced as the first sound of the following syllable, there is a choice to be made: Should the consonant be written *patchim*, keeping it an integral part of the last syllable of the stem, or should it be written as the initial consonant of the following syllable, the way it is actually pronounced?

Let us look for a moment at the first orthographic problem. The way Hangŭl is written today, any consonant can be written *patchim* to close the syllable. However, as will be explained in Chapter 3, Korean consonants are not pronounced with a release in this final position, and as a result, the distinctions between stops, fricatives, and affricates are neutralized there. This means that when written as *patchim*, the letters ㅅ, ㅈ, ㅊ, ㅋ, ㅌ, ㅍ, and ㅎ

(*s, c, ch, kh, th, ph,* and *h*) do not represent phonemically distinct consonants. For example, the letter ㅅ *(s)* written at the end of the syllable 빗 *(pis)* is pronounced the same as the letter ㄷ *(t)*, as are also the ㅈ *(c)* of 빛 *(pic)*, the ㅊ *(ch)* of 꽃 *(kkoch)*, and the ㅌ *(th)* of 밭 *(path)*. The pronunciation of all five of these letters is the same in that position. Similarly, ㅋ *(kh)* is pronounced like ㄱ *(k)*, and so on. If the neutralization were reflected in how the words were written and the consonants transcribed the way they were pronounced, the number of consonants that could be written *patchim* would be greatly restricted. However, modern Korean orthography does not take this neutralization into account. What is written represents not the actual pronunciation of the consonant in each phonological environment, but rather the basic, or underlying, form. In a word, the transcription is morphophonemic. In the following examples, the forms in (a) represent the actual phonemic shapes, while those in (b) represent how these words and phrases are written in Hangŭl:

(1) a. pat to 'the field, too . . .';   pat-twuk 'the field dike'
   b. path to   path-twuk
   (밭도)   (밭둑)

(2) a. kkot kwa 'flowers, and . . .';   kkot-pakwuni 'flower basket'
   b. kkoch kwa   kkoch-pakwuni
   (꽃과)   (꽃바구니)

(3) a. teptolok 'until it covers . . .';   tepkay '(bed) covers'
   b. tephtolok   tephkay
   (덮도록)   (덮개)

The treatment is the same in the case of double consonants and consonant clusters. In the following examples, (a) again represents the phonemic shape, while (b) is the morphophonemic one written in Hangŭl:

(4) a. pak kwa 'the outside and . . .'   kap to 'the price, too . . .'
   b. pakk kwa   kaps to
   (밖과)   (값도)

(5) a. huk-temi 'a pile of dirt'   epta 'not have, exist'
   b. hulk-temi   epsta
   (흙더미)   (없다)

The difference between what is written and the actual pronunciation is especially great in forms where ㅎ *(h)* is used as *patchim*. In some cases, the difference is so great, it can be difficult to see how the identity of the underlying consonant was determined.

(6) a. nokho 'place, and . . .';   nothaka 'having placed, . . .';   nonnunta
                                                                    'places'
    b. nohko   nohtaka   nohnunta
       (놓고)   (놓다가)   (놓는다)

This morphophonemic orthography is not the only way Korean has been written, however. Transcribing the underlying forms was not standard practice until the early years of the twentieth century, when, following a number of orthographic experiments, the Unification of Hangŭl Orthography was established in 1933. Before that, from the time the Korean alphabet was invented until the beginning of the twentieth century, the orthographic rule that was followed in almost all texts[8] was the so-called Rule of Eight Final Sounds (八終聲法). According to this rule, only eight consonant letters, ㄱ, ㄴ, ㄷ, ㄹ, ㅁ, ㅂ, ㅅ, and ㅇ *(k, n, t, l, m, p, s, ng)*, could close the syllable as *patchim*. (And, in the latter part of this premodern era, only seven consonants were used, as the letter ㄷ *(t)* ceased being used in this position.) This older, traditional orthography reflected the neutralization mentioned above and thus transcribed the actual pronunciation more faithfully. In contrast, the modern orthography transcribes, as much as possible, each morpheme in a single, unvarying form. In other words, the old orthography was much more of what is known as a phonemic orthography, while the modern orthography is morphophonemic. The change in orthography thus represented a different concept of writing. The decision to allow any consonant to be written at the end of the syllable as *patchim* was a product of this newer way of thinking.

The decision whether to write phonemically or morphophonemically involves more than the neutralization mentioned above, however. There are also a number of related problems, such as that of assimilation. Let us look at some examples. (More details will be given in chapter 3.)

One type of assimilation occurs when a stop occurs before a nasal and the stop becomes nasalized.

(6) a. kwung-mul 'broth'   mengnunta 'eats'
    b. kwuk-mul   meknunta
       (국물)   (먹는다)

(7) a. pam mata 'each field'   ennunta 'acquires'
    b. path mata   etnunta
       (밭마다)   (얻는다)

(8) a. im man 'just a leaf'   emnun 'being non-existent'
    b. iph man   epsnun
       (잎만)   (없는)

(9) a. kkom-mangwul 'flower bud' wunnunta 'laughs'
    b. kkoch-mangwul   wusnunta
       (꽃망울)   (웃는다)

Another kind of assimilation occurs when the nasal consonant *n* assimilates to an adjacent *l*.

(10)a. welli 'principle'	tal-lim 'the dear moon'	hallunta 'licks'
b. wenli	tal-nim	halthnunta
(원리)	(달님)	(핥는다)

In a completely phonemic orthography, the forms given in (a) of the above examples would be those that were transcribed. However, none of these cases of assimilation are reflected in the modern Hangŭl orthography, and even the older, traditional orthography did not represent them completely.

Thus far we have looked at one of the two orthographic points in contention. Now let us turn to the other problem of Korean orthography, that of how to write a consonant at the end of a syllable when the following syllable begins with a vowel. In the modern orthography, such consonants are almost always written as *patchim* at the end of the first syllable. However, in the early years following the invention of the Korean alphabet, the practice was to write the consonant at the beginning of the second syllable.[9] After that early period in the fifteenth century, there was a gradual tendency toward leaving the consonant at the end of the first syllable. But the general rule did not change until the Unification of Hangŭl Orthography in 1933, when the outline of today's modern orthography was adopted. Let us look at some examples of these two types of orthography. The forms in (11a) show how the noun *os* 'clothing' is written in today's orthography before a variety of particles beginning with a vowel, as well as before the copula *i(ta)*; (12a) shows the verb stem *cap-* 'grab' written with vowel-initial endings. The forms in (11b) and (12b) show how the earlier orthography worked.

(11)a. 옷이,	옷을,	옷으로,	옷에서,	옷이다
os i	os ul	os ulo	os eyse	os ita
b. 오시,	오슬,	오스로,	오세서,	오시다
o-si	o-sul	o-sulo	o-seyse	o-sita

(12)a. 잡아,	잡아라,	잡으니,	잡으면,	잡았다
cap-a	cap-ala	cap-uni	cap-umyen	cap-assta
b. 자바,	자바라,	자브니,	자브면,	자봤다
ca-pa	ca-pala	ca-puni	ca-pumyen	ca-passta

Of these two types of orthography, the older, traditional one reflects pronunciation more faithfully. From the phonological point of view, there is no syllable boundary dividing a *patchim* consonant and a following vowel, because the consonant is actually pronounced as the initial consonant of that second syllable. The reason for choosing the modern type of orthography and writing the consonant *patchim* is to keep the spelling of the morpheme the same no matter how it is actually pronounced. As was mentioned above, the basic principle of today's Hangŭl orthography is to always write each morpheme with a single unchanging shape.

Not only does this modern orthographical rule apply to inflectional forms, as shown in the preceding examples, but it also applies to the morphemes within a derived word. For example, the two suffixes *-i* and *-um*,[10] are written as forms separate from the rest of the word, as can be seen in (13). However, the application of the rule in such cases is not absolute. Other, similar suffixes—such as *-em, -ay, -wung,* and *-umeli*—are not written separately, as we see in (14).

(13) a. 웃음 'laughter', 울음 'crying', 믿음 'belief', 얼음 'ice', 죽음 'death'
    wus-um   wul-um   mit-um   el-um   cwuk-um
    (*wus-* 'laugh', *wul-* 'cry', *mit-* 'believe', *el-* 'freeze', *cwuk-* 'die')
  b. 높이 'height', 깊이 'depth', 길이 'length', 땀받이 'undershirt'
    noph-i   kiph-i   kil-i   ttam-pat-i
    (*noph-* 'be high', *kiph-* 'be deep', *kil-* 'be long', *ttam-pat-* 'sweat-receive')

(14) a. 무덤 'grave', 마개 'stopper', 마중 'meeting', 귀머거리 'deaf person'
    mu-tem   ma-kay   ma-cwung   kwi-me-keli
    (*mut-* 'bury', *mak-* 'stop', *mac-* 'meet' *kwi-mek-* 'be deaf')
  b. 너무 'too much', 도로 'again', 불긋불긋 'reddish'
    ne-mu   *to-lo*   *pul-kus pul-kus*
    (*nem-* 'go over', *tol-* 'turn', *pulk-* 'be red')
  c. 지붕 'roof', 바깥 'outside', 이파리 'small leaves', 끄트머리 'the end part'
    ci-pung   pa-kkath   i-phali   kku-thumeli
    (*cip* 'house', *pakk* 'outside', *iph* 'leaf', *kkuth* 'end')
  d. 미덥다 'be trustworthy', 우습다 'be laughable'
    mi-tepta   wu-supta
    (*mit-* 'believe', *wus-* 'laugh')

The difference in the way these words are written has to do with the productivity of the suffix. While the suffixes *-um* and *-i* can be used relatively freely to derive nouns from verbs and adjectives, the others cannot. (Cf. chapter 4.) In the mind of the speaker (and the user of the orthography), the words *wus-um* 'laughter' and *noph-i* 'height' can be thought of as regular derivations of the verb *wus-* and the adjective *noph-*, much as are the predicative forms *wus-uni, wus-ela, noph-ase,* and *noph-umyen.* But words like *makay* 'stopper' and *mutem* 'grave' are not derived productively. The decision to write them without showing the suffix separated was based upon the assumption that most people think of them as single, indivisible words. Their etymologies were thought not to be obvious.

Here we can see that spellings were not always chosen to elucidate meanings. Sometimes the rule of keeping single, invariant forms for morphemes was abandoned in favor of a phonemic notation. Such is also the case with the inflection of the irregular verbs. Here, it is the actual pronunciation that is transcribed. Although, as we have seen, phonological processes such as neutralization and assimilation are ignored in favor of preserving uniform shapes for the morphemes, the decision was made to record the actual phonemic shapes of the irregular verbs. Notice that the spellings given in (a) and not (b) were chosen for the verb forms in (15) through (17):

(15) *tep- / tew-* 'be hot'
　　a. 덥다,　　　　더우니,　　　　더워서
　　　　tep-ta　　　　te-wuni (← -uni)　　te-wese (← -ese)
　　b. 덥다　　　　덥으니　　　　덥어서
　　　　tep-ta　　　　*tep-uni　　　　*tep-ese

(16) *ci(s)-* 'build'
　　a. 짓고,　　　　지으니,　　　　지어서
　　　　cis-ko　　　　ci-uni　　　　ci-ese
　　b. 짓고,　　　　짓으니,　　　　짓어서
　　　　cis-ko　　　　*cis-uni　　　　*cis-ese

(17) *tut- / tul-* 'hear'
　　a. 듣고,　　　　들으니　　　　들어서
　　　　tut-ko　　　　tul-uni　　　　tul-ese
　　b. 듣고　　　　듣으니　　　　듣어서
　　　　tut-ko　　　　*tut-uni　　　　*tut-ese

Besides the two issues discussed above, another point of controversy about modern Hangŭl orthography is the problem of word spacing. Though writing in traditional times had no spaces at all, modern Korean writing requires spacing based on the unit of the word. The question that arises is what constitutes a word.

For the purpose of spacing, particles are not thought of as independent words but are written solid, as part of the preceding word. Once this convention has been stipulated, the principles of word spacing in Korean become relatively simple. In English, the treatment of compounds can present a problem because it is not consistent; sometimes a compound is written solid, sometimes with a space, and sometimes with a hyphen—as we see in the words *bathroom, high chair,* and *ape-man.* Hangŭl does not have this problem. The rule is to treat compounds always as single words and write them solid. Yet even so, word spacing is still, by far, the most difficult aspect of Korean orthography to master. It is where the most confusion can be found in the orthography of printed media, such as books and newspapers.

The reason that word spacing presents so many difficulties is that it derives from a fundamental problem in linguistics, for one of the hardest tasks in linguistic analysis is the definition of a word. It is not easy to draw boundaries in any language between what is a word and what is not a word, and Korean is no exception. It is simple to say that compounds should be written solid as a single word, but it is far from simple to distinguish in such cases whether one is actually dealing with a compound or with a phrase. For example, there are people who write 여름 방학 *(yelum panghak)* 'summer vacation' as a phrase composed of two words, but there are also people who write 여름방학 *(yelumpanghak)* 'summervacation' as a single, compound word.

It is also difficult, for example, to draw a clear boundary between what is a particle and what belongs to another word class. Many other forms besides particles do not occur independently, and for the nonspecialist it is not easy to tell these apart. For example, the noun *swu* 'way, means' occurs exclusively as a post-modifier in constructions together with verbal forms ending in *-nun* or *-l.* Therefore, even though the rules of orthography require the word spacing of (18a), many Koreans will write the sentence as in (18b), choosing to divide the form before the particle *cocha* 'even' rather than make the required break in the middle of this set construction.

(18) a. 나는 울 수조차 없다. 'I can't even cry.' [Lit., 'I don't even have a crying way.']

nanun wul swucocha epsta

b. 나는 울수 조차 없다.

nanun wulswu cocha epsta

In Korean, an auxiliary verb, such as *pota* 'try (doing)', occurs after the main verb; for example, *wus-e poala* 'Make a smile' (literally, 'try laughing'), *mek-e poala* 'Try some [food]' (literally, 'try eating'). Since the two verb forms often bond together as a lexical unit, there is a tendency to write such constructions solid as a single word. The orthographic rule for Hangŭl has until recently specified that a space must be written between the main verb and the auxiliary, but the new Hangŭl Orthography (한글 맞춤법) of 1989 takes this tendency into account and permits the constructions alternatively to be written solid.

On a practical level, the problems with word spacing are not very serious because Hangŭl is written in syllabic units. Koreans are not particularly conscious of the need for spaces. As was pointed out above, there is no word spacing at all in older texts, yet most Koreans do not experience any great difficulty reading the texts. There is none of the confusion that is caused when English is spelled without spaces. In newspapers, therefore, where there is little flexibility in the use of space on the page, word spacing is completely inconsistent and used only where convenient. Magazines, too, tend to use far fewer spaces than are found in the textbook.

There are also differences between North Korea and South Korea in the use of word spaces. North Korea tends to require fewer spaces between words than does South Korea. Words written with spaces in South Korea are often written solid in North Korea. In the following example, (19a) represents a sentence as it actually appeared in a North Korean work, while (19b) represents how the sentence would be written according to South Korean orthographic rules:

(19)a. 이러한 형태는 전통적인 방언소유자들속에서만 잔재적으로
       남아있는것으로서 극히 드물게 쓰이고있을뿐이다.
       (Hwang Taehwa 1986:117)
       Ilehan hyengthaynun centhongcekin pangensoyucatulsokeyseman
       cancaycekulo namaissnunkesulose kukhi tumulkey ssuikoissulppu-
       nita.

     b. 이러한 형태는 전통적인 방언 소유자들 속에서만 잔재적으로
       남아 있는 것으로서 극히 드물게 쓰이고 있을 뿐이다.
       Ilehan hyengthaynun centhongcekin pangen soyucatul sokeyseman
       cancaycekulo nama issnun kesulose kukhi tumulkey ssuiko issul
       ppunita.
       'These kinds of forms are only used extremely rarely as things that re-
       main vestigially only among [speakers] of traditional dialects.'

Another salient feature of North Korean orthography deserves mention here. In North Korea, beginning in 1966, an etymological *l-* at the beginning of words has been restored in the spellings of many words.

In the Korean language, there is a constraint against the occurrence of the consonant *l-* (ㄹ) in word-initial position. (Cf. Chapter 3.) With the exception of modern loanwords such as *latio* 'radio', *leypeyl* 'level', and *lenchi* 'lunch' and proper names such as *Loma* 'Rome', *Lenten* 'London', and *Lesia* 'Russia', *l-* does not occur at the beginning of a word. From very early on, an initial *l-* found in many of the borrowed readings of Chinese characters was either lost, or became *n-* in initial position, and the original consonant *l-* is only preserved in non-initial syllables in Sino-Korean compounds. Some examples of modern character readings with etymological *l-* are given in (20).

(20)a. 樂 *nak-* / *-lak: nak*(wen) 'paradise'; (o) *lak* 'pleasure'
     b. 勞 *no-* / *-lo: no*(tong) 'labor'; (kwa) *lo* 'overwork'
     c. 禮 *-yey* / *-lyey: yey*(uy) 'politeness'; (sil) *lyey* 'rudity'

Etymological spellings used in North Korea are shown in (21a); the South Korean equivalents are given in (21b):

(21)a. NK: 락원 'paradise';   로동 'labor';   례의 'politeness'
       lakwen   lotong   lyeyuy
     b. SK: 낙원 'paradise';   노동 'labor';   예의 'politeness'
       nakwen   notong   yeyuy

Another common example of this kind of etymological spelling is the North
Korean spelling 리 *(li)* for the surname 李 (rendered variously as *Lee, Rhee,
Yi, Ri,* etc., in English). The South Korean spelling of the name is 이 *(i)*.
A related phonological constraint on initial consonants is against the
occurrence of *n-* before *-i* or *-y*. Thus, in Sino-Korean vocabulary, original occurrences of *n-* have been lost. But again, as with initial *l-*, North Korean pol-
icymakers have chosen etymological spellings, as seen in the examples below:

(22) a. 女 *-ye / -nye: ye*(ca) 'woman'; (nam) *nye* 'male and female'
   b. 尿 *-yo / -nyo: yo*(so) 'urea'; (pang) *nyo* 'urination'
   c. 年 *-yen / -nyen: yen*(sey) 'age'; (o) *nyen* 'five years'

(23) a. NK: 녀자 'woman';   뇨소 'urea';   년세 'age'
         nyeca   nyoso   nyensey
     b. SK: 여자 'woman';   요소 'urea';   연세 'age'
         yeca   yoso   yensey

   The thought behind the North Korean etymological spellings is that a
morpheme should always be spelled the same way, regardless of its changes
in pronunciation. At first, these spellings seem to reflect an attitude consistent with the basic, morphophonemic principles of Hangŭl orthography.
But when one examines them a bit more closely, one discovers quickly that
in fact they are not in accord with the thinking of Hangŭl orthography and
that they are a treatment that goes beyond practicality.
   As we have seen above, the Hangŭl spellings 믿음 *(mit-um)* 'belief' and
웃음 *(wus-um)* 'laughter' are constructed to reflect the etymologies of the
words—that is, what morphemes they are composed of—but the spellings of
the words 무덤 *(mutem)* 'grave' and 마중 *(macwung)* 'meeting' are not. It is
not an easy task to reveal the etymologies of forms that are not derived productively, and an orthography that attempts to do so is not an effective one.
In many cases, it is not obvious that a Chinese character reading should have
an initial *l-* or *n-*. It is far more difficult to know that the morphemes *li* and
nyo found in the words *(l)ibal* 'haircut' and *(n)yoso* 'urea' have an etymological *l-* and *n-* than it is to know that the words *mutem* 'grave' and *macwung*
'meeting' are derived from *mut-* 'bury' and *mac-* 'meet'. It is for this reason
that, from the point of view of practicality, the North Korean orthography is
burdensome to the user.
   Moreover, not only does North Korea use the archaic spellings 로동, 례
의, 녀자 *(lotong, lyeyuy, nyeca),* and so on, but policy also requires that the
words actually be pronounced that way, even though such pronunciations
were lost several hundred years ago. For the most part, North Koreans seem
to make the effort to do so. Still, adopting such prescriptive pronunciations
is like asking speakers of English to pronounce the initial *k-* found the spellings *knight, knack,* and *knee.* Even given the desire to do so, it is not easy to re-
introduce such sounds into natural speech and be completely consistent.[11]

2.4 An Evaluation of Hangŭl Orthography

The orthography used in the modern Hangŭl writing system went through a long process of trial and error before reaching its present form. For many years, controversy centered around the two points of contention discussed in the preceding section, with disputes raging back and forth and strong opinions on both sides. In fact, it is difficult to say that the fires of controversy have completely died down even to this day.

One important principle of Hangŭl orthography is syllabic writing. Hangŭl orthography has many unusual features, but the clustering of letters into syllables is one that over the years has continually come under criticism.

The criticism of syllabic writing begins with the observation that it is a hindrance to mechanization (Ch'oe Hyŏnbae 1937). If the letters of Hangŭl were arranged linearly the way Roman letters are, only forty letters would have to be kept in printers' fonts. However, in Korean print shops today as many as two thousand five hundred print keys have to be prepared for printing because a different one has to be prepared for every syllable. (If it is necessary to represent dialect pronunciations or other special sounds, then additional keys have to be made for each of those.) This typesetting problem is a major inconvenience of syllabic writing. Another disadvantage is that it requires additional time for picking type. The syllabic nature of Hangŭl has also proved more than a little inconvenient in the construction of typewriters. Quite recently, these problems have been largely solved with the development of the computer, but there is no question that clustering the letters into syllables has long been a hindrance to the mechanization of the writing system.

The significance of this typesetting inconvenience, however, can be exaggerated. After all, a work is written by one or, at most, three or four authors; but when printed, that same work can be read by many thousands of people. How much does a little inconvenience for the typesetter matter if the needs of so many readers are served? In other words, when evaluating the effectiveness of a writing system, the mechanics of reading are far more important than the mechanics of writing. When weighing the relative merits of a writing system, one must always consider it first from the standpoint of the reader.[12]

For this reason, the judgment that syllabic writing is a hindrance to mechanization needs to be put into a little perspective. Even if syllabic writing does present some inconvenience for mechanization (and this problem has largely been resolved thanks to the computer), the evaluation of the orthography becomes quite different if it has some advantage for the reader. The question should be: Which is more convenient for the reader, syllabic writing or in-line writing? This is the question upon which evaluations of printing and all forms of mechanized writing must turn.

In our opinion, the syllabic system used in Hangŭl orthography is particularly well adapted to the Korean language. Because Korean is an agglutinative language in which particles and suffixes are added one after the other to a stem, there are a very large number of inflected forms, and in in-line writing it can often be difficult even to distinguish where one inflec-tional form ends and another begins. Grouping the letters into syllables is an effective solution to this problem. The following example shows alterna-tive ways of writing some of the inflectional forms of the verb *nulk-* 'to age'; (1a) is in-line, (1b) is phonemic, and (1c) is morphophonemic:

(1) a. ㄴㅡㄹㄱㄴㅡㄴㄷㅏ,   ㄴㅡㄹㄱㅡㄴㅣ,   ㄴㅡㄹㄱㅓㅅㅓ,   ㄴㅡㄹㄱㅓㅆㄷㅏ
    n u l k n u n t a   n u l k u n i   n u l k e s e   n u l k e ss t a

b. 능는다,   늘그니,   늘거서,   늘걷다
    nung-nunta   nul-kuni   nul-kese   nul-ketta

c. 늙는다,   늙으니,   늙어서,   늙었다
    nulk-nunta   nulk-uni   nulk-ese   nulk-essta

In (1c), the stem of the verb *nulk-* has a consistent visual form. In this case, the morpheme is more easily recognized by the reader than when it has a changing shape, as in (1b) — and far more quickly perceived as a unit than in the in-line writing of (1a). There has not been enough research on the efficiency of the kind of syllabic writing found in Hangŭl (Taylor 1980), but from the point of view of morpheme recognition we believe that the ver-dict on this kind of writing must be positive.

Moreover, the striking difference in compactness reveals much about the nature of the Korean alphabet. The writing system was not designed to be written in-line, and spreading the letters out in a linear fashion as in (1a) alters a fundamental feature of their structure. Were in-line writing to be adopted, as a practical measure, many of the letters — especially the horizon-tal vowels — would need to be redesigned.

The assessment of the present Hangŭl orthography has to be a positive one. In some cases the spellings may be at some remove from the actual pro-nunciations, but the practice of keeping a single, consistent shape for a mor-pheme is effective for readability. And if this principle of morpheme representation is the one that is adopted into a writing system, it is difficult to imagine a better orthography than the present one used for Hangŭl.

A phonemic script can also serve logographically, with the morpheme as the unit of representation rather than pronunciation, and such writing can be more effective than a straightforward phonemic one. Only recently has this concept of writing begun to spread in Western academic circles, where it had long been taken for granted that the only measure of the value of a script was how accurately it represented pronunciations. For the most part, thinking had been based on the idea that writing only has the mission of rendering sounds visible. The assumption was that when people read and understand meaning, they first transpose the letters into sounds and then grasp the meaning through the sounds. This thinking also tied into the ten-dency, as was described above, for the efficiency of a writing system to be judged from the point of view of the writer. Thus, since efficiency in writing was the objective, reasoning centered on the idea that transcriptions of pronunciations are easier to learn and to write. This view of writing affected language policies worldwide. The enthusiasm for a straightforward phonemic representation was the thought that underlay, for example, the numerous movements for the reform of English spellings.

However, in recent years perceptions about the mechanics of writing have begun to change. People have begun to realize that, as the degree of dependence on writing grows in civilized society and a proficient level of reading is reached, the writing system develops in its own characteristic way and comes to transmit meaning without a complete dependence on pronunciation. Let us look at an example from English. No matter how the -*ed* of *wanted, passed,* and *called* is pronounced, the meaning of the form can be perceived by the eye without recourse to the actual details of the pronunciation. Rather than transcribe each occurrence as -*id, -t,* or -*d,* it is better to fix the form as an unchanging -*ed.* Establishing a uniform shape is a more effective way of transmitting the meaning of this past tense morpheme than writing each and every phonemic variant.[13]

From very early on, Hangŭl orthography has made use of this principle. It is fundamentally a morphophonemic script. In addition, it incorporates into its basic design the clustering of letters into syllables, a practice that makes it possible to maximize morphemic representation. In this way, Hangŭl orthography represents logographic units using phonemic symbols.

2.5 The History of the Korean Alphabet

There is historical documentation of the invention of Hangŭl. More than is true of most writing systems, it is possible to know how and when the Korean alphabet was created, who invented it, and by what principles.

2.5.1 The Origin of the Korean Alphabet

In Volume 102 of the *Annals of King Sejong* (世宗實錄), the entry for the twelfth month of the twenty-fifth year of Sejong's reign reads as follows:

(1)

是月上親制諺文二十八字其字倣古篆分爲初中終聲合之然後乃成字凡于文字
及本國俚語皆可得而書字雖簡要轉換無窮是謂訓民正音

'This month, His Highness personally created the twenty-eight letters of the Vernacular Script (*Ŏnmun*). Its letters imitate the Old Seal, and are divided into initial, medial, and terminal sounds. Once one combines them they form a syllable. All [sounds] in both Chinese characters and in the rustic language of this country may be written. Although they are simple and fine, they shift and change [in function] without end. These are called the "Correct Sounds for the Instruction of the People."'[14]

The twenty-fifth year of Sejong's reign was 1443. However, since time was kept by the lunar calendar, the entry for the twelfth month also extended over into 1444. For this reason, accounts of the date vary. In South Korea, it is customary to attribute the invention to 1443, but in North Korea, and in some Western works as well, the date given is 1444. The first ten days of the month were in 1443, and the rest, from the eleventh on, were in 1444. One cannot know which of the two years is correct.

According to this entry from the dynastic records, the person who created the alphabet was the reigning monarch of the time, the king posthumously known as Sejong. There are varying interpretations of this text. One that has gained particularly wide acceptance is that, even though the entry attributes the invention to the king, the alphabet was actually created by a number of scholars who served as advisors to the king. According to this widespread interpretation, the alphabet was referred to as the "personal creation" of the king only because it was the custom to ascribe such accomplishments to the monarch. However, such was not the case in Korea. No other accomplishments or inventions during Sejong's remarkable reign were referred to this way, as his "personal creation." The entry is unique in all the records of that period.

Quite recently, through a thoroughgoing examination of the textual record, it has been convincingly shown that the alphabet was not a collaborative creation.[15] The numerous alphabetic projects carried out during Sejong's reign did not begin until after the entry cited above had been written, and by that time the invention of the alphabet was an accomplished fact. We do not know how long the preliminary research on writing systems lasted; there are no records predating the dynastic entry given above. But the identity of the inventor is clear. King Sejong created the alphabet himself, and he accomplished this task working in isolation, keeping the project secret from all but perhaps the crown prince and his other sons.

The skepticism that has been shown over the years about Sejong as inventor derives from the commonsense reasoning that it would have been difficult for the king to have invented the new letters by himself. He was, after all, a reigning monarch, busy with everyday affairs of state. However, there are ample firsthand accounts from other scholars of the time, as well as from Sejong himself, that show the king's superior learning and reveal in some detail his theories regarding orthography. The linguistic scholars who surrounded him were brilliant young men in the Academy of Worthies (Chiphyŏnjŏn, 集賢殿) such as Chŏng Inji, Sin Sukchu, Sŏng Sammun, and Pak P'aengnyŏn, who worked at Sejong's bidding. But these advisors did not participate in the invention of the alphabet. The conclusion from the textual record is inescapable. Sejong was a scholar of phonology and writing without parallel in Korean history, and the alphabet was indeed his personal invention.

The dynastic record cited in (1), above, also informs us that the original name of the Korean alphabet was *Hunmin chŏngŭm* ("the Correct Sounds for the Instruction of the People," 訓民正音). As a name, *Hunmin chŏngŭm* is somewhat long and cumbersome (it is often abbreviated to just *Chŏngŭm*), but the fact that it was the name chosen for the script is important. By calling it 'the Correct Sounds for the Instruction of the People', Sejong showed that he had created the new writing system with the intent of bringing literacy to the ordinary citizens of the kingdom, the "common people" who were not of the intellectual elite proficient in Literary Chinese. In addition, however, the alphabet is also referred to in this entry as *Ŏnmun* (諺文). This other name for the alphabet was constructed as a word parallel to *Hanmun* (漢文), 'Chinese writing', in order to contrast the new letters with those used for literary writing, Chinese characters. It meant 'vernacular writing', or local writing. The name *Ŏnmun* subsequently eclipsed *Hunmin chŏngŭm* and became the common name used for the alphabet in traditional times. And, as was mentioned at the beginning of this chapter, it was not until this century, sometime around 1913, that the name *Hangŭl* emerged. In 1927 the magazine entitled *Hangŭl* began publication, and from that time on, the word gradually spread in usage. Today it is used in South Korea to the total exclusion of other terms. In North Korea, on the other hand, the name was never adopted. There the word used for the alphabet instead is *Chosŏngul* 'Chosŏn writing'.

The information given in the dynastic record about the new writing system is cursory. Besides the date of its announcement, the identity of the inventor, and the name of the writing system, the entry tells us that there were twenty-eight letters in the alphabet. It also informs us that the letters are divided into initials, medials, and terminals that can be combined to form a syllable. It goes on to say that they can be used to write any sound. However, the entry does not show what the letters looked like; it gives no concrete description of their shapes; nor is there any basic information about the use of the letters, how they were to be grouped into syllables, and the like.

Detailed information about the alphabet was first revealed a little over two and a half years later, in the first part of the ninth lunar month of 1446, when the document known as the *Hunmin chŏngŭm* ("The Correct Sounds for the Instruction of the People," 訓民正音) was published. This document, which carried as its title the name of the new letters themselves, had been written by Sejong himself. It was a kind of handbook for learning the alphabet.

The *Hunmin chŏngŭm* itself was a very short work, only about seven pages long, including the preface. But attached to it, and really forming a single document with it, was a much longer and detailed text called the *Hunmin chŏngŭm haerye* ('Explanations and Examples of the Correct Sounds for the Instruction of the People', 訓民正音解例). This "*Haerye* Text" was not written by the king, but by a group of young scholars from the Academy of Worthies commissioned by him. In contrast with the brief outline sketched in the *Hun-*

min chŏngŭm, the *Haerye* presented a scholarly treatise on the principles and
theories that underlay the new writing system. It showed how the alphabet was
to be employed and gave concrete examples of its use, and it is from this work
that the details of the Korean alphabet as originally conceived are known.

It is often said that the Korean alphabet was invented in 1443 (or
1444), but it was with the publication of the *Hunmin chŏngŭm* and the *Hunmin chŏngŭm haerye* in 1446 that the script was made known to the world. The
South Korean holiday *Hangul-nal*, "Alphabet Day," is celebrated each year
on 9 October, because that date is intended to coincide with the promulgation of the *Hunmin chŏngŭm*.[16]

Nevertheless, whether the Korean alphabet is dated to 1443/44 or to
1446, the fact that the date of its invention can be celebrated is what is special. Most of the writing systems of the world were developed over long periods of time, and even were it true that they were invented by someone at
some particular point in time, the circumstances usually can no longer be
known. That is the situation to which Coulmas (1989:3) was referring in the
following passage:

(2) Of course [writing] was not invented in the sense that one day someone decided that writing was what was needed, and sat down at a desk to invent it.

However, that is exactly what did happen in the case of the Korean alphabet.
The *Hunmin chŏngŭm* and the *Hunmin chŏngŭm haerye* give us the facts, in
great detail, about its provenance.

2.5.2 The Design Principles for the Letter Shapes

The heart of the *Hunmin chŏngŭm haerye* is the section entitled "Explanation of the design of the letters" ("Chejahae," 制字解). This part of the document provides detailed and in-depth explanations of the linguistic and
philosophical principles forming the basis of the letter shapes and structure.
For our purposes here, in examining the design principles of the letters, we will
concentrate principally on the linguistic explanations found in the document.

The twenty-eight letters of the Korean alphabet were not created by designing each letter separately. Rather, the letters were produced in a two-stage process, in which a number of basic letters were designed first, then the
remaining letters were derived from these basic shapes. Of the seventeen
consonant letters (called, in the nomenclature of the time, "initials" (初聲),
five were created as the basic letters. The shapes of these basic letters were
based upon the organs of articulation pronouncing the consonants. The explanations given in the "Chejahae" are as follows:

(1) 牙音 ㄱ 象舌根閉喉之形
    舌音 ㄴ 象舌附上顎之形
    脣音 ㅁ 象口形

齒音 ㅅ 象齒形
喉音 ○ 象喉形

'The molar sound ㄱ [k] depicts the outline of the root of the tongue blocking the throat.
The lingual sound ㄴ [n] depicts the outline of the tongue touching the alveolar ridge.
The labial sound ㅁ [m] depicts the outline of the mouth.
The dental sound ㅅ [s] depicts the outline of the incisor.
The laryngeal sound ○[ø] depicts the outline of the throat.'[17]

Let us examine first the explanations given for the last three letter shapes. Here the text says that the letter ㅁ is an outline drawing of the lips, the speech organs used in the pronunciation of the labial consonant *m*. The letter ㅅ, representing the "incisor" (in modern terminology, the dental) consonant *s,* was made in the shape of a tooth, the place where the sound is modulated when the consonant is pronounced. The laryngeal ○ was made to represent the round shape of the throat.

The first two letters ㄱ [k] and ㄴ [n] were also made in imitation of the speech organs used in the production of the sounds, just as the other three were. However, these two cases are somewhat different because the tongue, the speech organ involved in the articulation, was not portrayed at rest, but rather depicted in the act of producing the sound. In other words, the "molar sound" (that is, the velar) ㄱ was made in imitation of the "root of the tongue" (the dorsum) closing the oral cavity to make the sound [k]; the "lingual (apical or alveolar) sound" ㄴ shows the tongue making contact with the alveolar ridge, as it does when the sound [n] is pronounced. The articulatory gestures the two consonants represent are illustrated in figures 1 and 2, below:

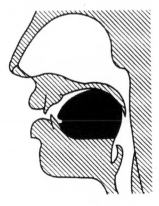

Figure 1 The shape of the tongue used in the pronunciation of English [ŋ] (Jones 1957: 171)

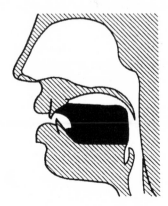

Figure 2 The shape of the tongue used in the pronunciation of English [n] (Jones 1957: 169)

Each of the remaining consonant letters was made by adding strokes to the letter from which it was derived. The process was as follows:

(2) basic + 1 stroke + 2nd stroke

  ㄱ → ㅋ   k → kh

  ㄴ → ㄷ → ㅌ (ㄷ→ㄹ)   n → t → th (t →l)

  ㅁ → ㅂ → ㅍ   m→ p → ph

  ㅅ → ㅈ → ㅊ (ㅅ→ㅿ)   s → c → ch (s → z)

  ㅇ → ㆆ → ㅎ (ㅇ→ㆁ)   ø → q → h (ø → ng)

The "Chejahae" passage from which this information comes is the following:

(3) ㅋ 比 ㄱ 聲出稍려 故加劃 ㄴ而ㄷ ㄷ而ㅌ ㅁ而ㅂ ㅂ而ㅍ ㅅ而ㅈ
  ㅈ而ㅊ ㅇ而ㆆ ㆆ而ㅎ 其因聲加劃之義皆同 而唯ㆁ 爲異 半舌音ㄹ 半齒
  音ㅿ 亦象舌齒之形而異其體 無加劃之義焉

  'The sound of ㅋ [k^h] is a little more severe than that of ㄱ [k]; therefore a stroke is added.

   ㄴ [n] then ㄷ [t]; ㄷ then ㅌ [t^h].

   ㅁ [m] then ㅂ [p]; ㅂ then ㅍ [p^h].

   ㅅ [s] then ㅈ [c]; ㅈ then ㅊ [c^h].

   ㅇ [ø] then ㆆ [q]; ㆆ then ㅎ [h].

  The appropriety of adding strokes in accordance with the sound is in all these cases the same; only ㆁ [ng] constitutes an exception. The semilingual sound ㄹ [l] and the semi-incisor sound ㅿ [z] likewise depict the outline of the tongue and incisor, only the form is altered; in these cases there is no appropriety of adding strokes.'[18]

In this crucial passage, the "Chaejahae" tells us that each letter made by adding a stroke was of the same type as the basic letter from which it was derived. In other words, both ㅋ *(kh)* and ㄱ *(k)* were "molar sounds"; ㅁ *(m)*, ㅂ *(p)*, and ㅍ *(ph)* were labials; and so on. Each time a stroke was added, the type of consonant remained the same, but the sound became "a little more severe." This increased "severity" of sound is what the addition of strokes represented. However, the consonants ㄹ *(l)* and ㅿ *(z)* were exceptions, because the addition of strokes did not make them "more severe." The consonant ㆁ *(ng)* was exceptional for yet another reason. Though it actually represented a "molar sound" (a velar) and as such should have been derived from ㄱ *(k)*, its form was modeled instead on the laryngeal ㅇ. The editors of the *Hunmin chŏngŭm haerye* understood this inconsistency but explained their decision as follows:

(4) 唯牙之ㆁ 雖舌根閉喉聲氣出鼻 而其聲與ㅇ相似 . . . 今亦取象於喉

  'As for the molar ㆁ [ng], the root of the tongue blocks the throat and the breath of enunciation is emitted through the nose; nonetheless, the enunciation resembles that of ㅇ [Ø]. . . . [So] we have taken the depiction [for ㅇ] from the throat . . .'[19]

The *Haerye* editors wanted to show a relationship between initial *ng-* and zero. They knew that as an initial, the use of *ng-* had a certain artificiality about it. Korean words did not have an initial *ng-* in the fifteenth century any more than they do today, and, word-initially at least, the symbol ㆁ was used only to spell certain words from Chinese. It was not many years before the graphic distinction between ㆁ *(ng)* and ㅇ (ø) disappeared completely, and the two symbols were merged into one. Subsequently, this unified symbol was used as a "zero consonant" in initial position, and as the symbol for *-ng* in final position, just as the letter still is today.

There are eleven letters representing vowels (the *Haerye* referred to them as "medial sounds": 中聲). Of these eleven, three are the basic symbols, from which all the other vowel letters were derived. These three basic letters are · [ʌ], — [ɨ], and ㅣ [i]. The *Haerye* explanations are as follows:

(5) · 舌縮而聲深 天開於子也 形之圓 象乎天也
　　 — 舌小縮而聲不深不淺 地闢於丑也 形之平 象乎地也
　　 ㅣ 舌不縮而聲淺 人生於寅也 形之立 象乎人也

　　　'With · [ʌ], the tongue retracts and the sound is deep. Heaven commences in the First Epoch. The roundness of the outline is a depiction of Heaven.

　　　With — [ɨ], the tongue retracts a little and the sound is neither deep nor shallow. Earth opens in the Second Epoch. The flatness of the outline is a depiction of Earth.

　　　With ㅣ [i], the tongue does not retract and the sound is shallow. Man is born in the Third Epoch. The uprightness of the outline is a depiction of Man.'

These explanations are not like those given for the consonants. Though they begin with brief descriptions of pronunciation and sound, they are primarily philosophical rationalizations, not linguistic analysis. Instead of depicting articulations, the vowel symbols represent abstract philosophical concepts. According to this *Haerye* passage, these basic shapes were not intended to represent articulatory gestures; rather, they were constructed to symbolize the natural pattern of the three great powers of the Neo-Confucian universe: Heaven, Earth, and Man.

The eight remaining vowel symbols were complex symbols, devised by combining · with — or ㅣ . The first four of these complex symbols combined a single occurrence of · with one of the other two vowels:

(6) · + — → ㅗ [o]
　　 · + ㅣ → ㅏ [a]
　　 · + — → ㅜ [u]
　　 · + ㅣ → ㅓ [ə]

The second four vowel symbols added one more dot · :

(7) · + ᆠ → ᆢ [yo]
· + ᅡ → ᅣ [ya]
· + ᅮ → ᅲ [yu]
· + ᅥ → ᅧ [yə]

Although the vowels in this second group of four were presented as unitary symbols, the sound that was being transcribed was actually a glide-vowel combination, [y] plus one of the other four "complex" vowels.[20]

In any event, the cosmological symbolism begun with the basic vowels continued with the complex vowels, as "Heaven" combined with "Earth" or "Man." As an example, let us look at the explanation given for the first of these vowel derivations:

(8) ᅩ 與 ·同而口蹙 其形則·與 一 合而成 取天地初交之義也
'ᅩ [o] is the same as · [ʌ], only the mouth is contracted. Its outline is formed by combining · with ㅡ. We take the appropriety of Heaven's initial conjugation with Earth.'

Still, the Neo-Confucian cosmology did no damage to the linguistic facts; rather, it harmonized smoothly with them. A good example of this synthesis can be seen in the division of the vowels into *yin* and *yang* categories: Symbols in which the dot appeared above or to the right (ᅩ, ᅡ, ᅭ, and ᅣ) were determined to be *yang* vowels, and the symbols where the dot was below or to the left (ᅮ, ᅥ, ᅲ, and ᅧ) were *yin* vowels. This treatment not only reflected the philosophical background of the *Hunmin chŏngŭm*, but it also reflected structurally the system of vowel harmony found in Korean in the fifteenth century (cf. chapter 7).

For the modern Korean reader, or for anyone familiar with modern *Hangŭl*, the most striking aspect of the Korean alphabet as seen in the *Hunmin chŏngŭm* (cf. figure 3) is the appearance of the letters. As Sejong originally conceived them, the shapes of the letters are uncompromisingly geometric. Lines are straight, angles sharp, and circles perfectly round. Spare, rational, and systematic, they stand in sharp contrast to the smooth and flowing lines of Chinese, or even to the softened lines of modern Hangŭl.

The Korean alphabet began to change in appearance soon after the *Hunmin chŏngŭm* was published. In the *Hunmin chŏngŭm*, and in one other early text,[21] the vowel letter · [ʌ] is a perfectly round black dot everywhere it is used. In slightly later texts, such as those shown in figure 4, the vowel itself is still a round black dot, but when combined in the complex letters, it has become a solid line; for example, ᅩ is now ㅗ, ᅡ is now ㅏ, and so on. By the time texts such as those in Figure 5 were printed, the vowel letter itself had changed, from perfectly round to a tear-shaped mark like a stroke used in Chinese calligraphy: · → ⸝ . Though actually printed with wood blocks, these latter texts show in the shapes of the letters the influence that the writ-

Figure 3 A page from the *Hunmin chŏngŭm* (1446)

ing brush had already begun to exert upon the appearance of the Korean alphabet. In subsequent years, Korean writing conformed ever more to the medium, and before long, the letters of the alphabet came to be written, as well as printed, as calligraphic brush strokes rather than as the original, more geometric lines and dots. These smooth brush strokes make up the alphabet that people are familiar with today.

The *Haerye* also provided explanations for letters besides the 28 discussed above. Although it was said that "His Highness [had] personally created the twenty-eight letters of the Vernacular Script," in actuality, a number of other letters had been constructed as well. First of all, there is the letter 붕, made by writing the laryngeal ㅇ below the labial ㅂ [p]. The structure of this letter was intended to indicate that the lips were touched more "lightly" than was the case with ㅂ [p]. While ㅂ [p] transcribed the labial stop [p], 붕 transcribed the labial fricative [ß]. The difference was that in the pronunciation of the latter, the lips did not close tightly enough to close off the flow of air. In addition to 붕, a number of other "light" letters were made in this way; e.g., 동, 푱, and 뭉. However, these latter symbols were used only to transcribe prescriptive pronunciations for Chinese characters and not to write the Korean language itself.

Also not included in the twenty-eight letters were double consonants such as ㄲ, ㄸ, ㅃ, ㅆ, ㅉ, and ㆅ. These geminate symbols, said to represent "congealed" (凝) sounds, were also used prescriptively in the early texts, to transcribe what were thought of as the proper pronunciations of Chinese

Figure 4 Wŏrin chŏn'gang chi kok (1448)   *Figure 5 Wŏrin sŏkpo* (1459)

characters. It was only much later, in this century, that the letters were used consistently to represent what are now referred to as the "hard sounds" (된 소리), the reinforced or tense consonants of modern Korean (cf. chapter 3).

In addition, the *Haerye* provided for eighteen vocalic nuclei made by combining vowel letters. These were presented in three groups, as shown in (9), below. For the sake of convenience, the letters are shown here in their modern shapes. (Six of the vocalic combinations, which were not used to write Korean even then, are omitted.)

  (9) a. two-letter combinations: ㅘ[wa], ㅝ[wə]
      b. one-letter combinations with ㅣ [i]:
        ㅢ[ʌy], ㅢ[ɨy], ㅚ[oy], ㅐ[ay], ㅟ[uy], ㅔ[əy], ㅒ[yay], ㅖ[yəy]
      c. two-letter combinations with ㅣ [i]:ㅙ[way], ㅞ[wəy]

As we have seen above, the principles upon which the letters were designed can be summarized in two categories. One is that each basic letter has a definite source for its design, whether that was an imitation of the speech organs or of the cosmological principles of Heaven, Earth, and Man; the other principle is that each of the twenty-eight letters was not created individually and independently, but rather, once a few basic letter shapes had been designed first, the rest of the letters were derived from them, creating structural relationships between the letters. The concept of patterning the shapes of letters on the speech organs is extraordinary, as is also the idea of deriving letter shapes in a two-stage process. The Korean alphabet is often said to be a scientific writing system, and it is. The descriptions of the articulatory gestures used in pronouncing ㄱ [k] and ㄴ [n] are particularly worth notice in this regard.

The possibility that the creation of the Korean alphabet was influenced by Chinese characters continues to be a subject of controversy. One issue is the curious statement, found in both the *Haerye* and the *Annals of King Sejong* (cf. 2.5.1, above), that the letters of the alphabet "imitate the Old Seal." Even at the time, "Old Seal" (古篆)was taken to mean a style of Chinese writing. But it is far from clear what the term, or those passages, meant. Most experts have assumed that "Old Seal" referred to one of two Chinese calligraphic styles known as "Large Seal" and "Small Seal." But the term is a general one and not a precise name for those styles; if there is any resemblance of the Korean letters to any Chinese calligraphic style at all, it is an extremely superficial one. The meaning of the passages is still debated. Many other suggestions about Chinese influence have also been put forward, some concrete, some more abstract and systematic. Many have pointed out that the letter depicting the mouth, ㅁ [m], looks more like the Chinese character for 'mouth', 口, than it does the shape of the lips; the letter depicting a tooth, ㅅ [s], resembles one of the elements that make up the Chinese character for 'tooth', 齒. More subtle are arguments about the principles underlying the construction of the letters. The idea of creating basic letters, then deriving more complex symbols either by adding strokes or combining basic symbols, is much like structural principles found in the traditional graphic analysis of Chinese characters (六書).[22] These arguments cannot be dismissed out of hand. At the time the alphabet was invented, there was already in place in Korea a long and stable tradition of writing, and it would have been difficult for Koreans to completely ignore those graphic principles with which they had grown up and with which they were intimately familiar. The arguments are ones of historical and cultural continuity. Moreover, there may well have been influences on the alphabet from elsewhere in the region. It has been well documented that Sejong and his assistants had thoroughly researched the writing systems used in that part of the world, including alphabetic ones of Indian origin, and it stands to reason that this research would have played a role in the design of the new letters. The resemblances of some of the letter shapes to those of the hP'agspa alphabet used by Khubilai Khan are particularly striking.[23]

Nevertheless, none of these suggestions, for Chinese or for any other influence, diminishes in any way the creative nature of what Sejong had done. Nothing invented is ever created out of thin air; there is always an intellectual history to be considered. But there is also no reason to doubt that the origin of the Korean alphabet is anything other than what the *Haerye* said it was. The principles explained there are consistent with the structure of the script, and with what is known about the background and culture of the time. Sejong designed a simple and efficient writing system for the Korean people that was like no other, and that is still unique. Whatever else is said or claimed about it, the invention of the Korean alphabet will always be counted among the most remarkable events in the long history of writing on this planet.[24]

2.5.3 Special Features of the Korean Alphabet

In examining the design principles of the Korean alphabet we have seen that its graphic structure is unique, and that many of its other characteristics are unusual as well. Here we will expand on some of these points. First let us look at the composite nature of the letters. The letters of the Korean alphabet were designed in a two-stage process, in which one part of a composite letter has the function of representing certain phonological information. For example, although ㅋ [kʰ] is a single letter, one of the strokes that compose it is an element representing the phonological feature of aspiration. The stroke is the same as one of the strokes that make up the letter ㅌ [tʰ]. It is difficult to find another writing system in which letters can be analyzed into features smaller than a phoneme. In a similar way, vowels such as ㅛ [yo] and ㅑ [ya] are also single letters, but one of their strokes represents the semivowel [y]. This characteristic makes the Korean alphabet unlike any other.

Chao (1968:107) has described this graphic structure in a rather humorous way:

> The system of phonetic symbols in Korean (called *Han-gŭl* or *ŏnmun*) is interesting in two respects. First, it is much more of an alphabet than the Japanese syllabic *kana*. Secondly, from the point of view of the design of symbols, it is a writing system in which parts of unit symbols represent analytically features of the sounds. Except for sporadic cases in Chinese, no other system of writing in the world does that. One cannot say, for example, that the consonant *b* in English is voiced when the stem is up and voiceless when the stem is down, that is *p*, since the symbol for the voiced dental consonant *d* with stem down would be *q*, which, if this graphic analysis were valid, should represent the voiceless dental consonant [t]. In the Korean system, on the other hand, even parts of symbols are sometimes phonetically relevant. For example, the symbol for the tense consonant phonemes are made of doublets of the symbols for the corresponding non-tense consonants, such as ㅅ for ordinary *s*, ㅆ for tense *s* (usually romanized as "*ss*"), ㄱ for *k* or *g* and ㄲ for tense *k* ("*kk*"), etc.; a certain modification of a vocalic syllable stands for a preceding front semivowel, for example ㅏ for *a*, ㅑ for *ya*, ㅓ for *ŏ*, ㅕ for *yŏ*, ㅗ for *o*, ㅛ for *yo*, etc.'

Sampson (1985) approaches this design feature with more seriousness. In his classification of the writing systems of the world, he establishes a completely new and separate category, called "featural writing," solely to classify Hangŭl. Sampson's classification system is illustrated in figure 6. He reserves this special treatment for Hangŭl because elements of the letters represent distinctive features, the phonological units smaller than phonemes.

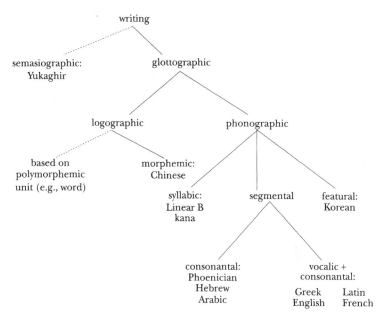

Figure 6 Sampson's Classification of Writing Systems (reproducted from DeFrancis 1980:60)

Is Hangŭl actually "featural writing"? To the extent that writing is considered syllabic or phonemic according to what unit each letter as a whole represents, Hangŭl is a phonemic system. However, since parts of the Hangŭl letters do have significance, classification in a special category of this kind is not without justification. The structure of Hangŭl is not like that of other phonemic systems. Readers of Hangŭl letters can intuit from the letter shapes that ㄱ [k] and ㅋ [kʰ] represent one series of sounds and that ㄴ [n], ㄷ [t], and ㅌ [tʰ] represent a separate series of sounds. Also, compared with ㅏ [a], ㅓ [ə], ㅗ [o], and ㅜ [u], the letters ㅑ [ya], ㅕ [y] , ㅛ [yo], and ㅠ [yu] have the same added stroke; similarly, it can be just as easily recognized that ㅏ [a] and ㅑ [ya], and ㅗ [o] and ㅛ [yo], are letters tied together by their shapes. These relationships derive from the fact that one of the strokes within each of these letter is more than a simple, meaningless stroke; instead, the mark represents a distinctive feature.

Next, as another of Hangŭl's distinguishing features, let us take another look at the clustering of symbols into syllables. As was pointed out above, this writing of letters together in syllabic units was described in volume 102 of the *Annals of King Sejong* (see 2a, below). It is interesting that this brief passage, which offers almost no other concrete information about the new letters, lays down rules for writing in syllables. These rules for syllabic writing are elaborated in more detail first in the *Hunmin chŏngŭm* (cf. 2b) and then in the "Explanation of the Combining of the Letters" (合字解) section of the *Hunmin chŏngŭm haerye* (cf. 2c).

(2) a. 分爲初中終聲 合之然後 乃成字
'[All letters] are divided into initial, medial, and terminal sounds. Once one combines them they form a syllable.' (*Annals of King Sejong* 102)

b. 終聲復用初聲 ... ‧ㅡㅗㅜㅛㅠ附書初聲之下 ㅣㅏㅓㅑㅕ附書於右 凡字 必合而成音
'For the terminal sounds, one again uses the initial sounds ... [The medial sounds] ‧, ㅡ, ㅗ, ㅜ, ㅛ, and ㅠ are written just under the initial sound, while ㅣ, ㅏ, ㅓ, ㅑ, and ㅕ are written just to the right. Letters must always join and form a [syllable] sound.' *Hunmin chŏngŭm*, p. 4a.

c. 初中終三聲 合而成字 ... 中聲則圓者橫者在初聲之下 ‧ㅡㅗㅜㅛㅠ是也
縱者在初聲之右 ㅣㅏㅑㅓㅕ是也 ... 終聲在初中之下
'The three sounds, initial, medial, and terminal, combine to complete the syllabic symbol. ... Among the medial sounds, the round one and horizontal ones stand below the initial sound; these are ‧ [ʌ], ㅡ [ɨ], ㅗ [o], ㅜ [u], ㅛ [yo], and ㅠ [yu]. ... The vertical ones stand at the right of the initial sound; these are ㅣ [i], ㅏ [a], ㅑ [ya], ㅓ [ə], and ㅕ [yə]. ... The terminal sounds stand below the initial and the medial.' (*Hunmin chŏngŭm haerye*, "Explanation of the Combining of the Letters")

Sejong and his assistants took great pains to explain these conventions carefully and in detail because of the special way the symbols had to be used. The letters were certainly phonemic, but they were also designed to fit into syllables. The forms of the vowels (the medials) were made completely different from the consonants (the initials), and the shapes of all were designed with syllabic writing as a precondition. The position of the letter in the syllable determined its general shape.

The influence of Chinese characters in this syllabic design was apparent, and, indeed, it could hardly have been otherwise. In any literate society, the form that writing takes influences how people conceive of language, and Korea was no different. In the West, where roman letters are written in a linear, "typewriter" fashion, language is thought of as being linear. People believe they hear a consonant, then a vowel, and so on down the line to the end of the utterance, when in fact, as even the most elementary spectrographic analysis shows, what they actually hear is multidimensional, with acoustic cues for consonants and vowels overlapping in complex ways. In traditional Korea, as in all societies where writing was done with Chinese characters, the syllable was the basic unit of writing. In Chinese writing each and every symbol represented exactly one syllable, no more, no less. In East Asia, the syllable was basic, it was unchanging, it was a constant of language itself. We do not know if syllabic clustering makes reading more efficient or if it makes it less efficient (in all likelihood it probably does not matter). Still, there is no culturally unbiased reason to assume that linear writing is in any way more natural. Even entertaining the idea that the letters of the Korean alphabet should have, or could have, been written in a line is a modern prejudice arising out of familiarity with Western styles of writing. From the point of view of acoustic phonetics, clustering and overlapping phonemic symbols actually symbolize more faithfully the multidimensionality of natural speech.

Practical considerations reinforced the conformity of the Korean writing system to the Chinese character. In texts of the time, Chinese characters and alphabetic writing were customarily mixed together, and Chinese characters offered no flexibility in the shape they took. It was the alphabet that had to conform. Moreover, one of the original functions for which the alphabet was devised was to indicate the pronunciations of Chinese characters, and to that end each pronunciation for each character had to be a separate unit. The weight of the Sinitic vocabulary in the Korean lexicon also had an effect, for writing such words in any other units except syllables would have seemed extremely unnatural.

In any event, this combining of alphabet with syllable cluster has resulted in an extremely unusual kind of writing. When making typeface, the word *hankul* ('Hangŭl') requires that two type keys be made, one for *han* (한) and one for *kul* (글). In this case, what is the linguistic term for these clusterings of symbols that represent *han* and *kul*? They aren't letters, they aren't alphabetic symbols, nor are they syllabary symbols or characters. Is Hangŭl an alphabetic syllabary as Taylor (1980) suggests? There is no term that quite fits. In making the computer code for Hangŭl, a controversy has arisen over whether to construct the code around composites of the letters or around complete syllables. If coding is done for complete syllables, the units of input would be shapes like 한 *(han)* and 값 *(kaps)*. This kind of controversy, which probably exists only in Korea, arises completely out of the two-level, double-unit orthography found in Hangŭl. In addition, as was discussed earlier, there are also the nettlesome problems of dictionary ordering and how to write *patchim* consonants. In a word, the clustering of symbols into syllables is the most salient feature of Hangŭl and the factor most responsible for why its usage is unlike that of other alphabets.

2.6 The Use of Chinese Characters

In discussing Korean writing, the importance of Chinese characters should not be overlooked. Before the invention of the alphabet, Literary Chinese

served as the written language of Korea. These East Asian graphs were also
used for transcribing Korean. There was no other writing system. During
this long period of time countless Chinese vocabulary items came into Korea as borrowings, and not only do words composed of them comprise a very
large part of the Korean lexicon even today (cf. chapter 4), but such words
are still on occasion written in Chinese characters. When deciding on a personal name, when making up a new name for a school, a government
agency, or a shop, when deciding on a new technical term—even though
the name is usually written in Hangŭl—the determination of the name itself
tends to be done on the basis of Chinese characters. It is true that Chinese
characters are used far less often in modern Korea than in Japan, and, in recent years, their relative importance has been diminishing steadily. Still,
Chinese characters occupy an important place in Korean literary life even
today. In this chapter we will start by looking at the role of Chinese characters in the past, then examine the influences they continue to exert in modern times.

2.6.1 Transcriptions of Korean

We do not know just when Chinese characters were transmitted to Korea. However, it can be inferred that usage on the Korean peninsula had
reached a considerable level around the third century A.D., and that by approximately the fourth or fifth century, all three kingdoms, Koguryŏ,
Paekche, and Silla, were actively using Chinese characters. In A.D. 375, the
dynastic history known as *Sŏgi* was compiled in Paekche; an inscription on
the wall of a Koguryŏ fortification, written in so-called "popular" Literary
Chinese (俗漢文) and containing native Korean elements, has been esti-
mated to have been written in 446; in Silla, in the 4th year of the reign of
King Chijŭng (A.D. 503), the Chinese title *wang* was adopted for the king;
and, again in Silla, the dynastic history of that kingdom was compiled in 545.
Such historical facts make us aware of how much Chinese characters had
taken root in these lands.

From the beginning, knowledge of Chinese characters seems to have
had two functions in Korea. One was to accommodate and read works written in Literary Chinese, and, at the same time, to write narratives and keep
records in that language. The other was to write down Korean. This second
function began more than anything with the need to record proper names.
This was because, even though the historical records were written in Literary
Chinese, the local names that appeared in them needed to be written in
ways that indicated their pronunciation. This method, in which the Sinitic
characters served as phonograms, was like that already used in China to
record foreign names such as India and Kāsgapa (India was usually written
'seal-measure' (印度), and 'Kās(gapa)' with a character (迦) used only for
transliterating Sanskrit sounds). In such cases the meanings associated with
the characters had nothing to do with the word being transcribed. Only the

sounds counted. Use of the characters to record words phonetically was a time-honored East Asian practice, and Koreans readily adopted it to write down their own names. The meanings later read into such transcriptions are ones that often were never intended. One glaring example is the name of the oldest Korean state for which there are historical records, Chosŏn (朝鮮). Contrary to popular Western belief, the name Chosŏn does not mean 'Morning Calm'. The characters cannot possibly have that interpretation.[25] Moreover, in this Chinese transcription they were almost certainly being used as phonograms anyway, chosen only for their sounds, to represent the sounds of a native Korean name. Whatever Chosŏn might once have meant, that meaning of this ancient Korean word was forgotten long ago. 'Morning Calm' is a romantic fantasy based upon a misunderstanding of the Chinese writing system. Korea is "The Land of the Morning Calm" only in Westerners' imaginations.

There are two ways that Chinese characters were used to transcribe Korean names. One was to use them as phonograms, to represent sounds. As was mentioned above, this method was already used by the Chinese (to write 'India', for example). An example of a Korean use of phonograms can be found in the transcription of the Silla place name *Kiltong*[26] 'Long Piece', 吉同 (the characters were those for the Sino-Korean morphemes *kil* 'lucky' and *tong* 'together'). The other method of transcription, which was developed by Koreans, was to use the characters as a kind of rebus for writing Korean words. In this case, the characters were chosen for the meanings associated with them. For example (assuming modern pronunciations for the name), *Pam-kokay* 'Chestnut Hill' could be written with the characters 栗峴 because the Chinese words they represented meant 'chestnut' and 'steep hill'. In this method of transcription, called *hun* (訓) in Korean, the pronunciations of the Chinese characters are ignored. We have already seen examples of this usage in section 2.1, above, in connection with the names for the Hangŭl letters. It will be recalled that Ch'oe Sejin wrote the letter names *sios* (ㅅ) and *tikut* (ㄷ) in Chinese characters. In those transcriptions, he used the character 衣 (*uy* 'clothing') to illustrate the final *-s* of *sios* because it could be read as the Korean word *os* 'clothing'; similarly, 末 (*mal* 'end') illustrated final *-t*, because it could be read as Korean *kut(h)* 'end'. These were *hun* readings of the characters. This method of transcription is roughly similar to the use of the symbol 3 or (Roman numeral) *III* to represent the English word *three*. The *hun* reading of 3 in French is *trois*; and, in German, *drei*. In *Xmas*, the *hun* reading of *X* is [krɪs] (*Christ-*).

The *hun* method of reading characters has completely disappeared from modern Korean life. But *hun* (or rather, in Japanese pronunciation, *kun*) readings are still a part of everyday life in Japan, where native words continue to be written with Chinese characters; for example *yama* 'mountain' with the character 山 (*san*), *higashi* 'east' with the character 東 (*tō*), and so on. How the Japanese usage began, and to what extent it owes its origins to practices on the Korean peninsula, is a complex issue that will not be addressed here.

It was possible to mix both phonograms and *hun* readings in the representation of a single word. For example, the place name *Kiltong* 'Long Piece' mentioned above was not only written 吉同; it also appeared as 永同, using the character 永 (*yeng* 'long time, forever') for its *hun* reading, the Korean word *kil* 'long'. The first king of Silla is known to the world in modern times by the name "Hyŏkkŏse" *(hyekkesey)*. That is because the characters used to write his name, 赫居世, are read with the modern Sino-Korean readings, *hyek, ke,* and *sey*. But the modern pronunciation of the king's name cannot possibly represent anything close to what it actually was, for the first and last characters were apparently intended to be given *hun* readings representing native Silla morphemes. We know that to be true because the name is also written completely in phonograms as 弗矩內, *pulkwunay*. Thus, the character 赫 (*hyek* 'bright, glorious, awe-inspiring') was read *hun*-style as the Silla word **pol(k)-* 'bright, shining', and 世 (*sey* 'world, generation') as Silla **nay* 'long time, age', We can surmise that the name meant something like '(Monarch of) the Shining Age'.

We can see that the use of Chinese characters to write Korean was not simply a matter of "borrowing" characters. The writing system, originally devised to represent Chinese, did not lend itself well to the representation of languages as different in structure from Chinese as Korean. Still, in spite of the difficulties, the ancient Koreans turned this unwieldy script to their own ends and adapted it into the fiber of their literary lives. Nor did they stop with the representation of proper names. They also used Chinese characters to write ordinary Korean words. For example (in approximately the thirteenth century), we find transcriptions like the phonogramic 多里甫里, *talipwoli* 'flatiron', the *hun* rebus 板麻 *nesam* '(a type of) ginseng', and the mixed transcription 末栗 *malpam* 'water caltrop' (from *mal* 'end' and *yul* 'chestnut'). Centuries before Hangŭl was invented, Koreans had developed writing styles and conventions for representing elements in their own language. And, as early as the Silla period, they were even able to write literature in Korean.

2.6.1.1 Hyangch'al

The most highly developed form of Korean transcription in Chinese characters can be found in the vernacular poetry known as *hyangga* (鄉歌, "local songs"). The *hyangga* were a form of Silla verse of which only twenty-five examples have been preserved. The oldest of these twenty-five are the fourteen verses found in the *Samguk yusa* (三國遺事, "Recollections of the Three Kingdoms"). One of the *Samguk yusa* verses has been attributed to a Paekche prince, but the others are said to have been written by Silla poets between A.D. 600 and 879, mostly in the eighth century. The remaining eleven *hyangga* were recorded in the biography of the priest Kyunyŏ (均如傳). Though these latter verses were apparently written in the early Koryŏ period between 963 and 967, they are also considered Silla poetry. Together, the twenty-five *hyangga* are the oldest extant forms of completely Korean writing and the oldest literary compositions in Korean that have been passed down to us. Interpretation of these short poems is not an easy task. Mysteries abound, and much remains undeciphered. As a representative *hyangga*, let us look at the "Song of Ch'ŏyong" (處容歌), which is reproduced below. Although the "Song of Ch'ŏyong," found in volume 2 of the *Samguk yusa*, is one of the best understood *hyangga* (a fifteenth-century version has been preserved), it too presents difficulties, especially in understanding the sound system that underlies it. The readings on the right represent the interpretations given in Kim Wanjin 1980, with romanization according to the Yale system of transcribing the fifteenth-century alphabet. The translation is from David McCann 1997.

東京明期月良	Tongkyeng polki tala
夜入伊遊行如可	Pam tuli nwotitaka
入良沙寢矣見昆	Tuleza caloy pwokwo
脚烏伊四是良羅	Kalwoli neyh ilela
二 隱吾下於叱古	Twuβulun nayhayeskwo
二 隱誰支下焉古	Twuβulun nwukihaynkwo
本矣吾下是如馬於隱	Pwontoy nayhaytamalonon
奪叱良乙何如爲理古	Azanol estiholitkwo

The Song of Ch'ŏyong

In the bright moon of the capital
I enjoyed the night until late
When I came back and looked in my bed
There were four legs in it.
Two are mine,
But the other two—Whose are they?
Once upon a time what was mine;
What shall be done, now these are taken?

The syntax and inflection of this poem are purely Korean. The Chinese-style grammar seen in other early works is not to be found here. This kind of transcription, in which the word order is completely Korean, is called *"hyangch'al"* (鄉札). The name, which means simply "local letters," comes to us from a text written in the early Koryŏ period,[27] and we do not know if the name was used before that time. No Silla source mentions it—or even whether the Sillans had a special name for this kind of writing. In any case, *hyangch'al* is the term preferred today by modern Korean philologists.

Hyangch'al was a mixed style of writing. Nouns and the stems of verbs were generally transcribed by using *hun* readings of the characters, while grammatical forms such as auxiliaries, particles, and verb endings were

written with characters used as phonograms. For example, in the "Song of
Ch'ŏyong" cited above, there is the verbal form *pwokwon* 'looking . . .',
which is transcribed 見昆. In this transcription, the *hun* character 見 (*kyen*
'see') represents the stem of the verb *pwo-* 'look', and the phonogram 昆
(*kwon* 'elder brother; descendant; swarming') represents the inflectional
ending *-kwon*. The copular form *neyh ilela* '(they) were four!' is transcribed
四是良羅. Here 四 (*sa* 'four') represents Korean *neyh* 'four'; 是 (*si* '(this)
is') represents the Korean copula *i-*; and the phonograms 良羅 represent
the inflectional ending *-lela*. *Hyangch'al* phonograms were also used to transcribe consonants that closed the syllable. For example, in the form *nay-
hayeskwo* (吾下於叱古), the character 叱 (*cil* 'to abuse') was used to
transcribe the syllable-final *-s*. This practice of transcribing syllable-final
consonants was used fairly widely as a way of specifying more clearly what
word was intended. For example, *pam* 'night' was written 夜音 (*ya* 'night',
um 'sound'); *kwulum* 'cloud' was 雲音 (*wun* 'cloud', *um* 'sound'); and the
verb stem *is-* 'be, exist' was 有叱 (*yu* 'exist', *cil* 'to abuse'). The verbal form
kesk.a 'breaking off, . . .' was written 折叱可 (*cel* 'break off', *cil* 'to abuse', *ka*
'add'). With the exception of this practice of writing terminal consonants
with a separate character, the system almost always equated one character
to one syllable. With this same one exception, the system was not unlike the
man'yōgana style of writing found in Japan.

　　Hyangch'al was a way of writing natural Korean in more or less complete form. With it, it was possible to represent modifiers, suffixes, particles,
and all the inflectional endings that characterized the language.

　　However, the *hyangch'al* system of writing did not flourish long. It developed and grew during the Unified Silla period; it is said to have been standardized around the end of the seventh century, and it was then used for the
publication of an anthology of native poetry entitled *Samdaemok* (三代目)
"Collection from the Three Periods (of Silla History)" in 888 (the source
from which our fourteen Silla poems ultimately come). Later, during the
Koryŏ period, *hyangch'al* was used sporadically to transcribe native poetry
but after the early part of the period generally fell into disuse. The *hyangch'al*
writing system thrived during the Unified Silla period. But literary activity in
that medium, though highly creative and vigorous at first, did not continue
at nearly the same level. Part of the reason may have been an increasingly
complex Korean syllable and the difficulty of writing with Chinese characters consonant clusters such as that found in *kesk.a* 'breaking off, . . .'. The
system depended basically upon the representation of a syllable with a single
character, and the Korean language contained syllables far too complex in
structure to be accommodated easily with the stock of available phonograms. Writers perhaps felt the limitations of the *hyangch'al* system. (The
contrast with the situation in Japan is striking. Beginning with what was essentially the same transcription system, but with a language characterized by
a much simpler syllable structure, the early Japanese developed the syllabic
writing system that is still in use today.)

Korean Writing 51

But the greatest reason for the demise of *hyangch'al* was probably the influence and authority of the Chinese writing system. It was through Literary Chinese that civilization had been brought into Korea, and carrying on a literary life using that standard medium was both practical and efficient, a factor that may have convinced Koreans it was better to give up altogether such a clumsy method of writing as *hyangch'al*. As can be seen even from the few examples we have looked at, *hyangch'al* was very cumbersome. There is no evidence that the *hyangch'al* system was ever used for anything except the representation of poetry, where the form of the language itself was essential. For other kinds of writing, the same meaning could be expressed perfectly well in Literary Chinese, and writers may well have felt the effort required to transcribe *hyangch'al* was just too great. This conclusion is supported by the fact that *idu* and *kugyŏl*, two methods of writing that will be discussed presently, were used far longer, into later ages. In any event, one feels a sense of loss that earlier Korean was not more abundantly preserved in *hyangch'al* script.

2.6.1.2 Kugyŏl

Hyangch'al was a bold and vigorous method of writing that represented completely Korean word order; but there were also more subtle and passive ways of writing Korean with Chinese characters. The most passive way of all was with *kugyŏl*.

Kugyŏl were Korean markers added to a purely Chinese text. In Korea, when reading a text written in Literary Chinese, there was a convention for adding Korean grammatical elements in appropriate places to aid in reading the text. These added elements were called "*kugyŏl*" (口訣) or, and perhaps more frequently, *t'o* (吐). Though both terms were written in Chinese characters, they were apparently both native words. *Kugyŏl (kwukyel)* is the modern Sino-Korean reading of characters chosen to gloss the native word *ipkyec* 'oral embellishment'; the etymology of *t'o* is obscure, but the textual meaning, which survives in the modern language, seems to have been 'grammatical particle'. The word *kugyŏl* is preferred today as the term for these textual intercalations.

To understand the role of *kugyŏl*, let us look at how they might be used to elucidate a sentence from the English-language canon (the meanings of the hypothetical *kugyŏl* are indicated below the line):

In the beginning *ey* God *i* created the heaven and the earth *hasyessta*.
         at   SUBJECT   (respectfully) did

Note that if the intercalated elements are taken away, what remains is completely English, without the remotest trace of Korean. That was just how *kugyŏl* were used in Chinese texts. Now let us look at an actual example of *kugyŏl* taken from the *Tongmong sŏnsŭp* (童蒙先習), a primer of Chinese used in traditional Korea. The *kugyŏl* in this example are underlined. (In the translation, the parenthetic words are meant to suggest the functions of the *kugyŏl* in the text.)

天地之間萬物之中厓　唯人伊　最貴爲尼　所貴乎人者隱　以其有五倫也羅

	ey	i	honi	nun	la
	at	SUBJ.	does, and so ...	TOPIC	is

'In the multitude of the myriad things midst heaven and earth (at that place), Man (he) is the most noble (and so): What is noble in man (it) is his possession of the Five Human Relationships (it is).'[28]

If the *kugyŏl* are removed, the sentence is completely standard Chinese. Thus, it can be seen that these *t'o* were only supplements to the Chinese text, and the information they provide about Korean is limited. Still, it is nevertheless true that *kugyŏl* were one common way of representing Korean elements with Chinese characters. Just as was the case with *hyangch'al*, some *kugyŏl* characters were phonograms, and others were given *hun* readings. It is unfortunately difficult to date most of the *kugyŏl* practices and conventions, however, because the examples that have come down to us are not of great antiquity.

One interesting feature of *kugyŏl* is that many of the most common graphs could be abbreviated. For example, the *kugyŏl* used in the text cited above were sometimes abbreviated to 厂 (厓), 亻 (伊), ㇏ (爲), ヒ (尼), 𡰩 (隱), and ㆍ (羅). To the extent that *kugyŏl* were customarily written as smaller characters inserted into the Chinese text, there was probably a need to simplify them by omitting some of the strokes. Here is how our text would appear with abbreviated *kugyŏl*:

天地之間萬物之中厂　唯人亻　最貴㇏　所貴乎人者𡰩　以其有五倫也 ㆍ

Such abbreviated *kugyŏl* were normally not part of the printed text itself. Rather, they were marks brushed in later by hand, most likely by the book's owner, as a kind of private punctuation to help in understanding the text. Such was the practice in traditional Korea, and countless Chinese-language books, including ones printed well into the twentieth century, were marked and punctuated this way.

These simplified *kugyŏl* look very much like Japanese *katakana*. Some of the resemblances are only superficial; *kugyŏl* ㇏ (ho-), for example, looks like *katakana* ソ (so); ヒ (ni) looks like ヒ (hi < fi); and so on. But many other symbols are identical in form and value. For example, among the *kugyŏl* in the example given above, 亻, which was abbreviated from 伊, represents the syllable *i*; there is also 夕 (ta) from 多, カ (ka) from 加, ヤ (ya) from 也, and so on. These are the same as their Japanese equivalents. We do not know just what the historical connections were between these two transcription systems. The origins of *kugyŏl* have never been accurately dated. But there are many who believe, in Japan as well as Korea, that the beginnings of *katakana*, and the orthographic principles they represent, should be traced at least in part to earlier practices on the Korean peninsula.

2.6.1.3 Idu

Among the ways of transcribing Korean with Chinese characters, there was a third kind of writing, a method not so vigorously faithful to the representation of Korean grammar as *hyangch'al*, yet not so passive as *kugyŏl*, either. This middle level of transcription was known as *idu* (吏讀, 'clerk readings'). In its broader meaning, the term *idu* is used to include both *hyangch'al* and *kugyŏl*, and in that sense, it refers to any kind of representation of Korean with Chinese characters. But in its narrower meaning, *idu* refers to a kind of transcription that, unlike the addition of *kugyŏl*, did not leave an original Literary Chinese text intact; at the same time, however, it normally left some of the Chinese elements in the text. There was a lot of middle ground between *hyangch'al* and *kugyŏl*, and *idu* covered it all.

The origin and age of the word *idu* are obscure. The most common form of the word is 吏讀 *(idu)*, and that particular transcription first occurs rather late, after the alphabet was invented, in the anti-alphabet memorial of Ch'oe Malli of 1444.[29] But the word was also written in other ways, as *it'o* (吏吐), *ido* (吏道), *it'u* (吏套), *isŏ* (吏書), etc. All of these forms begin with the morpheme 'clerk', and since *idu* was in fact used most often by government clerks, there is little reason to doubt that that is what the morpheme meant. But the second syllable appears written so many different ways, it may well have been native in origin. In any case, we do not know which, if any, of these words for *idu* was used in the Silla period. The oldest attestation of a name of any kind seems to be *isŏ*, found in a text written around 1287. Another early form was *ido*, which appears in the 1395 Korean "translation" of the Ming legal code.

Both of these passages (and countless others as well) relate that *idu* was invented by the famous seventh-century monk Sŏl Ch'ong. But the story is only a legend. Sŏl Ch'ong could not possibly have invented the system, because there are textual examples that predate him. The *Samguk yusa* reports, without mentioning *idu* explicitly, that Sŏl Ch'ong used "local speech" to read the Nine Classics, and that he glossed and interpreted the classical Confucian literature in his own language.[30] Perhaps the legend about Sŏl Ch'ong arose because his Korean-language interpretations and pedagogical work had such influence on those who came after him. He may have played a role in systematizing transcription conventions. Most modern Korean scholars, however, believe he was more deeply involved with *kugyŏl* than with *idu*.[31]

The way *idu* was used is more difficult to understand than *hyangch'al* or *kugyŏl*. Again, let us look at some simple English examples to illustrate the differences; such examples, however, can only suggest some of the range of *idu*:

(1) *Kugyŏl:*   God *i* created the heaven and the earth *hasyessta.*
(2) *Hyangch'al:* *Hanunim i hanul kwa ttang ul changco hasyessta.*
            God SUBJ heaven and earth OBJ create (resp.) did
(3) *Idu:*   a. God *i hanul kwa ttang ul* create *hasyessta.*
            b. *Hanunim i* heaven and earth *ul changco hasyessta.*

In its early stages, *idu* began as subtle Koreanizations of Literary Chinese, with a few Korean elements added to Chinese-language texts; but in later ages, *idu* transcriptions began to include elements little different from *hyangch'al.* In the examples below, (5) is an excerpt (6:3) from the 1395 *idu* translation of the Ming legal code; the underlined elements are *idu,* and the readings for them are given in italics underneath. The original Chinese text is given in (4):

(4) 雖 犯   七 出   有 三 不 去
    tho' violate 7 go-out exist 3 not go
    'Even though there may be a violation of the "Seven Reasons for Divorcing a Wife," there are three (causes) not to go.'

(5) 必于 七 出   乙   犯爲去乃   三 不 去 有去乙
    pilok   *ul*   *hokena*   *iskenul.*
    tho' 7 go-out OBJ violate do, but 3 not go   exist

It can be seen that the original text has been radically altered in the *idu* translation. The Chinese word for 'although' is replaced by a Korean equivalent, 必于 *(pilok);* the Korean object marker 乙 *(ul)* is added after the grammatical object; and the verbs are Koreanized with inflectional endings completely like *hyangch'al.* At the same time, however, the original Chinese elements 七出 and 三 不去 are left unchanged, in their original order. This mixing of pure Chinese words and phrases together in the same sentence with Korean words and Koreanized syntax and morphology is what distinguishes *idu* from *hyangch'al.*

The *idu* system had reached this level of development by about the eleventh century, and it continued in this form without great change until the end of the nineteenth. Note, especially, that it was employed actively as a writing system long after the invention of the alphabet. In a part of the world where the only serious writing was Chinese, *idu* had the advantage of representing Korean, while at the same time, unlike *hyangch'al,* maintaining the comfortable feel of written Chinese.

Idu and *hyangch'al* differed from the beginning both in motivation and objective. *Hyangch'al* was simply a borrowing of letters with no thought at all given to a Chinese form; in contrast, *idu* always began from a base of written Chinese. Whether that Chinese was of the Koreanized kind known as "Popular" Chinese (俗漢文), or whether it was a matter of translating standard Literary Chinese such as that seen in (4) and (5), above, *idu* always had this kind of Chinese connection. We have said that the failure of *hyangch'al* to develop as a writing system was due primarily to the influence and authority of written Chinese. That being the case, then why did *idu*, which was also a way of representing Korean, continue to have such a vigorous existence? The reason was surely its written Chinese base. The literate upper classes did their writing easily and without inconvenience in Chinese and were satisfied with it. They felt no need to resort to a different method of expressing themselves. But those who were not so at home with Literary Chinese must have wanted to find a way of Koreanizing that written medium that was easier to use. The method that fit this need was *idu*. *Idu*, in other words, was much like the Koreanized English Koreans today sometimes call "Konglish." The fact that *idu* was principally used by lower-level government officials and clerks reinforces this characterization.

Even after the invention of the alphabet, Literary Chinese was translated using *idu* as well as with the alphabet. This fact also helps in understanding the nature of *idu*. During the Imjin Wars with the Japanese at the end of the sixteenth century, the Korean king issued a message to the people and ordered that it be presented in three different kinds of writing. This incident shows that even though writing continued on as ever in Chinese, there was a class of people for whom it had to be simplified, and that *idu* was, in the final analysis, a variety of written Chinese that satisfied this need.

Unlike *hyangch'al* and *kugyŏl*, which are really technical terms used for clarity by Korean philologists, *idu* remains an everyday word. In its broader meaning, it is known and used by anyone in South Korea with a high school education. For the public at large, *idu* is any use of Chinese characters for representing native words, and in this vague and ill-defined way, *idu* represents Korea's Sinitic tradition to most modern Koreans.

2.6.2 Literary Chinese and Chinese Characters

Literary Chinese was the written language of Korea in traditional times. It was the medium through which Chinese civilization was accommodated, and from very early on it maintained a position of clear superiority over the transcription of Korean. Writing Korean with Chinese characters never did become a full-scale writing instrument. The great Buddhist priest Wŏnhyo (617-686) left a number of excellent volumes of writing from the Silla period that still have influence today, but it is difficult to imagine him writing them in *hyangch'al* or *idu*. Such works were always written in Literary Chinese. It was Literary Chinese that very early on brought Korea into what was considered the civilized world.

The position of Literary Chinese changed little after the invention of the alphabet. Buddhist and Confucian books and Chinese poems were translated into Korean using the alphabet, and literature such as poetry and fiction were written in Korean, but works of learning continued as before to be written in Literary Chinese. The much-lauded writings of T'oegye (1501-

1570) and Yulgok (1536-1570), the great Confucian scholars of the Chosŏn period, the treatises of the Sirhak scholar Chŏng Yagyong (1762-1836), and other such works were written in Literary Chinese. The administration of the country was no exception, and the official *Annals of the Chosŏn Dynasty (Chosŏn wangjo sillok)* were recorded completely in standard, Literary Chinese. Before the establishment of today's modern schools and continuing well into the twentieth century, the principal schools of Korea were the *sŏdang* (private grammar schools) and *sŏwŏn* (private academies) for studying Chinese and the Chinese classics. The alphabet was something one learned by oneself if at all, and the only vehicle of education was written Chinese. In Korea at that time, the role of written Chinese was very much like that of Latin in Western societies. One absolutely had to have an extensive knowledge of Chinese to succeed in life. The civil service examination for advancing men of talent was given in standard written Chinese, and almost all government documents were composed in Chinese (royal mandates issued from the king directly to the people, however, were written with the alphabet). Literary Chinese, as Korea's standard writing system, occupied a position superior to the alphabet as late as the twentieth century. Even though Koreans were in possession of the clearly more efficient Korean alphabet, they were still not able to escape the fetters of the traditional writing system.

And yet, the written Chinese used in Korea had in fact, to an extent, become Koreanized. The readings of the characters were not Chinese, but rather distinctively Korean. To be sure, right after the invention of the alphabet, there was an effort to restore the pronunciations of the characters to those used in China. The *Tongguk chŏngun* (東國正韻, 'The Correct Rhymes of the Eastern Country') of 1447, though incorporating some actual Korean readings of the time, was a prescriptive dictionary of character readings corrected to follow those of Chinese; and the alphabetic works published around this time all had the pronunciations of the Chinese characters contained in them transcribed according to this *Tongguk chŏngun* system. This attempt at reform, however, continued for only about fifty years before being abandoned in favor of the actual, Korean-style readings. The native readings of Chinese characters were too deeply ingrained in Korean language and society to be changed. In a very real way, Chinese characters were not a foreign writing system at all, any more than the "Roman" alphabet is foreign to writers of English today. And yet, the grammatical structure of Literary Chinese was so distinctly different from the language Koreans spoke, and so much of its vocabulary unlike that of everyday Korean life, written Chinese could never, in spite of the familiarity of the script, be anything other than the written form of someone else's language.

Koreans finally broke free from the bonds of this foreign writing system with the growth of national awareness around the time of the Reform of 1894 *(kabo kyŏngjang)*. Somewhat earlier, from May of 1886 for about three years, the newspaper *The Independent (Tongnip sinmun)* had been published completely in Hangŭl without the use of any Chinese characters, but that had been a civilian venture. It was in December 1894 that a Royal decree at last came down ordering that all government documents be printed in the "national letters," that is, in Korean. At the time, what was considered Korean writing was a prose style filled with Chinese characters with a little bit of Hangŭl mixed in. But it provided the impetus for change, and in 1910 a movement was initiated to unify the spoken and written language. The idea was to bring what was written more in line with the way people talked, and gradually, writing in that spirit increased. At the very least, the movement brought about a complete release from the restraints of Literary Chinese.

However, escaping the bonds of Literary Chinese was a different matter from stopping the use of Chinese characters. A large part of the Korean vocabulary was made up of Sino-Korean, and because of that, even if Korean were written completely in Hangŭl and no Chinese characters used at all, the sentences would still contain a mixture of words made up of the readings of Chinese characters. As shown in example (1), these Sino-Korean words could be written either in Hangŭl or in Chinese characters, and no matter which way the words were transcribed, the sentence would still be completely Korean. The choice was similar to deciding whether to write "number one" or "number 1" in English.

(1) a. 나무는 덕을 가지고 있다.
    b. 나무는 德을 가지고 있다.
    Namu nun tek ul kaciko issta.
    tree TOPIC virtue OBJ having exist
    'Trees have virtue.'

If the above sentence is written as in (1b) by mixing in a Chinese character, it does not mean that the language is influenced by written Chinese. The sentence is not Literary Chinese; it is Korean; what it represents is completely natural, spoken Korean and is therefore in no way out of line with the idea of unifying the spoken and written languages. So far as the language is concerned, Korean can be said to have completely escaped the bonds of Literary Chinese. But it has not broken free of the bonds of Chinese characters; for they are still, to this day, very much in use.

We have mentioned that the frequency with which Chinese characters are used is gradually decreasing. In the past, Sino-Korean words were almost always written with Chinese characters, but in more recent years, there has been an effort to keep representation with Chinese characters to a minimum. Sino-Korean words are written more and more often in Hangŭl. Now, characters felt to be needed for better understanding are often written in parentheses after the Hangŭl. The following examples reflect the general trend over the past four decades (the Sino-Korean words not written with Chinese characters are underlined):

(2) a. 이와 같이 複合語의 成分이 되는 單語의 原意나 原形이 變하는

것은, 結局 그 成分 사이의 結合을 一層 緊密鞏固하게 하여, 새로운 한
單語로서의 資格을 强化하려는 것이라고 볼 수 있다. (Yi Hŭisŭng
1955:251)
b. 韓國 文化의 여명기라고 부를 수 있는 新石器時代는 대략 B.C.
3,000년 내지 2,000년 경부터 시작된 것으로 추측된다. (Yi Kibaek
1967:14)
c. 암산(暗算)의 실수가 계산의 불능을 말해 준다고 볼 수 없듯이
기억력의 제한에 의한 언어의 오산(誤算)도 그것이 언어능력을 반영
해 주는 것이라고 볼 수는 없다. (Kim Chinu 1985:16)

To an extent, the proportion of Chinese characters mixed into the text is
largely determined by individual taste (or philosophy). There are many Koreans who as a matter of principle advocate using only Hangŭl, and for
them, Chinese characters are taboo. Most South Korean daily newspapers
are printed with a mixture of Chinese characters, but, again, there are also
newspapers that make a point of printing only Hangŭl. Nevertheless, even
given this leeway for personal preference, the decline in the proportion of
Chinese characters found in print reflects, far more than individual inclina-
tion, the trend of the time. When it appeared in 1955, example (2a), above,
was considered perfectly normal written style, but today, if anything were
published with that many Chinese characters in it, it would seem far too
"heavy" to its readership. However, if examples (2b) or (2c) had appeared in
the same era as (2a), the underlined words would almost certainly have been
written in Chinese characters. The spirit of the time overrides whatever in-
clination the author might have and determines what society will accept.

The newspaper is a medium that persists more than others in using a
mixture of Chinese characters. This seems to be due to the character of the
medium. Newspapers are usually not something one reads carefully. One
runs the eye quickly over the page, skimming from headline to headline,
and in this process the right mixture of Chinese characters makes words
stand out and is clearly a help in understanding quickly what the articles are
about. Also, the conciseness of Chinese-character expressions is particularly
effective for headlines. In the following headlines, both taken from the 30
January 1994 edition of the *Tonga ilbo,* the logographic nature of the Chinese characters works much like that of the Arabic numeral:

(3) a. 美 9명 사망   'In U.S., 9 Dead'
       U.S.   people dead
    (b. 미 구명 사망)

(4) a. 和 獨 곳곳 교통 두절   'Holland, Germany: Transportation Many
                                Places at Standstill'
       Hol. Germ. places traffic stoppage
    (b. 화 독 곳곳 교통 두절)

Like Chinese characters, Arabic numerals serve as logograms; and '250
Missing', for example, is more effective as a headline than 'Two Hundred

Fifty Missing'. That holds true whether the language is English or Korean. But there is another aspect of newspaper Korean that makes the logogram effective. On the newspaper page, where space is at a premium, rules of word spacing are usually ignored. Such rules are considered too restrictive. Instead, the visual boundaries between Chinese characters and Hangŭl serve to demarcate word divisions, and the result is an overall saving of space. This function is one of the factors influencing editorial decisions in favor of using Chinese characters.

Still, even in newspapers, where the utilization of Chinese characters is the most effective, a gradual decline in use can be seen. According to one statistical study, the rate of Chinese character use in the 1990s had decreased to only 72.92 percent of what it had been from 1910 through 1970. The decline can be seen throughout Korean society. In many aspects of life Chinese characters are hardly in evidence at all. The level of usage seen in example (2b), above, is maintained in some professional publications of the humanities or social sciences, while general educational materials have gravitated to about the level of (2c). Even when writers compose manuscripts with a mixture of Chinese characters, the characters are changed to Hangŭl by the publishers and the characters put in parentheses. The excuse given by the publishers is that too many Chinese characters depress sales. Korean society has changed to that extent. In addition, beginning in the 1970s, the South Korean government adopted a policy that all government documents should be written completely in Hangŭl. Middle school and high school textbooks are written so as not to exceed the level of usage of (2c), and elementary school textbooks are always written completely in Hangŭl.

These matters are controlled by government regulations, of course. But it has also become difficult to find Chinese characters even on billboards and signs along the street. In particular, signs on government and other public offices are always in Hangŭl. Traffic signs and the like are the same. As we mentioned at the beginning of this chapter, North Korea completely abolished Chinese characters in 1949 and has not used them since. South Korea did not adopt such a radical policy, choosing to follow a more natural course of events instead. But now, in South Korea, too, it can be said that literary activity is carried on in many fields without using Chinese characters even in a supplemental way.

In this respect Korea stands in contrast with Japan. Figure 7 shows a portion of the Korean and Japanese texts found in the instruction manual for an American-made computer printer (the instructions are printed in six languages, English, French, German, Spanish, Korean, and Japanese). While the Korean instructions are printed entirely in Hangŭl, the Japanese text is filled with a mixture of Chinese characters. If all the words of Sino-Korean origin in the Korean text had been printed in Chinese characters, the Korean text would have approximately the same proportion of Chinese characters in it as the Japanese.[32] But writing all the words in Hangŭl causes no inconvenience whatsoever to Korean readers, who are now completely accustomed to reading texts without Chinese characters.

取り扱い上の注意	취급방법
實際に使用するまでツールを剝がさないでください。緑か黒の部分だけを持つようにしてください。銅製の部分が他の部分と接觸しないよう注意してください。落としたりすると、構造上の破損、及びイソク漏れなどの原因になります。破損したカートリッツは使用しなでください。	사용하실 때까지 밀폐된 잉크통을 뜯지 마십시오. 잉크통을 집을 때는 초록색 혹은 검정색으로 된 부분만 집으십시오. 구리로 된 부분은 아무것에도 닿지 않게 하십시오. 잉크통을 떨어트리면 구조상으로 고장을 일으켜 잉크가 샐 수도 있습니다. 파손된 잉크통은 사용하지 마십시오.

Figure 7 Instructions in Japanese and Korean for a Computer Printer

Nevertheless, the question as to whether Korean has completely escaped the influence of Chinese characters is something entirely different. These traditional graphs have left an indelible mark on the Korean lexicon, as we have already said. The majority of the entries in dictionaries are of Sino-Korean origin, and words continue to be coined out of Sino-Korean elements. Also, the mystique of Chinese characters and the traditional meanings and nuances they bring with them have special significance for names. Genealogies and the identification of family relationships still play an important role in the structure of Korean society, and insofar as they continue do so, they will be bound to the graphs with which Korean names are written.

In 1957 the South Korean Ministry of Education chose eighteen hundred characters for inclusion on a list of 'Commonly Used Chinese Characters' (常用漢字), and in 1972, eighteen hundred characters were selected for educational purposes in middle and high schools. In 1967 the Korean Newspaper Guild made up its own list of two thousand 'Commonly Used Chinese Characters'. These are the general guidelines for Chinese character usage that have currency in South Korea today.

References

An Pyŭnghŭi 1977; Chao 1968; Ch'oe Hyŏnbae 1937; Coulmas 1989; DeFrancis 1989; Henderson 1982; Jones 1957; Kang Sinhang 1987; Kim Wanjin 1980; Ledyard 1966; McCann 1997; Nam P'unghyŏn 1981; Ramsey 1987; Sampson 1985; Taylor 1980; Vachek 1945-1949, 1973, 1976; Yi Hŭisŭng and An Pyŏnghŭi 1989; Yi Iksŏp (Lee Iksop) 1986, 1992; Yi Kimun (Lee Ki-Moon) 1972a, 1997.

3
Phonology

The sound system described in this chapter is that of standard Korean. By "standard Korean" we mean the variety of the language that is given official status by the government of the Republic of Korea and that is recognized as standard by South Koreans. It is based upon the older, upper-class variety of speech used in the city of Seoul, a speaking style and pronunciation that has long enjoyed enormous prestige.[1]

Few younger speakers, even those born and raised in the city of Seoul, maintain all of the phonological values and distinctions considered standard; speech in that dynamic metropolis of over 8 million has absorbed too many influences from elsewhere in Korea, particularly from Kyŏngsang in the southeast, to preserve, museumlike, the older dialect unchanged. Still, the government and its agencies, as well as the public media, have not always adjusted the standard to accommodate changes in Seoul speech. In our presentation of the Korean sound system in this chapter, we will simply note some of the more salient points at which the official standard and actual usage have diverged.

3.1 The Sound System

Korean has nineteen consonants. The table below is a display of those consonants, arranged by place and manner of articulation. The phonemes are represented in Hangŭl and Yale Romanization:

Consonants

	Lax	*Reinforced*	*Aspirate*	*Nasal*	*Liquid*
labial	ㅂ p	ㅃ pp	ㅍ ph	ㅁ m	
dental	ㄷ t	ㄸ tt	ㅌ th	ㄴ n	ㄹ l
alveolar affricate	ㅈ c	ㅉ cc	ㅊ ch		
velar	ㄱ k	ㄲ kk	ㅋ kh	ㅇ ng	
fricative	ㅅ s	ㅆ ss	ㅎ h		

The Korean consonant system has an unusual distinction. The lax consonants *(p, t, s, c, k)* and the reinforced consonants *(pp, tt, ss, cc, kk)* contrast

by an articulatory feature not found in most other languages. The lax consonants are pronounced weakly, with minimal muscular activity. The reinforced consonants are pronounced with great muscular tension, both at the
point of articulation and throughout the vocal tract, and the tensity continues into the vowel, giving it a throaty, or laryngeal, quality. This difference in
the tensity of articulation is what distinguishes the two series of consonants.
Both contrast with the third series, the aspirated consonants *(ph, th, ch, kh),*
which are characterized by long aspiration, often heard as velar friction.

In initial position all three series are unvoiced. There is no voicing
contrast in Korean. The lax, or "plain," consonants are pronounced in initial position with a slight puff of air and a voicing delay of about 30 to 50
msec., while the aspirated consonants are pronounced with strong aspiration lasting about 100 msec. In most varieties of English, voiceless consonants are pronounced with about 70 to 85 msec. of voicing delay and
aspiration, about midway between the Korean values; as a result, English
speakers are often unable to hear the distinction between the lax and aspirated consonants. On the other hand, English speakers identify the Korean
reinforced consonants with the voiced consonants of their own language,
even though, in actuality, the reinforced consonants are voiceless as well as
unaspirated, with voice onset occurring almost simultaneously with the articulation of the consonant. The reinforced consonants are similar to the
voiceless consonants of French *(p, t, k)* or the unaspirated consonants of
Mandarin Chinese.

Here are some minimal triplets illustrating these contrasts:

(1) a. tal (달) 'moon' : thal (탈) 'mask' : ttal (딸) 'daughter'
    b. pul (불) 'fire' : phul (풀) 'grass' : ppul (뿔) 'horn'
    c. kayta (개다) 'spread out' : khayta (캐다) 'dig' : kkayta (깨다) 'break'
    d. cata (자다) 'sleep' : chata (차다) 'kick' : ccata (짜다) 'wring out'

In medial position between voiced sounds, the lax consonants are phonetically voiced. Thus, the word /papo/ 'simpleton' is pronounced [pabo];
/koki/ 'meat' is [kogi]; and so on. The voiced sounds [b, d, j, g] are regular
and predictable allophones of the phonemes /p, t, c, k/; the voicing heard
here is not used to distinguish meaning. In syllable-final position, the only
lax consonants that occur are *p, t,* and *k;* and in that position the consonants
are unvoiced and unreleased. When the lips close to articulate the final *-p* of
cip 'house', for example, they remain closed, no breath of air escaping even
in the most careful articulation. The situation is quite different from that of
English, and especially of French, but it is similar to that of Cantonese and
other southern varieties of Chinese.

The phonetic values of the reinforced consonants and the aspirated
consonants remain essentially the same in medial position. However, the reinforced consonants are, in addition, articulated long, as their geminate
transcription would suggest. For the /pp/ of *appa* 'dad', for example, the

lips are kept closed longer than they are for the /p/ of *apeci* 'father'. Reinforced consonants and aspirated consonants do not occur in final position. The reinforced and aspirated consonants written in that position in Hangŭl (or Yale Romanization) are phonetically realized as such only when followed by a vowel; e.g., 앞에 *(aph ey)* 'in front' is pronounced [apʰe]. Otherwise, when actually occurring in final position, these consonants are realized as the homorganic lax consonants; e.g., 앞 *(aph)* 'front' is pronounced [ap] (cf. 3.3.1, below).

The three-way distinction described above does not apply to the dental fricatives. There are only two of these: *s* and *ss*. The missing consonant is said to be the aspirate since *s* is normally treated as belonging to the lax series. In initial position, however, *s* is followed a strong pulse of air (though considerably less in medial position). It is also curious that, unlike all the other lax consonants, /s/ does not voice between vowels. It is always pronounced as a voiceless fricative. There is no phonetic [z] in Korean.²

It is difficult to hear the difference between *s* and *ss*. But reinforced *ss* often seems more like the "s" of English than does *s*, perhaps because the slight aspiration of this Korean *s* sounds so unlike English. In any event, when speaking English, Koreans often pronounce English "s" with the reinforced quality of the *ss* in their own language. Also, the lax, or plain, *s* is palatalized before *i* and *wi*; reinforced *ss* is usually not. For this reason, English speakers often "hear" the difference between *si* (시) 'poem' and *ssi* (씨) 'seed' as that of English *she* vs. *see*. In many dialects spoken south of Seoul, principally in Kyŏngsang, the distinction between *s* and *ss* is not maintained. It seems to be fragile among many younger-generation Seoul speakers, as well.

The affricates, *c, ch,* and *cc,* are always palatalized (except, apparently, for some Seoul speakers, before unrounded back vowels).³ Also, since there is no *z* in Korean, Koreans "hear" English "z" as /c/; thus, Koreans with insufficient mastery of English sounds pronounce English "zoo" in a way that Americans hear as "Jew." Americans, for their part, rarely hear or pronounce the palatal quality of the Korean affricates, giving them instead a more apical quality plus rounding. Thus, Korean *cip* (집) 'house' becomes in an American mouth the same as the American "cheep" or "chip."

Between vowels, as in *tali* (다리) 'bridge', the liquid /l/ is pronounced like the tongue-tip [r] of Spanish or Japanese: [tari]. Here the consonant is a quick tongue tap against the alveolar ridge. At the end of a word, as in *tal* (달) 'moon', /l/ is pronounced somewhat like an English "light" *l*, except that the tip of the tongue is brought up higher, behind the alveolar ridge: [tal]. The two sounds, [r] and [l], do not contrast, and what Americans hear as [l] between vowels is a long, double /ll/, consisting of an *-l* at the end of the first syllable, plus an *l-* at the beginning of the following syllable, for example, *ppalli* (빨리) 'quickly'. As was mentioned in chapter 1, a salient typological feature of Korean, typically found in the Altaic languages, is that liquids (such as *r* and *l*) ordinarily do not occur at the beginning of a word. The liquid /l/ is found at the beginning of a word only in modern loans, where what is heard is usually the [r] allophone; for example, *leyice* (레이저), meaning both 'razor' and 'laser', is pronounced [reijə]. The nasal consonants *m* and *n* can have a slightly oral release. The word *mu* (무) 'white radish', for example, is sometimes pronounced with what sounds like a short *b* between the consonant and vowel: [mᵇu]; *ney* (네) 'yes' sounds like [nᵈe] from some speakers. The nasal *ng* is different. It does not occur at the beginning of a word, and it is always completely nasalized. It is never pronounced with an oral release.

Vowels. According to the government document "Standard Pronunciation" *(P'yojun parŭm-pŏp)* published in 1989, there are ten vowels in standard Korean. In the table below, these vowels are arranged according to tongue position. The phonemic symbols are those of Yale Romanization; the phonetic values are enclosed in square brackets:

	Front		Mid	Back
	unrounded	*rounded*		
High	ㅣ i [i]	ㅟ wi [ü]	ㅡ u [ɨ]	ㅜ wu [u]
Mid	ㅔ ey [e]	ㅚ oy [ö]	ㅓ e [ə]	ㅗ o [o]
Low	ㅐ ay [ɛ]		ㅏ a [a]	

The monophthongs shown above represent a kind of ideal system. These phonetic values are maintained, to be sure, by many speakers of the central, Kyŏnggi area around Seoul. But, in some cases, other pronunciations are more common. In particular, the compilers of "Standard Pronunciation" recognized that /wi/ (위) and /oy/ (외) can also be pronounced as the diphthongs [wi] and [we] and added a proviso to that effect. In actuality, these two diphthong values are heard much more often than the equivalent monophthongs.

The distinction between /ay/ and /ey/ is considered an earmark of standard, Seoul speech. Since the distinction has been lost throughout much of the country south of Seoul, the ability to hear and make the difference is a source of pride to old-time natives of the city. However, in spite of themselves, younger speakers are seldom able to actually hear the difference. Because the two vowels are spelled differently in Hangŭl (ㅐ vs. ㅔ), most literate Koreans know which value a word is supposed to have from its spelling. But how they actually speak is something else. So many Seoulites are not able to hear a difference between the familiar forms *nay ka* (내가) 'I' and *ney ka* (네가) 'you', a new form for 'you', *ni ka*, has emerged to replace *ney ka* in colloquial use. The same is true for *nayq kes* (내것) 'mine' and *neyq kes* (네것) 'yours'; 'yours' is now *niq kes*. Speakers of English can see evidence of the merger of these two vowels in the fact that speakers of "standard" Korean often cannot distinguish between the English words *pet* and *pat*, *men* and *man*, *bend* and *band;* they confuse the names *Meg* and *Mag;* they misspell *Nelson* as *Nalson*, *radical* as *redical; practice* as *prectice;* and so forth. For most, the pronunciation of both 애 and 에 is a uniform [e]. The vowel /e/ (ㅓ) is pronounced in two different ways. The phonetic value [ə] prescribed in "Standard Pronunciation" is actually somewhere between these two pronunciations. When short, as in words like *mes* 'attractiveness' or *thel* 'hair', it is pronounced a little farther back in the mouth, somewhere near the value [ʌ]: [mʌt], [tʰʌl]. But when long, as in *sēm* 'island', *hēnpep* 'constitution', *cēkta* 'be few', or (especially when emphasized) *tēlepta* 'be dirty' or *kēcis-mal* 'lie, falsehood', it is pronounced somewhat higher in the mouth than [ə], near the pronunciation [ɨ]. Only older speakers, however, maintain this allophonic difference clearly; younger speakers, in contrast, tend to pronounce the vowel in all cases with the tongue slightly retracted, and with a phonetic value near [ɔ].

The vowel /u/ [ɨ] is pronounced with the middle of the tongue raised high in the mouth, keeping the lips completely unrounded. Rounding the lips, as is automatically done when this vowel follows a labial consonant such as *p* or *m*, changes /u/ [ɨ] to its rounded equivalent, /wu/ [u].

Complex vowels. Korean has two semivowels, *w* and *y*, and these combine with vowels to form eleven diphthongs:

> *y*-onglide: ya, ye, yo, yu, yay, yey (ㅑ , ㅕ , ㅛ, ㅠ, ㅒ , ㅖ)
> *w*-onglide: wa, we, way, wey (ㅘ, ㅝ , ㅙ, ㅞ)
> *y*-offglide: uy (ㅢ)

The diphthong *uy* is a spelling pronunciation that has been reintroduced into the standard language. In older, unself-conscious Seoul speech unaffected by the spelling, what is written that way is never a diphthong. In initial position, as in *uysa* 'doctor' or *uyca* 'chair', it becomes the single vowel /u/ [ɨ]: [ɨsa], [ɨdʒa]. In noninitial position, as in *kanguy* 'lecture' or *mincwu-cwuuy* 'democracy', it is pronounced as the vowel *i*: [kaŋi], [mindʒudʒui]. It is always a monophthong in this older, more natural variety of Seoul speech. But for most younger and middle-aged Seoul speakers, the pronunciation has become a normal part of the language. In initial position especially, it is regularly pronounced [ɨy]. However, there are still exceptions. In spellings such as *huyta* (희다) 'be white', *hwanhuy* (환희) 'joy, ecstasy', *mu.nuy* (무늬) 'pattern', the vocalic sequence remains just a spelling; it is pronounced as [i] in all these cases. The genitive marker *uy* (의), as in *sewul uy yeys ilum* 'the old name of Seoul' or *chensa uy nalkay* 'the wings of an angel', is sometimes given a spelling pronunciation, but that is usually evidence of overcareful speech. In unguarded, more natural conversation it is a homophone of the locative marker *ey* (에). Seoul schoolchildren still confuse the spellings of these two particles in their written compositions, showing that the distinction has still not become part of the language.

The two vocalic sequences *yay* and *yey* do not occur after a consonant.

What is spelled that way—for example, *kyeysan* (계산) 'reckoning', *sikyey* (시계) 'clock', *cihyey* (지혜) 'wisdom'—is actually pronounced without the *y*-onglide: [kesan], [ʃige], [tʃihe]. The sequence *yay* only occurs after a consonant as a contraction; for example, *kyay* (걔) is from *ku ai* 'that child', *cyay* (쟤) 'that child (over there)' is from *ce ai*. But here, too, the sequence is only a written form for the *y* is always lost after the consonant.

Vowel length. Words are distinguished by vowel length in Korean. The functional load of this distinction is not great and it is not written in Hangŭl orthography.[4] But vowel length is indicated in most better Korean dictionaries, usually with a colon after the syllable; for example, 말: (māl) 'speech'. A few other dictionaries place a long mark—a macron—over the syllable, which is how they are indicated in the romanized forms in 2, below. Here are a few common words distinguished by vowel length:

> (2) a. mal 'horse' : māl 'speech'
> b. nwun 'eye' : nwūn 'snow'
> c. pam 'night' : pām 'chestnut'
> d. saki 'porcelain' : sāki 'morale'
> e. toyta 'become' : tōyta 'be thick, hard'

Vowel length is maintained only in the first syllable of a word. If a word with an underlying long vowel appears in noninitial position in a compound, the vowel becomes short. For example, *nwūn* 'snow', *māl* 'speech', and *pām* 'chestnut' have basic long vowels, but in the compounds *ches-nwun* 'first snow', *kēcis-mal* 'lie, untruth', and *ssangtong-pam* 'double chestnut', their vowels are all short. In many dictionaries, some non-initial syllables are marked long; for example, *pōhō* (보:호:) 'protection', *mopāng* (모방:) 'imitation', *meli-māl* (머리-말:) 'preface'. But these markings are based on the etymologies and do not represent actual pronunciations. The syllables are pronounced short.

Vowel length is not the same for every Seoul speaker. Some speakers retain the etymological vowel length better than others, and the tendency is toward the loss of more and more of these distinctions. In general, vowel length seems to be more stable and better maintained in verb stems than in nouns.

3.2 Syllable Structure

A Korean syllable can begin with zero or any one of the nineteen consonants. The vocalic element that follows can be one of the ten vowels or eleven diphthongs (counting *uy*). After the vowel, in final position, the syllable can be open or else closed by one of the seven consonants *p, t, k, m, n, ng, l*.

This syllable shape is more complex than that of such languages as Japanese or Mandarin Chinese. While there are only about 1,200 syllabic distinctions in Mandarin and a mere 113 distinct moras in Japanese, there are between 3,000 and 4,000 distinct syllables in Korean.[5] But the Korean syllable is simpler than that of most European languages like English, principally because of the absence of consonant clusters. A syllable in the modern Korean language cannot begin with a sequence such as *spr-* or *kl-*, nor can it end with one. This difference in the syllable structure of Korean and English means that many English monosyllables are borrowed into Korean as polysyllabic words. For example, the Korean words for "cream," "spring," and "text" are *khulim, suphuling,* and *teyksuthu.* The vowel *u* is inserted between the consonants, creating extra syllables, so that the words can be accommodated into the Korean phonological structure.

Many clusters are written at the end of syllables in Hangŭl orthography; for example, 닭 *(talk)* 'chicken', 없다 *(eps.ta)* 'not exist', 훑는다 *(hwulth.nunta)* 'is thrashing'. But the words are not actually pronounced this way. The Hangŭl is a representation of the basic forms of the morphemes, not their isolated pronunciation. When an overloaded syllable like this occurs before a consonant or a pause, one of the consonants is dropped. For example, *talk* 'chicken' is pronounced [tak]; *eps.ta* 'not exist' is pronounced [əp.tˀa]. But when the syllable occurs before a vowel, the last consonant spills over the syllable boundary and is pronounced as part of the following syllable; for example, *eps.umyen* (없으면) 'if [it] doesn't exist, . . .' is pronounced [əp.si.myən]. In this case, there is still only one consonant at the end of the first syllable.

There are rules governing which consonant at the end of a syllable gets deleted and which is retained.[6] The basic rule is that all except the first are dropped. Here are a few examples:

(1) a. neks (넋) 'spirit' → ne*k*
   b. a*nc.*nunta (앉는다) 'is sitting' → a*n*.nunta
   c. ka*ps* (값) 'price' → ka*p*

Clusters with the liquid *l* are more complex, however. In the clusters *-ls* and *-lth,* the cluster follows the basic rule, and all but the first consonant are dropped. The same is true of *-lp* in the one noun example occurring in the modern language, *yetelp* 'eight', which is pronounced [yədəl]. For nouns that end in *-lk,* however, it is the *l* that is dropped; for example, *talk* 'chicken' is [tak], *hulk* 'earth' is [hik]. For verb stems ending in *-lk, -ls, -lp,* or *-lph,* the standard treatment is to drop the *l.* But when the cluster *-lk* appears before a *k* (as in 4, below), it is an exception; in this case the *l* is retained. The examples in (2), (3), and (4), below, illustrate these rules.

(2) yete*lp* (여덟) 'eight' → yete*l*
   oyko*ls* (외곬) 'single way' → oyko*l*
   ha*lth.*nunta (핥는다) 'is licking' → ha*l.*nunta

(3) ma*lk*.ta (맑다) 'is clear' → ma*k*.ta
     cē*lm*.ta (젊다) 'is young' → cē*m*.ta
     pa*lp*.ci (밟지) '[you] step on [it], I suppose' → pa*p*.ci
     u*lph*.ta (읊다) 'recite (poetry)' → u*p*.ta[7]

(4) ma*lk*.key (맑게) 'clearly' → ma*l*.kkey
     pa*lk*.kwuna (밝구나) '[It's] bright, I see' → pa*l*.kkwuna

The rules described above produce the forms considered standard. But
there is nevertheless considerable variation to be heard in the way speakers
pronounce such words. It is not uncommon, for instance, to hear *il.ta* 'read'
instead of the nominally standard *ik.ta* (it is written *ilk.ta*). Also, in some people's speech the more complex, underlying cluster is actually pronounced,
with both *l* and *p* heard in forms such as *palp.ta* 'trample, step on'. Such pronunciations are probably induced by spellings, however, and are, accordingly, considered somewhat artificial.

The velar nasal *ng* [ŋ] is not found at the beginning of a word. It can
be pronounced at the beginning of a syllable only if the syllable is noninitial,
such as in *mangaci* 'colt' or *inge* 'carp'. The aspirated and reinforced consonants, as well as the fricatives and affricates, do not occur at the end of a syllable (cf. section 3.3.1, below).

3.3 Phonological Processes

We have outlined the kinds of syllables that occur in Korean. But the pronunciation of any given syllable can change depending on the phonological
environment in which it appears. When morphemes and words appear in
context, the underlying forms are subject to a number of morphophonemic
rules, some of which we have already described in our discussion of consonant dropping at the end of syllables. In this section we will describe other
important processes that apply to strings of consonants and vowels.

3.3.1 Neutralization

In Korean, final consonants are never released. The slight puff of air
sometimes heard in English after a consonantal closure like that of the *-t* in
belt is impossible in Korean. At the end of a syllable, Korean obstruents must
be articulated with complete closure and stoppage of airflow, and, as a result, many consonants cannot be pronounced in that position. The consonant *s*, for example, does not occur there. The hissing of air escaping
between tongue tip and alveolar ridge is only possible when [s] is followed
by a vowel, and so English words such as *gas* gain an extra vowel and syllable
(*kaysu*, 개스) when borrowed into Korean.

Complete closure of obstruents at the end of a syllable results in the neutralization of many consonantal distinctions. We have said at the beginning of this chapter that only seven consonants can close the syllable: *p, t, k, m, n, ng, l.* All the other consonants merge with these seven in that position. The following examples illustrate how these mergers are realized:

(1) a. pue*kh* (부엌) 'kitchen' → pue*k*, pa*kk* 'outside' → pa*k*
    b. pa*th* (밭) 'field' → pa*t*
    c. a*ph* (앞) 'front' → a*p*

(2) a. o*s* (옷) 'clothes' → o*t*, i*ss*.ta 'be, exist' → i*t*.ta
    b. ce*c* (젖) 'breast' → ce*t*
    c. pi*ch* (빛) 'light' → pi*t*

As can be seen from these examples, the aspirates and reinforced consonants merge with the homorganic lax consonants (-*kh* becomes -*k*, etc.), and the dental affricates (*c*, etc.) and fricatives *(s, ss)* all uniformly become the dental stop *t.* The neutralization of these distinctions can result in the creation of homonyms. The word *iph* 'leaf', for example, sounds like the word *ip* 'mouth' before a pause or juncture. The words *nas* 'sickle', *nac* 'day', and *nach* 'face' are all pronounced [nat].

The distinctions between syllable-final consonants exist only when the consonants appear before a particle or verb ending that begins with a vowel. The word *kkoch* (꽃) 'flower' becomes *kkot* in isolation; that is, its final consonant is neutralized to /t/. The basic, final consonant /ch/ can be heard only before particles such as *i* or *ulo: kkoch i* [kʔotʃʰi], *kkoch ulo* [kʔotʃʰiro]. In these cases, the "final" consonant is no longer final; it has phonologically become the initial consonant of the particle.

The rules for neutralization are different for compound nouns. These cases require a two-step process. First, neutralization takes place under all conditions in compounds. In other words, there is a juncture, or word boundary, between the elements of the compound that triggers neutralization. But then the boundary disappears and *liaison* takes place, the neutralized consonant spilling over to become the initial consonant of the second element.

(3) a. ce*c*(##)emi (젖어미) 'breast' 'mother' → ce*t*##emi → ce.*t*emi [tʃədəmi] 'wet-nurse'
    b. ke*th*(##)os (겉옷) 'outer' 'clothes' → ke*t*##os → ke.*t*os [kədot] 'overalls'
    c. mulu*ph*(##)alay (무릎아래) 'knee' 'below' → mulu*p*##alay → mulu.*p*alay [murɨbarɛ] 'below the knee'

As was explained in chapter 2, Korean orthography before this century usually reflected the neutralization of syllable-final consonants. However, in modern Hangŭl orthography, the policy is to write the underlying forms of these consonants instead. Pronunciation adjustments are left up to the native speaker, for whom they are largely unconscious and auto-matic. The nonnative learner, however, must learn and internalize the rules in order to read Hangŭl effectively. Hangŭl spellings are not tran-scriptions of pronunciations.

3.3.2 Assimilation

A number of phonological changes are subsumed under the label of assimilation. What they have in common is that these changes are induced by neighboring phonemes. Again, as in neutralization, Hangŭl ortho-graphic practice is to write the underlying consonants and vowels, not the sounds that result from assimilation.

Nasal Assimilation. An important morphophonemic rule in Korean is nasal assimilation. When a stop occurs before a nasal, it assimilates the nasaliza-tion and becomes the corresponding nasal phoneme; that is, *p, t, k* become *m, n, ng.* In the following examples, note that neutralization and cluster re-duction occur before the assimilation:

(1) a. kwu*k*-mul (국물) 'soup-water' → kwu*ng*mul 'broth'
me*k*-nunta (먹는다) 'eat-ing' → me*ng*nunta 'is eating'
b. pue*kh* man (부엌만) 'kitchen only' → pue*k*.man → pue*ng*man 'just the kitchen'
c. mu*kk*-nunta (묶는다) 'bind-ing' → mu*k*.nunta → mu*ng*nunta 'is bind-ing'

(2) a. pa*t*-nunta (받는다) 'receive-ing' → pa*n*nunta 'is receiving'
b. pu*th*-nunta (붙는다) 'stick-ing' → pu*t*.nunta → pu*n*nunta 'is sticking'

(3) a. pe*p*-mang (법망) 'law-net' → pe*m*mang 'the reaches of the law'
tōp-nunta (돕는다) 'help-ing' → tōmnunta 'is helping'
b. a*ph*-matang (앞마당) 'front-yard' → a*p*.matang → a*m*matang 'front yard'
c. e*ps*-nun (없는) 'not exist-ing' → e*p*.nun → e*m*nun 'not existing'

Peculiarities of l. The behavior of *l* has some distinctively Korean properties. One is that it causes a neighboring *n* to assimilate so that is also pronounced as a lateral. In other words, what is morphophonemically (and normally written in Hangŭl as) *-nl-* or *-ln-* is phonemically /ll/. Here are examples:

(4) a. na*n.lo* (난로) → na*llo* 'stove', kwe*n.lyek* → kwe*llyek* 'power'
b. kha*l-n*al (칼날) 'knife-edge' → kha*llal* 'blade of a knife'
ha*lth-n*unta (핥는다) 'lick-ing' → ha*l.n*unta → ha*ll*unta 'is licking'

However, there are some interesting exceptions to this rule. In the following examples—all of which involve Sino-Korean—the underlying *-nl-* is not replaced by /ll/, but by /nn/ instead. In all of these forms, the first part of the compound is a common, two-syllable word, and the second element is a monosyllabic suffix.

(5) sayngsa*n-l*yang (생산량) 'production volume' → sayngsa*nn*yang
ipwe*n-l*yo (입원료) 'hospital-admission charges' → ipwe*nn*yo 'hospital charges'
hoyngta*n-l*o (횡단로) 'traversing road' → hoyngta*nn*o '(street) crossing'
Sinmu*n-l*o (신문로) 'Sinmun Road' → sinmu*nn*o

Sometimes the surface forms defy etymology. The everyday word *kollan* 'difficulty', which is spelled *kon.lan* (곤란) in Hangŭl, has no etymological *l* in it anywhere; it is composed of the Sino-Korean morphemes *kon* (困) + *nan* (難). The second morpheme, with the initial *n*, occurs in such words as *kan-nan* (艱難) 'hardships' and *swunnan* (殉難) 'martyrdom'. The word *kollan* is aberrant.[8]

What all of these forms share, even the exceptions mentioned above, is a constraint against the contiguity of *l* and *n;* the two phonemes cannot be pronounced together. This constraint is the reason why, when Koreans speak English, an American ear will sometimes hear "Seoul Lational University" instead of "Seoul National University." In Korean, Marilyn Monroe's last name is spelled *monlo* (몬로) but is phonemically /monno/.[9]

The phoneme *l*, in fact, is broadly constrained. It cannot follow any other consonant except *l*. We have seen examples of the assimilation that occurs when it follows *n*. If, in its underlying form, *l* follows some other consonant, the *l* changes to an *n*. Then the preceding consonant is subject to nasal assimilation:

(6) tok.lip (독립) → tok.nip → tongnip 'independence'
kok.lyu (곡류) → kok.nyu → kongnyu 'grains'
ap.lyek (압력) → ap.nyek → amnyek 'pressure'
sip-li (십리) → sip.ni → simni 'ten miles'

Changes such as these are often the source of linguistic difficulties for non-Koreans. Until a decade or two ago, the Korean Ministry of Education advocated a romanization system that, while linguistically well motivated and easy to use, resulted in spellings that many Westerners found surprising and even jarring.[10] Like Hangŭl (and Yale Romanization), the romanization transcribed underlying forms, and, on signs and tourist maps, what was phonemically *songnisan* became 'Sog-ri Mountain', *tongnimmun* became 'Dog-rib Gate'. Partly because of problems such as these, the Ministry of Education adopted the McCune-Reischauer system of romanization, which reflects more directly the phonemic shapes.

Palatalization. When a stem-final *t* or *th* is followed by a particle or other enclitic beginning with the vowel *i* (or *y*), the consonant assimilates to the palatal articulation of the vowel. Then the closure is released with affrication. In other words, *t* becomes *c*, and *th* becomes *ch*.

(7) a. pa*th* i (밭이) → pa*ch* i [pat͡ʃʰi] 'field [subject]'
so*th* imyen (솥이면) → so*ch* imyen 'if it's a kettle, . . .'
ka*th*.i (같이) → ka*ch*i 'together'
b. mita*t*.i (미닫이) → mita*d* 'sliding door'
kwu*t*.i (굳이) → kwu*d* 'firmly'
c. kwut.hita (굳히다) → kwu.thita → kwuchita 'firm up, harden'
tat.hita (닫히다) → ta.thita → tachita 'be shut'

Looked at historically, this two-step process of palatalization and affrication has played a role in transforming the phonological structure of many words and morphemes; for example, the older verb *tita* is now *cita* 'become'. What was historically *tyenti* first changed to *cyenci*, then to what is now *cenci* 'heaven and earth'. (Cf. chapter 7.) Today, however, the synchronic changes seen in (7), above, are limited to the boundaries between morphemes. The apical consonants in the words *titita* 'tread on', *thi* 'mote', or *tti* 'sash', for example, do not become affricates because, in the modern language, affrication of apical stops does not occur within the same morpheme. (Historically, the example words did not undergo the processes of palatalization and affrication because the forms of the words at the time were *tuytuyta, thuy,* and *ttuy.*)

However, palatalization without accompanying affrication is a general and widespread phenomenon in the phonology of modern Korean, and most apical consonants have a palatal allophone before *i* or *y*. We mentioned in our description of the phoneme *s* that it was pronounced [ʃ] before *i*. The phonemes *n* and *l* also have palatal allophones, [ɲ] and [ʎ], before *i* or *y* (the tongue-tap [r] allophone of /l/ does not palatalize, however).

(8) a. nam.nye (남녀) → [namɲə] 'male and female'
o.ni (오니) → [oɲi] 'since [he] comes, . . .'
b. il.li (일리) → [ilʎi] 'some reason'
tal.lyek (달력) → [talʎək] 'calendar'

Labial Assimilation. When the unrounded vowel *u* [ɨ] occurs after a labial consonant, *p, ph, pp,* or *m,* or after the semivowel *w,* it rounds and becomes the phoneme *wu* [u]. For example, what is underlyingly, and written, *cip un* (집 은) 'house [as topic]' is phonemically *ci.pwun* (지 분). The verb stem *kam-* 'to wind' plus the ending *-umyen* becomes phonemically *ka.mwu.myen* (가무면) 'when [you] wind [it]'.

As a result of this assimilation, the two vowels /u/ and /wu/ do not contrast after a labial. Since the pronunciation is the same, there is no need to write two different vowels. In Yale Romanization, the vowel [u] is normally transcribed as *wu*, because the Yale symbol *u* is in other cases used to represent the vowel [ɨ]. But after a labial, where [ɨ] does not appear, Yale saves a letter by writing [u] as *u* instead of *wu;* for example, *pul* (불) 'fire', *mul* (물) 'water', and so on.

3.3.3 Restrictions on Initial Consonants

Certain sounds do not normally occur in initial position in Korean (Cf. chapter 1). The consonant *l* is the best known of these. There are no native Korean words that begin with this consonant. Modern borrowings, however, do not follow this pattern, and there are many loan words in Korean today beginning with *l-;* for example, *leykhotu* [rekʰodɨ] 'record', *lain* 'line', *lekpi* 'rugby', *laion* 'lion', *ling* 'ring', *langteypu* 'rendezvous'. But note that even words of Western origin, at least those borrowed during the early period of contact, show resistance to this sound; a variant form of *latio* 'radio', for example, is *nacio;* a Western lamp is either *lamphu* or *nampho.* Still earlier borrowings—specifically from Chinese sources—never have an *l-* at the beginning of the word. The general situation is that what was an initial *l-* in the Chinese original has either changed to *n-* or been lost in Sino-Korean words. The rule is this: an initial *l-* dropped when it was followed by *i* or *y;* before all other vowels it changed to *n-*. Nevertheless, this constraint against initial *l-* does not meant that the *l-* in the etymology was necessarily lost entirely. For whenever that particular Sino-Korean morpheme came in noninitial position in a word, there, in the middle of the word, the *-l-* could appear. There was no constraint on *l* in that position. And because most morphemes were found in many different words, the initial was usually preserved morphophonemically. The following examples illustrate the situation:

(1) a. *nay.il* (來日) 'tomorrow', *no.in* (老人) 'old person', *nak.wen* (樂園) 'Eden'

b. mi.*lay* (未來) 'future', hay.*lo* (偕老) 'age together', o.*lak* (娛樂) 'pleasure'

(2) a. _i.chi (理致) 'logic', _yek.sa (歷史) 'history', _yey.sik (禮式) 'ceremony'

b. to.*li* (道理) 'reason', i.*lyek* (履歷) 'career', hon.*lyey* (婚禮) 'wedding'

Like *l,* the consonant *n* is another phoneme that does not normally come in word-initial position when followed by an *i* or *y.* Again, modern loans from Western languages are not subject to the constraint: *nyusu* 'news', *nikheyl* 'nickel'; nor are mimetics such as *nyam-nyam* 'yum-yum'. However, the examples in (3), below, show what happens to Sino-Korean morphemes that underlyingly begin with *ni-* or *ny-*:

(3) a. _ye.seng (女性) 'woman', _yen.mal (年末) 'year end', _ik.myeng (匿名) 'pseudonym'

b. nam.*nye* (男女) 'male and female', sin.*nyen* (新年) 'new year', un.*nik*
(隱匿) 'concealment'

The morphophonemic rules applying to initial *l-* and *n-* are linked and
can be conflated. First, initial *l-* changes to *n-*. Then, before *i* or *y*, initial *n-* is
deleted. We can use examples taken from (2a) to show how the rules apply:

(4) a. li.chi → ni.chi → i.chi 'logic' (이치)
     b. lyek.sa → nyek.sa → yek.sa 'history' (역사)

Note that the forms *nichi* 'logic' and *neksa* 'history' can be found in some
modern dialects (cf. 9.3.4), which show the *n-* of the intermediate stage of
derivation.

Names are considerably more complex. When a given name follows a
surname in the natural Korean order, the constraints ordinarily apply to
the initial consonant of the given name. For example, what is underlyingly
Choy Lyongho (崔龍浩), with an initial *l-*, is pronounced *Choy Yongho*. But for
given names consisting of only a single character, the underlying form is often realized phonemically: *Choy Lyong* (崔龍). There is also considerable
variation in the pronunciation of the second character in given names. For
example, the name 崔五龍, which according to the rules governing initials
should be pronounced *Choy O.lyong*, can also be pronounced *Choy O.yong*.
The name 崔元龍, which underlyingly is *Choy Wenlyong*, should be pronounced *Choy Wellyong*, but *Choy Wen.yong* is often what one hears instead.
Moreover, *Choy O.nyeng* (崔五寧), which has no etymological *l* in it anywhere, is sometimes pronounced as if it did, as *Choy O.lyeng*. This same morpheme *nyeng* (寧) is also found in the place name *Hoy.nyeng* (會寧), and in
this case, too, it is pronounced as if it began with an *l-*, as *Hoy.lyeng*. There
are many idiosyncratic readings like these to be found in the pronunciations of proper nouns.

3.3.4 Syncope, Contraction, and Epenthesis

Dropping, contraction, or insertion of a consonant or vowel occurs
widely in Korean. Some of these changes are conditioned phonologically,
and some are limited to certain words or types of words. Some processes of
both kinds will be discussed here.

Disappearing h. Between vowels, or between a vowel and *y, w, m, n, ng*, or *l*,
the consonant *h* will drop when the word is spoken at normal conversational
speed. For example. what is written *manh.i* (많이) 'much' is ordinarily pronounced [māni]; *kyel.hon* 'marriage' is [kyəron].[11]

Disappearing w. After a *p, ph, pp, m, o*, or *wu*, a *w* will drop at normal conversational speed. For example, *sip wen* '₩10' often becomes *sipen* [ʃibən]; *sam wel* 'March' becomes *samel* [saməl]¹²

Reduction of cye, chye, *and* ccye. Standard Hangŭl Orthography *(Han'gŭl match'umpŏp t'ongiran)* requires that a *y* be written in certain kinds of verbal contractions. For example, when the verb stem *kali-* 'to choose' is followed by the ending *-ela,* the change *kali-* + *-ela* → *kalyela* 'Choose!' takes place, and it is written showing the contraction *-li.e-* to *-lye-* (가려라).

However, since the affricates *c, ch,* and *cc* are always pronounced with palatal articulation, a *y* occurring after one of these consonants is not distinctive. In other words, *cy-,* for example, is pronounced exactly like *c-.* In Standard Hangŭl Orthography, a *y* in that position is supposed to be written to show the contraction, but, recognizing that the pronunciation is not distinctive, the official document also allows the word to be written without the *y*:

(1) a. *kaci-* + *-ela* 'take it!' is written *ka.cyela* (가져라) or *ka.cela* (가저라)]
    b. *chi-* + *-ese* 'hit, and . . .', written *chye.se* (쳐서) or *che.se* (처서)
    c. *cci-* + *-ess.ta* 'steamed', written *ccyess.ta* (쪘다) or *ccess.ta* (쩠다)

Since there is no distinction in Korean between *cy-* and *c-,* it might therefore seem strange that many Koreans insist on transcribing English "j" with a Hangŭl *cy-.* For example, the name "John" is habitually written by many as *cyon* (죤) or *cyan* (쟌), even though official and semi-official sources these days prefer the simpler *c*—as in *Con Leynon* (존 레논), 'John Lennon' (the spelling usually found in Korean newspapers). Perhaps, since no modern Korean word could be spelled that way, the insertion of the *y* serves simply to make the word look and feel foreign.

Dropping of l before a t, n, s, *or* c. In some compound words, the consonant *l* drops before one of the coronal consonants, *t, n, s,* or *c*:

(2) a. *sol* (솔) 'pine' + *namu* 'tree' → *so.namu* (소나무) 'pine tree'
    mal (말) 'horse' + *so* 'cow' → *ma-so* (마소) 'horses and cattle'
    yel- (열다) 'to open' + *tat-* (닫다) 'to shut' → *ye.tat-* (여닫다) 'to open and shut [a door]'
    b. *ttal* (딸) 'daughter' + *-nim* '[respect]' → *tta-nim* (따님) '[your] esteemed daughter'
    panul (바늘) 'needle' + *-cil* [suffix] → *panu-cil* (바느질) 'sewing'

But the consonant *l* does not drop in all, or even most, words; for example, *mal-sol* 'horse brush'; *pal-tung* 'instep'; *pul-noli* [pullori] 'fireworks display'; and so on. Where *l* is lost depends on the word and is not phonologically predictable; for example, while the *l* does drop in *mu-com* 'athlete's foot' (from *mul* 'water' and *com* 'mildew'), it does not in *mul-cip* 'blister' (literally, 'water-enclosure'). In Sino-Korean words, the *l* ordinarily stays put, and the following coronal consonant is reinforced: *pal.tong* [palt?ong] 'start', *mul.cil* [multʃ?il] 'matter', and so on. The lexical items in which the *l* drops must all be memorized.

Reinforcement. When two lax consonants occur together within a word, the second must always be pronounced with reinforcement. The addition of reinforcement to the consonant is automatic.

> (3) a. *kwuk-pap* (국밥) → *kwuk.ppap* 'boiled rice served in soup'
>   *pat-ko* (받고) → *pat.kko* → *pa.kko* [pak?o][13] 'receiving'
>   *pep-tay* (법대) → *pep.ttay* 'law school'

Sometimes the cluster of two lax consonants comes from the neutralization or dropping of other consonants, but the result is the same.

> (4) a. *yeph-cip* (옆집) → *yep.cip* → *yep.ccip* 'the house next door'
>   *kkoch-pakwuni* (꽃바구니) → *kkot.pakwuni* → *kkot.ppakwuni* → *kko.ppak-*
>   *wuni* [k?op?aguni] 'flower basket'
>   b. *talk-sal* (닭살) → *tak.sal* → *tak.ssal* 'chicken meat'
>   *eps-ta* (없다) → *ep.ta* → *ep.tta* 'not exist'

In neither Hangŭl nor romanization is the reinforcement in any of these clusters written; 'law school' in Hangŭl is 법대, in Yale Romanization, *pep.tay*, in McCune-Reischauer, *pŏptae*; nothing in any of these transcriptions overtly shows that the cluster is phonemically /ptt/. Transcription of the reinforcement is not necessary because it is completely automatic here.

However, in other cases reinforcement is not automatic. After an *-l*, for example, most (noncoronal) lax consonants remain lax consonants: *wel.pu* [wəlbu] 'monthly installment', *phal.ko* [pʰalgo] 'selling, and . . .'. Nevertheless, in some lexical items otherwise unexpected reinforcement does occur, and a consonant following *l* is, on the contrary, reinforced. The most salient examples of this are verbal forms with the prospective modifier *-l: kal kos i →* *kal.kko.si* [kalk?oʃi] 'place to go'; *mannal salam → mannal.ssalam* [man-nals?aram] 'a person to meet'; *hal kes ul → hal.kkesul* [halk?əsɨl] 'something to do'; *hal pa lul → hal.ppalul* [halp?arɨl] 'way to do'. In Hangŭl, the reinforcement associated with the prospective modifier is not transcribed; there is nothing in the way the forms are written that gives any indication of the reinforcement. Koreans, of course, have no trouble reading the constructions properly because, as native speakers, they know instinctively that the prospective modifier always induces this pronunciation in a following lax consonant. But for Westerners, the Hangŭl can cause pronunciation problems. In this case romanization can help because it usually indicates whatever is phonemically distinct. Yale Romanization, for example, shows the reinforcement with a special morphophonemic symbol, *q*, so that the prospective modifier is not *-l*, but rather *-lq*. Compare:

	Hangŭl	Yale
'place to go'	갈 곳이	kalq kos i
'person to meet'	만날 사람	mannalq salam
'things to do'	할 것을	halq kes ul
'way to do'	할 바를	halq pa lul

In the original form of the Korean alphabet as used in the fifteenth century, the symbol " ᅙ " *(q)* was often employed to show this reinforcement; for example, *mwo.mol mwot mi.tulq ke.si.ni* (모ᄫ 몯 미긇 거시니) 'the body is not to be trusted' [*Sŏkpo sangjŏl* 6:11b (1447)].[14] In modern Hangŭl, however, the symbol is no longer used. Hangŭl is easy to read only for people who know the language.

Reinforcement also does not ordinarily occur after a nasal: *tan.pal* 'short hair'; *kum.pang* 'just now'; *pang.sik* 'method'. But, at the end of a verb stem it does, and an *n-* or an *m-*, on the contrary, causes consistent reinforcement: *sin-ko* → *sin.kko* 'putting on [shoes], and . . .'; *tetum-taka* → *tetum.ttaka* 'groped, and then . . .' . Since this reinforcement was not indicated in texts of the fifteenth century, nor is it found in some modern regional dialects, it is probably something that developed after the fifteenth century in Seoul.[15] To add to the mystery, it is curious that the reinforcement does not occur when the stem is followed by the suffix *-ki-*, a morpheme used to indicate a causative or passive construction: *an-* 'embrace' + *-ki-* → *an.ki-* 'have [someone] hold in the arms'; *kam-* 'wind [something]' + *-ki-* → *kam.ki-* 'be wound'. Again, Hangŭl gives no clue to these differences in pronunciations.

Noun Compounds and the "Genitive s. " The situation in noun compounds is still more complex. Phonologically unpredictable reinforcement occurs quite often in compounds, much of it because of the otherwise hidden presence of the "genitive particle *s*," *sai-sios* (사이ㅅ) in Korean. This "genitive *s*" is believed to have once been pronounced as an [s], and it is still written that way, with the Hangŭl letter " ㅅ ". But it is never pronounced as a sibilant in modern Korean,[16] for the only way it is usually realized is as reinforcement of the following consonant. Here is a typical example: *sai s kil* (사잇길) 'the way between' is pronounced [saikʔil] (it is a synonym for *sai uy kil* (사이의길)). This nearly hidden morpheme is written *patchim* in Hangŭl in case the first element of the compound ends in a vowel; for example, *pays sakong* (뱃사공) 'boatman', *pays kil* (뱃길) 'shipping route', *kosos cang* (고숫장) 'letter of complaint', *congis cang* (종잇장) 'sheet of paper', *thes path* (텃밭) 'backyard vegetable plot'. But in case the syllable ends in a consonant, Hangŭl gives no indication of the reinforcement. In Yale

Phonology

Romanization, the morphophonemic symbol *q* is used for this purpose (as it is also in the previous examples, instead of the *s* we have written). Here are some compounds like this:

	Hangŭl	*Yale*	*Pronunciation*
'inner room'	안방	anq pang	anppang [ampˀaŋ]
'ophthalmology'	안과	anq kwa	ankkwa
'pupil of eye'	눈동자	nwunq tongca	nwunttongca
'sleepyhead'	잠보	cam-qpo	camppo
'Korean sushi'	김밥	kimq pap	kimppap
'riverside'	강가	kangq ka	kangkka
'sound of water'	물소리	mulq soli	mulssoli

In noun compounds where the genitive *s* is followed by an *n* or *m*, it assimilates to that consonant. Sometimes these occurrences of the morpheme are transcribed in Hangŭl, and sometimes they are not.

	Hangŭl	*Yale*	*Pronunciation*
'seawater'	바닷물	pataq mul	patammul
'gum' [tooth-body]	잇몸	iq mom	immom
'sea chantey'	뱃노래	payq nolay	paynnolay
'rear paddy'	뒷논	twiq non	twinnon

In North Korean orthography, the genitive *s* in all these forms was formerly transcribed with an apostrophe: 안'방, 김'밥. The North Korean apostrophe is an innovation that may have nothing to do with Korean tradition, but it is a convenience not found in Hangŭl.

In addition to reinforcement caused by the (unwritten) genitive particle, there are also a number of nouns where the etymological source of the reinforcement is unclear. Here are some examples of those:

	Hangŭl	*Yale*	*Pronunciation*
'Chinese characters'	한자	hanqca	hancca
'letters'	글자	kulqca	kulcca
'grammar'	문법	munqpep	munppep
'a stroll'	산보	sanqpo	sanppo
'condition'	조건	coqken	cokken
'popularity'	인기	inqki	inkki
'decision'	결정	kyelqceng	kyelcceng

The reinforcement found in these words is not written in Hangŭl, and it is indicated with an apostrophe only in some cases, but not in all, in North Korean orthography.

n-epenthesis. If the second member of a compound noun begins with an *i* or *y*, an *n* is inserted; for example, *aph-i* → *aph-ni* (→ *amni*) 'front teeth'. Historically, this *n* originated as the initial consonant of the noun (so that 'teeth' was originally *ni*), but it was subsequently lost in that position and after that showed up only in these compound words. However, these are not the only places the *n* is found. There are also many nouns that begin with *i* or *y* that never had an initial *n*, and now these, too, by analogy, often gain an unexpected *n* when they form compounds:

	Hangŭl	Yale	Pronunciation	Etymology
etymological *n*				
'front teeth'	앞이	aphq (n)i	amni	ni 'teeth'
'flower petal'	꽃잎	kkochq iph	kkonnip	niph 'leaf'
'sesame leaf'	깻잎	kkayq iph	kkaynnip	niph 'leaf'
no etymological *n*				
'things to come'	앞일	aphq il	amnil	il 'work'
'internal medicine'	내복약	naypokq yak	naypongnyak	yak 'medicine'
'business use'	영업용	yengepq yong	yengemnyong	yong 'usage'

3.3.5 Verb Stems

There are a number of phonological idiosyncracies to be found in the shapes of verb stems. The listings here generally follow those of Martin 1954 and 1992.

Final -*h*. Some of the most rancorous disputes in the debates about orthography have been over the *h* that comes at the end of certain verb stems. This *h* was of course not among the seven consonants that were traditionally written *patchim*, at the end of the syllable, but even after the decision in the 1930s to allow the transcription of other syllable-final consonants, there was still great resistance against this one consonant, some scholars insisting that it should remain the sole exception to the practice of morphophonemic writing. Finally, however, determining that there was no easy alternative, the decision was made to allow *h* to be written *patchim*.

The problem was, and is, that this consonant is never actually an *h* phonemically. Written as such, it is an abstraction, because it is always pronounced as something else. When a verb stem ending in this -*h* is followed by *t*, *c*, or *k*, the *h* is realized as aspiration on that following consonant:

(1) a. *noh.ko* (놓고) → *no.kho* [nokʰo] 'placing'
    noh.teni (놓더니) → *no.theni* [notʰəni] 'having placed . . ., and then . . .'
    noh.ci (놓지) → *no.chi* [notʃʰi] 'places . . ., [I suppose]'

  b. *manh.ta* (많다) → *man.tha* [mantʰa] '. . . are many,'
    manh.ci (많지) → *man.chi* [mantʃʰi] '. . . are many, [I suppose]'

Before any other consonant, the *h* behaves like a *t*:

(2) a. *noh.so* (놓소) → *not.so* → *no.sso* [nosʔo] '[he] places . . .'
       noh.nunta (놓는다) → *not.nunta* → *non.nunta* [nonninda] 'is placing
       . . .'

When followed by a vowel, the *h* is dropped. It does not in every case
disappear without a trace, however. Verb stems that end in a vowel ordinarily contract when followed by the vowel *-a: ka.a la* → *ka la* 'go!'; *po.a* →
p(w)a 'look'; *o.a* → wa 'come'.[17] But when the stem *cōh-* 'be good', for example, is followed by the infinitive ending *-a*, the phonemic result is *cō.a*, with
two full syllables, and the vowel length intact. This *cō.a* can, for some speakers, contract to the monosyllable *cwa*, but that is usually only in rapid or
sloppy speech and is looked down on even then as substandard. In any case,
the *h* is never pronounced.

There are no nouns in the modern language with a final *h* (which is
probably part of the reason for the earlier resistance against writing an *h* at
the end of verb stems). But there are a few lexical items that show where one
once existed. For example, *swu.thalk* 'rooster' is plainly composed of *swu*
'male' and *talk* 'chicken'; the aspiration of the *t* is evidence for earlier *swuh*
'male'. The etymology is supported by *swu.khay* 'male dog' (*kay* 'dog') and
swukhes 'male' (*kes* 'thing'). Similarly, *am.thalk* 'hen', *am.khay* 'bitch', and
am.khay 'female' point to earlier *amh* 'female'. Such words as these are completely frozen in the lexicon, however, and the *h* at the end of nouns is no
longer a productive part of the language.

Final -p/-w. A *-p* written in Hangŭl at the end of a verb stem can be of two
kinds. One is a consonant that remains a *-p* before all endings; the other
weakens to a *-w* before a vowel.

-p:	*kwup-* (굽다) 'be bent'	*kwup.supnita*	*kwupko*	*kwup.e* (굽어)
-p/-w:	*kwūp/kwuw-* (굽다) 'bake'	*kwūp.supnita*	*kwūpko*	*kwuwe* (구워)
	nwup/nwuw- 'lie down'	*nwup.supnita*	*nwupko*	*nwuwe* (누워)

These two consonantal types have different etymological origins; the
fifteenth-century source of the *w* was the consonant [ß] (written with the
symbol " ᄫ "), which later weakened to the semivowel. For details, see
chapter 7.

Final -t/-l. A *-t* written at the end of a stem can also be of two kinds. One always remains a *-t;* the other weakens to an *-l* [r] before a vowel.

-t:	*tat-* (닫다) 'close'	*tat.supnita*	*tat.ko*	*tat.e* (닫어)
-t/-l:	*tut-* (듣다) 'listen'	*tut.supnita*	*tut.ko*	*tul.e* (들어)

Again, for etymological details see chapter 7.

Dropping of final -s. An *-s* written at the end of some stems drops before a vowel.

-s:	*wus-* (웃다) 'laugh'	*wūs.sumnita*	*wūt.ko*	*wus.e* (웃어)
-(s):	*pu(s)-* (붓다) 'swell'	*pūs.supnita*	*pūt.ko*	*pu.e* (부어)

The disappearing *s* was a *z* (written " ᅀ ") in the fifteenth century (cf. chapter 7).

l-stems. The most complex and irregular consonantal behavior is that of the liquid *l*. We have already mentioned one stem type with an *l*, the one in which *l* alternates with *t*. There are at least three other types, too.[18] Here are examples of the three types, listed by the forms given in Korean dictionaries:

(1) *l* drops before *n, l, p, s,* but appears before other consonants or a vowel: *tul.ta* (들다) 'cost': *tu.na, tup.nita, tu.sita, tu.sey, tul.ko, tul.ci, tul.e, tul.essta.*

(2) These verb stems all end in *-lu-*. When followed by the infinitive ending *-e* or the past marker *-ess-*, the *u* drops and the *l* doubles: *hulu.ta* (흐르다) 'flow': *hulu.na, hulup.nita, hulu.ko, hulu.ci, hulle, hullessta.*

(3) These verb stems also end in *-lu-*. But when followed by the infinitive ending *-e* or the past marker *-ess-*, the *u* does not drop, and another *l* is added: *phulu.ta.* (푸르다) 'be blue': *phulu.na, phulup.nita, phulu.ko, phulu.ci, phulu.le, phulu.lessta.*

There are only three verbs of this last type: *nwulu-* (누르다) 'be yellow', *ilu-* (이르다) 'reach', and *phulu-* (푸르다) 'be blue'.

Disappearing vowel. When a stem-final *-u-* appears before an ending beginning with a vowel, it is always dropped. The vowel in the stem *phu-* 'scoop up' is written as /wu/ (" ㅜ ") in Hangŭl, but it drops, too, and this behavior shows that the vowel is actually /u/ (cf. section 3.3.2, "Labial Assimilation," above, for remarks on the pronunciation).

ssu- (쓰다) 'use': *ssu-* + *e la* → *sse la, ssu-* + *-essta* → *ssess.ta* (썼다)
phu- (푸다) 'scoop up': *phu-* + *e la* → *phe la, phu-* + *-essta* → *phess.ta* (펐다)

Weakening vowel. When a stem-final *i, o,* or *wu* is followed by the infinitive ending *-e* or *-a*, the vowel shortens to a semivowel, *i* changing to a *y*, and *o* or *wu* changing to a *w*. As phonological compensation for the syllabic compression, the remaining syllable is pronounced long — but only if it is the first syllable in the word:

phi.e se (피어서) → *phyē se* 'bloom, and so...'; *culki-e la* → *culye la* 'enjoy!'
po-a la (보아라) → *pwā la* 'look!'; *ssawu-e se* → *ssawe se* 'fight, and so . . .'

When the vowel *i* follows a stem-final vowel, it, too, will weaken to a *y*.
Again, the remaining syllable is ordinarily pronounced long:

pha- (파다) 'dig' + *-ita* → *phāyta* 'be dug'
sso- (쏘다) 'shoot' + *-ita* → *ssōyta* 'be shot'

(Notice, however, such syllables are phonetically monophthongized in
modern Korean; for example, *phāyta* is [pʰɛda].)

There are a number of other small-scale alternations to be found in
the phonology of modern Korean. However, since most native speakers are
not consciously aware of them, they need not be discussed here.

References

Austerlitz, et al. 1980; Hŏ Ung 1965; Kim Chin-W. 1965; Kim-Renaud 1974;
Lee Sang Oak (Yi Sangŏk) 1990, 1994; Martin 1954, 1992; Ramsey 1978, 1996; Yi
Hŭisŭng and An Pyŏnghŭi 1989; Yi Kimun (Lee Ki-Moon), Kim Chinu, and Yi
Sangŏk 1984; Yi Pyŏnggŭn 1979

4
Words and Parts of Speech

In this chapter, and in chapters 5 and 6 that follow, we will describe the general grammatical structure of Korean. Here, in the first of the three chapters, we look at morphology. We examine the structure of words and morphemes and the various parts of speech found in Korean, and at the end of the chapter, we take up the rather special topic of loans from other languages. Particles and verb endings are a complex topic that will be treated in some detail separately, in chapter 5. Chapter 6 provides a brief overview of syntax and syntactic processes.

4.1 The Basic Structure of Words

In Korean, just as in most other languages, there are *free morphemes*, which can be used as independent words, and *bound morphemes*, which must be combined with other morphemes in order to be used as free-standing words. The nouns *namu* 'tree', *salang* 'love', *na* 'I', and *tases* 'five',[1] and the adverbs *acwu* 'very', *cokum* 'a little', and *kyewu* 'almost' are free morphemes. In contrast, verb and adjective stems are all bound morphemes. That is, stems such as *mek-* 'eat' and *phulu-* 'blue' cannot function independently as words, but must necessarily be combined with suffixes, as in *mek-ni, mek-ko, phulu-ta, phulu-myen*, to function as words. Korean verbs and adjectives are characterized by this structural feature. It makes them quite unlike verbs and adjectives in English.

Particles are grammatical elements that show the syntactic role of the noun phrase or add to its meaning. They are not free-standing words and are phonologically more tightly bound to the noun than English prepositions. However, they do not attach as rigidly to the noun as the case endings of German. In German, a case ending is bound so tightly to the stem of the noun that nothing can be inserted between the two. The case ending is an integral part of the noun. In Korean, another element often comes between the subject marker and the noun, as in *yeki-kkaci-ka* 'up to here'. The same is true of the object marker; for example, *chayk-man-ul* 'only the book'. Also, unlike case marking in German, these particular Korean particles can even be omitted entirely. Particles are more independent entities than suffixes. For this reason (as will be explained in detail later), particles are treated in most Korean grammars as independent parts of speech.

In addition to suffixes, the concept of 'root' is necessary to an understanding of how Korean grammarians treat the structure of Korean words.
Though this concept has had many different meanings in its usage by Western scholars, it will be used here in the way it is used in Korea. Like stems,
roots have no independent existence and form the central part of the word,
but, unlike a stem, a verbal root refers to an element to which an inflectional
suffix cannot be directly bound. For example, the bound morphemes
kkaykkus- and *thwutel-* are found combined with *hata* 'does, is' and *-kelita*
'does repeatedly' in the verb forms *kkaykkus-hata* 'is clean' and *thwutel-kelita*
'grumble'. These two morphemes are not prefixes; they are clearly the ker-
nels of the words. Yet, they do not themselves inflect—there are no forms
like ˟*kkaykkus-umyen* or ˟*kkaykkus-uni*, ˟*thwutel-ese* or ˟*thwutel-ko*. Only by combining with *ha-* or *keli-* can they be inflected, as in *kkaykkus-hamyen*, *kkaykkus-
hani*, *thwutel-kelyese* (< *thwutel-keli-ese*) or *thwutel-keliko*. In these cases, *kkaykkus-
ha-* and *thwutel-keli-* are the stems, and *kkaykkus-* and *thwutel-* are the roots.

In Korean, the concept of 'root' is especially useful for handling the
massive Sino-Korean vocabulary. In Literary Chinese one character generally represents one word, but when Sinitic vocabulary was borrowed into Korean, what was represented by a single character was often a bound
morpheme that could not be used by itself as a word. Of course, among Chinese characters there are also many that function independently as words in
Korean (for example, 門 *mun* 'door', 冊 *chayk* 'book', 窓 *chang* 'window', 房
pang 'room', 床 *sang* 'table', 賞 *sang* 'award'), but most Chinese characters
form words by combining with another Chinese character. In such cases,
since each Chinese character cannot take an inflectional suffix, it cannot be
called a "stem," nor is it itself an affix. The term used by Korean grammarians for these kinds of Sino-Korean morphemes is *root*. In the Sino-Korean
words *en.e* (言語) 'language', *swucok* (手足) 'limbs (hands and feet)', *pumo*
(父母) 'parents', and *wangpok* (往復) 'round trip', *en-*, *-e*, *swu-*, *-cok*, *pu-*, *-mo*,
wang-, and *-pok* are all examples of roots.

When it is necessary to combine into a single term the concepts of
both 'stem' and 'root', we will use the term *base*. The base contrasts with the
affix. There are two types of affixes: *inflectional affixes* and *derivational affixes*.
Derivational affixes are used to generate words. Since there are no infixes in
Korean, the only derivational affixes in the language are prefixes and
suffixes. (Cf. 4.4.2.) Inflectional affixes always occur as suffixes; they attach
to bases to show how the words function in the sentence. These inflectional
affixes are called "verb endings" in most Korean grammars; here, except in
special cases, we will follow this conventional usage, using the term to refer
to the inflectional endings attached to verbs, adjectives, and the copula.

There are very few Korean *prefixes*. They never change the part of
speech of the word, but function only to limit its meaning. *Suffixes* are a much
more important element of the Korean language. Not only are they greater in
number and type, but they also function far beyond simply limiting the meaning. Suffixes are used in a broad range of ways, functioning for such processes

as changing the part of speech, or changing a verb into a causative or passive. In addition, when we remember that the inflectional endings of verbs, adjectives, and nouns (+ copula) are suffixes, we begin to see what an extraordinarily large number of grammatical functions depend on the use of suffixes.

4.2 Parts of Speech

In most Korean grammars, the parts of speech are divided into nine classes: *nouns, pronouns, numbers, verbs, adjectives, prenouns, adverbs, interjections,* and *particles.* These traditional grammars (which are ultimately based upon Western grammatical categories) have not gone unchallenged, however. Alternative analyses have often been suggested. One important alternative is one that recognizes a primary word-class difference between uninflected words and inflected words—that is, between nouns and verbs.[2] In this alternative framework, the term "noun" is used in a broader sense to include not only nouns in the narrower meaning found in traditional grammars, but also pronouns and numbers. Similarly, verbs and adjectives are classed together as "verbs" in the broader sense of inflecting forms.

In the present work, however, we will use the traditional nine-class system in describing the Korean lexicon. The parts of speech and the terms are familiar ones that one is most likely to encounter in Korea. Still, for the sake of convenience, verbs and adjectives will be treated under the same heading since they are virtually identical in structure. The same is true of prenouns and adverbs. A description of exclamations will be omitted. Particles will be discussed in a separate section in chapter 5.

4.2.1 Nouns

In a well-formed Korean sentence, nouns are generally marked by case particles. These postposed case particles express the grammatical functions of the nouns. However, since particles are not always absolutely necessary for grammatical functions to be clear, they can also sometimes be omitted, as shown in examples (1b) and (1c).

(1) a. 민호가 수미를 사랑한다.
    Minho *ka* Swumi *lul* salang-hanta.
      SUBJ   OBJ loves
    'Minho loves Swumi.'
  b. 민호가 수미 사랑한다.
    Minho *ka* Swumi salang-hanta.
  c. 민호 점심 먹었니?
    Minho cemsim mek.ess.ni?
         lunch ate?
    'Did Minho eat lunch?'

Nouns also function as the sentence predicate by linking up with *ita,* the *copula.* For example, *(Swumi nun haksayng) ita* '(Sumi) is (a student)'. In having inflection the copula is like a verb, but, unlike a verb stem, *i-* has no conceptual meaning. It serves only to predicate the noun to which it attaches. What is peculiar about the copula among inflecting forms is that it attaches to the noun tightly, like a particle. For this reason—because the copula and the noun are inseparable—Korean grammarians have generally not treated the copula as a separate word. They prefer to think, rather, that the entire noun-plus-copula phrase (*haksayngita* 'is-a-student') is the predicate. In other words, according to most Korean grammarians, the noun is directly predicated, and the *i-* is only an inserted linking vowel. The idea that the copula is actually a separate word was originally proposed by Ch'oe Hyŏnbae and his disciples. That idea has since gained support in many circles. But scholars such as Yi Sungnyŏng of Seoul National University and his followers have continued to maintain that the *i-* is merely a vowel used to link the predicated noun to its inflectional endings.

Another characteristic of nouns is that they are modified by *prenouns,* such as <u>*say*</u> *cikcang* '<u>*new*</u> workplace', <u>*yele*</u> *nala* '<u>*various*</u> countries', <u>*i*</u> *kapang* '<u>*this*</u> briefcase'. This modification by prenouns is actually a more typical characteristic of nouns than is their use with particles since particles also link up with other forms besides nouns (cf. 5.1). To illustrate this point, notice that there are cases where derived nouns and verbal nouns, both of which consist of verb or adjective stems combined with *-um* or *-ki,* are difficult to distinguish from each other. In such cases, the two can be differentiated by whether or not they are modified by prenouns. As can be seen in (2), below, the two are distinguished by the fact that derived nouns are modified by prenouns, while verbal nouns are modified by adverbs. Thus, modification by a prenoun makes it clear that the word is a noun.

(2) a. 그는 호탕하게 <u>웃음</u>으로써 어색한 상황을 벗어나려고 했다.
　　　　Ku nun *hothang-hakey wusum ulosse* esayk-han sanghwang ul
　　　　　　　　　heartily　　laughing
　　　　pes.e na.lyeko hayssta. (verbal noun, modified by an adverb)
　　　　'He tried to get out of an uncomfortable situation by *laughing heartily.*'

　　b. 그의 호탕한 <u>웃음</u>은 보는 사람까지 즐겁게 한다.
　　　　Ku uy *hothang-han wusum un* po.nun salam kkaci culkepkey
　　　　　　　　　hearty　　laugh
　　　　hanta. (derived noun, modified by a prenoun)
　　　　'His *hearty laugh* makes people watching happy.'

There are types of nouns that, even though they are undeniably nouns, do not appear independently in the sentence but must instead be preceded by a modifier. These are the *bound nouns* such as *kes, i, pun, tey, cwul, swu, ttay, mun, ttalum, ppun, kim,* and *li.*

(3) 가진 것을 다 내어 놓아라.
Kacin *kes* ul   ta nay.e noh.ala.
having THING   all
'Take out everything you have.'

(4) 김 박사는 외로운 이들을 위해 좋은 일을 많이 하신 분이시다.
Kim paksa nun oylowun *i* tul ul wi-hay coh.un il ul manh.i hasin *pun* isinta.
    lonely ONE benefitting good deeds much did PERSON is
'Dr. Kim is a person who has done many good things for the lonely.'

(5) 나는 아직 수영할 줄을 모른다.
Na nun acik swuyeng-hal *cwul* ul molunta.
I   still swim WAY not-know
'I still don't know how to swim.'

(6) 나는 그 이유를 도무지 알 수가 없었다.
Na nun ku iyu lul tomuci al *swu* ka eps.essta.
I   that reason utterly know   WAY not-is
'I didn't have the least idea what the reason was.'

(7) 좀더 넓은 데로 가자.
Com te   nelp.un *tey* lo   kaca.
little more wide   PLACE-to let's-go
'Let's go to where there's a little more room.'

(8) 이번 여행은 나쁜 날씨 때문에 고생이 많았다.
I pen yehayng un napp.un nalssi *ttaymun* ey   kosayng i manh.assta.
this time trip   bad weather   because-of   hard-time be-much
'We had a very hard time on the trip this time because of the bad weather.'

(9) 뉴욕에 온 김에 워싱톤까지 구경하고 가야겠다.
Nyuyok ey on *kim* ey   wesingthon kkaci kwukyeng-hako kayakeyssta.
New York came WHILE Washington until sight-seeing must-go
'As long as I'm in New York, I might as well visit Washington.'

On the basis of form and function, it is clear that these words are nouns because they are modified by prenouns and followed by postposed particles. However, many are semantically unlike nouns. Not only are they not used independently, but they also do not have a specific, "nominal" type of reference—such as do *il* 'thing', *kos* 'place', *nayyong* 'content', and *salam* 'person', for example. Instead, what they refer to is abstract, generalized, and unspecified.

Moreover, though there are exceptions (such as *kes* 'thing'), most of these bound nouns are characterized by a limitation on how they function syntactically—some can only serve as subjects, some as objects, some as

predicates, and so on. For example, *cwul* only appears in constructions
where it is an object (cf. 5, above), and *swu* is only used as a subject (as in 6).

One type of bound noun is the *classifier*. A classifier is a word that is
suffixed to numerals when counting. It is chosen strictly by the type of noun
being counted because noun and classifier must always be in agreement. For
example, 'five soldiers' can be expressed as *kwun.in tases myeng* ('soldier +
five + PERSON') but never as ^x*kwun.in tases kay* or ^x*kwun.in tases mali*, because the classifier *kay* is used for inanimate objects, and the classifier *mali*
is used for animals. Some common classifiers are shown in (10), below:[3]

> (10) 개 *kay* (general classifer), 마리 *mali* (for animals), 명 *myeng* (for people),
> 그루 *kulwu* (for trees), 자루 *calwu* (for objects with a handle, writing in-
> struments, etc.), 켤레 *khyelley* (for pairs of shoes or socks), 벌 *pel* (for sets),
> 채 *chay* (for buildings, houses), 단 *tan* (for bundles, bunches), 접 *cep* (for
> hundred counts of fruits or vegetables), 두름 *twulum* (for strings of twenty
> fish or dried vegetables), 권 *kwen* (for bound volumes), 장 *cang* ('sheets',
> for thin flat objects), 리 *li* ('miles'), 살/세 *sal/sey* (for years of age).

Here are some examples of how nouns are counted:

> (11) 사과 열 개 *sakwa yelq kay* 'ten apples', 소 열 마리 *so yel mali* 'ten oxen', 군
> 인 열 명 *kwun.in yelq myeng* 'ten soldiers', 소나무 열 그루 *sonamu yelq kulwu*
> 'ten pine trees', 연필 열 자루 *yenphil yelq calwu* 'ten pencils', 운동화 열 켤
> 레 *wuntonghwa yel khyelley* 'ten pairs of sneakers', 양복 열 벌 *yangpok yelq pel*
> 'ten suits', 집 열 채 *cip yel chay* 'ten houses', 오징어 열 두름 *ocinge yelq twu-
> lum* 'ten strings of (twenty) squid', 책 (노트) 열 권 *chayk (nothu) yelq kwen*
> 'ten books (notebooks)', 종이 열 장 *congi yelq cang* 'ten sheets of paper'.

> (12) 시장에 가서 양파 다섯 개, 파 한 단, 마늘 한 접을 샀다.
> Sicang ey kase yangpha tases *kay,* pha han *tan,* manul han *cep* ul sassta.
> market   go onions   5   scallion 1   garlic 1   bought
> 'I went to the market and bought five onions, one bunch of scallions, and
> one bulb (one hundred) of garlic.'

For further discussion of classifiers and counting, cf. 4.2.3, below.

In contrast with the complexity of classifiers, the grammatical category
of "number" does not exist in Korean. That is to say, the difference between
singular and plural is not reflected in the noun or in any morphological
form. Whether one says *Sakwa lul han kay mekessta* 'I ate one apple' or *Sakwa
lul tases kay mekessta* 'I ate five apples', the form of *sakwa* 'apple(s)' does not
change. There is a suffix *-tul* that is used to mark plurals, but it is only used
for special purposes, so that, for example, in the sentence *Musun chayk ul
kuleh.key manh.i sassni?* 'Why did you buy that many books?' one expresses
the meaning of 'books' with the word *chayk* not *chayk-tul*. There is also no
grammatical category of "gender" in Korean, and the question of whether

sakwa 'apple' or *chayk* 'book' or *Han kang* 'the Han River' is masculine or feminine or neuter does not arise. As a consequence, it should be noted that another characteristic of Korean nouns is that they are not governed by number or gender. Such concepts as "concrete" and "collective" also have no particular meaning for Korean nouns.

Proper nouns deserve special mention. Korean personal names are constructed in the order of surname first, followed by the given name. Surnames almost all consist of one syllable, and given names are almost all made up of two syllables. As a result, virtually all Korean names consist of three syllables, and only rarely does one meet a name of two syllables or four syllables. Since women by custom do not take their husband's surname when they marry, there are almost no cases where the length of a name breaks out of this pattern. However, names of two and four syllables may be rare, but they do exist. The forms of the names given in 13a, below, are typical, and the examples in 13b, c, and d illustrate the other possibilities.

(13)a. 주-시경 Cwu Sikyeng, 이-순신 Yi Swunsin
   b. 김-구 Kim Kwu, 정-철 Ceng Chel
   c. 선우-휘 Senwu Hwi, 황보-인 Hwangbo In
   d. 독고-영재 Tokko Yengcay, 남궁-옥분 Namkwung Okpun

The order of place names is also exactly the opposite of that of English. The large unit of area comes first, and the names are in order of increasingly small size. For example, when one writes the address on a letter, one writes <*Kangwen-to Kanglung-si Yongkang-tong* 213-*penci*> 'Kangwŏn Province, Kangnŭng City, Yonggang Tong (district), Number 213'. In expressing time, also, the order is from big to small, as <*1965-nyen 5-wel 4-il ocen 6-si 20-pun*> '1965, May 4, 6:20 A.M.' Since names, as we have seen, are in the final analysis also ordered with the large unit first, we can see that in Korean the general rule is that units are ordered from large to small.

4.2.2 Pronouns

Pronouns are a special type of noun. They have the syntactic characteristics of nouns; their grammatical functions are specified by postposed particles, and they are modified by prenouns. The reason pronouns are treated as a separate word class in traditional Korean grammars is largely because of the influence of Western grammatical categories. Nevertheless, for our purposes here, it is useful to follow the traditional treatment and highlight pronouns by describing them separately.

First, the most representative pronouns found in Korean are given in the following list.

(1) First person: 나 na, 저 ce; 우리 wuli, 저희 cehuy
   Second person: 너 ne, 자네 caney, 당신 tangsin, 댁 tayk, 어르신 elusin; 너희 nehuy

Third person:(human) 애 yay, 이이 i i, 이분 i pun; 걔 kyay, 그이 ku i, 그
분(그) ku pun (ku); 쟤 cay, 저이 ce i, 저
분 ce pun
(inanimate)이것 i kes; 그것 ku kes; 저것 ce kes
(location)여기 yeki; 거기 keki; 저기 ceki
reflexive: 자기 caki, 저 ce, 당신 tangsin

What must first be noted about this chart is that the selection of the appropriate pronoun depends upon the speech style level in the honorific system. Such distinctions in the second-person pronouns are rather
complicated and will be treated later, in section 7.1. As for the first-person
pronouns, *ce* 'I' and *cehuy* 'we' are humble forms of self-deprecation. When
talking to a friend, one speaks as in (2a), and to one's teacher or grandfather, one must speak as in (2b).

(2) a. 나(우리)는 안 가겠다.
       Na (Wuli) nun an kakeyssta.
       I we TOPIC not will-go
       'I (We) are not going.'

     b. 저(저희)는 안 가겠어요.
       Ce (Cehuy) nun an kakeyss.eyo.
       I we TOPIC not will-go (polite)
       'I (We) are not going.'

The first-person pronoun *wuli* 'we/us' has a special usage beyond
marking a simple plural. When referring to family or household, the plural
form *wuli* 'our' is used instead of the singular form *na uy/nay* 'my': *wuli apeci*
'our (=my) father', *wuli enni* 'our (=my) older sister', *wuli cip* 'our (my)
home', or even *wuli manwula* 'our (=my) wife'. A singular pronoun would be
completely out of place in this in-group context. The expression *nay cip* certainly exists, but it refers to a building, 'my HOUSE', not 'my HOME'. Similarly, expressions such as *nay cip malyen* 'preparations for my house' refer to
a physical object instead of a family unit.[4] The pronoun *wuli* 'our' also has
a variety of other in-group usages. Expressions such as *wuli nala* 'our country, Korea', *wuli tongney* 'our (=my) neighborhood', and *wuli sensayng-nim*
'our (=my) teacher' express common bonds to country, neighborhood, and
teacher. In cases such as these, *wuli* expresses the meaning of 'my' with implications of deference and sharing.
    In a sense, there are no third-person pronouns in Korean. The forms
used to denote third-person are not separate lexical items, but rather are
formed by combining the demonstrative prenouns *i* 'this', *ku* 'that' and *ce*
'that (over there)' with bound nouns.[5] The deictic use of (1) *i*, (2) *ku*, and
(3) *ce* depends on the distance between the referent and the speaker; they indicate, respectively, (1) close proximity, (2) middle proximity, and (3) dis-

tant proximity. In other words, *i* refers to an object close to the speaker, *ku* to an object close the listener, and *ce* to an object at a distance from both speaker and listener. These prenouns are combined with the bound nouns *i* and *pun* for people, and with *kes* to indicate inanimate objects; the noun *i* is language indicating a fairly high social rank, but *pun* is used when referring to someone for whom the highest honorific is appropriate. Since the pronouns *yay*, *kyey*, and *cyey* are contractions of *i ay* 'this child', *ku ay* 'that child', and *ce ay* 'that child (over there)', they are used by adults to refer to children, or by children or young people to refer to close friends. The expressions *i nom*, *ku nom*, and *ce nom* are also used with affection by adults to refer to their own children or children of their own children's age; but the expressions must be treated with care because they are otherwise used to refer to animals or as terms of deprecation. The words *yeki* 'here', *keki* 'there', and *ceki* '(over) there' also etymologically consist of the deictic elements *i*, *ku*, and *ce*. They come from the forms in Middle Korean in which the prenouns were combined with the morpheme *-ngekuy*: *ingekuy* 'this place', *kungekuy* 'that place', *cengekuy* 'that place (over there)'. But in the modern language, the prenouns are completely fused into the words.

(3) (내가 가지고 있는) 이것과 (네가 가지고 있는) 그것을
(Nay ka kaciko issnun) *i kes* kwa   (ney ka kaciko issnun) *ku kes* ul
I   having   this THING and you having   that THING
'this thing (I have) and that thing (you have)'

다 팔면 저것을 살 수 있을까?
ta phalmyen, *ce kes* ul sal swu iss.ul kka?
all sell-if   that THING buy WAY is?
'If we sell all *these things* and all *those things*, will we be able to buy those things (over there)?'

(4) 그이는 제 남편이고, 이분은 제 친정 아버지세요.
Ku i nun cey namphyen iko, *i pun* un cey chinceng apeci sey yo.
that ONE my husband is-and that ONE my own-home father is
'*That's* my husband, and *this* is my (own) father.'

또 애는 제 아들이고, 쟤는 걔 사촌 누나 얘 요.
Tto, *yay* nun cey atul iko,   *cyay* nun *kyay* sachon nwuna yey yo.
also this(-child) my son is-& that(-child) his first-cousin older sister is
'Also, *this* is my son, and *that's* his (older female) first cousin.'

(5) 저놈 잡아라. 이놈 단단히 혼을 내야 해요.
Ce nom cap.ala! . . . *I nom* tantan-hi hon ul nayya hay yo.
that fellow grab!   this fellow firmly spirit give-out-must
'(pointing at a thief) Catch *that guy*! . . . (pointing at the captured thief) *This guy* has to be taught a good lesson [i.e., made to suffer].'

(6) 거기는 여기보다 훨씬 더 추운 곳이니 겨울 옷을 많이 가져 가거라.

Keki nun *yeki* pota hwelssin te chwuwun kos ini kyewul os ul manh.i kacye
kakela.

there here than much-more cold place is-so winter clothes much having
go

'It's much colder *there* than *here*, so take a lot of winter clothes.'

Reflexive pronouns are again different. On the one hand, Korean
does not have distinct first- and second-person reflexive pronouns; instead,
na 'I, me' and *ne* 'you' serve as reflexives. On the other hand, for third-person pronouns, there are distinct words such as *caki, ce,* and *tangsin* that are
used as reflexives. For this reason it is often said that third-person pronouns
are the only reflexive pronouns in Korean. These reflexives are differentiated according to the honorific rule governing the antecedent; therefore, *ce*
is used when referring to a person of lower social rank than is indicated by
caki, and *tangsin* is used as a reflexive when the antecedent merits a term of
respect. In other words, the use of *tangsin* as a reflexive differs from other
uses of this pronoun (as will be seen in section 7.1, below). Nevertheless, it
must still be treated with caution. Though *tangsin* is a term of respect when
used as a reflexive, it still cannot be used when talking about a person who
has a public rank such as *sacang-nim* 'company president', *cangkwan-nim*
'officer', or *cangkwun-nim* 'general'. Even as a reflexive, *tangsin* is generally
restricted in use mostly to persons in a private relationship to the speaker,
such as family or relations.

(7) a. 그때는 나는 내 이름도 쓸 줄 몰랐어.

Ku ttay nun na nun *nay* ilum to ssul cwul mollass.e.

        I   my

'At that time I didn't even know how to write *my own* name.'

b. 너는 네가 이 세상에서 가장 잘났다고 믿니?

Ne nun *neyka* i seysang eyse kacang cal nasstako mitni?

you   you this world in most well turned-out believe?

'Do you think *you*'re better than everybody else in this world?'

(8) a. 민호는 {제, 자기}가 제일 잘났다고 믿는다.

Minho nun {*cey, caki*} ka ceyil cal nasstako mitnunta.

           himself

'Minho thinks that he *(himself)* is better than everybody else.'

b. 할아버지께서는 당신이 옳다고 믿으시는 일은 그대로 하시고야 만다.

Halapeci kkeyse nun *tangsin* i olhtako mit.usinun il un kutaylo hasiko
ya manta.

                himself

'Grandfather has to do exactly whatever he *(himself)* believes is right.'

Besides the pronouns listed in (1), above, there are also pronouns such as *amu* 'any', *nwukwu* 'who', *mues* 'what', and *enu kes* 'which'. These words serve as both *question words* and *indefinite pronouns*. Note, for example, that *nwukwu* and *mues* are used in two different meanings; one is in the meaning of the interrogative pronouns 'who' and 'what', and the other is in the meaning of 'somebody' and 'something'. For example, in (10a) *nwukwu uy* can be seen to be used in the sense of the former ('who'), but *nwuka* is used in the sense of the latter ('somebody'); in (10b), if the sentence ends with a falling intonation, *mues* means 'what', but if the sentence has a rising intonation, *mues* is not an interrogative but is used in the meaning of 'something'. In addition, if these words are combined with a special particle, as they are in (11), they are used in the meaning of an indefinite pronoun, 'anybody' or 'anything'. Another idiosyncracy is that when *nwukwu* 'who' combines with the subject particle ka, the form is realized as *nwuka: nwukwu + ka* → *nwuka*.

(9) a. 누가 우승했니?
   Nwuka wusung-hayssni?
   '*Who* won?'

   b. 오늘 점심은 무엇을 먹을까?
   Onul cemsim un *mues* ul mek.ul kka?
   '*What* shall we eat for lunch today?'

   c. 금년 수학여행은 어디로 가니?
   Kumnyen swuhak yehayng un *eti* lo kani?
   '*Where* are you going on (your) school trip this year?'

   d. 너는 어느 것을 갖겠니?
   Ne nun *enu kes* ul kackeyssni?
   '*Which* will you have?'

(10)a. 이 사건이 누구의 실수 때문이었는지 누가 대답해 보아라.
   I saqken i *nwukwu uy* silswu ttaymun iessnunci *nwuka* taytap-hay poala.
   '*Somebody* answer *whose* fault this incident is.'

   b. 저런 식으로 해서 무엇이 될까?
   Celen sik ulo hayse *mues* i toyl kka?
   '*What* will come of it if they do it that way?' /
   'Will *something* come of it if they do it that way?'

(11)a. 만 18세가 넘은 사람이면 누구나(누구라도, 누구든) 응시할 수 있다.
   Man 18-sey ka nem.un salam imyen *nwukwu na (nwukwu lato, nwukwu tun)* ungsi-hal swu issta.
   '*Anybody* who is a person over eighteen can take the examination.'

b. 나는 무엇이나 잘 먹는다.

Na nun *mues ina* cal meknunta.

'I (enjoy) eating *anything*.'

As we have seen, there are many types of pronouns in Korean. But there are also many restrictions on their usage. A noun in a preceding sentence is usually more often repeated than pronominalized. Moreover, as will be explained in (7.1), a second-person pronoun is normally not used to refer to someone who must be respected; there are many instances where one can only use a noun to refer to such a person. In the following examples, there is no possibility that *kamca* 'potato', *emeni* 'mother', or *sensayng-nim* 'teacher' could be replaced by a pronoun. On the whole, Korean is a language in which the use of pronouns is restricted. Another way to describe this characteristic of Korean is to say that it is a language in which pronominalization is not as active a process as it is in other languages.

(12) 나는 감자가 많이 나는 고장에서 태어나서 감자를 무척 좋아 한다. 그리
고 감자를 좋아 하는 사람을 만나면 해 마다 감자를 선물로 보내고 싶
어진다.

Na nun *kamca* ka manh.i nanun kocang eyse thaye nase *kamca* lul muchek
coh.a hanta. Kuliko *kamca* lul coh.a hanun salam ul mannamyen hay
mata *kamca* lul senmul lo ponayko siphecinta.

'Since I was born in a place where they grow a lot of *potatoes*, I really like
them. Moreover, whenever I meet someone who likes *potatoes*, I want to
send them *some* as a present every year.'

(13) 나는 어머니를 사랑한다. 어머니가 없는 세상은 상상조차 할 수 없다.
어머니는 정말 대지와도 같다.

Na nun *emeni* lul salang-hanta. *Emeni* ka epsnun seysang un sangsang cocha hal swu epsta. *Emeni* nun ceng-mal tayci wato kathta.

'I love (my) *mother*. I can't even imagine a world without *her*. *She's* really
like the earth to me.'

(14) 선생님은 어렸을 때 선생님 용모에 자신이 있으셨어요?

Sensayng-nim un elyess.ul ttay *sensayng-nim* yongmo ey casin i iss.usyess.e yo?

[Speaking to one's teacher:] 'When *you* were a child, were *you* proud of
how (you) looked?'

4.2.3 Numerals

Since grammatical function is expressed by attaching case particles, Korean numerals are similar enough to be classed together with nouns and pronouns. However, a few features distinguish this word class from other kinds of words, and in this section we will examine some of these characteristics.

There are two parallel sets of Korean numerals: one of native origin, and one of Chinese origin. These two sets of numerals are shown in (1), below. The largest numeral of native origin is *cumun* '1,000', but it is only found in older texts. In modern Korean, both this word and the native word for '100', *on*, have been replaced by Sino-Korean. As a result, one can only count to '99' *(ahun ahop)* using native numerals; past that number one must make use of Sino-Korean numerals. For example, '101' can be read as *payk hana* (SK + native), or as completely Sino-Korean, *payk il;* '225' can be read *i payk sumul tases* (SK + SK + native + native) or as completely Sino-Korean, *i payk i sip o.* In addition, numbers written in Arabic numerals, such as '2, 8, 26', are regularly read as Sino-Korean *(i, phal, isip lyuk).*

(1) Korean Numerals

	Native numerals		Sino-Korean numerals		
1	하나	hana	일	一	il
2	둘	twul	이	二	ī
3	셋	sēys	삼	三	sam
4	넷	nēys	사	四	sā
5	다섯	tases	오	五	ō
6	여섯	yeses	육	六	ˡyuk
7	일곱	ilkop	칠	七	chil
8	여덟	yetel(p)	팔	八	phal
9	아홉	ahop	구	九	kwu
10	열	yel	십	十	sip
11	열하나	yel-hana	십일	十一	sip-il
12	열둘	yelq-twul	십이	十二	sip-i
...					
19	열아홉	yel-ahop	십구	十九	sip-kwu
20	스물	sumul	이십	二十	ī-sip
30	설흔	sel(h)un	삼십	三十	sam-sip
40	마흔	mahun	사십	四十	sā-sip
50	쉰	swīn	오십	五十	ō-sip
60	예순	yeyswun	육십	六十	ˡyuk-sip
70	일흔	ilhun	칠십	七十	chil-sip
80	여든	yetun	팔십	八十	phal-sip
90	아흔	ahun	구십	九十	kwu-sip
100	(온)	(on)	백	百	payk
1,000	(즈믄)	(cumun)	천	千	chen
10,000	—		만	萬	man
100,000			십만	十萬	sip man
1,000,000			백만	百萬	payk man
10,000,000			천만	千萬	chen man
100,000,000			억	億	ek
1,000,000,000,000			조	兆	co

As can be seen from the above list, the formation of higher numerals in both systems is more regular than that of English. Instead of special words for numbers eleven through the teens ("eleven," "twelve," "thirteen," etc.), Korean numerals are structured "ten-one," "ten-two," "ten-three," and so on. Sino-Korean numerals are more regular still. In the Chinese system, multiples of ten ("twenty," "thirty," "forty," etc.) are simple juxtapositions: "two-ten," "three-ten," "four-ten," and so on.

The two Korean numeral systems differ in a number of ways. First, there is a difference in the way ordinals are formed. The native ordinals are formed with the suffix *-ccay*, as in *twul-ccay* 'second' and *seys-ccay* 'third'. The exception is *hana* 'one' because the ordinal 'first' is not *ˣhana-ccay* (or *ˣhan-ccay*), but rather the special form *ches-ccay*. From the ten units on, however, *han* is used instead of *ches-*, and *twu* is used for 'two' instead of *twul*—as in *yel han-ccay* 'eleventh', *yel twu-ccay* 'twelfth', *sumul han-ccay* 'twenty-first', and *sumul twu-ccay* 'twenty-second'. In contrast with this native system, the Sino-Korean ordinals are expressed by attaching the prefix *cey-* (第) to the basic numeral, as in *cey-il* 'first', *cey-i* 'second', *cey-sip.o* 'fifteenth'.

There are cases where the use of Sino-Korean numbers and native numbers are also distinguished by the context of the sentence. For example, when counting a small number of objects, native numbers are used, as in *sakwa twu-kay* '2 apples', while in contrast, when the number is large, Sino-Korean numbers tend to be preferred. When asking how old someone is, the answer can be the completely native number *yetun-twul* '82', but one will more often hear as the answer, *phalsip twul* (with a mixture of SK + native). In addition, Sino-Korean is ordinarily preferred when making mathematical calculations, as in *il te-haki sam un sa* (1 + 3 = 4) or *i phal un siplyuk* (2 x 8 = 16).

Sino-Korean numerals and native numerals are also differentiated by their concord with classifiers. First, when counting without using a classifier, native numerals are used, as in (2), below. But when the classifier is a Western loanword, Sino-Korean is used, as in (3). In other cases, as in (4), the most natural usage is generally to combine native numerals with native classifiers, and SK numerals with SK classifiers. Native classifiers adhere rigidly to this concord. However, SK classifiers do not since there are many cases, particularly with larger numbers, where SK classifiers are allowed to combine with native numerals. For example, both SK and native numerals are permissible in *swin-kay/ osip-kay* 'fifty (general objects)', *ilkop-myeng/ chil-myeng* 'seven (people)', *selhun-kwen/ samsip-kwen* 'thirty (volumes)'. Other SK classifiers, such as *-cang* (for thin, flat objects), only combine with native numerals in most number constructions: *congi sek-cang* 'three sheets of paper', but not *ˣcongi sam-cang*. Yet, for multiples of ten, SK numerals are permissible with *-cang*: *isip-cang* 'twenty sheets', *samsip-cang* 'thirty sheets', and so on. The rules of concord for SK classifiers are often quite complex.

(2) 학생 다섯/ˣ학생 오
haksayng tases/ ˣhaksayng o
student five (N) / five (SK)
'five students'

(3) 밀가루 칠 킬로그램/ˣ밀가루 일곱 킬로그램
milkalwu chil-khillokulaym/ ˣmilkalwu ilkop-killokulaym
flour   7 (SK)   / flour   7 (N)
'7kg. of flour'

(4) a. 연필 아홉 자루/ˣ연필 구 자루
yenphil ahop-calwu/ ˣyenphil kwu-calwu
pencil   9 (N)-(N)/ pencil   9 (SK)-(N)
'nine pencils'

b. ˣ열다섯 리/ 십오 리
xyel tases-li/ sip.o li
15 (N)-(SK)/ 15 (SK)-(SK)
'fifteen *li* (Chinese miles)'

c. 쉰 다섯 살/오십오 세
swin tases-sal/ osip o-sey
55 (N)-(N)/ 55 (SK)-(SK)
'fifty-five years old'

Number constructions are an important structural feature of the Korean language. As can be seen in the above examples, number expressions can be formed by using a native numeral alone or by combining a numeral with a classifier. Most classifiers are bound morphemes. But many ordinary nouns, such as *salam* 'person', *kulus* 'vessel', *can* 'cup', *khep* ' (Western) cup', *thong* 'bucket', *toy* (a container used as a quantity measure [0.477 gal.]), *mal* (a larger container; 10 *toy*), and *kamani* 'a type of straw bag (containing 10 *mal*)', can also serve as classifiers, whether the noun in the construction is countable or not. Here are some typical number expressions using such nouns as classifiers: *wuyu (khephi, swul) han-can* 'one cup of milk (coffee, liquor)', *mul han-khep* 'one cup of water', *ssal han-kamani (-mal, -toy)* 'one bag *(mal, toy)* of rice', and *elun tases-salam* 'five adults'.

There are several different patterns for Korean number constructions. These can be divided into four types:

(5) a. Noun-Numeral: 학생 셋이 찾아왔다.
Haksayng seys i chac.a wassta.
student   3
'Three students came to visit.'

b. Noun-Numeral-Classifier: 학생 세 명이 찾아왔다.
Haksayng sey-myeng i chac.a wassta.
student   3-PERSON
'Three students came to visit.'

c. Numeral-Noun: 세 학생이 찾아왔다.
Sey haksayng i chac.a wassta
3   student
'Three students came to visit.'

d. Numeral-Classifier-*uy*-Noun: 세 명의 학생이 찾아왔다.
Sey-myeng uy haksayng i chac.a wassta.
3-PERSON OF student
'three students came to visit.'

The differences between these patterns are first of all phonological. Before a classifier, the native numerals *hana* 'one', *twul* 'two', *seys* 'three', and *neys* 'four' take on the forms *han-*, *twu-*, *sey- (se-, sek-)*, and ney- *(ne-, nek)*. For example, *(haksayng) hana* 'one (student)', in which a bare numeral follows the noun, is alternatively expressed as *(haksayng) han-myeng*. In similar fashion, *haksayng twul* 'two students' becomes *haksayng twu-myeng;* and *haksayng seys (neys)* becomes *haksayng sey (ney)-myeng*. Moreover, when the classifier is the native measure *-mal* (4.765 gal.), *seys* 'three' becomes *se-*, for example, *ssal se-mal* '3 *mal* of rice', *poli se-mal* '3 *mal* of barley'. When the classifier is the native measure *-toy* (0.477 gal.) or *-ca* (0.944 ft.), the numeral *seys* 'three' becomes *sek-* and *neys* 'four' becomes *nek-*, for example, *ssal sek (nek-)toy* '3 (4) *toy* of rice', *pitan sek (nek-)ca* '3 (4) *ca* of silk'. In Korean grammars, it is usual to treat *han-*, *twu-*, *sey- (se-, sek-)*, and *ney- (ne-, nek-)* as prenouns because they cannot take particles and always function as modifiers of nouns. Here, however, we will consider them only as variants of the numerals. The topic will be discussed in more detail later, in section 4.2.5.

The usages and conditions for selecting each of the four patterns shown above are slightly different. As the most widely used pattern in modern Korean, pattern (5b) is used with no special restrictions. The use of pattern (5a) is more restricted. It is a natural number construction for counting people; for example, *haksayng twul* 'two students' and *kwun.in tases* 'five soldiers' are idiomatic Korean. But it can only be used when the noun can be counted: ˣ*molay hana* ('one sand') and ˣ*mul yeses* ('six waters') are quite nonsensical; and even for many countable nouns, the pattern is not used: ?*nolwu tases* 'five deer' and ?*chayk twul* 'two books', sound unnatural. Moreover, pattern (5a) only permits native numbers, and forms such as ˣ*haksayng i* ('two students') and ˣ*kwun.in o* ('five soldiers') are ungrammatical.

Pattern (5c) was used extensively in Middle Korean, but now its use has diminished to include only native numerals combined with a limited number of nouns. The expressions *twu (tases, selhun) nala* 'two (five, thirty) countries', *sey hakkyo* 'three schools', *ney haksayng* 'four students', and *twu thokki* 'two rabbits' are commonly used. But, although ?*tases thokki* 'five rabbits' and ?*selhun haksayng* are grammatical, the expressions are unnatural; and ˣ*sey* sonamu ('three pines'), ˣ*tases yenphil* ('five pencils'), and ˣ*o haksayng* ('five students'), for example, are quite ungrammatical.

Pattern (5d) is mostly a written instead of a colloquial usage. It cannot be used for counting; instead, it is an expression used when the construction refers to the entire phrase as a single unit. Thus, the most natural context for this pattern is as a "topic."

(6) ˣ시장에 가서 일곱 개의 오이, 세 쪽의 생강을 사 오너라.

ˣSicang ey kase ilkop-kay uy oi, sey-ccok uy sayngkang ul sa onela.

seven-UNIT cukes three-CLOVE ginger

('Go to the market and buy seven cucumbers and three cloves of ginger.')

(7) a. 열 개의 인디언 인형

Yel-kay uy Intien Inhyeng [The title of Agatha Christie's novel]

ten-UNIT Indian doll

'Ten Little Indians'

b. 7인의 신부

"Chil-in uy Sinpu" [A movie title]

seven-PEOPLE bride

"Seven Brides for Seven Brothers"

Besides the above, other differences between the patterns can be seen in examples (8) and (9), below. Specifically, the phrase *haksayng twul* 'two students' in (8) does not refer to some specific students, but means rather that any of them can be sent as long as they are students, so, *haksayng* 'students' in this case has an indefinite reference. In (9), by contrast, *twu haksayng* '(the) two students' is used in a restricted context where both the speaker and listener know exactly who the phrase refers to. Put another way, patterns (5a) and (5b) are used when the meaning of the noun is indefinite, and pattern (5c) forms the contrast with these patterns, when the reference is definite.

(8) 원고 정리할 학생 둘만(학생 두 명만) 보내 주세요.

Wenko cengli hal *haksayng twul man (haksayng twu-myeng man)* ponay cwusey yo.

student two only   student two-PERSON only

'send (me) *(any) two students* to put the manuscript in order.'

(9) 두 학생이 일을 잘 해서 다음에 또 부탁해야겠어요.

Twu haksayng i il ul cal hayse taum ey tto puthak-hayyakeysseyo.

two student

'*The two students* work so well I'll have to ask them to help next time, too.'

We can see from the above that plural expressions in Korean are made by combining numbers and nouns. Note, however, that in none of those cases does the so-called plural marker, the suffix *-tul*, appear. As pointed out in 4.2.1, there is no grammatical category of number in Korean, and whether one says *han haksayng* 'one student' or *sey haksayng* 'three student(s)', the noun *haksayng* undergoes no change in form. In fact, in an expression like *twu salam* 'two people', where the plural is specified by a definite number, the plural suffix *-tul* would be ungrammatical. The suffix is principally used in sentences like <u>*Salam-tul*</u> *i manh.i moyesskwuna* '(I see) a lot of <u>*people*</u> have showed up', where the plural is a generalized one with no specific number given. And even in such a case one could also say simply <u>*Salam*</u> *i manh.i moyesskwuna*, without using the suffix. It is true that in the difference between *tangsin* 'you' and *tangsin-tul* 'you all', *-tul* is used to specify plurality. But *-tul* is not an obligatory nominal suffix used to represent anything like a grammatical category of number.

4.2.4 Verbs and Adjectives

Verbs and adjectives function as predicates. Their grammatical functions are expressed by inflectional endings, and that is their most fundamental characteristic: By their very nature, verbs and adjectives always appear with inflectional endings. A stem cannot stand alone.

As was mentioned briefly in the introduction (1.4), Korean verb endings are numerous and complex. Endings will be discussed in more detail separately in section 5.2; here they will only be outlined briefly.

Korean endings can be divided into *final endings* and *prefinal endings*. *Final endings* can be subdivided into those that end a sentence and those that end the verb form but not the sentence. In (1), below, *-uni, -ko* and *-ta, -ni* are final endings; among these, *-ta* and *-ni* end the sentence, while *-uni* and *-ko* do not. The forms *-keyss-* and *-si-* are prefinal endings since they must necessarily be followed by another ending.

(1) a. 네 합격 소식을 들으니 무척 기쁘다.
       Ney hapkyek sosik ul tul.*uni* muchek kippu*ta*.
                      hear-since   happy-.
       'I'm very happy to hear you passed the exam.'
       [Lit.: 'Hearing your passing-exam news, (I'm) very happy.']

     b. 네 합격 소식을 듣고 누나가 무척 기뻐하겠다.
        Ney hapkyek sosik ul tut*ko* nwuna ka muchek ki.ppe ha*keyss*ta.
                       hear-and -   FUTURE-.
        'Your (older) sister will be very happy when she hears you passed the exam.'

     c. 네 합격 소식을 듣고 할머니께서 얼마나 기뻐하시니?
        Ney hapkyek sosik ul tut*ko* halmeni-kkeyse elmana kipp.e ha*sini*?
        'How happy your grandmother must be to hear you passed the exam.'

Prefinal endings indicate *tense* and *subject honorification*. In the above examples, the prefinal endings -*keyss*- and -*ass/ess*- specify the tense (or aspect), and -*si*- functions to honor the subject. *Sentence-final endings* function to show the *speech style* appropriate in the honorific system for the listener, and to show the *sentence type*. In example (2), below, (2a) is declarative, (2b) interrogative, and (2c) imperative. Each of these sentence types is further divided into three levels according to the social rank of the listener. Tense, style, and sentence type are determined by the resulting paradigmatic ending.

(2) a. 읽는다/ 읽네/ 읽습니다
Ilk-nunta/ Ilk-ney/ Ilk-supnita
'(He/she)'s reading.'

b. 읽니/ 읽나/ 읽습니까
Ilk-ni/ Ilk-na/ Ilk-supnikka
'Are you reading?'

c. 읽어라/ 읽게/ 읽으십시오
Ilk-ela/ Ilk-key/ Ilk-usipsio
'Read!'

Korean verbs and adjectives resemble each other closely in how they inflect and how they function in the sentence. It is not simple to distinguish between these two word classes—so much so, the question is often included as a problem on grammar examinations for Korean students. There are several clear differences, however. First, adjectives are distinguished from verbs in that they do not have imperative or propositive forms. For example, sentences such as ×*Khi ka cak.ala* ('Be short!') or ×*Khi ka cak.ca* ('Let's be short!') are impossible. In addition, adjectives do not take the progressive endings -*nta/nunta, -nun*. Verbs have inflected forms such as *ttwi-nta* 'is jumping', *ilk-nunta* 'is reading', *ttwi-nun* 'jumping', and *ilk-nun* 'reading', but examples of the corresponding adjectival forms are *kippu-ta* 'is happy', *cak-ta* 'is small', *kippu-n* 'happy', and *cak-un* 'small'. The classification of verbs and adjectives as separate parts of speech can be said to be based upon these small differences. Verbs and adjectives are often grouped together and spoken of as *inflecting words* (*yongen* 用言), and this is because verbs and adjectives have far more common features than differences. And, instead of "inflecting word," the term "verb" can also be used in this broader sense that includes not only what are usually called "verbs" but also "adjectives." (When classed as a type of verb, an adjective is usually referred to as a "descriptive verb.")

A fundamental principle of Korean grammar is that verbs and adjectives function as predicates; but there are also cases where they link up with other verbs or adjectives and enhance the meaning of that other form. These *auxiliary verbs* (*poco tongsa*) and *auxiliary adjectives* (*poco hyengyongsa*) follow the *main verb* (*pon-tongsa*), for which they provide support. Most (but not all) auxiliary verbs can also function as main verbs, but the meaning is usually different. In the following examples, the verbs *pwa* ('see'), *cwunta* ('give'), and *kani* ('go') serve as auxiliaries in (a) and as main verbs in (b), and the differences in meanings are striking. Number (6) is an example using *siphta* ('want to . . .'), a form that can only be used as an auxiliary verb.

(3) a. 이 불고기 좀 먹어 봐. 너무 짜지 않니?
　　　I pulkoki com mek.e *pwa*. Nemu ccaci anh.ni?
　　　　　　　　　　eating try
　　　'Taste this pulgogi. Isn't it too salty?'

　　b. 이 불고기 좀 봐. 색깔이 예쁘지?
　　　I pulkoki com *pwa*. Sayk.kkal i yeyppuci?
　　　　　　　　　　see
　　　'Look at this pulgogi. Isn't the color pretty?'

(4) a. 나는 가끔 동생에게 만화를 읽어 준다.
　　　Na nun ka.kkum tongsayng eykey manhwa lul ilk.e *cwunta*.
　　　　　　　　　　　　　　　reading provide (do as a favor)
　　　'I often read the comics for my younger brother/sister.'

　　b. 나는 가끔 동생에게 용돈을 준다.
　　　Na nun ka.kkum tongsayng eykey yongton ul *cwunta*.
　　　　　　　　　　　　　　　give
　　　'I often give my younger brother/sister spending money.'

(5) a. 일이 계획대로 잘 되어 가니?
　　　Il i kyeyhoyk taylo cal toy.e *kani*?
　　　　　　　　　　becoming continue (progressively)
　　　'Is (your) work progressing as well as you had hoped?'

　　b. 너는 왜 안 가니?
　　　Ne nun way an *kani*?
　　　　　　·not go
　　　'Why aren't you going?'

(6) 나는 금강산에 가고 싶다.
　　Na nun Kumkangsan ey kako siphta
　　　　　　　　　　go   want-to
　　'I want to go to the Diamond Mountains.'

The inflecting forms of Korean also include the *copula* (계사), a form used to predicate nouns. Because Korean grammarians ordinarily do not treat the copula as a separate word, we have mentioned it briefly in our discussion of nouns, in 4.2.1, above.

The stem of the Korean copula is *i-*. This stem takes inflectional endings just as verbs and adjectives do. However, unlike verbs and adjectives, the copula cannot be used independently, but must rather be combined with nouns like a particle. It cannot appear at the beginning of the sentence, nor can there be a pause between it and the preceding noun. Moreover, following a noun ending in a vowel, the stem *i-* is ordinarily omitted (as in examples 7b, 8b, and 10, below). Therefore, in Korean schoolbook grammars, the copula is treated as a type of particle. In Korean orthographic practice, it is written solid with the preceding noun, just as are particles.

The copula has an inflectional system that is closer to that of adjectives than that of verbs. It does not take imperative or propositive endings—which can be surprising for English speakers because of sentences like *"Be* a man!" and "Let's *be* friends." Instead of processive endings like those of verbs (*-nta* and *-nun*), the copula takes only nonprocessive endings like those of adjectives. Some concrete examples of copular sentences are given below.

(7) a. 이것이 오늘 신문이다.
    Ikes i onul sinmun *i*ta.
    'This *is* today's newspaper.'

   b. 한국의 대표적 상록수는 소나무다.
    Hankwuk uy tayphyo-cek sanglokswu nun sonamu 'ta.
    'The (most) representative Korean evergreen is the pine.'

(8) a. 깨어 보니 그것은 모두 꿈이였다.
    Kkay.e poni kukes un motwu kkwum *iyess*.ta.
    'When I woke up, it *was* all a dream.'

   b. 여기가 옛날에는 바다였다.
    Yeki ka yeys-nal ey nun pata '*yess*.ta.
    'In ancient times this *was* a sea.'

(9) a. 내가 시인이라면 이럴 때 얼마나 좋을까?
    Nayka siin *i*lamyen ilul ttay elmana coh.ulkka?
    'It would be nice to *be* a poet at times like this.'

(10) 일본이 한자를 들여간 것은 한국으로부터였다.
    Ilpon i hanqca lul tul.ye kan kes un Hankwuk ulo puthe '*yess*.ta.
    'Japan's taking in Chinese characters *was* from Korea.'

As these examples illustrate, the copula has a number of phonological and structural idiosyncracies. For one thing, when the copula stem *i-* combines with the past marker *-ess-*, as in (8b), the resulting form *iess-* contracts to *yess-*. Even more idiosyncratic is the fact that following the copula stem *i-* the ending *-ta* becomes *-la*, as in (9). In (10), the copula combines with preceding particles.

Negative constructions with the copula are different from those of verbs and adjectives. When the copula is negated, the stem *i-* is replaced by the form *ani-*,[6] and the nominative case particle *i/ka* is added to the preceding noun. This kind of construction is something that is not seen with negated forms of verbs or adjectives. Negations and negative constructions will be discussed in more detail later, in section 6.6; here it should only be noted that these constructions evidence a distinct difference between the nature of the copula and that of verbs and adjectives.

(11)a. 이것은 오늘 신문이 아니다.
　　　　 Ikes un onul sinmun i anita.
　　　　　　　　　　　 newspaper SP not-is
　　　　 'This is not today's newspaper.'

　　 b. 여기가 옛날에는 바다가 아니었니?
　　　　 Yeki ka yeys-nal ey nun pata ka aniess.ni?
　　　　　　　　　　　　　　　　 sea SP not-was?
　　　　 'In the old days, wasn't this a sea?'

　　 c. 당신이 미인이 아니라면 누가 미인이겠소?
　　　　 Tangsin i miin i anilamyen nwuka miin ikeyss.so?
　　　　　　　　 beauty SP not-is-if
　　　　 'If you're not a beautiful person, then who could be?'

4.2.5 Prenouns and Adverbs

Prenouns are parts of speech that do not change in form—in other words, they do not take case particles or inflectional endings—and they have the function of modifying a following noun or noun phrase. Prenouns can only be used in positions that modify nouns, and they are few in number. In fact, they form the smallest, and therefore the most unusual, word class found in Korean. The list given in (1), below, is almost exhaustive. In (2) a few examples of prenoun usage are given.

(1) a. 이 *i* 'this'; 그 *ku* 'that'; 저 *ce* 'that (over there)'
　　 b. 다른 *talun* 'other'; 딴 *ttan* 'other'; 여느 *yenu* 'ordinary, usual'; 어느 *enu* 'which; any', 무슨 *musun* 'what'; 웬 *weyn* 'a certain, some'; 각 *kak* 'each'; 별 *pyel* 'different'
　　 c. 모든 *motun* 'all'; 온 *on* 'all'; 갖은 *kac.un* 'assorted'; 온갖 *onkac* 'all sorts'; 전 *cen* (全) 'all'
　　 d. 새 *say* 'new'; 헌 *hen* 'old'; 옛 *yeys* 'ancient'; 순 *swun* 'pure'

(2) a. 이 옷이 그 구두와 잘 어울리겠다.
　　　　 I os i *ku* kwutwu wa cal ewullikeyssta.
　　　　 this   that
　　　　 'These clothes will go well with those shoes.'

b. 다른 나라에 가면 주로 무슨 음식을 먹니?
Talun nala ey kamyen cwulo *musun* umsik ul mekni?
other   what
'When you go to other countries, what food do you usually eat?'

c. 모든 걱정 버리고 새 각오로 새 세계를 개척하여라.
Motun kekceng peliko *say* kak.o lo *say* seykyey lul kaychek-hayela.
all   new   new
'Throw off all worries and, with new resolve, open up a new world.'

The principal function of prenouns is to delimit the noun. But, as we have shown above in the treatment of the pronouns *i kes* 'this (thing/fact)', *ku kes* 'that (thing/fact)', and *ce kes* 'that (thing/fact)', the deictics *i* 'this', *ku* 'that', and *ce* 'that (over there)' express the physical or psychological distance the noun has relative to the listener and the speaker. The words *ku* and *ce* both seem similar in meaning to English "that." However, anaphoric uses of "that" can only be translated as *ku (kes)*. For example, the famous soliloquy of Hamlet, "To be, or not to be: _that_ is the question" is translated as *Sanunya cwuknunya, ku kes* (*×ce kes*) *i muncey ta*. Moreover, the definite article "the" is also often translated as *ku*. For example, in the sentence *Yeys-nal ey han sonye ka sal.assnuntey, ku sonye nun acwu yey.ppess.ta* 'Once upon a time, there was a girl, and the girl was very beautiful', the phrase *han sonye* (literally, 'one girl') corresponds to "*a* girl", and the phrase *ku sonye* to "*the* girl". The prenoun *ce (kes)* can never be used anaphorically.

Adverbs are like prenouns in that they do not inflect and function to modify the word that follows. However, as can be seen in example (3), below, adverbs modify inflecting words like verbs and adjectives or (other) adverbs. In addition, as can be seen in (4), they also modify nouns and prenouns.

(3) a. 한국에서는 소나무가 가장 잘 자란다.
Hankwuk eyse nun sonamu ka *kacang cal* calanta.
                              most   well
'In Korea pines grow best.'

b. 어제는 좀 시원했는데 오늘은 몹시 무덥구나.
Ecey nun *com* siwen-hayssnuntey onul un *mopsi* mutepkwuna.
little   extremely
'Yesterday it was rather cool, but now it's extremely hot.'

c. 과연 우주는 끝이 없을까?
Kwayen wucwu nun kkuth i eps.ul kka?
indeed
'I wonder if the universe is indeed endless?'

(4) a. 그 사람도 꽤 부자인데 이 사람은 더 부자야.

> Ku salam to *kkway* puca intey i salam un *te* puca ya.
>   fairly rich-man   more
> 'that person is fairly rich, but this person is richer.'

b. 우리는 바로 저 집에서 살았다.
> Wuli nun *palo* ce cip eyse sal.assta.
>   precisely that house
> 'We lived in that very house.'

Korean has a richly developed system of *onomatopoeia* and *mimetics*, and from the point of view of function, these words belong to the class of adverbs. Onomatopoeia and mimetics are structurally characterized by reduplication. Besides being rich in number, they have also attracted interest because they are the last lexical class that preserves vowel harmony, and they are almost the only domain not penetrated by Sino-Korean. There will be an opportunity to discuss these again in the treatment of word formation (4.3.4).

(5) a. 아가들은 아장아장 걷고 오리들은 뒤뚱뒤뚱 걷는다.
> Aka-tul un *acang-acang* ketnuntey oli-tul un *twittwung-twittwung* ket-nunta.
> 'Babies walk *acang-acang*, but ducks walk *twittwung-twittwung*.'

b. 하늘하늘 춤추는 버들가지 위에서 꾀꼬리가 꾀꼴꾀꼴 노래한다.
> *Hanul-hanul* chwum chwunun petul-kaci wi eyse kkoy.kkol.i ka *kkoy.kkol-kkoy.kkol* nolay-hanta.
> 'On the willow branch dancing *hanul-hanul* sits the nightingale singing *kkoy.kkol-kkoy.kkol*.'

The adverb class includes *conjunctional adverbs* (접속부사), words that link logically a following sentence with a preceding sentence. These conjunctional adverbs include such words as *kuliko* 'moreover', *kulena* 'however', *kulentey* 'nevertheless', *kulemyen* 'thus', *kulemulo* 'therefore', *ttalase* 'accordingly', *tto* 'also', *hok.un* 'otherwise', *ohilye* 'rather', and *tekwuna* 'furthermore'. Among these, as can be seen in example (6), below, *kuliko, kulena, kulentey, kulemulo,* and *ttalase* form a special class of adverbs that are ordinarily used at the beginning of a new sentence after the first sentence is completed. (At one time, these words were classed separately as conjunctions, but these days conjunctions are almost never set up as a word class in Korean.)

(6) a. 인내는 쓰다. 그러나 그 열매는 달다.
> Innay nun ssuta. *Kulena* ku yelmay nun talta.
> 'Patience is bitter. *However,* the fruit is sweet.'

b. 지구는 하나다. 따라서 누구나 지구를 잘 보존하여야 한다.
> Cikwu nun hana ta. *Ttalase* nwkwuna cikwu lul cal pocon-hayeya hanta.
> 'The Earth is one. *Accordingly,* everyone must conserve it well.'

(7) a. 아이를 야단만 치면 오히려 역효과가 난다.

Ai lul yatan man chimyen, *ohilye* yekhyoqkwa ka nanta.

'If one only scolds a child, it will have *rather* the opposite affect.'

b. 비바람이 불고, 또 날까지 어두워 왔다.

Piq-palam i pulko, *tto* nal kkaci etwuwe wassta.

'The rain and wind blew, and it also grew dark.'

In defining prenouns and adverbs, we have said that they have no morphological variation. Their sole function is to modify the words that follow. However, there are also other parts of speech that modify words the same way. In the following examples, verbs and adjectives behave just like prenouns and adverbs:

(8) a. 가는 말이 고와야 오는 말이 곱다.

Kanun mal i kowaya *onun* mal i kopta.

[Lit., 'Only if the *going* words are nice will the *coming* words be nice.']

'Speak politely and people will speak politely to you.'

b. 작은 버릇이 큰 버릇이 된다.

Cak.un pelus i *khun* pelus i toynta.

'*Little* habits become *big* habits.'

(9) a. 뾰족하게 깎은 연필로 글씨를 깨끗하게 쓴다.

Ppyocok-hakey kkakk.un yenphil lo kulssi lul *kkaykkus-hakey* ssunta.

'(I) write *cleanly* with a sharp [*sharply* cut] pencil.'

b. 쉽게 할 일을 왜 어렵게 하려고 그러니?

Swipkey hal il ul way *elyepkey* halyeko kuleni?

[lit., 'Why are you trying to do something *with difficulty* that can be done *easily*?']

'Why are you making something easy into something difficult?'

Because these forms are actually verb and adjective stems with inflectional endings, they differ from prenouns and adverbs, which are invariant in form. Korean grammarians make this distinction by calling inflected forms such as *kanun* 'going', *onun* 'coming', *cak.un* 'little', and *khun* 'big' adnominals (*kwanhyeng-e* 관형어), instead of "prenouns" (*kwanhyeng-sa* 관형사). These same grammarians refer to inflected forms such as *kkaykkus-hakey* 'cleanly' and *swipkey* 'easily' as adverbials (*pusa-e* 부사어), instead of "adverbs" (*pusa* 부사).

4.3 Word Formation

Here we will look at the ways in which Korean words are formed through compounding and derivation. These processes are usually referred to as

"word formation." For Korean grammarians, this concept of 'word formation' contrasts with what is called "inflection"; accordingly, inflectional endings fall outside the scope of the present discussion.

When words are classified according to the categories of word formation, they can be divided into *simple words* and *complex words*. A simple word
is a word composed of a single morpheme, and a complex word is one composed of two or more morphemes. In addition, complex words are further
divided into *compounds* and *derivatives*. A compound is a word whose structural elements are composed entirely of bases or units larger than bases,
while a derivative is a word whose structural elements include derivational
affixes.

Since simple words are composed of single morphemes, they need not
be discussed here. However, note that we treat verbs and adjectives, such as
ka-ta 'go', *wus-ta* 'laugh', *mantul-ta* 'make' *palk-ta* 'be bright', and *kanul-ta* 'be
thin', as simple words, in spite of the fact that they are made up of two morphemes, including the inflectional ending. Still, as we have explained
above, they are considered simple words because, from the perspective of
word formation, endings are not to be taken into account. Compounds and
derivatives will be discussed below in separate sections.

4.3.1 Compounds

The most productive type of compound is the compound noun. However, compounds occur richly in other word classes, too, and the type of
structure is also extremely varied. The following shows the representative
compounding types arranged according to each part of speech.

(1) Compound Nouns
   a. *Noun + Noun:* 손목 *son-mok* 'wrist (hand-neck)'; 고무신 *komu-sin* 'rub-
      ber shoes'; 어깨동무 *ekkay-tongmu* 'childhood friend (shoulder-com-
      rade)'; 기와집 *kiwa-cip* 'house with a tile roof (tile-house)'; 산나물 *san-
      namul* 'wild herbs (mountain-vegetable)'
   b. *Noun + "genitive" s + Noun:* 콧날 *khos-nal* 'ridge of the nose (nose-s-
      edge)'; 시냇물 *sinays-mul* 'stream (brook-s-water)'; 담뱃대 *tampays-tay*
      'cigarette butt'; 등불 *tungq-pul* 'lamp light', 물개 *mulq-kay* 'seal (water-
      s-dog)'
   c. *Prenoun + Noun:* 새언니 *say-enni* 'stepsister (new sister)'; 첫사랑 *ches-
      salang* 'first love'; 옛날 *yeys-nal* 'the old days (ancient days)'; 이것 *i kes*
      'this (thing)'; 그분 *ku pun* 'he/him (that [respected] person)'
   d. *Inflected modifier + Noun:* 굳은살 *kwut.un sal* 'callus (hardened flesh)';
      작은아버지 *cak.un apeci* 'father's younger brother (little father)'; 어린
      이 *elin i* 'child (young one)'; 건널목 *kennel mok* 'railroad crossing
      (crossing neck)'; 올해 *ol hay* 'this year'[7]

e. *Inflecting stem + Noun:* 곶감 *koc-kam* 'dried persimmon (skewer-persimmon)'; 접칼 *cep-khal* 'folding knife'; 묵밭 *muk-path* 'fallow field'; 늦더위 *nuc-tewi* 'late (summer) heat'

f. *Adverb (or Adverbial root) + Noun:* 살짝곰보 *salccak-kompo* 'a slightly pock-marked face'; 곱슬머리 *kopsul-meli* 'curly hair'; 산들바람 *santul-palam* 'gentle breeze'; 뾰죽구두 *ppyocwuk-kwutwu* 'pointy shoes'

g. *Adverb + Adverb:* 잘못 *cal-mos* 'error (well-not)'

h. *Verbal nominalization + Noun:* 갈림길 *kallim-kil* 'side road (split road)'; 디딤돌 *titim-tol* 'stepping stone'

i. *Noun + Verbal nominalization:* 말다툼 *mal-tathwum* 'argument (word-fight)'; 보물찾기 *pomul-chacki* 'treasure hunt'; 줄넘기 *cwul-nemki* 'jump-rope'

(2) Compound Verbs

a. *Noun + Verb (Subject + Predicate):* 힘들다 *himtulta* 'difficult (strength-takes)'; 빛나다 *pichnata* 'shine (light-gives off)'; 겁나다 *kepnata* 'be afraid (fear-gives off)'; 멍들다 *mengtulta* 'get bruised (bruise-get)'

b. *Noun + Verb (Object + Predicate):* 본받다 *pon-patta* 'imitate (model-receive)'; 힘쓰다 *him-ssuta* 'try hard (strength-use)'; 등지다 *tung-cita* 'betray (back-become)'; 선보다 *sen-pota* 'have a prospective marriage interview (interview-see)'

c. *Noun + Verb (Adverbial + Predicate):* 앞서다 *aph-seta* 'go in front of (front-stand)'; 뒤서다 *twi-seta* 'go behind (behind-stand)'; 마을가다 *maul-kata* 'visit (one's) neighborhood (village-go)'; 거울삼다 *kewul-samta* 'take a lesson from (mirror-take as)'; 벗삼다 *pes-samta* 'make friends (friend-take as)'

d. *Inflected form of verb + Verb:* 돌아가다 *tol.a kata* 'go back (turning + go)'; 갈아입다 *kal.a ipta* 'change clothes (exchanging + put on)'; 알아듣다 *al.a tutta* 'understand something said (knowing + hear)'; 파고들다 *phako tulta* 'investigate (dig and raise)'; 타고나다 *thako nata* 'be born with (get and be born)'

e. *Verb stem + Verb:* 굶주리다 *kwulm-cwulita* 'starve, be famished (go hungry + go hungry)'; 뛰놀다 *ttwi-nolta* 'frolic (jump + play)'; 부르짖다 *pulu-cicta* 'shout (call + yelp)'

f. *Adverb + Verb:* 가로막다 *kalo-makta* 'block the way (horizontally-block)'; 잘되다 *cal toyta* 'turn out well (well-become)'; 그만두다 *kuman twuta* 'quit (that much-put)'

(3) Compound Adjectives

a. *Noun + Adjective (Subject + Predicate):* 값싸다 *kaps-ssata* 'be (price-)cheap'; 배부르다 *pay-puluta* 'be (stomach-)full'; 맛나다 *mas-nata* 'be tasty'

b. *Noun + Adjective (Adverbial + Verb):* 눈설다 *nwun-selta* 'be unfamiliar (eye-strange)'; 남부끄럽다 *nam-pukkulepta* 'be (other-)shy'; 남다르다 *nam-taluta* 'be different from others'; 번개같다 *penkay-kathta* 'be extremely quick (lightning-like)'

    c. *Adjective stem + Adjective:* 굳세다 *kwut-seyta* 'be (hard-)strong'; 검붉다 *kem-pulkta* 'be dark red (black-red)'; 검푸르다 *kem-phuluta* 'be dark blue (black-blue)'; 희멀겋다 *huy-melkehta* 'be fair-skinned (white-clear)'

    d. *Reduplicative:* 크나크다 *khuna-khuta* 'be huge'; 머나멀다 *mena-melta* 'be very far'; 붉디붉다 *pulkti-pulkta* 'be very red'; 검디검다 *kemti-kemta* 'be very black'

(4) Compound Adverbs

    a. *Noun + Noun:* 밤낮 *pam-nac* 'day and night (night-day)'; 오늘날 *onul-nal* 'nowadays (today-day)'; 여기저기 *yeki-ceki* 'here and there (this place-that place)'

    b. *Prenoun + Noun:* 한바탕 *han-pathang* 'for a time (big-spell)'; 한층 *han-chung* 'still more (one-storey)'; 요즈음 *yo-cuum* 'these days'

    c. *Prenominal form of verb + Bound noun:* 이른바 *ilunpa* 'so-called'; 이를테면 *ilultheymyen (ilul + the + imyen)* 'so to speak'

    d. *Adverb + Adverb:* 곧잘 *kot-cal* 'quite well'; 잘못 *cal-mos* 'mistakenly'; 좀더 *com-te* 'some more'

    e. *Reduplicative:* 오래오래 *olay-olay* 'for a long, long time'; 소근소근 *sokun-sokun* '(whispering sound)'; 반짝반짝 *panccak-panccak* '(flashing)'; 꼼지락꼼지락 *kkomcilak-kkomcilak* '(squirming)'

Some remarks should be added about the structural characteristics of Korean compounds. From a syntactic point of view, some compounds are structured like phrases, and some are not. The type of compound that is structured like a phrase is a *syntactic compound* (or a *phrasal compound*); the type that is not like a phrase is known as an *asyntactic compound* (or a *close compound*). For example, *him-ssuta* 'try hard' is a syntactic compound, as we can see from the fact that *him* 'strength' is sometimes overtly marked (by a particle) as an object, *him ul ssuta* (힘을 쓰다); *nwun-selta* 'be unfamiliar' is often expanded to *nwun ey selta* (눈에 설다) ('be strange to the eye'). However, some typical asyntactic compounds in the above examples are the compound nouns *khos-nal* 'bridge of the nose' and *sinays-mul* 'stream' of (1b), and *cep-khal* 'folding knife' and *muk-path* 'fallow field' of (1e); the compound verbs *kwulm-cwulita* 'starve' and *ttwi-nolta* 'frolic'; and the compound adjectives *kwut-seyta* 'be strong' and *kem-pulkta* 'be dark-red'. These never occur structurally as phrases but, instead, can only have the unique structure of compounds. For example, if *cep-khal* 'folding knife' were a phrase, then it should also occur as ˣ*cepnun khal* or ˣ*cepun khal;* similarly, *kem-pulkta* 'dark-red' should also appear as ˣ*kemkey pulkta* or ˣ*kemko pulkta*. If *son-mok* 'wrist' were a phrasal compound, then we would expect to see ˣ*son uy mok*.

    The asyntactic compounds of (1b), such as *khos-nal* 'ridge of the nose', *sinays-mul* 'stream', *tungq-pul* 'lamplight', and *mulq-kay* 'seal', are compounds containing the so-called "genitive *s*" or "medial *s*" (사이ㅅ). As we have seen in chapter 3, this "genitive *s*" is realized as reinforcement of the following consonant, even though it is written in Hangŭl as an *s* at the end of the first syllable. The *s* is not transcribed in Hangŭl in the compounds *tungq-pul* (등불) 'lamplight' or *mulq-kay* (물개) 'seal' because there is no space left underneath the syllable where it could be written. Nevertheless, the reinforced pronunciation is still there, as the forms in Yale Romanization remind us. Since this genitive *s* does not occur in noun phrases, it can be considered a kind of marker of asyntactic compounds. In any event, the syntactic and semantic function of this genitive *s* is not completely clear; and, as can be seen in the pairs of words in (5), below, its occurrence is also not phonologically predictable.

(5) a.

With "*genitive s*"	Without "*genitive s*"
뱃머리 *pays-meli* 'prow (boat-head)'	소머리 *so-meli* 'ox head'
처갓집 *chekas-cip* 'wife's home'	기와집 *kiwa-cip* 'tile(-roofed) house'
솔방울 *solq-pangwul* 'pine cone'	말방울 *mal-pangwul* 'horse bell'
봄비 *pomq-pi* 'spring rain'	산성비 *sanseng-pi* 'acid rain'
물고기 *mulq-koki* 'fish (water-meat)'	불고기 *pul-koki* 'pulgogi (fire-meat)'

Besides compounds that contain an occurrence of "genitive *s*" such as the above, there are also many other compounds with phonological shapes not predictable from their component parts. In some cases, sounds are interpolated, such as is done with the genitive *s;* in other cases, sounds are replaced by different sounds. Since these kinds of sound changes do not occur when the words form phrases, the phenomenon is unique to compounds. Here are some examples:

(6) a. 꽃잎 *kkoch-iph* 'flower petal': /kkonnip/ (MK *kosniph* < *koc* + *niph*)
물약 *mul-yak* 'liquid medicine': /mullyak/

b. 안닭 *am-thalk* 'hen' (*am* 'female' + *h* + *talk* 'chicken') (MK *amh* 'female')
안팎 *an-phakk* 'inside and outside' (*an* 'inside' + *h* + *pakk* 'outside') (MK *anh*)

c. 좁쌀 *cop-ssal* 'hulled millet' (*co* 'millet' + *p* + *ssal* '(uncooked) rice')
접때 *cep-ttay* 'that time' (*ce* 'that' + *p* + *ttay* 'time')

d. 섣달 *set-tal* 'December' (*s ēl* 'New Year's' + *tal* 'month')
숟가락 *swut-kalak* 'spoon' (*swul* 'spoon' + -*kalak* [long, thin object])
이튿날 *ithut-nal* 'second day' (*ithul* '2 days' + *nal* 'day')

e. 소나무 *so-namu* 'pine tree' (*sol* 'pine' + *namu* 'tree')
화살 *hwa-sal* 'arrow' (*hwal* 'bow' + *sal* 'arrow')
싸전 *ssa-cen* 'rice store' (*ssal* 'rice' + -*cen* 'shop')

f. 까막까치 *kkamak-kkachi* 'crows and magpies' (*kkamakwi* 'crow' + *kkachi* 'magpie'
엊저녁 *ec-cenyek* 'last evening' (*ecey* 'yesterday' + *cenyek* 'evening')
엉덩방아 *engteng-panga* 'fall on one's behind' (*engtengi* 'buttocks' + *panga* 'mortar, mill')

Examples like those in (6a) have already been discussed in chapter 3. In (6b, c, d), the shape differences have historical explanations. They result from the fact that the compounds are not synchronically generated, but are, instead, older compounds now completely lexicalized. In (6b), for example, the seemingly interpolated *h* is actually the modern trace of a consonant once found at the end of the first noun: for example *anh* 'inside'. Once the compound *an-phakk* was formed, *h* now occurred in the middle of this new, compound word, protected from the historical change that caused the consonant *h* to be lost whenever it was found at the end of words. Thus: *anh + pask* → *an-phask* > *an-phakk*. The examples in (6c) are similar. But in these cases, the consonant *p* was once an initial consonant, occurring at the beginning of consonant clusters in the Middle Korean words *psol* 'rice' and *pstay* 'time'. Though inexplicable from the point of view of the modern language, these consonants are like shadows of the earlier shapes of Korean words, and their examination can help us to reconstruct what the language was once like.

The explanation for (6d) is slightly more complex. Here, the two parts of the compound were first linked by genitive *s*, and in front of this *s*, *-l* elided; then the *s* assimilated to the following consonant. The original identity of the genitive *s* is further hidden because it is written with a *t* in modern Hangŭl orthography.

The development of (6e) is similar but somewhat less involved. In these compounds, word-final *-l* elided before the dental consonants *n*, *s*, and *c*. The complication comes from the fact that in most modern Korean compounds *-l* does not normally elide in these phonological environments; for example, *pul-noli* 'fireworks display (fire-play)', *pul-napi* 'tiger moth (fire-butterfly)', *pul-catongcha* 'fire engine (fire-car)', *ssal-cip* 'rice shop (rice-house)', *hwal-siwi* 'bowstring'. Again, the compounds must be treated as unproductive, historical relics.

In (6f) the final vowel of the first noun in the compound is lost. It is not clear why this syncope takes place.

Unlike asyntactic compounds, the formation of *phrasal compounds* is structurally like that of phrases. For example, *pam-nac* 'day and night', *cak.un-apeci* 'father's younger brother (little-father)', *thako-nata* 'be born with (get and-be born)' have structures like *sinlang sinpu* 'bride (and) groom', *malk.un hanul* 'a clear sky', *thako kata* 'go by __ (get on ___ and go)'. For this reason there are cases where it is difficult to determine whether a given structure is a compound or a syntactic phrase. Of course, lexicographers, typesetters, and others who use the modern written language must nevertheless make sharp, but sometimes arbitrary, distinctions. First, since a compound is considered a word, it is given an entry in the dictionary; since a phrase is not considered a word, it will not be found there. A compound is supposed to be written solid in modern Hangŭl orthography, while a phrase is written with a space. In addition, a useful rule of thumb in making such decisions is that, for the most part, another word cannot be inserted into the middle of a compound, while it can in the case of a phrase. The following examples illustrate this syntactic difference:

(7) a. 민수는 밤낮(×밤과 낮) 공부만 한다.

Minswu nun pam-nac (×pam *kwa* nac) kongpu man hanta. (compound)

night-day night and day

'All Minswu does is study night and day.'

b. 춘분에는 밤 낮 (밤과 낮)의 길이가 같다.

Chwunpun ey nun pam nac (pam *kwa* nac) uy kil.i ka kath.ta. (phrase)

'At the spring solstice night and day are the same length.'

(8) a. 우리의 첫사랑(×첫 우리 사랑)을 곱게 간직하자.

Wuli uy ches-salang (×ches wuli salang) kopkey kancik-haca. (compound)

first-love (×first our love)

'Let's treasure the memory of our first love.'

b. 너의 첫 방학(첫 겨울 방학)을 알차게 보내라.

Ne uy ches panghak (ches kyewul panghak) ul alchakey ponayla. (phrase)

first vacation (first winter vacation)

'spend your first vacation (first winter vacation) fruitfully.'

In (1) through (4), above, numbers (3d) and (4e) are structures we have called "reduplicatives." Some adjectival forms, such as *khuna-khuta* 'ever so big' and *kemti-kemta* 'ever so dark', contain an inserted element such as *-na-* or *-ti-*, but these, too, are nevertheless compounds made up of repetitions of the base. This type of compound, with two occurrences of a given stem, is often called a "reduplicative compound." As has been pointed out above (4.2.5), reduplication, with mimetics and onomatopoeia at its center, is an extremely complex and important process in Korean. Because of their complexity and number of types, we treat reduplicative compounds in a separate section, below.

4.3.2 Reduplicative Compounds

Reduplicative compounds can consist of a simple, unchanged repetition of the stem or a repetition of only a part of the base; also, as was pointed out above, some other, short element can be inserted between the two occurrences of the stem. Thus, Korean reduplicatives can be roughly divided into the three types: *complete reduplication, transformed reduplication,* and *interposed reduplication*. First, let us look at some examples of how complete reduplicatives are structured:

(1) a. 집집 *cip-cip* '(each) house'; 나날(<날날) *na-nal* (< *nal-nal*) 'every day'; 구석구석 *kwusek-kwusek* 'every corner'; 마디마디 *mati-mati* 'every joint'; 차례차례 *chalyey-chalyey* 'in regular sequence'; *kwup.i-kwup.i* 굽이굽이 'at every turn'; *kaci-kaci* (kac-kaci) 가지가지(갖가지) 'all kinds'

b. 고루고루 *kolwu-kolwu* 'very evenly'; 오래오래 *olay-olay* 'a long, long time'; 가득가득 *katuk-katuk* 'filled completely to the brim'; 길이길이 *kil.i-kil.i* 'for many, many years to come'

c. 쿵쿵 *kwung-kwung* 'bang, bang!'; 바스락바스락 *pasulak-pasulak* '(with a rustling sound)'; 중얼중얼 *cwungel-cwungel* 'mumble, mumble'; 덜그럭덜그럭 *telkulek-telkulek* 'rattle, rattle'; 아장아장 *acang-acang* 'todderingly (as a baby walking)'; 깜박깜박 *kkampak-kkampak* 'flickeringly'; 꾸벅꾸벅 *kkwupek-kkwupek* '(bowing, bobbing one's head)'; 넘실넘실 *nemsil-nemsil* '(rhythmically overflowing)'; 한들한들 *hantul-hantul* 'waveringly'; 빙글빙글 *pingkul-pingkul* 'round and round'; 획획 'jerkily'; 뭉게뭉게 *mungkey-mungkey* 'densely clouded'; 어슬렁어슬렁 *esulleng-esulleng* 'sluggishly'

d. 띄엄띄엄 *ttuyem-ttuyem* 'intermittently'; 구불구불 *kwupul-kwupul* 'twisting and turning'; 드믄드믄 *tumun-tumun* 'thinly, sparsely'; 넓적넓적 *nelpcek-nelpcek* 'all flatly'

The examples in (1a) are noun reduplications, (1b) adverb reduplications, and (1c) mimetics and onomatopoeia with reduplications of the root; these are but a small sampling of these types of reduplicative compounds. The examples in (1d) have a rather distinctive structure consisting of a reduplicated form combining a verb stem with a type of suffix.

Reduplicative compounds function principally as adverbs. With the exception of forms such as those illustrated in (1a), all of the above types are only used adverbially. Moreover, even the compounds in (1a) are used more often as adverbs than as nouns; when the form itself will not serve as an adverb, it can assume the function of an adverb by combining with the adverbial suffix *-i;* for example, *cip-cip-i* (집집이), *na-nal-i* 나날이. The following sentences illustrate how these noun reduplications work:

(2) a. 한강물 굽이굽이에 우리 역사의 슬픈 사연이 서려 있다.
Hankang-mul *kwupi-kwupi* ey wuli yeksa uy sulphun sayen i selye iss.ta.
twists-and-turns LOCATIVE
'The sadness of our history is enswathed in the twists and turns of the Han River.' [reduplicative used as a noun]

b. 한강물이 굽이굽이 흘러간다.
Hankang-mul i *kwupi-kwupi* hulle kanta.
twisting-and-turning
'The Han River flows twisting and turning.' [reduplicative used adverbially]

(3) a. 나는 그 무렵 시험 준비로 나날을 뜬눈으로 보냈다.

Na nun ku mulyep sihem cwunpi lo *na-nal ul* ponayss.ta.

day-day OBJECT

'In those days I spent day after day without a wink of sleep in preparation for the exam.' [reduplicative used as a direct object]

b. 봄이 되니 수풀 색이 나날이 달라진다.

Pom i toyni swu.phul sayk i *na-nal-i* tallacinta.

day-day-ADVERBIAL

'Since spring has come, the colors of the forest change day by day.' [reduplicative used adverbially]

Next, let us consider *transformed reduplicatives*. Since one of the constituent elements changes slightly, transformed reduplicatives are descriptive of a more varied appearance than complete reduplicatives. For example, the complete reduplicative *pulkus-pulkus* (from *pulk-* 'be red') describes a uniform red color, but *wulkus-pulkus*, with the first element phonologically altered, describes an appearance that is not only red but also has an admixture of various other colors.

In a transformed reduplicative, either of the two occurrences of the morpheme can be phonologically altered. As can be seen in (4a), the vowel can change, or, as in (4b), the consonant can change; or, alternatively, as can be seen in (4c), the whole syllable can completely change.

(4) a. 실룩샐룩 *sillwuk-sayllwuk* 'twitchingly'; 티격태격 *thikyek-thaykyek* 'bickeringly', 삐뚤빼뚤 *ppittwul-ppayttwul* 'unsteadily'; 싱글생글 *singkul-sayngkul* 'grinningly'; 찌그락째그락 *ccikulak-ccaykulak* '(thumping sound)'; 흘깃할깃 *hulkis-halkis* 'casting sidelong glances at'

b. 올망졸망 *olmang-colmang* 'in clusters'; 옹기종기 *ongki-congki* 'in small, tight groups'; 우글쭈글 *wukul-ccwukul* 'crumpled, wrinkled'; 우물쭈물 *wumul-ccwumul* 'waveringly'; 아둥바둥 *atwung-patwung* 'desperately'; 우락부락 *wulak-pulak* 'roughly'; 울룩불룩 *wulluk-pulluk* 'uneven, rough'; 얼룩덜룩 *ellwuk-tellwuk* 'mottled'; 오순도순 *oswun-toswun* 'chummily'; 알뜰살뜰 *alttul-salttul* 'thriftily'

c. 어슷비슷 *esus-pisus* 'much the same'; 안절부절 *ancel-pucel* 'fidgety'; 옥신각신 *oksin-kaksin* 'haggling'; 싱글벙글 *singkul-pengkul* 'grinningly'; 갈팡질팡 *kalphang-cilphang* 'flustered'

In the transformed reduplicatives given above, it can be seen what tendencies there are in the alternations between sounds. For example, looking at the vowel alternations, we can see that the vowels of initial syllables gravitate toward *i* or *u*, while vowels of latter forms are all *ay* or *a*. The basic canonical shape of these reduplicatives is built on a contrast of high vowel versus low vowel in the two parts. However, in the consonant alternations, the initial member of the reduplicative tends overwhelmingly to begin with a vowel or a semivowel, while the latter member begins with a consonant, usually one of the obstruents, *p, c,* or *t*. The forms with syllable alternations show a similar tendency.

Korean reduplicative compounds can also be made up of the reduplication of only part of one of the constituent elements. In (5), below, *khwung-cak-cak* 'rat-a-tat' represents a reduplication of only the second syllable of *khwungcak* 'id.'; *twu-twungsil* 'floating airily' repeats only *twu-* of *twungsil* 'floating lightly'; while *phu-tu-tuk* 'flying up fluttering' has a piece of the second syllable reduplicated between the two syllables of the word *phutuk* 'fluttering'. It is difficult to call forms such as these pure reduplication, but they can be thought of as one type of transformed reduplicatives.

(5) 쿵작작 *khwungcak-cak* 'rat-a-tat'; 얼씨구씨구 *elssikwu-ssikwu* 'yip-yippee!'; 두둥실 *twu-twungsil* 'floating airily'; 땍때굴 *ttayk-ttaykwul* 'tum-tum-tumbling'; 푸드득 *phutu-tuk* 'flying up fluttering'

Next, let us look at *interposed reduplications*. Interposed reduplications are so called because of the interposition of a third element between the reduplicated parts of a base, and in these strings, the interposed element takes either the shape *-ti-* or *-na-*, two forms that are difficult to classify as endings or suffixes. The form *-ti-* rather freely combines with various adjective stems, while *-na-*, in contrast, has a very restricted distribution with only a restricted number of adjective stems. In any event, these interposed reduplications involve the reduplication of adjective stems and only form adjectives; in this respect they contrast with the majority of reduplicative compounds, which are used as adverbs.

(6) a. 쓰디쓰다 *ssu-ti-ssuta* 'be as bitter as gall' (from 쓰다 *ssuta* 'be bitter'); 달디달다 *tal-ti-talta* 'be sugary sweet' (달다 *talta* 'be sweet'); 곱디곱다 *kop-ti-kopta* 'be extraordinarily beautiful' (곱다 *kopta* 'be pretty'); 길디길다 *kil-ti-kilta* 'be endlessly long' (길다 *kilta* 'be long'); 깊디깊다 *kiph-ti-kiphta* 'be very deep' (깊다 *kiphta* 'be deep'); 붉디붉다 *pulk-ti-pulkta* 'be deep red' (붉다 *pulkta* 'be red')
     b. 기나길다 *ki-na-kilta* 'be very long'; 크나크다 *khu-na-khuta* 'be enormous' (크다 *khuta* 'be big'); 머나멀다 *me-na-melta* 'be far, far away' (멀다 *melta* 'be far')

4.3.3 Derivatives

Korean derivatives can be divided into those derived by *prefixes* and those derived by *suffixes*. However, as was pointed out above (4.1), suffixes play a much more important role in Korean than prefixes. The derivatives created by suffixes are far more numerous, and the types of derivation by suffixes are much more varied. Prefixes, however, do not function to change the word class of the base, and they are not very large in number. First, let us look at a list of typical prefixes along with some examples of words derived with them:

(1) a. *kwun-* 'excess': 군소리 *kwun-soli* 'unnecessary remark' (소리 *soli* 'sound'); 군불 *kwun-pul* 'fire for heating an *ondol*' (불 *pul* 'fire'); 군침 *kwun-chim* 'excess saliva' (침 *chim* 'saliva'); 군입 *kwun-ip* 'snacking' (입 *ip* 'mouth'); 군손질 kwun-soncil 'unnecessary handling' (손질 *soncil* 'handling')

b. *mayn-* 'bare': 맨손 *mayn-son* 'empty hand' (손 *son* 'hand'); 맨발 *mayn-pal* 'barefoot' (발 *pal* 'foot'); 맨입 *mayn-ip* 'empty stomach' (입 *ip* 'mouth'); 맨정신 *mayn-cengsin* 'clearhead(ed)' (정신 *cengsin* 'mind'); 맨땅 *mayn-ttang* 'bare ground'; 맨밥 *mayn-pap* 'plain rice (without side dishes)'

c. *mat-* 'eldest': 맏형 *mat-hyeng* 'oldest brother'; 맏아들 *mat-atul* 'oldest son'; 맏딸 *mat-ttal* 'oldest daughter'; 맏며느리 *mat-myenuli* 'oldest daughter-in-law'; 맏물 *mat-mul* 'first fruits' (물 *-mul* 'stuff')

d. *phus-* 'unripe': 풋과일 *phus-kwail* 'unripe fruit'; 풋나물 *phus-namul* 'young herbs'; 풋사랑 *phus-salang* 'puppy love'; 풋내기 *phus-nayki* 'novice' (-내기 *-nayki* '-person'); 풋내 *phus-nay* 'smell of young greens' (-내 *-nay* '-smell')

e. *olun-* 'right': 오른손 *olun-son* 'right hand'; 오른발 *olun-pal* 'right foot'; 오른팔 *olun-phal* 'right arm'; 오른쪽 *olun-ccok* 'right side'

f. *oyn-* 'left': 왼손 *oyn-son* 'left hand'; 왼발 *oyn-pal* 'left foot'; 왼팔 *oyn-phal* 'left arm'; 왼새끼 *oyn-saykki* '(straw) rope (wound) left-handed'

g. *swu(h)-* 'male': 수캐 *swu-khay* 'male dog' (개 *kay* 'dog'); 수탉 *swu-thalk* 'rooster' (닭 *talk* 'chicken'); 수평아리 *swu-phyengali* 'male chick' (병아리 *pyengali* 'chick'); 수놈 *swuq-nom* 'male (animal)'; 수키와 *swu-khiwa* 'convex tile' (기와 *kiwa* 'tile')

h. *am(h)-* 'female': 암소 *amq-so* 'cow', 암탉 *am-thak* 'hen'; 암캐 *am-khay* 'bitch'; 암놈 *am-nom* 'female (animal)'; 암키와 *am-khiwa* 'concave tile'

i. *oy-* 'outside': 외할머니 *oy-halmeni* 'grandmother (on mother's side)'; 외할아버지 *oy-hal.apeci* 'grandfather (on mother's side)'; 외삼촌 *oy-samchon* 'uncle (on mother's side)'; 외사촌 *oy-sachon* 'cousin (on mother's side)'; 외가 *oyq-ka* 'home of one's mother's parents'

j. *si-* 'in-laws . . .': 시부모 *si-pumo* 'husband's parents'; 시어머니 *si-emeni* 'husband's mother'; 시아버지 *si-apeci* 'husband's father'; 시동생 *si-tongsayng* 'husband's younger sibling'; 시집 *si-cip* 'husband's home'

k. *tes-* 'additional': 덧신 *tes-sin* 'overshoes'; 덧니 *tes-ni* 'snaggletooth' (이/니 *i/ni* 'tooth'); 덧문 *tes-mun* 'outer door'; 덧나다 *tes-nata* 'get worse' (나다 *nata* 'become'); 덧바르다 *tes-paluta* 'coat (something)' (바르다 *paluta* 'apply (liquid)')

l. *hes-* 'fruitless': 헛수고 *hes-swuko* 'wasted effort'; 헛소문 *hes-somun* 'empty rumor'; 헛일 *hes-il* /hennil/ 'useless work'; 헛딛다 *hes-titta* 'lose one's footing' (디디다 *titita* 'to step, tread'); 헛짚다 *hes-ciphta* 'guess wrong' (짚다 *ciphta* 'rest (on), lean (on)')

m. *cis-* 'roughly': 짓누르다 *cis-nwuluta* 'squash' (누르다 *nwuluta* 'press down'); 짓밟다 *cis-palpta* 'trample underfoot' (밟다 *palpta* 'step on')

As can be seen from these examples, a noun with a prefix remains a noun, a verb with a prefix remains a verb. A given prefix attaches to a set part of speech; only in (1k) and (1l) do we see prefixes that combine with two different parts of speech. And even in these cases we find that they only combine with nouns and verbs; from the point of view of distribution, prefixes have a narrow range of application.

Now let us turn to derivations by *suffixes*. Derivational suffixes number in the hundreds, and they are also much more productive. They also combine with many different stems, and, in addition, a single suffix is often found combined with two or more bases. Their functions are varied, and, unlike prefixes, which only add to the meaning, suffixes not only add to the meaning, but they can also change the syntactic category. The following representative examples are arranged according to the part of speech of the derived forms:

(2) Derived Nouns

a. *-i:* 넓이 *nelp.i* 'width' (넓 - *nelp-* 'to be wide'); 길이 *kil.i* 'length'; 높이 *noph.i* 'height'; 깊이 *kiph.i* 'depth'; 놀이 *nol.i* 'game' (놀 - *nol-* 'to play'); 먹이 *mek.i* 'feed' (먹 - *mek-* 'to eat'); 개구리 *kaykwuli* 'frog' (개 골개골 *kaykol-kaykol* 'croak! croak!'); 뻐꾸기 *ppekkwuki* 'cuckoo' (뻐꾹 뻐꾹 *ppekkwuk-ppekkwuk* 'cuckoo! cuckoo!')

b. *-(u)m:* 웃음 *wus.um* 'laughter' (웃 - *wus-* 'to laugh'); 울음 *wul.um* 'crying'; 믿음 *mit.um* 'belief'; 기쁨 *kippum* 'happiness'; 슬픔 *sulphum* 'sadness'; 삶 *salm* 'life'

c. *-kay/key:* 덮개 *tephkay* 'cover' (덮 - *teph-* 'to cover)'; 지우개 *ciwukay* 'eraser' (지우 - *ciwu-* 'to rub out'); 찌개 *ccikay* 'tchigae, Korean stew' (찌 - *cci-* 'to steam, cook (with water)'; 지게 *cikey* 'Korean carrying frame' (지 - *ci-* 'carry (on the back)'); 집게 *cipkey* 'tweezers'

d. *-cil:* 가위질 *kawi-cil* 'using scissors' (가위 *kawi* 'scissors'); 톱질 *thop-cil* 'sawing'; 부채질 *puchay-cil* 'fanning'; 이간질 *ikan-cil* 'alienating' (이간 *ikan* 'alienation')

e. *-po:* 잠보 *cam-po* 'sleepyhead'; 겁보 *kep-po* 'coward, fraidy cat'; 꾀보 *kkoy-po* 'shrewd person, guy with an angle'; 털보 *thel-po* 'hairy guy'; 울보 *wul-po* 'crybaby'; 느림보 *nulim-po* 'slowpoke'

f. *-kkwuleki:* 잠꾸러기 *cam-kkwuleki* 'sleepyhead'; 심술꾸러기 *simswul-kkwuleki* 'mean person'; 욕심꾸러기 *yoksim-kkwuleki* 'greedy person'

g. *-cayngi:* 멋쟁이 *mes-cayngi* 'a fashionable person'; 거짓말쟁이 *kecismal-cayngi* 'liar'; 심술쟁이 *simswul-cayngi* 'a dog in the manger'; 욕심쟁이 *yoksim-cayngi* 'greedy person'

h. *-ca* (者): 기술자 *kiswulca* 'technician' (기술 *kiswul* 'skill'); 과학자 *kwahakca* 'scientist'; 학자 *hakca* 'scholar, academic'; 지휘자 *cihwica* '(orchestra) director'

i. *-sa* (師): 교사 *kyosa* 'instructor'; 목사 *moksa* 'pastor'; 미용사 *miyongsa* 'beautician'; 이발사 *ipalsa* 'barber'

j. *-swu* (手): 목수 *mokswu* 'carpenter'; 조수 *coswu* 'helper, aide'; 운전수 *wuncenswu* 'driver'; 기수 *kiswu* 'flagman'; 나팔수 *naphalswu* 'bugler'

(3) Derived Adjectives

a. *-lop/low-:* 향기롭다 *hyangki-lopta* 'be fragrant' (향기 *hyangki* (香氣) 'fragrance'); 해롭다 *hay-lopta* 'be harmful' (해 *hay* (害) 'harm'); 슬기롭다 *sulki-lopta* 'be wise' (슬기 *sulki* 'wisdom'); 외롭다 *oy-lopta* 'be lonely' (외- *oy-* 'single')

b. *-tap/taw-:* 정답다 *ceng-tapta* 'be on friendly terms' (정 *ceng* (情) 'feelings'); 꽃답다 *kkoch-tapta* 'be flowerlike'; 신사답다 *sinsa-tapta* 'be gentlemanly'

c. *-sulep/sulew-:* 복스럽다 *pok-sulepta* 'be fortunate' (복 *pok* (福) 'good fortune'); 탐스럽다 *tham-sulepta* 'be attractive, tempting' (탐 *tham* (貪) 'covetousness'); 어른스럽다 *elun-sulepta* 'be grownup-like'; 창피스럽다 *changphi-sulepta* 'be embarrassing'

d. *-ha-* (from *hata* 'do, be'): 깨끗하다 *kkaykkus-hata* 'be clean'; 조용하다 *coyong-hata* 'be quiet'; 튼튼하다 *thunthun-hata* 'be sturdy'; 알쏭달쏭하다 *alssongtalssong-hata* 'be motley'

e. *-ci-:* 값지다 *kaps-cita* 'be expensive' (값 'price'); 멋지다 *mes-cita* 'be lovely' (멋 'good taste'); 건방지다 *kenpang-cita* 'be conceited, impudent'; 야무지다 *yamu-cita* 'be solid, firm'; 앙칼지다 *angkhal-cita* 'be spirited, aggressive'

f. *-talah-:* 기다랗다 *ki-talahta* 'be long and tedious' (길다 *kilta* 'be long'); 굵다랗다 *kwulk-talahta* 'be very thick' (굵다 *kulkta* 'be thick'); 널따랗다 *nel-ttalahta* 'be extensive, spacious' (넓다 *nelpta* 'be broad'); 좁다랗다 *cop-talahta* 'be narrowish' (좁다 *copta* 'be narrow')

(4) Derived Adverbs

a. *-i:* 같이 *kath.i* 'alike, together' (같- *kath-* 'to be together, the same'); 굳이 *kwut.i* /kwuci/ 'firmly, obstinately' (굳- *kwut-* 'to become hard, firm'); 바삐 *pappi* 'busily' (바쁘- *pappu-* 'to be busy'); 많이 *manh.i* 'many, much' (많- *manh-* 'to be many, much'); 높이 *noph.i* 'high', 고이 *koi* 'beautifully, well'; 깨끗이 *kkaykkus.i* 'cleanly'

b. *-hi:* 천천히 *chenchen-hi* 'slowly'; 쓸쓸히 *ssulssul-hi* 'cheerlessly' (쓸쓸하다 *ssulssul-hata* 'be lonely, cheerless'); 넉넉히 *neknek-hi* 'amply' (넉넉하다 *neknek-hata* 'be ample, sufficient'); 조용히 *coyong-hi* 'quietly' (조용하다 *coyong-hata* 'be quiet'); 부지런히 *pucilen-hi* 'diligently' (부지런하다 *pucilen-hata* 'be diligent'); 무던히 *muten-hi* 'generously' (무던하다 *muten-hata* 'be generous')

c. *-lo:* 진실로 *cinsil-lo* 'truly' (진실 *cinsil* (眞實) 'truth'); 참으로 *cham-ulo* 'really' (참- *cham-* 'real'); 대대로 *taytay-lo* 'from generation to generation' (대 *tay* (代) 'generation'); 따로 *tta-lo* 'separately'; 주로 *cwu-lo* (主로) 'principally'

d. *-o/wu-:* 너무 *nemu* 'too much, excessively' (넘- *nem-* 'exceed'); 자주 *cacwu* 'often' (잦- *cac-* 'to be frequent'); 도로 *tolo* '(over) again' (돌- *tol-* 'to turn'); 바투 *pathwu* 'near (by)' (밭- *path-* 'to be very close')

(5) Derived Verbs

a. *-i/hi/li/ki-:* 쓰이다 *ssuita* 'be used' (쓰다 *ssuta* 'use'); 막히다 *mak.hita* 'be closed off' (막다 *makta* 'close off'); 잘리다 *callita* 'be cut off' (자르다 *caluta* 'cut off'); 빼앗기다 *ppayaskita* 'have (something) taken away' (빼앗다 *ppayasta* 'take (something) away')

b. *-i/hi/li/ki/ay/wu/kwu/chwu-:* 먹이다 *mek.ita* 'feed' (먹다 *mekta* 'eat'); 굽히다 *kwup.hita* 'bend (something)' (굽다 *kwupta* 'be bent'); 울리다 *wullita* 'make cry' (울다 *wulta* 'cry'); 웃기다 *wuskita* 'make laugh' (웃다 *wusta* 'laugh'); 없애다 *eps.ayta* 'get rid of' (없다 *eps.ta* 'not have, not exist'); 지우다 *ciwuta* 'make (someone) carry' (지다 *cita* 'carry on the back'); 세우다 *seywuta* 'stand (something) up' (서다 *seta* 'stand'); 돋구다 *totkwuta* 'raise' (돋다 *totta* 'rise'); 낮추다 *nacchwuta* 'lower' (낮다 *nacta* 'be low')

c. *-keli-:* 덜렁거리다 *telleng-kelita* 'tinkle, jingle' (덜렁덜렁 *telleng-telleng* 'jingle, jangle!'); 덤벙거리다 *tempeng-kelita* 'act carelessly' (덤벙덤벙 *tempeng-tempeng* 'carelessly'); 추근거리다 *chwukun-kelita* 'bother (someone) persistently' (추근추근 *chwukun-chwukun* 'persistently'); 두근거리다 *twukun-kelita* 'pulse, throb, beat fast' (두근두근 *twukun-twukun* 'pit-a-pat')

d. *-tay-:* 출렁대다 *chwulleng-tayta* 'undulate, roll' (출렁출렁 *chwulleng-chwulleng* 'undulating'); 구물대다 *kwumul-tayta* 'wriggle' (구물구물 *kwumul-kwumul* 'wriggling'); 빈정대다 *pinceng-tayta* 'tease' (빈정빈정 *pinceng-pinceng* 'teasingly'); 덜컹대다 *telkheng-tayta* 'clatter' (덜컹덜컹 *telkheng-telkheng* 'clatteringly'); 우쭐대다 *wuccwul-tayta* 'be conceited' (우쭐우쭐 'swaggeringly')

e. *-i-:* 끄덕이다 *kkutek.ita* 'nod at' (끄덕끄덕 *kkutek-kkutek* 'nodding'); 깜박이다 *kkampak.ita* 'blink, twinkle' (깜박깜박 *kkampak-kkampak* 'blinking, flickering'); 뒤척이다 *twichek.ita* 'rummage in' (뒤척뒤척 *twichek-twichek* 'rummaging'); 서성이다 *sesengita* 'pace back and forth' (서성서성 *seseng-seseng* 'pacing restlessly'); 들먹이다 *tulmek.ita* 'move up and down' (들먹들먹 *telmek-tulmek* 'moving up and down')

As can be seen in the above examples, a suffix can serve to change the word class; it can change an intransitive verb into a transitive verb or a transitive verb into an intransitive verb. We see that suffixes have far more functions in Korean than prefixes do. Moreover, they combine not only with nouns, verbs, and adjectives, but also with roots; they have a very broad distribution. In the above examples, the endings in (5a) change the verbs into passives, those in (5b) into causatives; these processes will be discussed in more detail below, in (6.3).

4.3.4 Special Derivatives

We have looked at derivations by affixes. However, in addition to these typical kinds of processes, Korean also makes use of derivation through internal change. Instead of utilizing affixes, these derivations take place through vowel or consonant alternations. Korean has many derivations of this kind, especially in the mimetics and onomatopoeia of the language. In this section, we will look briefly at how these special derivatives are formed in Korean. Here are some examples of vowel alternation:

(1) a. *a/e/u:* 까닥까닥/꺼덕꺼덕/끄덕끄덕 *kkatak-kkatak/ kketek-kketek/ kkutek-kkutek* (jerking, bobbing, nodding movement)

b. *o/wu/i:* 졸졸/줄줄/질질 *col-col/ cwul-cwul/ cil-cil* (trickling/ streaming/ dribbling)

c. *a/e:* 말짱하다/멀쩡하다 *malccang-hata/ melcceng-hata* 'flawless, spotless'; 빨갛다/뻘겋다 *ppalkahta/ ppelkehta* 'be bright red/reddish'; 파랗다/퍼렇다 *phalahta/ phelehta* 'be bright blue/bluish'; 간들간들/건들건들 *kantul-kantul/ kentul-kentul* 'swaying gently/wobbling'; 방글방글/벙글벙글 *pangkul-pangkul/ pengkul-pangkul* 'smiling sweetly/radiantly'; 산들산들/선들선들 *santul-santul/ sentul-sentul* 'blowing gently/softly'; 찰찰/철철 *chal-chal/ chel-chel* 'brimmingly/overflowingly'; 까칠까칠/꺼칠꺼칠 *kkachil-kkachil/ kkechil-kkechil* (worn/coarse appearance)

d. *a/u:* 가득하다/그득하다 *katuk-hata/ kutuk-hata* 'be full/brimming over'; 따갑다/뜨겁다 *ttakapta/ ttukepta* '(a small thing) is burning hot (to the touch)/(bigger thing) is hot (to the touch)'; 탄탄하다/튼튼하다 *thanthan-hata/ thunthun-hata* 'be compactly solid/sturdy'; 한들거리다/흔들거리다 *hantul-kelita/ huntul-kelita* 'flicker, waver/shake, tremble'; 날씬하다/늘씬하다 *nalssin-hata/ nulssin-hata* 'be delicate and slim/tall and slim'; 살금살금/슬금슬금 *salkum-salkum/ sulkum-sulkum* 'stealthily and catlike/quietly, furtively'; 달달/들들 *tal-tal/ tul-tul* 'thoroughly, excessively/annoyingly, rummaging'; 하늘하늘/흐늘흐늘 *hanul-hanul/ hunul-hunul* 'lightly, airily/slowly, sluggishly'

e. *ay/i:* 새카맣다/시커멓다 *say-khamahta/ si-khemehta* 'be jet-black/dirty black'; 매끄럽다/미끄럽다 *maykkulepta/ mikkulepta* 'be smooth/slick'; 뱅뱅/빙빙 *payng-payng/ ping-ping* '(something small) turning/ (bigger object) turning'; 뱅글뱅글/빙글빙글 *payngkul-payngkul/ pingkul-pingkul* 'turning round and round/ spinning'; 생글생글/싱글싱글 *sayngkul-sayngkul/ singkul-singkul* 'smiling affably/gently'; 탱탱/팅팅 *thayng-thayng/ thing-thing* 'blown up until the surface is taut/swollen'; 해해/히히 *hay-hay/ hi-hi* 'heh, heh/hee, hee'

f. *o/wu:* 도톰하다/두툼하다 *tothom-hata/ twuthwum-hata* 'be thick/heavy'; 노랗다/누렇다 *nolahta/ nwulehta* 'be bright yellow/yellowish'; 동그랗다/둥그렇다 *tongkulahta/ twungkulehta* 'be small and round/be round'; 고소하다/구수하다 *koso-hata/ kwuswu-hata* 'be savory/pleasant-tasting, be worth gloating about/be appealing'; 소복하다/수북하다 *sopok-hata/ swupuk-hata* 'be in neat heaps/be in piles'; 볼록하다/불룩하다 *pollok-hata/ pullwuk-hata* 'be convex/pooch out'; 통통하다/퉁퉁하다 *thongthong-hata/ thwungthwung-hata* 'be pleasantly round/be rotund'; 촉촉하다/축축하다 *chokchok-hata/ chwukchwuk-hata* 'be damp, moist/wet, dank'; 꼬불꼬불/꾸불꾸불 *kkopul-kkopul/ kkwupul-kkwupul* 'winding in tight curves/winding back and forth'; 쪼글쪼글/쭈글쭈글

ccokul-ccokul/ ccwukul-ccwukul 'finely wrinkled/crumpled'; 소근소근/
수근수근 *sokun-sokun/ swukun-swukun* 'whispering in a low voice/whispering, murmuring'; 모락모락/무럭무럭 *molak-molak/ mulek-mulek*
'puffing/billowing'; 보슬보슬/부슬부슬 *posul-posul/ pusul-pusul* 'raining in a light mist/slowly raining in small drops'; 폭신폭신/푹신푹신
phoksin-phoksin/ phuksin-phuksin '(small cushion, e.g.) is soft/(big futon, e.g.) is soft'; 풍당/풍덩 *phongtang/ phungteng* 'with a plop/with a
dull splash'

As can be seen in the above examples, the vowel alternations largely
reflect the relationships of Korean vowel harmony, in which *yang* vowels,
such as /ay/, /a/, and /o/, are in opposition to *yin* vowels, such as /ey/,
/e/, and /wu/. However, the *yang* vowels /ay/, /a/, and /o/, which are
front, mid, and back vowels in the Korean vowel system, are all articulated in
the lowest positions in the mouth, and so the alternations can also be analyzed as low (or open) versus high (or closed).

The opposition between *yang* vowels and *yin* vowels has long attracted
attention because of its relationship to phonetic symbolism. The vowel /i/
is a neutral vowel in the vowel harmony system, but for the purposes of phonetic symbolism it patterns as a *yin* vowel. Therefore, in the Korean system
of phonetic symbolism the *yin* and *yang* vocalisms are as follows:

yang: 아, 애, 야, 오, 외, 요, 와, 왜
        a, ay, ya, o, oy, yo, wa, way
yin: 어, 에, 여, 우, 위, 유, 워, 웨, 으, 이, 의
        e, ey, ye, wu, wi, yu, we, wey, u, i, uy

These vowels are in opposition to each other in the system of phonetic
symbolism. The *yang* vocalisms connote "bright, light, clear, small, few,
sharp, thin, strong, quick, new," while the *yin* vocalisms connote "dark,
heavy, cloudy, big, many, dull, thick, weak, slow, old."

(2) a. 할아버지께서 벙글벙글 웃으신다.
       Hal.apeci kkeyse pengkul-pengkul wus.usinta.
       'Grandfather laughs *pengkul-pengkul.*'
    b. 아기가 방글방글 웃는다.
       Aki ka pangkul-pangkul wusnunta.
       'Babies laugh *pangkul-pangkul.*'

(3) a. 삼각산 봉우리가 우뚝하다.
       Samkak-san pongwuli ka wuttwuk-hata.
       'The peak of Mount Samgak is *wuttwuk* [majestically towering].'
    b. 수미가 콧날이 오똑하다.
       Swumi ka khos-nal i ottok-hata.
       'The (ridge of) Sumi's nose is *ottok* [attractively prominent].'

Color terms show most graphically the opposition of vowels in the Korean system of phonetic symbolism. For the same basic color word, bright and dark colorations, deep and light shades can be distinguished; and, in this fine-tuned color terminology, vowel symbolism is what is used to express relative lightness and darkness. In the word pairs *ppalkahta/ppelkehta* 'red', *phalahta/phelehta* 'blue, green', and *nolahta/nwulehta* 'yellow', the *yang* forms *ppalkahta*, *phalahta*, and *nolahta* describe bright and vivid colors, while the *yin* forms *ppelkehta*, *phelehta*, and *nwulehta* describe dark and muddied colors.

(4) a. 봄이 되니 새싹이 파랗게 돋아난다.

    Pom i toyni sayssak i *phalahkey* tot.a nanta.

    'When spring comes, new shoots spring up *phalahkey* [bright, fresh green].'

   b. 수미가 넘어져서 무릎에 멍이 퍼렇게 들었다.

    Swumi ka nem.ecyese muluph ey meng i *phelehkey* tul.ess.ta

    'When Sumi fell down, her knee was bruised phelehkey [dark and purplish].'

(5) 노란색 벽지가 오래 되어서 누렇게 변했다.

   Nolan-sayk pyekci ka olay toy.ese *nwulehkey* pyen-hayssta.

   'The *nolan*-colored [bright yellow] wallpaper is so old it turned *nwulehkey* [faded, dull yellow].'

Let us now look at some examples of consonant alternation. There are not as many consonant alternations in Korean as vowel alternations, but the process is nevertheless quite productive. The alternations are between lax, "reinforced," and (heavily) aspirated consonants. A representative example is *kam-kam/kkam-kkam/kham-kham,* in which the variants are used to describe various shades of black. But this kind of three-way alternation, in which a single base form has variants from all three series of consonants, is rare. The most usual consonant alternation is a two-way one between lax and reinforced; there are also examples that contrast "reinforced" consonants and aspirated consonants, such as *saykkamahta/saykhamahta,* but these are more limited in number.

It is common for an originally lax consonant to become reinforced or aspirated in order to express emphasis or greater degree; but an original aspirate does not change to a reinforced or lax consonant in order to express less emphasis or less degree. The basic lexical item <u>k</u>amahta 'be black' becomes <u>kk</u>amahta when the object being described is jet black, or in order to express the speaker's feeling of a greater degree of blackness. But <u>ph</u>alahta 'be blue/green' cannot become ˣ<u>p</u>alahta or ˣ<u>pp</u>alahta. In consonant alternation, reinforcement connotes strength, and aspiration, something still more violent or strong.

(6) a. lax/reinforced: 발갛다/빨갛다 *palkahta/ ppalkahta* 'be bright red/

deep red, crimson'; 보얗다/뽀얗다 *poyahta/ ppoyahta* 'be hazy/completely fogged'; 서느렇다/써느렇다 *senulehta/ ssenulehta* 'be refreshingly cool/shiveringly chilly'; 뱅뱅/뺑뺑 *payng-payng/ ppayng-ppayng* 'round and round in lazy circles/in violent circles'; 생긋생긋/쌩긋쌩긋 *sayngkus-sayngkus/ ssayngkus-ssayngkus* '(smiling) sweetly/(smiling) brightly'; 숙덕숙덕/쑥덕쑥덕 *swuktek-swuktek/ sswuktek-sswuktek* 'whispering secretly/slyly'; 종알종알/쫑알쫑알 *congal-congal/ ccongal-ccongal* 'babbling/rattling on'

 b. lax/aspirated: 바르르/파르르 *palulu/phalulu* 'seething/boiling over'; 질벅질벅/질퍽질퍽 *cilpek-cilpek/ cilphek-cilphek* 'muddily/slushily'; 부석부석/푸석푸석 *pusek-pusek/ phusek-phusek* 'slightly swollen/grossly swollen'

 c. reinforced/aspirated: 뚱뚱하다/퉁퉁하다 *ttwungttwung-hata/ thwungthwung-hata* 'be fat/be puffy fat'; 시꺼멓다/시커멓다 *si-kkemehta/ sikhemehta* 'be dark and dirty black/be filthy black'; 땅땅/탕탕 *ttangttang/ thang-thang* 'bang-bang!/boom-boom!'

 d. lax-lax/reinforced-reinforced: 질금질금/찔끔찔끔 *cilkum-cilkum/ ccilkum-ccilkkum* 'shuffling/dragging'

 e. lax-lax/reinforced-aspirated: 경중경중/껑충껑충 *kengcwung-kengcwung/ kkengchwung-kkengchwung* 'jumping lazily/jumping energetically, in great leaps'

  We have looked briefly at the richness of internal change and phonetic symbolism in Korean. Let us now illustrate the workings of the system more systematically with an examination of some of the Korean color terminology. It can be seen that the richness of color terminology is not only the result of phonetic symbolism; it is also enhanced further by prefixes and suffixes used expressly to describe the brightness or darkness and the deepness or lightness of colors. Prefixes used in this way for colors include *say/si-, says/sis-;* and suffixes used to shade color terms include *-ah/eh-* and *-usulum-ha-*.

  The system of derivation looks as follows:

(7) deep ←————————————————→light

['red']

bright: 새빨갛다 – 빨갛다 – 발갛다 – (붉다) – 발그스름하다
   say-ppalkahta ppalkahta palkahta (pulkta) palkusulum-hata

dark: 시뻘겋다 – 뻘겋다 – 벌겋다 – (붉다) – 벌그스름하다
   sippelkehta ppelkehta pelkehta (pulkta) pelkusulum-hata

['blue']

bright: 새파랗다 – 파랗다 – (푸르다)– 파르스름하다
   say-phalahta phalahta (phuluta) phalusulum-hata

dark: 시퍼렇다 – 퍼렇다 – (푸르다)– 푸르스름하다
   si-phelehta phelehta (phuluta) phulusulum-hata

['black']

bright: 새카맣다–새까맣다–까맣다–가맣다–(감다)–가무스름하다
   say-khamahta say-kkamahta kkamahta kamahta (kamta) kamusulum-hata

dark: 시커멓다-시꺼멓다-꺼멓다-거멓다-검다-거무스름하다
si-khemehta si-kkemehta kkemehta kemehta kemta kemusu-
lum-hata

4.4 Loanwords

The vocabulary of Korean contains many loanwords. Before the nineteenth century, these borrowings came principally from Chinese, and the massive stock of Sinitic words and morphemes imported during traditional times is still very much a part of the language. Though basic vocabulary remains predominantly native Korean, in sheer quantity, Sino-Korean elements comprise the major part of the lexicon. Many words of Japanese origin were also used in Korean during the modernization period, from the late 1800s through the first half of the twentieth century. But in recent years, virtually all imports are from Western languages and, these days, overwhelmingly from English.

4.4.1 How Words Are Borrowed

Words borrowed into Korean take the shape of nouns. Verbs and adjectives in the language have distinctive inflecting shapes and, so far as is known, are all of native origin. A borrowed word cannot have one of those inflecting shapes, so if a borrowing is to be used as a verb or adjective, it must be followed by a special derivational suffix, the most common of which is etymologically to be identified with *hata* 'do/be'. For example, the Sino-Korean word *cenghwak* 'accuracy, precision' becomes *cenghwak-hata* 'be accurate, precise'; *kum-hata* 'forbid, prohibit'. Modern loans follow the same pattern: *sumaathu-hata* 'be smart, stylish'; *cemphu-hata* 'to jump'. Other morphological treatment is also possible. For example, some Sino-Korean roots are followed by *-sulepta* 'is like, seems' or *-lopta* 'is (characterized) by': *poksulepta* 'is happy-looking'; *hāy-lopta* 'is harmful'. Sino-Korean morphemes may function as adverbs with adverb-deriving suffixes such as *-i*, *-hi*, and *-lo:* for example, *chin-hi* 'intimately'; *il.il-i* 'one by one'; *cinsil-lo* 'truly, really'. No matter what the word may have been or what syntactic function it may have had in the original language, once it is borrowed into Korean, it must fit into these native rules of word formation.

As do speakers of other languages, Koreans try to approximate the sounds of the original language when borrowing words. But some foreign sounds cannot be accommodated easily within the Korean sound system. For example, Korean has no voiced consonants such as *b*, *d*, *g*, or *j* at the beginning of a word. Thus, the English 'bus' becomes *pesu* (or, colloquially, *ppesu*); 'date' is *teithu;* 'golf' is *kolphu;* 'gossip' is *kasip*. Occasionally, in some contact loans from English, voiced initials will be approximated by reinforced consonants; for example, (colloquially) *ppesu* 'bus'; *ppayk* (from English 'back') 'connections'; *ttaym* 'dam'; *kkem* '(chewing) gum'; *ccaym* 'jam'. To the ear of an English speaker, these reinforced consonants sound closer to the sounds being imitated, because they have no aspiration, and the voice onset time is the closest of all the consonant types to zero. In any event, the third series of consonants, the (heavy) aspirates, are reserved for representing (among other things) English *p, t, k*, and *ch;* for example, *phaiphu* 'pipe'; *phica* 'pizza'; *phathi* 'party'; *thail* 'tile'; *thengsuthen* 'tungsten'; *khoma* 'coma'; *khangkalwu* 'kangaroo'; *khemphyuthe* 'computer'; *chyokholeys* 'chocolate'; *chip* 'chip'. English *z* causes special problems since Korean does not have a voiced dental fricative, even in medial position. As a result, Koreans hear the English sound as closest to their own palatal affricate *c: cwūm-leyncu* 'zoom lens'; *ceylo* 'zero'; *leyice* 'laser'; *ciku-cayku* 'zig-zag'.

English labiodentals (*f* and *v*) and dental fricatives (written *th*) are also especially troublesome. Since Korean has nothing pronounced that way, *f* and *v* are usually approximated in Korean with bilabial stops, *ph* or *p*. Thus, 'foul' is *phawul;* and 'violin' is *paiollin*. Such Korean words are pronounced very differently from the English originals. Some more examples: *phawunteyisyen* [pʰaundeyʃɔn] 'foundation'; *phailling sisuthim* 'filing system'; *phaysyen* 'fashion'; *phayn* 'fan' (also, 'pan'); *pholwum* 'forum'; *phom* 'form'; *phinlantu* 'Finland'; *pailesu* 'virus'; *pakhangsu* 'vacation' (from French *vacances*); *pathikhan* 'Vatican'; *peythukhong* 'Viet-cong'; *peylpeythu* 'velvet'; *pinesu* 'Venus'. English *th* is in most cases rendered as *s* in Korean; for example, *sulil* 'thrill'; *heylsu khulep* 'health club'. But there are also other outcomes. English "thank you" sometimes finds its way into Korean conversations, where it is variously pronounced *ttayngkhyu* or *ssayngkhyu*.

Other English pronunciations that are difficult to accommodate are *l-* and *r-*. Native Korean words do not begin with a liquid, and as a result some early loans such as *nampho* '(kerosene) lamp' show a completely different sound in place of the *l-* in the original language (in this case, Dutch). The situation today is quite different of course, for there are many modern loans that begin with *l-*. Still, given the Korean sound system, there is no way of distinguishing between an initial *l* and an initial *r: laithe* 'lighter', *laymphu* 'lamp', *latio* 'radio', and *lokheys* 'rocket'.

Voicing distinctions at the end of a word are leveled; for example, 'bag' and 'back' are both pronounced *payk*. The ending consonant in such Korean words is an unreleased stop. An extra vowel is always added when the word to be borrowed ends in an affricate or fricative; for example, *khwicu* 'quiz', *phaysu* 'pass', and *sukhaphu* 'scarf'. The added vowel in almost all such cases is the minimal vowel *u*. The principal exceptions are after palatalized affricates, *c* and *ch*, when these consonants are used to represent English *j* (usually written with the letter *g*) or *ch*. In such cases the added vowel is usually an *i: pheyici* 'page'; *sukheychi* 'sketch'. (Note, however, that if the consonant is intended to represent English *ts*, the vowel is, again, *u: suphōchu* 'sports'.) When the English sound to be approximated is *sh*, the parasitic vowel can also be *i : saysi* 'sash'; *hulasi* 'flash'; *pangkullateysi* 'Bangladesh'.

Modern Korean does not have consonant clusters at the beginning of a word,[8] and clusters in other positions are relatively restricted as well. This means that in loans from English words with clusters, Koreans must insert extra vowels between the consonants so that they may be pronounced: *khullep(u)* 'club'; *misuthe* 'mister, Mr.'; *sukhulin* 'screen'; *suphenci* 'sponge'; *suthulaikhu* 'strike'.

4.4.2 Loans Past and Present

Koreans borrow principally from English these days, but, as we have said, most borrowing in the past came from Chinese. From very early on, cultural borrowings flowed from China into the Korean peninsula, accelerating in tempo as time went on. What undoubtedly began as contact borrowing gave way to the systematic importation of Sinitic vocabulary through the use of Literary Chinese writing and Chinese characters. Almost all borrowing from then on was modeled not on sounds per se, but rather on the phonological system that obtained in literary texts. In the strictest sense, then, these Sino-Korean morphemes were not loanwords at all, any more than the Latinate vocabulary in English is. They were literary elements that came out of the systematic study of texts.

The assimilation of Literary Chinese elements reached a significant level of refinement during the Unified Silla period. In A.D. 757 King Kyŏngdŏk issued an order that all place names in the land be given unified, Chinese-style readings. Until that time Chinese characters were read in a variety of ways, including as native Korean words (cf. 2.6.1, above). From what is preserved from before 757, it appears that the use and reading of Chinese characters in ancient Korea was much like that of Japan in those days—and considering the fact that many teachers of Literary Chinese in ancient Japan came from the Korean peninsula, it is reasonable that there should be such parallels. But King Kyŏngdŏk changed all that. Intimations of the ancient variety in Korean readings of Chinese characters are preserved in records of early place names. There are also a few relics of such unofficial usages of Chinese characters preserved today in the modern language. For example, the Copper Sparrow Ferry Crossing across the Han River into the city of Seoul has always been written with the Chinese characters 銅雀津址, which, if given standard readings, would be pronounced *Tongcak Cinci;* but people who live in the area read the name *Tongcayki Nalwu-the,* giving the characters for 'ferry crossing' (a compound which had never been used in China anyway) a native reading.[9] The wild and beautiful Mun'gyŏng Saejae, a mountainous area in North Kyŏngsang much celebrated in Korean song and verse, is often written with the characters 聞慶鳥嶺 and the last two of these characters read *hun*-style as the native morphemes for 'bird' and 'ridge'. Here and there, in out of the way places, there seem always to have been such informal readings of Chinese characters. But for the most part the pre-Kyŏngdŏk readings have been lost. From the time of King Kyŏngdŏk's reign down to the present day, the Korean readings of Chinese characters have been of a piece, unified, with regular correspondences to the system reflected in the ancient Chinese rhyme tables.

Still, there are also Chinese loanwords not associated with Chinese characters at all. The two most often cited examples of such loans are the words *pus* (< *pwut*) '(writing) brush' and *mek* 'ink (stick)'. These two words are considered native vocabulary and always written in Hangŭl. They are never linked to the characters 筆 (*phil*) and 墨 (*muk*) used to write the Chinese words. Other such early Chinese loanwords include *ca* 'ruler, measure'; *ce* 'flute'; *yo* 'mattress, futon'; and *po* 'cloth cover'. Later contact loans from Chinese include *popay* 'treasure', *thangken* 'a kind of horsehair skullcap', *no(kkun)* 'string, cord', *pitan* 'silk', *mumyeng* 'cotton cloth', *tahong* 'bright red(ness)', *thosi* 'tapered muffs worn like sleeves under the coat', *sangthwu* 'topknot', and many more.[10] Food terms such as *paychwu* '(Chinese) cabbage, bok choy' and *sangchwu* 'lettuce, endive' have Chinese sources,[11] as do *kaci* 'eggplant' and *kochwu* 'chili pepper'. *Sathang* 'sugar, candy' is from Chinese. *Pintay-ttek,* the flat Korean-style pancake made from mung beans, has a name that seems to mean 'bedbug cakes', but that is a folk etymology. From a work written in the sixteenth century we know that *pintay-* in this form did not originally mean 'bedbug' but was rather a borrowing of a Chinese word for 'cake'. Even *kimchi,* the Korean national dish (which used to be pronounced *timchoy*), is a native-sounding word made up from Chinese morphemes meaning 'steeped greens'.[12] The original Korean word for pickled vegetables, now usually found in compounds such as *oici* 'pickled cucumbers' or *cangacci* 'vegetables preserved in soy sauce', is *ci* (< *tihi*).[13]

Many more Chinese loanwords, of various kinds, are suspected to be lurking in native-seeming vocabulary. One conspicuous example of a suspected borrowing is the Korean word for Buddhist temple, *cel* (< *tyel*). By its very nature, this word is almost certain to be a loanword, most likely from Chinese, but the precise Chinese source is far from obvious.[14] Another example is the colloquial, often derogatory, word for 'Buddhist priest', *cwung.* (The term is considered impolite and avoided by Buddhists.) In the case of this word, the borrowing is also nativized because it apparently represents a nonstandard meaning assigned to the character 衆 'multitude, crowd'.[15]

Many other such early, native-sounding loans are associated with Buddhism. Buddhist words, which are almost always from Indic sources transmitted through Chinese, include such terms as *miluk* 'Maitreya', *poli* 'bodhi', and *posal* Bodhisattva'. Many of these terms represent character readings unlike those of standard Sino-Korean but have been preserved anyway because they were long ago assimilated into the colloquial language and have come to seem like native words. For example, if the word *miluk* 'Maitreya' (彌勒) were read with the usual Sino-Korean pronunciations, it would be pronounced ˣ*milyek;* similarly, *poli* 'bodhi' (菩提) would be pronounced ˣ*pocey.* The word *cimsung* 'animal, beast, brute' (< *cumsoyng*), is derived from the Buddhist term *cwungsayng* (衆生) 'sentient beings'. The usual word for 'Buddha' itself, *puche,* which in the earliest alphabetic texts (midfifteenth century) was written *pwuthye* (부텨), comes from an early, nonstandard variant of *pultha* (佛陀) 'Buddha'.[16]

Sinitic vocabulary came to have still more importance in Korea during the Koryŏ period. In 958 King Kwangjong established a civil service examination system based upon a Chinese model, and success in passing this examination depended upon detailed mastery of Chinese characters, a near-perfect memory of Confucian writings, and extraordinary skill in Literary Chinese composition. In this way, the examination system ensured that knowledge of Chinese became the measure, the *sine qua non,* of worldly success, a situation that remained in effect until the end of the Chosŏn period in the twentieth century.

Thus, throughout the entire traditional period, Literary Chinese served as the medium of communication not only with China and the rest of the world, but also among intellectuals within the country as well. Such was the importance, and unshakable prestige, of Chinese letters.

Later, during the thirteenth and fourteenth centuries, contact with the conquering Mongol rulers of Yuan dynasty China brought in loanwords from a new source, Mongolian. The principal imports from the Mongols were terms related to the political and social world of these horseback-riding warriors—such as the names of their government positions, types of horses and equestrian terminology, and the vocabulary of falconry. For example, the word *polamay* 'a hawk that is trained for hawking before it is a year old' is a hybrid made up of a borrowing from Middle Mongolian *boro* 'young falcon' and native *may* 'hawk'. Lee Ki-Moon has proposed a quite convincing list of fifty-three such loans from Mongolian.[17] Most of these highly specialized words have long since fallen into disuse, but a few, such as *polamay,* remain in the modern language. The exact, original meaning of *polamay* may not be not known to most modern Koreans (though they probably know that it means a kind of hawk), but it has retained its usefulness because the ROK air force has adopted it as a term used to refer to fighter pilots. The well-known word *olangkhay* 'barbarians', still retains a meaning close to its original sense, which is '(Manchurian) aborigines who lived north of the Tumen River; northern barbarians'.

A few loanwords from Jurchen, a northern language thought to be ancestral to Manchu, date from roughly the same period. These words marginally survive in some of the place names of Hamgyŏng Province, the northeastern part of the peninsula where the people who spoke this language lived until well into the fifteenth century. The name of the Tumen River (*Twuman-kang,* 豆滿江) flowing along Korea's northeastern border comes from the Jurchen word *tuman* 'ten thousand' (the river springs from many sources). Most such modern connections to Jurchen words are relatively tenuous. Chongsŏng, a town on the right bank of the Tumen, has a name written with characters that mean 'Bell City.' The gazetteer of the *Sejong sillok* records that the old name of this town was *Tongken* (童巾), then explains: "The northern barbarians call a bell a *"tongken"*; the prefecture [where the city is] is the location of [what is called] '*Tongken* Mountain'." In the Jurchen language *tungken* meant 'bell' or 'drum'.[18] In addition to place names, there are also a tiny number of possible cultural loans from Jurchen. The word *misi(s-kalwu)* '(powder of) roasted rice or barley (used for making a kind of tea)' is thought by many to be a loan from Manchu, but philological evidence is better that it is from the earlier Jurchen word *mušin*.[19]

At the beginning of the Qing period (1644-1911), when Manchus ruled Korea as well as China, Koreans had more significant contact with the Manchu language. Most of the words imported at that time were cultural loans that fell into disuse when the objects themselves stopped being used. *Nelkhwu*, taken from Manchu *nereku*, was the name of a kind of cape or coat used as rainwear; but since this type of raincoat has not been used for a very long time, no one today remembers the word for it. *Kamthwu* was the name of a kind of horsehair hat worn by officials during the late Chosŏn period; it was taken from the Manchu word for it, *kamtu*. Other Manchu words are remembered only in dialects. In North P'yŏngan and North Hamgyŏng, and in some southern regions with significant snowfalls, people still use a kind of horsedrawn sled known as (variously) *palkwi*, *palkwu*, or *palki*. These dialect words are variants of a very old borrowing from the Manchu word for the sled, *fara* (< *pāra*). In the same dialects, the word for a winter coat is *khwulwumayki*, *khwulwumay*, or *khwulimay*. These forms are taken from Manchu *kurume*. A much better known suspected loan is *swuswu* 'millet'; 'sorghum'.[20] The earlier Korean pronunciation of this word was *syusyu*, which is said to be from Manchu *šušu*, which in turn was taken from the Chinese word for 'sorghum', *shǔshǔ* (蜀黍 —these characters are read *chokse* in Sino-Korean).

It was during this same Qing period that Western ideas and objects first began to flow into Korea through China. Words for imported concepts had been either recently coined or calqued in China, or new meanings extended from older Chinese words. The vocabulary of Christianity was part and parcel of this process, and words such as *sengkyeng* 'Bible', *chencwu* 'the Lord of Heaven, God', *pok.um* 'the (Christian) gospel', and *sengmo* 'the Holy Mother' reached Korea during the seventeenth and eighteenth centuries. Christianity brought along other kinds of vocabulary as well. Among other things, Koreans had had no concept of a seven-day week until that time, and so the word *cwuil* 'week' also dates from that period. New technology, both high and low, produced new vocabulary such as *camyengcong* 'alarm clock' (with characters meaning 'self-sounding-bell') and *chenlikyeng* 'telescope' ('thousand-mile-mirror').

The situation vis-à-vis Japan was quite different. Linguistic evidence of contact during late traditional times is scanty, and very few examples of loanwords from Qing times have been authenticated. One clear exception is the word for tobacco. This New World plant had been introduced into southern Korean from Kyushu, and the name the Koreans associated with tobacco was the Japanese dialect word *tambako*. Koreans cut off the last syllable of the word, added their own nominal suffix *-i* (> *-y*), and created the form *tampay,* which is today the universal Korean word for 'cigarettes, tobacco'.

In the late nineteenth century, however, the political situation rapidly changed, and Japan began to eclipse China as the major source of new vocabulary. From that point until the end of World War II, the Japanese language remained a powerful influence on Korean. Though more important than is ordinarily recognized today, the resulting impact that Japanese had on the Korean lexicon was much less than that of Chinese. It was also borrowing of a different kind. Whereas the classical Chinese language had always been considered the framework and the source of Korea's own classical traditional, Japanese, particularly after the annexation of Korea by imperial Japan in 1910, was the language of the oppressor, necessary for social and economic survival but deeply resented all the while.

The Japanese language and even Japanese linguistic science in some cases became the tools of imperial policy. In 1910, in what was purported to be a scientific study, the famous and respected linguist Kanazawa Shōzaburō reached the conclusion that Korean was no more than a "dialect" of Japanese, like Ryukyuan. From a linguistic point of view, Kanazawa's conclusion was odd even by the standards of the day, but it fit the political spirit of the times and helped to pave the way for the kind of standardization policy in Korea that the Japanese government had been pursuing in the home islands. In the succeeding years under Japanese admininistration, schools in Korea stressed, along with vocational training, the teaching of the Japanese language as a vehicle for assimilating Korea into the empire. Finally, toward the end of the Pacific War, Japanese authorities initiated a policy aimed at the complete eradication of Korean culture—the infamous *munhwa malsal chŏngch'aek.* Under this policy, the teaching of Korean was terminated, and only Japanese was allowed to be spoken or written in the schools or used in any official or semi-official way. Although serious Japanese linguists such as Ogura Shinpei and Kōno Rokurō continued their research on the Korean language, the Japanese government itself pursued a heavyhanded policy aimed at suppressing the language. Korean linguists and language scholars were considered revolutionary secessionists, and many were arrested and thrown in jail, sometimes to die there, for nothing more serious than compiling a Korean-language dictionary.

Considered against this historical backdrop, it is understandable why Korean governments both North and South, as well as the majority of their citizenry, have in the postcolonial period tended to view Japanese loans as distasteful symbols of Japanese oppression and have tried to eliminate as many of them from the language as possible. The end of World War II ended the Japanese presence and many words associated with it.

Japanese institutions, especially of the symbolic kind, were among the first things to go. Shinto shrines, such as the imposing edifices that sat atop Namsan mountain overlooking the city of Seoul, were razed, and the word for these shrines, *jinja,* was Koreanized with Sino-Korean readings to *sinsa.*

In this way Koreans were relieved of the need to articulate the word even when talking about Japan. One of the most vivid memories one of us has from that period is that, immediately upon liberation from Japanese rule, groups of local citizens spontaneously rose up and chopped down the cherry trees that had been planted in front of his elementary school.[21] The flowering cherry was (and still is) of course the symbol of Japan, and during the Japanese period it was called by the Japanese name *sakura*, even though the tree grew natively and was much loved by the Korean people. After the restoration of independence, those flowering cherries that had not been symbolically cut down were called by their native name again, *pecnamu*, or *peckkoch*. *Karate* was an especially offensive word because it was associated with the Japanese military and police, and so, in the late 1950s or early 1960s, both fighting style and the word for it were replaced by the native equivalent, *thayqkwento* 'taekwondo'.

Japanese personal names and surnames, which Koreans had been obliged to adopt under Japanese rule,[22] were cast off immediately. Place names went back to their old Sino-Korean readings again, and *Fuzan* became *Pusan*, *Taikyū* changed back to *Taegu*, *Heiyō* became *P'yŏngyang*. Gone also was the Japanese name of the Korean capital *Keijō*, as well as the Koreanized pronunciation of that name, Kyengseng, as the city regained its original, completely native name of *Seoul*. Many Koreans even extended this renaming practice to Japan itself, preferring to treat Japanese place names as Sino-Korean; thus *Tokyo* became *Tongkyeng*, *Kyoto Kyengto*, and the like.

Many objects of Japanese culture that had seeped into and blended with modern Korean life were renamed, some immediately, others more gradually. Tatami mats, for example, had by the end of the Japanese period become part of the architecture of many Korean houses, and even today, neighborhood craftsmen make the mats, and people have them fitted into their houses and apartments. Koreans kept the mats but have the option of removing the Japanese flavor of the word *tatami* by substituting a native Korean coinage, *tosciph-cali*. The Japanese cushion for sitting on the floor is still sometimes referred to by the name *caputong*, but now Koreans increasingly use *pangsek* instead. The Japanese loan *cupong* 'trousers' coexists alongside native Korean *paci*—which, ironically, is a word that in the eighteenth century had been borrowed from Korean into Japanese.[23] A much-loved card game in Korea is *hwathwu*, a renamed version of Japanese *hanafuda*. The Japanese-style box lunch known as *bentō* was and is much favored by Koreans. But since liberation it has been called by another name, *pyentho* at first (with the first character pronounced as Sino-Korean!), then later, today, by the native word *tosilak*. Strangely enough, Koreanized Chinese restaurants habitually serve as a side dish *takkwang* '(Japanese) takuan pickled radish', which, in recent years, young people have taken to calling *tanmuci* (cf. remarks above on -*ci* as the original Korean word for *kimchi*). No longer is *yakki-mantwu* served in Chinese restaurants in Korea, since *yakki-* 'fried' was originally borrowed as a prefix from Japanese; for some time now, the word for those Chinese-style pot-stickers is *kwun-mantwu,* using the native prefix for 'fried', *kwun-. Waribashi,* the attached pair of wooden chopsticks made to be split and then used once, are standard fare in many Korean restaurants, but the usual term for these chopsticks these days is just *namu-ceskalak* 'wooden chopsticks'. Western-style beer, now *biiru* in Japan, was earlier in the century *mugishu,* (literally) 'barley liquor'; Koreans read the characters as Sino-Korean and called beer *maykcwu,* which is still the Korean word for this popular drink. OB, Koreans' favorite brand of beer, is named for the "Oriental Brewery," which branched off from the company that made Asahi beer during the Japanese period; the second most popular postwar brand was *Khulawun* ("Crown"), which was "Kirin" renamed. Japanese-style sake is *cengcong* in Korean, which is the Korean reading of the Chinese characters used to write the Japanese brand name, *(Kiku)masamune.* The old-fashioned coils burned like incense as a mosquito repellent were until recently *katoli-seynkko,* but now they are known simply as *moki-hyang* 'mosquito incense'.

The names of Western objects and concepts introduced during the Japanese period were treated similarly. Clocks and watches are *tokei* in Japanese; Koreans gave the Chinese characters with which the word was written Korean readings and they became *sikyey.* At the supermarket, a middle-aged shopper might ask for *tamaneyki,* from the Japanese compound meaning 'bulb scallions', but the sign over the onions will list them as *yangpha,* a word composed of Sino-Korean *yang-* 'Western' plus the native Korean word for 'scallions', *pha.* Fingernail clippers are *cumeykkili* (from *tsumekiri*) by older Koreans; their children use only the Korean calque, *sonthop-kkakk.i.* The Japanese-style *cenki-thama* 'light bulb' is more and more often called by the name *cenkwu.* A building located on a street corner was until quite recently called a *katos-cip,* from Japanese *kado* 'corner' plus Korean *cip* 'house'; but a few years ago the South Korean government offered in its place a native calque, *mothwungi-cip,* and no one under a certain age today remembers the older form. As recently as 1996 the word for 'elementary school' was changed from *kwukmin-hakkyo* 'national school' to *chotung-hakkyo* 'first-level school', because the former was the Sino-Korean reading of what had been the Japanese word. The banking term *swuhyeng* 'bill, draft, note' (a Sino-Korean reading of Japanese *tegata*) has now been completely replaced by *eum.* Recent borrowings like *kalaokhey* 'karaoke' (said to be from *kara* 'empty' plus *oke* 'orche(stra)') are so conspicuous they especially invite replacement with calques or new coinages; and, for example, signs on karaoke places advertise them to be *nolay-pang* 'song-rooms'. Relative usage of Japanese loans varies, and their replacement by native words follows a varied pace.

Nevertheless, there are many categories of Japanese loanwords still to be found in Korean, some obvious and direct, but others subtle and cloaked in forms that disguise Japanese as the source. Some obvious Japanese loans include: *kamani* 'straw (rice) bag'; *kapang* 'bag, briefcase'; *kotey* '(curling) iron'; *kwulwuma* 'pushcart, wheelbarrow' (from *kuruma,* the general Japanese word for 'vehicle'); *kwutwu* '(Western) leather shoes'; *nokata* 'construction laborer' (in Japanese, the meaning is 'outside or farm labor'); *sakhatachi* 'headstand'; *soteynasi* 'sleeveless (shirt)'; *swuli* 'pickpocket'; *tamusi* 'ringworm'; *ttayngttayngi* 'polka-dot pattern' (from Japanese *ten-ten* 'dot-dot' plus the Korean nominaling suffix -*i*); *wailo* 'bribe'; *wuwaki* 'jacket, coat'.

There are also grammatical and morphological calques, such as *kunye* 'she', which is patterned on Japanese *kanojo,* and -*ko issta* 'is (do)ing', which is possibly from -*te iru.* (These two Japanese constructions were in turn influenced by English usages.) *Say-chiki* 'cutting in line' is from Japanese *yokodori.*

Somewhat less obvious are Koreanized readings of the Chinese characters used to write the Japanese word: *aymay(-hata)* 'be vague'; *capci* 'magazine'; *hokseng* 'planet' (from *wakusei); h(w)al.in* 'discount' (from Japanese *waribiki*); *hyeycon* "with the compliments of the author" (an inscription in a book); *iltallak* 'stopping place' (from *ichidanraku*); *kkang(thong)* '(metal) can'; *konghay* 'pollution' (from *kōgai*); *maylipci* 'landfill' *(umetatechi); nangman* 'being romantic' (from Japanese *rōman*); *naptuk(-hata)* 'comprehend';*panchangko* 'Band-Aid' (from *bansōkō*); *senkyen ci.myeng* 'ESP' *(senken no mei); siksa(-hata)* 'eat'; *sinmun* 'newspaper'; *sinpun* 'social standing' (from *mibun*); *swuto(s-mul)* 'tap water'; *yuncwungcey* 'encircling dike' (from *wajūtei*). In addition to examples such as the above, there are literally many hundreds of words, constructed out of Chinese morphemes and written with Chinese characters, that were coined in Meiji Japan to accommodate Western words and concepts. This vocabulary of modern life, which for the most part was adopted by all East Asian countries including China, includes such now common terms as 'science', 'physics', 'art', 'philosophy', 'civilization', 'culture', 'folklore', 'communism', 'capitalism', 'stock market', *cohap* 'trade union' *(kumiai),* 'national language', 'subway', 'highway', *tayphyo* 'representative' *(daihyō),* 'telephone', 'electron', *chwiso* 'cancellation' *(torikeshi), thahyep* 'compromise' *(dakyō),* and so on.

Even less conspicuous are loanwords from Japan that the Japanese, in turn, either borrowed from the West or created out of Western roots: *alpaithu* 'part-time student worker' (German *Arbeit*); *apeykhu* 'date' (from French *avec*); *aphathu* 'apartment'; *ppang* 'bread' (Portuguese *pan*); *campa* 'jumper, jacket'; *komu* 'rubber' (from *gomu,* from French *gomme*); *leningsyechu* 'athletic shirt' (from 'running shirt'); *lasa* 'woolen goods' (Portuguese *raxa*); *leyci* 'cashier' (from a Japanese shortening of the English 'register');*matolosu* 'boatman, seaman' (from Dutch *matrous*); *maysu-khem* 'the media' (from 'mass communication'); *ningkeylu* 'I.V.' (from German *Ringer*); *olai* 'all right' (the signal given to a driver backing up that everything is clear); *pakhangsu* 'vacation' (from French *vacance*); *opa* 'overcoat'; *papali* 'trench coat' (from 'Burberry'); *paykmile* 'rearview mirror'; *phama* 'permanent wave'; *ppanchu* '(women's) panties'; *ppangkkwu* '(tire) puncture'; *ppeyncci* 'pliers' (from 'pinchers'); *ppin* 'pin'; *ppoi* 'bellhop' (from 'boy'); *saita* 'cider'; *sayllelimayn* 'salaried worker'; *tasu* 'dozen'; *theyleypi* 'television';

thurengkhu 'trunk, suitcase'; *tolansu* 'transformer'; *tulaipe* '(screw)driver'; *waisyassu* 'dress shirt' (from 'white shirt'). Often these words have been slightly rephoneticized to appear more like English. Adding to this impression that the words have nothing to do with Japan is the fact that most dictionaries list only the ultimate Western sources without mentioning the role of Japanese as intermediary.

In addition to loans known to the general public, there are many sets of complex and specialized terminology used in various Korean professions. The fashion industry and tailoring, for example, would have great difficulty functioning without using words assimilated during the Japanese period. Much the same is true of the manufacturing industry, architecture, and printing, and of professions such as barbering and hairdressing. But Japanese influence is seen not only in business modes that took shape in the first half of the twentieth century. The modern entertainment industry, for example, including television, continues to borrow terminology from Japan. Most such professions that use jargon borrowed from Japanese have at various times entertained proposals for lexical reform; on occasion, lists of native terms suggested as replacements have been distributed to their memberships. But to date most of these attempts at reform have not met with great success.

Today, like much of the rest of the world, South Korea is awash in a world culture dominated by English, particularly American English, and most of the new words from English are taken in by imitating the original sounds. Seldom are loans translated, or calqued, into native roots along the lines used in China, for example. Whereas the term the Chinese have coined for "computer software" is composed of native morphemes that mean, roughly, 'electric-brain soft-article' (*diànnǎo ruǎnjiàn*), Koreans use the culturally unbuffered term *khemphyuthe sophuthuwey.e*.

Through such unmitigated borrowing from a uniform source, the Korean language is being affected today by English, as it was in the past by Literary Chinese; as a result, the Korean lexicon now contains three distinct layers of vocabulary: native, Sino-Korean, and English. These three layers give Korean, in some cases, three nearly synonymous words or expressions for what amounts to the same concept. For example, the following words are distinguished in meaning, but in ways principally dictated by usage and context:

	Native	Sino-Korean	English loan
'skill'	caycwu 재주	kiswul 기술	theykhunik 테크닉 ("technique")
'meeting'	moim 모임	hoyhap 회합	mithing 미팅
'to cut'	caluta 자르다	celtan-hata 절단하다	khethu-hata 커트하다

In most cases, however, the newer layers of vocabulary have caused the older words to fall into disuse or to change in meaning. *Mey* (< *moy*), the native word for 'mountain', refers today only to the traditional Korean grave made in the shape of a mound; in the general meaning of 'mountain' it has been displaced by the Sinitic word *san*. Native *kyeycip* 'woman, girl, female' sounds disparaging and vulgar (*kyeycip-cil* means 'womanizing' or 'whoring') alongside the polite, more general Sino-Korean word *yeca*. But what was once the polite Sino-Korean address form *-yang* 'Miss', as in *Kim-yang* 'Miss Kim', has in Korean workplace usage completely given way, both lexically and syntactically, to the English term of address *Misu (Kim)*; the term *Kim-yang* today sounds hopelessly quaint and old-fashioned. The (relatively) new word *hotheyl* 'hotel' has caused the Sino-Korean word *yekwan* 'hostel, inn' to take on, in most cases, implications of cheap accommodations and outmoded facilities.

4.4.3 Sino-Korean

The Korean word for 'loanword' is *oylay-e*, while the word for 'Sino-Korean' is *Hanqca-e*. For Koreans, the two are totally different concepts. Sino-Korean words do not have the same feel of foreignness about them that modern, Western loans do. Sino-Korean morphemes combine freely with native morphemes; they are fully assimilated into the language.

One reason for this difference is the special nature of Sino-Korean vocabulary, which we have already remarked on several times (cf. 2.6, above). Sino-Korean vocabulary is not composed of borrowings in the usual sense of the word but represents, rather, the Korean versions of East Asian literary vocabulary. What is called "Sino-Korean" *(Hanqca-e)* consists of the Korean readings of Chinese characters and the compounds formed from those elements. The Korean pronunciations of Chinese characters are not Korean imitations of sounds heard spoken by Chinese; they derive instead from the system codified in rhyming dictionaries and rhyme tables that then developed along lines unique to the Korean language. The meanings of Sino-Korean elements derive originally from those found in classical Chinese sources as well, but they, too, became assimilated early on into the Korean language and developed along uniquely Korean lines. As we have said, Sino-Korean vocabulary should be considered "loanwords" only to the extent that the Latinate vocabulary and coinages found in English are thought of as loans.

Only about 10 percent of the words classified as basic vocabulary are Chinese in origin.[24] However, in sheer volume, there are more Sino-Korean words in Korean than native vocabulary. The largest Korean dictionary compiled to date, *Uri-mal k'un sajŏn*,[25] is reported to contain among its entries 74,612 words of native origin, 85,527 Sino-Korean words, and 3,986 loanwords. The stock of Sino-Korean words is enormous, far greater in size than that of modern loanwords.

Virtually all the Sino-Korean words in the dictionary are compounds of two monosyllabic, Sinitic morphemes. In rare cases, a word may consist of three morphemes; other morphemes serve as prefixes or suffixes for these two-syllable compounds. But the basic Sino-Korean word unit is two syllables long. The ease with which Koreans have combined and recombined Sino-Korean morphemes into compounds over the years is part of the reason for the proliferation of such words in the lexicon.[26] The morpheme *ho* 'good, liking' (好), which in Korean is not a word by itself, appears in numbers of compounds such as *hokam* 'good impression', *hoki* 'good opportunity', *ho.lyey* 'good example', *hosa* 'happy event', *hoswu* 'good move', *houy* 'good will', *ho.yen* 'good acting', *hoin* 'good person', *hopu* 'good and bad', *hophyeng* 'favorable criticism', *hoo* 'likes and dislikes', *hosayk* 'licentiousness (i.e., liking beauty)'. It is also used as a prefix: *ho-kyengki* 'prosperity (i.e., good business)', *ho-sicel* 'good season'. A word such as *hakkyo* 'school' consists of two morphemes. But in forming compounds related to school things, only one of the two morphemes is used as the combining form. Thus, the resulting secondary compounds are also usually two syllables long. Here are some of the many words formed with *hak-*, the first morpheme of 'school': *haksayng* 'student', *hakkwa* 'school subject', *hakkwu* 'school zone', *hakki* 'school term', *haknyen* 'school year', *haklyek* 'scholarly ability', *haklyeng* 'school age', *hak.wen* 'educational institute', *hakcem* 'academic credit', *panghak* 'school vacation', *thonghak* 'attending school', *thoyhak* 'leaving school', and so on. And here are some of the words formed with the second morpheme of 'school', *-kyo*: *kyoka* 'school song', *kyoki* 'school banner', *kyopok* 'school uniform', *kyochik* 'school regulations', *kyocang* 'school principal', *kyohun* 'school precepts'. Most Sino-Korean morphemes can appear initially or finally in a compound. They do not change in shape; there are almost no morphological rules that apply. Word formation is simple and relatively unrestricted.

Compounding with native Korean morphemes is much less utilized. Compared to Sino-Korean compounds, which are usually concise and simple, complex concepts expressed as native terms tend toward longer, morphologically complex phrases. For example, *paywum-the*, used in some circles as a native equivalent of *hakkyo* 'school', is composed of the verb stem *paywu-* 'learn', plus the nominal suffix *-m*, plus the suffixation of the noun *-the* 'place'. In recent decades, in the nativist spirit of Ch'oe Hyŏnbae, many neologisms made up of native roots have been suggested for Sino-Korean terms, but the complexities of word formation have proved a difficult hurdle to overcome. Some of the creations, especially early ones coined by Ch'oe himself, are needlessly cumbersome. Still remembered as particularly outrageous are Ch'oe's prim euphemisms for *ppanchu* 'panties' and *pulaca* 'brassiere': *uttum-kalikey* 'the first-place concealer' and *pekum-kalikey* 'the second-place concealer'. Even so, one sees today, especially in public spaces, an ever-increasing number of creations out of native roots. In the Seoul subway system, what one finds written on signs instead of the compact Sino-Korean word *chulkwu* 'exit' is *nakanun kos*, literally, 'the going-out place'. *Tulekanun kos* 'the going-in place' has similarly replaced *ipkwu* 'entrance'.[27]

References

Ch'ae Wan 1983, 1986; Kang Sinhang 1985, 1991; Kim Ch'angsŏp 1981; Kim Kwanghae 1989; Kim Wanjin 1970; Kim Yŏngsŏk and Yi Sangŏk (Lee Sang Oak) 1992; Miller 1967; Nam Kisim (Nam Ki Shim) and Ko Yŏnggŭn 1985; Nam P'unghyŏn 1985; No Myŏnghŭi 1990; Sim Chaegi 1982, 1987; Sŏ Chaegŭk 1970; Song Ch'ŏrŭi 1992; Yi Hŭisŭng 1955; Yi Iksŏp (Lee Iksop) 1968, 1982, 1986; Yi Iksŏp (Lee Iksop) and Im Hongbin 1983; Yi Kimun (Lee Ki-Moon) 1991a, 1991b; Yi Sŏkchu 1989.

5

Phrase Structure

Korean is known as an "agglutinative language." This typological classification is primarily based upon the fact that verbs and adjectives are conjugated by affixing, or sticking on, endings. The stems of Korean verbs and adjectives, regardless of their syntactic position, require endings, and the addition of these endings determines the grammatical function and meaning of the resulting word. This kind of structure is typical of an agglutinating language. At the same time, however, Korean is also a language in which various particles are used as postpositions for nouns. This combining of particles with nouns is very similar to the conjugation of verbs and adjectives by adding endings. The difference is that verb and adjective stems cannot stand alone, and to function in a sentence, they must necessarily be combined with endings. In contrast, nouns appear in isolation; it is not necessary that they be followed by particles. Even so, from the standpoint of general linguistic typology, this addition of particles can be considered a form of agglutination. In word formation there is clearly a structural resemblance between the use of particles and the use of inflectional endings. In preceding chapters we have often tied the two processes together; in this chapter we will continue to do so. We will begin our discussion of Korean grammar by describing particles and endings and how they are used.

5.1 Particles

The principal function of most particles is to express the syntactic role of the noun or noun phrase to which they are attached. Such particles are ordinarily called "case particles" (격조사) by Korean linguists. In addition, however, there are grammatical elements called "special particles" (특수조사) that have nothing to do with expressing case and, instead, are used only to add to the meaning—they are used for emphasis and focus. Still other particles are similar to, and difficult to distinguish from, nouns and nounlike suffixes; some verbal constructions also resemble particles. These special particles and related constructions will be discussed separately, in section 5.1.2. Here, however, unless specifically stated otherwise, the term "particle" should be taken to mean case particle.

Case particles resemble in many ways the declension endings of Western languages such as German or Latin. Like declension endings, particles cannot be used in isolation and appear in sentences combined with nouns. They do not qualify as independent words. But a Korean particle is separable from the noun in a way that a declension ending is not. The noun to which a case particle would normally be attached can also be used in a sentence without the particle—that is, the particle can be omitted. Therefore, the noun does not depend on the particle for its status as a word. It can stand by itself as an independent word in the sentence. In contrast, the declension endings of Indo-European languages are integral and inseparable parts of the noun. A noun in German or Latin does not appear in the language without being marked for case; in contrast, a Korean noun quite normally and regularly does. Korean particles and Indo-European declension endings are fundamentally different in this respect.

Another important difference is that in Korean, these same basic case particles are not only suffixed to nouns; they are also used in constructions with other types of words and phrases for a variety of purposes besides case marking. In (1), below, the particle *i/ka* marks the "nominative case"—that is, it is used to show that the noun is the subject of the sentence. But in (2) the same particle is not being used to mark a case; instead, it follows the inflectional ending in a negative construction, where, according to some researchers, it functions to emphasize the adjective being negated.[1] In (3), the "accusative marker," *(l)ul,* functions primarily to mark with emphasis the preceding clause as the object of the verb 'to think.' The complexity of usages like these is beyond the scope of the present discussion.[2]

(1) 장미꽃이 아름답다.
Cangmi-kkoch *i* alumtapta.
rose-flower-*i*
'The roses [subject] are beautiful.'

(2) 장미꽃이 예쁘지가 않다.
Cangmi-kkoch i yeyppuci *ka* anhta.
pretty-*ci-ka*
'The roses are not pretty.'

(3) 무슨 꽃이 가장 아름다운가를 생각해 보아라.
Musun kkoch i kacang alumtawun ka lul sayngkak-hay poala.
beautiful-*ka-lul*
'Think about which flowers are the most beautiful.'

As was mentioned above, case particles may also be omitted. Ordinarily, case relationships are marked in Korean by postposed particles, especially in cases where abiguity would otherwise arise. But there are times when morphological marking is not necessary, and word order or semantic content alone is sufficient to mark these relationships. In (5), below, the meaning of the sentence is clear without case particles. But the same is not

true in (6) and (7). In these latter examples, there are a number of noun
phrases with several possible interpretations, and it is impossible to determine by word order alone how they are related in the sentence. Their relationships must be clarified with particles. As can be seen in (6), when the
nominative, genitive, and accusative cases appear in the same sentence, it is
natural to leave out all but one of the three particles, and, of the three, the
one most naturally used in such cases is the nominative particle. Also, if only
the accusative case were to be marked, as in (6d), the meaning would be understood to be a long, complex phrase modifying 'book': X 가 순이의 동생
의 책을 읽는다 *X ka Swuni uy tongsayng uy chayk ul ilknunta* '(Some unspecified person) is reading Swuni's (younger) sibling's book'. Such an interpretation would not be the meaning intended for the sentence.

(5) a. 영이가 학교에 간다.
      Yengi *ka* hakkyo *ey* kanta
      'Yŏngi *[nom.]* is going to school *[locative]*.'
   b. 영이 학교 간다.
      Yengi hakkyo kanta
      'id. [but more casual]'

(6) a. 순이의 동생이 책을 읽는다.
      Swuni *uy* tongsayng *i* chayk *ul* ilknunta.
      'Suni's *[gen.]* sister *[nom.]* is reading a book *[acc.]*.'
   b. ?순이의 동생 책 읽는다.
      ?Swuni *uy* tongsayng chayk ilknunta.
   c. 순이 동생이 책 읽는다.
      Swuni tongsayng *i* chayk ilknunta.
      'Suni's sister *[nom.]* is reading a book.'
   d. ˣ순이 동생 책을 읽는다.
      ˣSwuni tongsayng chayk *ul* ilknunta.
                    book *[acc.]*

(7) a. 목수가 助手와 나무로 책상을 만든다.
      Mokswu *ka* coswu *wa* namu *lo* chayksang *ul* mantunta.
      'The carpenter *[nom.]* along with the helper *[comitative]* is making a
      table *[acc.]* out of wood *[instrumental]*.'
   b. ˣˣ목수 조수 나무 책상 만든다.
      ˣˣMokswu coswu namu chayksang mantunta.
      [ungrammatical with no case particles marking the nouns]

Marking noun phrases with all the case particles is the rule in the written language, where not doing so would be considered a serious lapse in
style. The omission of particles is generally confined to the colloquial, spoken language and usually to cases where the sentences are short. The particles most frequently omitted without causing ambiguity are the particles

that mark the nominative, accusative, and genitive cases: *i/ka*, *(l)ul*, and *uy*. But, given the right context, it is also possible to leave out other particles as well.[3] Of course, deletion is not possible in every case, and the context must in any event be right for it to happen, but Korean case particles are considerably more subject to ellipsis than their counterparts are in Japanese. The much ballyhooed structural resemblance between Korean and Japanese breaks down somewhat at this point.

(8) Korean: a. 그것은 개한테 주고, 이것은 사람이 먹어.
          Kukes un kay *hanthey* cwuko, ikes un salam i mek.e.
          'That (you) give to the dogs *[locative]*, this, people eat.'
      b. 그것은 개 주고, 이것은 사람이 먹어.
          Kukes un kay cwuko, ikes un salam i mek.e.
          'That (you) give (to) the dogs, this, people eat.'

(9)   Japanese: ?Sore wa inu yatte, kore wa hito ga taberu.
           ('id.') [not grammatical without the locative particle]

In particle ellipsis, syntactic and semantic structures and pragmatic factors interact with the inflectional elements in complex ways. As a result, the conditions for ellipsis vary according to which case marker is to be elided. Moreover, the basic meaning may remain the same with or without the particle, but the presence or absence of the particle changes the stylistic nuance. In cases such as (10), where the context is clear without the particle, the use of the particle adds emphasis to the noun phrase. In the two suggested responses (*a* and *b*), Speaker B adds a case particle to focus attention on what it is that she is asking about. In the first, *(a)*, she verifies what it was that was said to have been broken by adding the accusative marker *ul;* in *(b)*, she shows her concern not for the broken cup but for the well-being of Suni; she asks about Suni and places stress on her as the subject by using the nominative marker *ka*.

(10) Speaker A: 엄마, 순이 유리컵 깼어요.
          Emma, Swuni yuli-khep kkayss.e yo. [no case particles]
          'Mama, Suni broke the glass cup.'

    Speaker B: a. 유리컵을 깼다고? 그 예쁜 컵을?
          Yuli-khep *ul* kkayss.tako? Ku yeyppun khep *ul?*
          'Broke the glass cup *[acc.]*, you say? That pretty cup *[acc.]*?'
      b. 순이가 (유리컵 깼다고)? 어디 다치지는 않았니?
          Swuni *ka* (yuli-khep kkaysstako)? Eti tachici nun
          anh.ass.ni?
          'Suni *[nom.]* (broke the glass cup, you say)? Did (she) get
          hurt?'

Martin (1992:195-96) lists forty-four "particles proper." By "particles proper" Martin means the basic particles that could not be analyzed as an extended usage of some other part of speech. In what follows, we will examine the most common and important of these particles proper. First, let us look at some of the characteristics of the case particles: the markers of the nominative, accusative, genitive, locative, instrumental, comitative, and vocative cases.

5.1.1 Case Particles

5.1.1.1 Nominative Case Particles

The particles marking the nominative case in Korean are *i/ka* and *kkeyse*. The shape of the particle *i/ka* is determined phonologically. Following a vowel, the particle is *ka;* and following a consonant, the particle is *i*. The honorific particle *kkeyse* substitutes for *i/ka* following a noun representing an esteemed and honored person.

(1) 비가 온다.
Pi *ka* onta.
'It's raining.' [Lit. 'rain *[-ka]* is coming.']

(2) 바람이 시원하다.
Palam *i* siwen-hata.
'The wind *[-i]* is (refreshingly) cool.'

(3) 할아버지께서 오랫만에 유쾌하게 웃으신다.
Hal.apeci *kkeyse* olays-man ey yukhway-hakey wus.usinta.
'Grandfather *[-kkayse]* is finally laughing happily.'

Another nominative marker is the particle *eyse*, which can be used to mark an impersonal, collective noun as the subject. But *eyse* is basically a locative marker, and its usage as a nominative case particle must be treated as a special, oblique marking for subjects when they are groups or institutions.

(4) a. 자선 단체에서 고아원에 위문품을 보냈다.
Casen-tanchey *eyse* koawen ey wimun-phum ul ponaysta.
'The charitable institution *[-eyse]* sent gifts to the orphanage.'
b. 국회에서 새 예산안을 만장일치로 통과시켰다.
Kwukhoy *eyse* say yeysan-an ul mancang-ilchi lo thongkwa-sikyessta.
'The National Assembly *[-eyse]* passed the new budget unanimously.'

A noun phrase marked by *i/ka* is not necessarily a subject—at least in the semantically based case grammar preferred by many linguists. For example, in the sentence, *A ka B ka toynta* 'A becomes B', or *A ka B ka anita* 'A is not B', B is not the subject of the verb, but rather a complement.

(5) 김씨 아들이 사장이 되었다.
Kim-ssi atul *i* sacang *i* toy.ess.ta.
'Mr. Kim's son *[-i]* became the company president *[-i]*.'

But even when the predicate does not need a complement, there are times when two noun phrases are marked by the particle *i/ka*. Such sentences are known as "double-subject" constructions:

(6) 목사가 어떻게 재산이 많겠니?
Moksa *ka* ettehkey caysan *i* manhkeyss.ni?
'How can a preacher be rich?'
[Lit., 'preacher *[-ka]* how wealth *[-i]* be much?']

(7) 영희가 얼굴이 참 예쁘구나.
Yenghuy *ka* elkwul *i* cham yeyppukwuna.
'Yŏnghŭi is really pretty.'
[Lit., 'Yŏnghŭi *[-ka]* face *[-i]* really is pretty.']

(8) 한강이 홍수가 가장 자주 난다.
Hankang *i* hongswu *ka* kacang cacwu nanta.
'The Han River floods most often.'
[Lit., 'The Han River *[-i]* a flood *[-ka]* most often happens.']

Double-subject constructions are quite natural and common in Korean. But, contrary to appearances, it is not actually the case that a single predicate has two subjects. Rather, the constructions are examples of a subject-verb or subject-adjective combination functioning as the predicate in a larger sentence. For example, the entire phrase *elkwul i yeypputa*, which literally means 'face is pretty', is the predicate in (7), where it is used in the meaning of '(someone or something) is (face-)pretty'. In (7), in other words, the speaker is not just talking about Yŏnghŭi's face being pretty, but rather about Yŏnghŭi herself. If Yŏnghŭi's face were intended as the subject, the sentence would be, *Yenghuy uy elkwul i yeypputa*, 'Yŏnghŭi's face is pretty'.[4]

(9) 학생이 두 명이 지각했다.
Haksayng *i* twu myeng *i* cikak-hayss.ta.
'Two students were late.'
[Lit., 'Students *[-i]* two-PERSONS *[-i]* were late.']

Number (9) is another example of a double-subject construction, but the structure in this case is somewhat different. Here, the nominative particle attaches to both the noun phrase and the number phrase to lend more emphasis to the number. In this type of construction, the particle in question can also be the accusative marker *(l)ul*; for example, *Cangmi-lul yel songi-*

lul kkekk.essta '(I) picked ten roses'. Thus, double objects as well as double subjects occur with number constructions. It is also common to omit one of the two occurrences; the dropping of either particle produces a natural, idiomatic utterance. For example: *Haksayng twu myeng-i/Haksayng-i twu myeng cikak-hayssta* 'Two students were late'; *Cangmi-lul yel songi/Cangmi yel songi-lul kkekk.essta* '(I) picked ten roses'.

As we have seen from the above examples, there are Korean predicates that have what appear to be two subjects. It is even more common in Korean for a sentence to have no subject expressed at all. One reason for subjectless sentences in Korean is that a subject understood from context is quite frequently omitted. But deletion cannot always be used as an explanation because it is sometimes difficult to determine what subject, if any, the speaker had in mind. In such cases it is a moot question as to whether a subject has been deleted or whether there was ever a subject at all, at any level. Perhaps it is better not to look for a hidden subject when none is apparent. In other words, some Korean predicates simply occur without a subject.

In the exchange in (10), a first-person subject, and then a second-person subject has been omitted. However, in (11), the predicate *khunil-ita* (큰 일이다) 'be a serious matter' has no subject expressed, and it is not at all clear what the wording of that subject would be, were one to assume that it had been deleted.

(10)A: 어디 가니?
Eti kani?
'Going somewhere?'

B: 응, 학교에 가.
Ung, hakkyo ey ka.
'N. Goin' to school.'

(11)청소년들이 너무 무기력해서 (X가?) 큰일이다.
Chengsonyen-tul i nemu mukilyek-hayse (X ka?) khun-il ita.
'Since young people are too spiritless, (it?) is a serious matter.'
['It's awful that young people are so spiritless.']

The particle *i/ka* not only has the grammatical function of marking a subject; it also has semantic content. First of all, *i/ka* is used to mark new information; second, it also conveys the meaning of exclusivity—in other words, *X-ka* means something like 'it's not something else, but just *X* to which the predicate applies'. In a neutral context not compatable with such intepretations, the particle can be omitted and the subject left unmarked; but an occurrence of *i/ka* that expresses new, exclusive information cannot be dropped. (Of course, since it conveys new information, the noun phrase with which *i/ka* is used also cannot be deleted.)

(12) A: 흥부와 놀부 중에 누가 재산이 많으니?

　　　 Hungpu wa Nolpu cwung ey nwu*ka* caysan i manh.uni?

　　　 'Between Hŭngbu and Nolbu, who[-*ka*] has the most wealth?'

　　 B: 놀부가 재산이 많다. / ˟놀부__ 재산이 많다.

　　　 Nolpu *ka* caysan i manh.ta. / ˟Nolpu __ caysan i manh.ta

　　　 '*Nolbu*[-*ka*] has the most wealth.' / [ungrammatical]

(13) A: 이 세상에서 제일 아름다운 사람은 누구지?

　　　 I seysang eyse ceyil alumtawun salam un nwukwu ci?

　　　 'Who is the most beautiful person in the world?'

　　 B: 백설공주가 제일 아름다워요. /˟백설공주__ 제일 아름다워요.

　　　 Payksel-kongcwu *ka* ceyil alumtawe yo. / ˟Payksel-kongcwu ceyil
　　　 alumtawe yo

　　　 '*Snow White*[-*ka*] is the most beautiful.'/ [ungrammatical]

In addition, as can be seen in the following examples (and as was mentioned at the beginning of this section), *i/ka* is also used with verbal inflections. In cases such as these, the particle cannot be considered a nominative case marker.

(14) 요즘은 밥이 통 먹히지가 않아.

　　 Yocum un pap i mek.hici *ka* anh.a.

　　 these-days rice at-all be-eaten-*ci-ka* NEG

　　 'These days I just can't eat anything at all.'

(15) 나는 그 사람을 만나고 싶지가 않아.

　　 Na nun ku salam ul mannako siphci *ka* anh.a.

　　 I　　 that person-ul meet　　 want-*ci-ka* NEG

　　 'I just don't want to *see* that person.'

In examples like these, the particle *lul* can be used instead of *ka* with almost no difference in meaning: 요즘은 밥이 통 먹히지를 않아 *Yocum un pap i mek.hici lul anh.a* 'These days I just can't eat anything at all'. Just as *i/ka* is not a nominative case marker in such cases, neither is *lul* an accusative case marker here. In these kinds of constructions, case particles are used to add emphasis and shift focus in various complex ways; but how the usages should best be analyzed remains the topic of considerable debate in linguistic circles.

5.1.1.2 Accusative Case Particles

The particle that is used to mark the direct object of a transitive predicate is *ul/lul*. Following a vowel, the particle has the shape *lul*, and following a consonant, the shape is *ul*. (For the sake of convenience, we will generally refer to the particle shape as *lul*.)

(1) 순이가 책을 읽는다.
    Swuni ka chayk *ul* ilknunta.
          chayk-*ul*
    'Suni is reading a book[-*ul*].'

(2) 순이가 차를 마신다.
    Swuni ka cha *lul* masinta.
          cha-*lul*
    'Suni is drinking tea[-*lul*]'

A *lul*-marked noun phrase can also appear in a sentence with an intransitive verb in case the verb is a verb of movement. In such constructions, *lul* functions to mark a locative. The verbs of movement that take a *lul*-marked noun phrase include: *kata* 'go'; *kie kata* 'crawl'; *tanita* 'attend, make a trip'; *ketta* 'walk'; *kenneta* 'cross over'; *nalta* 'fly'; *naylye kata* 'go down'; *tol.a tanita* 'return'; *oluta* 'go up'; *ttenata* 'leave, depart'; *cinata* 'pass'. The *lul*-marked noun phrase can be one of several things: a place noun, a noun expressing the extent of space or the duration or frequency of time, or a noun marking the purpose of the verb of movement.

(7) 순이가 {학교, 시장, 외국}를 자주 간다.
    Swuni ka {hakkyo, sicang, oykwuk} *lul* cacwu kanta.
    'Suni often goes to {school, the market, foreign countries}.'

(8) 순이가 {두 시간, 10km}를 걸었다.
    Swuni ka {twu sikan, 10km.} *lul* kel.ess.ta.
    'Suni walked for {two hours, 10km.}.'

(9) 순이가 오늘도 {등산, 영화 구경, 해수욕, 낚시}를 갔다.
    Swuni ka onul to {tungsan, yenghwa, kwukyeng, hayswuyok, nakksi} *lul* kassta.
    'Suni went {mountain climbing, movie viewing, sea bathing, swimming} today, too.'

In sentences such as (8), in cases where *lul* marks the duration of time that the verb of movement took, the locative particle *ey* can be used in the place of *lul*, but the meaning of the resulting sentence is different. For example, (8), with particle *lul*, means 'Suni walked for two hours', but the same sentence with particle *ey* means 'Suni walked it (= the distance) in two hours'. However, when *lul* in this kind of syntactic pattern marks distance (that is, space), it cannot be replaced by either the locative marker *ey* or its sometimes synonym *(u)lo:* *Swuni ka 10km. ey kel.essta.

Sentences such as (9) are again different. Here the noun phrase expresses the purpose of the verb of movement, and no other particle besides *lul* can be used with it. For example, *tungsan-ey kanta ('go mountain climbing') and ×*tungsan-ulo kanta* ('id') are both ungrammatical. The meaning of sentences such as (9) is one of going to a specific place where the action can be carried out; for example, in (9), Suni would be going to the *mountains* where she can go mountain climbing, or to the *theater* where she can see a movie. But the implied place noun is usually left unstated because it is taken from such a restricted set of possibilities (the fishing hole to go fishing; the mountains to go mountain climbing; the beach to go sea bathing), stating it overtly would be largely redundant. It would only distract from the activity focused upon in the sentence.

5.1.1.3 *Genitive Case Particles*

The genitive case is marked by the particle *uy*. Since the particle serves to link two noun phrases, its function is different from an ordinary case particle, which is used to mark the grammatical relationship between a noun phrase and the predicate. Moreover, the variety of semantic relationships that can obtain between these two noun phrases linked by *uy* is extremely broad and difficult to delineate with a simple definition. Here are some representative usages and semantic interpretations of this particle:

(1) 이것은 나의 책이다.
     Ikes un na *uy* chayk ita.
     'This is *my* book.' [possession]

(2) 순이는 나의 친구다.
     Swuni nun na *uy* chinkwu 'ta.
     'Suni's *my* friend.' [relationship]

(3) 지리산의 천왕봉이 구름에 덮였다.
     Cili-san *uy* chen.wang-pong i kwulum ey teph.yess.ta.
     'Ch'ŏnwang Peak *in* the Chiri Mountains was enveloped in clouds.' [location]

(4) 제주도의 조랑말이 천연기념물로 지정되었다.
     Ceycwu-to *uy* colang-mal i chen.yen kinyem-mul lo ciceng toy.ess.ta
     'The ponies *of* Cheju Island have been designated a precious natural resource.' [origin, source]

(5) 충무공의 거북선이 지폐 도안으로 채택되었다.
     Chwungmu-kong *uy* kepuk-sen i ciphyey toan ulo chaythayk-toy.ess.ta.
     'The Turtle Boats *of* Admiral Yi Sunsin were chosen as the design to be printed on bank notes.' [creator, originator]

(6) 우리 팀의 주장이 은퇴했다.
     Wuli thim *uy* cwucang i unthoy-hayssta.
     'The captain of our team retired.' [membership]

(7) 창 밖에서 사랑의 노래를 부르는 사람이 누굴까?

Chang pakk eyse salang *uy* nolay lul pulunun salam i nwukwu 'l.kka?

'Who could be singing a song *of* love outside the window?' [object of reference, i.e., depicting or referring to something]

(8) 카 레이서가 사막에서 죽음의 여행을 마치고 돌아왔다.

Kha leyise ka samak eyse cwuk.um *uy* yehayng ul machiko tol.a wass.ta.

'The automotive racers returned having completed a journey *of* death in the desert.' [figure of speech, simile]

(9) 이제 남북한의 통일도 멀지 않았다.

Icey Nam-Puk Han *uy* thongil to melci anh.ass.ta.

'Now the unification *of* North and South Korea is not far off.' [goal, result]

(10) 그 때의 서울은 아주 달랐다.

Ku ttay *uy* Sewul un acwu tallass.ta.

'Seoul *at* that time was very different.' [time]

(11) 그 여자는 백설공주의 미를 가지고 있다.

Ku yeca nun Payksel-kongcwu *uy* mi lul kaciko iss.ta.

'She has the beauty *of* (like) Snow White.' [similarity]

In quantified expressions such as that of (12), the particle *uy* has no particular semantic content; it is being used, rather, only to link the number phrase with the noun phrase. In (13) the usage is similar; *uy* has no particular semantic function in this case, either. Since the semantic connection between the two noun phrases is clear, the context does not become confused even if the connection is not overtly indicated; as a result, *uy* only serves the weak function of directly linking the two noun phrases.

(12) 한 잔의 차가 생활에 여유를 준다.

Han can *uy* cha ka saynghwal ey yeyu lul cwunta.

'A glass *of* tea gives leisure to life.'

(13) a. 독서의 계절

tokse *uy* kyeycel

'a season *for* reading books' [i.e., 'a good time for reading books']

b. 사랑의 상처

salang *uy* sangche

'an injury *of* love' [i.e., 'hurt caused by love']

Besides being used in constructions such as the above, *uy* is also used to express a vague, general relationship between two noun phrases rather than a strictly defined one. The phrase *onul uy yoli* (literally, 'today *uy* cooking, food') can mean any one of a number of things: 'the food that will be eaten today'; 'the food that will be prepared today'; 'the food suitable to be eaten today'; 'the cooking that will be introduced today (as in a televised cooking demonstration)'; 'the food that was eaten today'; 'the best-tasting food that was/will be eaten today'; and so on.

The particle *uy* is frequently postposed to a noun plus particle (or particle sequence) to link the phrase to the noun that follows. The resulting linkage is much like that described in the preceding paragraph. In (14) and (15), below, the phrases *Hawai eyse* 'in Hawaii' and *pata lo puthe* 'from the sea' can modify a verb, but they cannot be direct modifiers of a noun. In this respect, Korean structure contrasts with that of English, where prepositional phrases such as *in Hawaii* and *from the sea* modify nouns directly, without an interceding preposition: <u>a night *in Hawaii*</u>, <u>a gift *from the sea*</u>. (Constructions such as ^{xx}*a night of in Hawaii* and ^{xx}*a gift of from the sea* would not only be ungrammatical; they would almost be uninterpretable.)

(14) a. 그 신혼부부는 하와이에서 하룻밤을 보냈다.
      Ku sinhon pupu nun Hawai eyse halwus-pam ul ponayss.ta.
      'The newlyweds spent a night in Hawaii.'
   b. 하와이에서의 하룻밤은 인상에 남는다.
      Hawai eyse *uy* halwus-pam un insang ey namnunta.
      'The night in Hawaii was memorable.' [Lit., 'The night *of* in Hawaii . . .']

(15) a. 이 진주는 바다로부터 받은 선물이야.
      I cincwu nun pata lo puthe pat.un senmul iya.
      'This pearl is a gift received from the sea.'
   b. 이 진주는 바다로부터의 선물이야.
      I cincwu nun pata lo puthe *uy* senmul iya.
      'This pearl is a gift from the sea.' [Lit., '. . . a gift *of* from the sea.']

From usages such as these it can be seen that the basic function of *uy* is to link a noun phrase to another noun phrase. The two noun phrases linked by *uy* are not so much to be thought of as modifier-modified as simply a longer noun phrase that then can function as a syntactic unit.

5.1.1.4 *Locative Case Particles*

The locative case expresses location, extent of time, of space, or of direction. The particle most commonly used to mark the locative case is *ey*. Other particles used as locative markers include: *eykey, kkey, hanthey,* and *tele.*

As can be seen in the following examples, the particle *ey* is used in a wide variety of contexts. However, the differences in interpretation are not so much due to any multiple meanings of *ey* itself, as to the combinations of the noun phrases and predicates linked in these contexts. For example, with the existential predicate *issta* 'is, exists', *ey* marks location: *A ka B ey issta* 'A is at B'. But with verbs of movement, the particle shows destination: *A ka B ey kanta* 'A is going to B'.

(1) 산에 나무가 많다.
San *ey* namu ka manh.ta.
'There are a lot of trees *on* the mountains.' [location]

(2) 순이가 학교에 간다.
Swun.i ka hakkyo *ey* kanta.
'Suni is going *to* school.' [destination]

(3) 내일 오후 두 시에 만납시다.
Nayil ohwu twu-si *ey* mannapsita.
'Let's meet *at* two tomorrow afternoon.' [point in time]

(4) 이 시계는 하루에 1분씩 빨리 간다.
I sikyey nun halwu *ey* 1-pun ssik ppalli kanta.
'This watch gains a minute a day (Lit., *in* one day).' [duration of time]

(5) 구청에서 10m에 한 그루씩 가로수를 심었다.
Kwucheng eyse 10m *ey* han-kulwu ssik kalo-swu lul sim.ess.ta.
'At the district office, they planted trees *at* 10m intervals.' [extent of space]

(6) 순이는 천둥소리에 깜짝 놀랐다.
Swun.i nun chentong soli *ey* kkamccak nollass.ta.
'Suni was startled *by (at)* the sound of thunder.' [cause]

The particle *ey* also combines with certain inflected forms of verbs to form various idiomatic expressions. These include: *-ey pi-haye* 'compared to'; *-ey tay-haye/kwan-haye* 'concerning, about'; *-ey ttala* 'depending on, according to'; *-ey uy-hay* 'because of, is (done) by'; *-ey uy-hamyen* 'according to'; and the like. In these cases the locative meaning of *ey* has almost been lost.

(7) 형에 비하여 동생이 낫다.
Hyeng *ey pi-ha.ye* tongsayng i nasta.
'*Compared to* (his) older brother, the younger brother is not so bad.'

(8) 거북선이 이순신 장군에 의해 만들어졌다.
Kepuk-sen i I Swunsin Cangkwun *ey uy-hay* mantul.ecyess.ta.
'The Turtle Boats *were* created *by* General Yi Sunsin.'

(9) 나는 한국 역사에 대해 아는 것이 별로 없다.
Na nun Hankwuk yeksa *ey tay-hay* anun kes i pyello eps.ta.
'I know almost nothing *about* Korean history.'

The particles *eykey, kkey, hanthey,* and *tele* have often been treated as datives. However, the only difference between them and the particle *ey* is that they are only used with animate nouns, while *ey* is only used with inanimates. Since their basic function is the same, there is no need to set up a separate dative case in Korean. All of these particles can be classified as locative markers.

(10)a. 민호가 순이에게 물을 주었다.
      Minho ka Swun.i *eykey* mul ul cwuess.ta.
      'Minho gave some water *to* Suni.'

   b. 민호가 화초에 물을 주었다.
      Minho ka hwacho *ey* mul ul cwuess.ta
      'Minho gave some water *to* the flowers.'

(11)a. 이번 사고의 책임은 너에게 있다.
      I pen sako uy chayk.im un ne *eykey* issta.
      'The responsibility for this accident is yours (lit., *on* you)'

   b.이번 사고의 책임은 행정 당국에 있다.
      I pen sako uy chayk.im un hayngceng tangkwuk *ey* iss.ta.
      'The responsibility for this accident lies with (Lit, is *on*) the administrative authorities.'

The particle *kkey* is an honorific morpheme. It functions like *eykey* with nouns of honorification. The general rule is that, if a noun requires *kkeyse* as a subject marker, it will take *kkey* instead of *eykey* in the locative position.

(12)a. 어머니가 민호를 시장에 심부름을 보냈다.
      Emeni ka Minho lul sicang *ey* simpulum ul ponayss.ta.
      'Mother sent Minho on an errand *to* the market.'

   b. 어머니가 민호를 할아버지께 심부름을 보냈다.
      Emeni ka Minho lul hal.apeci *kkey* simpulum ul ponayss.ta.
      'Mother sent Minho *to* his grandfather on an errand.'

The particles *hanthey* and *tele* are more restricted in application than *eykey*. *Hanthey* has almost the same distribution as *eykey*, but it is more colloquial and more often used in informal speech. *Tele* is like *hanthey* in that it is also colloquial and informal, but it is used in more circumscribed contexts than either *eykey* or *hanthey*. *Tele* can only be used in reference to humans and only when the verb has to do with speaking: *mal hata* 'say'; *mut.ta* 'ask'; and the like.

(13) 순이가 민호 {에게, 한테, *더러} 장미꽃을 주었다.
      Swun.i ka Minho {*eykey, hanthey,* *tele}* cangmi-kkoch ul cwuess.ta.
      'Suni gave some roses *to* Minho.' [-*tele* ungrammatical here]

(14)자세한 것은 순이 {에게, 한테, 더러} 물어 봐.
Casey-han kes un Swun.i {eykey, hanthey, tele} mul.e pwa.
'Ask *(to)* Suni about details.'

The morpheme *-se* combines with locative markers to form the complex particles *ey se, eykey se,* and *hanthey se.* The resulting particles are used to indicate a starting or origination point or the location of an activity.

(16)순이가 도서관에서 책을 본다.
Swun.i ka tosekwan *eyse* chayk ul ponta.
'Suni is reading a book *in* the library.' [location of the activity]

(17)순이가 부산에서 왔다.
Swun.i ka Pusan *eyse* wass.ta.
'Suni came *from* Pusan.'

(18)민호는 순이 {에게서, 한테서} 재미있는 이야기를 들었다.
Minho nun Swun.i {eykey se, hanthey se} caymi issnun iyaki lul tul.ess.ta.
'Minho heard an interesting story *from* Suni.'

The origination-point meaning of these particles is apparent from the English equivalent 'from'. But, in their respective functions of marking a location, it is often difficult for English speakers to understand the difference between *ey* and *eyse*. The basic difference is that *ey* marks a static location, while *eyse* marks the location of an activity.

(19)a. 교실에 아무도 없다.
Kyosil *ey* amu to eps.ta.
'There's no one *in* the classroom.' [static location]

b. 교실에서 공부하자.
Kyosil *eyse* kongpu-haca.
'Let's study *in* the classroom.' [location of an activity]

But there are also action verbs that are used, in some situations, with *ey* instead of *eyse*.

(20)a. 교실에 모여라.
Kyosil *ey* mo.yela.
'Gather (together) *in* the classroom.'

b. 교실에 두어라.
Kyosil *ey* twuela.
'Put (it) *in* the classroom.'

The difference is that, although 'gather' and 'put' are action verbs, the location marked by *ey* describes not where the action takes place, but the end point, the destination, of the activity.

5.1.1.5 *Instrumental Case Particles*

The instrumental case is marked by the particle *(u)lo*. As is the case with many other particles, the shape is determined by the phonological environment. But the phonological conditions are not quite the same. Whereas the shape of most particles depends on whether the particle follows a consonant or a vowel, the shape of the instrumental is *lo* not only after a vowel, but also following the consonant /l/; the alternate shape *ulo* follows all other consonants. (In the discussion that follows, *lo* should be understood as shorthand for both shapes).

The particle *lo* is typically used together with a transitive verb and its object, but there are also a wide variety of other patterns in which it appears. Because of this variety, the particle can have a number of different meanings, which traditional Korean grammars treated as different particles. There were said to be several different particles pronounced *lo*, each with a separate case function: instrumental *lo*, causative *lo*, locative *lo*, and so on. In recent years, however, the tendency has been to analyze all these occurrences of *lo* as one and the same particle, with the semantic differences arising from the relationship between the noun and the following predicate.

First, let us look at some examples of *lo* used with a transitive verb and its object. When the nouns in this pattern are concrete, the noun marked by *lo* shows the material or ingredients out of which something is made, or the instrument used in the action of the verb:

(1) 두부는 콩으로 만든다.
Twupu nun khong *ulo* mantunta.
'(They) make tofu *out of* soy beans.' [component material]

(2) 영희가 가위로 색종이를 오렸다.
Yenghuy ka kawi *lo* sayk-congi lul olyess.ta
'Yŏnghŭi cut out colored paper *with* a pair of scissors.' [instrument]

However, if the noun marked by *lo* represents an act of some kind or is an abstract noun, the noun phrase indicates the means or method through which the action of the verb is accomplished. After such an occurrence of *lo* the morpheme *-sse* can be added to emphasize more strongly the 'means' interpretation.

(3) 이순신 장군은 죽음으로(써) 나라를 지켰다.
I Swunsin Cangkwun un cwuk.um *ulo* (-sse) nala lul cikhyess.ta
'General Yi Sunsin *through* his death saved the country.' [means]

A change in the syntactic order can affect the meaning of the phrase. A *lo*-marked noun phrase that follows the direct object becomes the complement of the verb when that verb is one of certain verbs that occur in this pattern: *ppopta* 'choose'; *samta* 'take as'; *kyelceng-hata* 'decide'; *ceng-hata* 'decide (on)'; *senchwul-hata* 'choose (as)'; *chwutay-hata* 'be presided by'; *sayngkak-hata* 'think (of)'; *yekita* 'consider'; *chwikup-hata* 'treat (as)'; and so on. If the noun that is marked by *lo* in this pattern is a person, then the meaning expressed by *lo* is something like 'qualified to be':

(4) 이사회에서 그를 사장으로 선출했다.
Isa-hoy eyse ku nun sacang *ulo* senchwul-hayss.ta
'In the board of directors meeting he was chosen *as* company president.'

(5) 민수가 순이를 아내로 삼았다.
Minswu ka Swun.i lul anay *lo* sam.ass.ta.
'Minsu took Suni *as* his wife.'

(6) 동창회 모임 시간을 12시로 결정했다.
Tongchang-hoy moim sikan ul 12-si *lo* kyelceng-hayssta.
'(They) decided *on* 12 o'clock as the time of the alumni meeting.'

(7) 그들은 결혼식 장소를 시민공원으로 정했다.
Ku-tul un kyelhon-sik cangso lul Simin Kongwen *ulo* ceng-hayss.ta.
'They decided *on* People's Park as the place for the wedding.'

When verbs describing a change in the situation, such as *pyen-hata* 'change', *tulenata* 'be revealed', *palkhyecita* 'be disclosed' are used with *lo*, the particle marks the result of the change.

(8) 여우가 처녀로 변했다.
Yewu ka chenye *lo* pyen-hayss.ta
'The fox changed *into* a young girl.'

(9) 소문이 사실로 드러났다.
Somun i sasil *lo* tulenass.ta.
'The rumor was revealed *as* the truth.'

The particle *lo* is also used to mark cause or reason; it is also used in this function in patterns like *-lo in-haye* 'by reason of' and *-lo malmiam.a* 'on account of.

(10) 황영조 선수의 우승(으로/으로 인하여/으로 말미암아) 온 나라가 기쁨에 들떴다.
Hwang Yengco senswu uy wusung (*ulo/ ulo in-ha.ye/ ulo malmiama*) on nala ka kippum ey tulttess.ta.

'*Because of* Hwang Yŏngjo's victory, the entire country was giddy with happiness.' [Hwang Yŏngjo was the Korean runner who won the marathon at the Barcelona Olympics in 1992.]

(11) 민호가 독감(으로/으로 인하여/으로 말미암아) 결석하였다.
Minho ka tokkam *(ulo/ ulo in-ha.ye/ ulo malmiama)* kyelsek-ha.yess.ta.
'Minho was absent *because of* a cold.'

In addition, in examples such as (12), *lo* functions to express a locative. In this case, as a locative marker, *lo* indicates general direction. *Cilum-kil lo kata* (지름길로 가다) can *only* be translated as an instrumental, '*by* a shortcut' or '*by means of* a shortcut', never as a locative.

(12) 순이는 친구를 만나러 사직 공원으로 갔다.
Swun.i nun chinkwu lul mannale Sacik Kongwen *ulo* kass.ta.
'Suni went *to* Sajik Park to meet her friend.'

(13) 순이가 지름길로 학교에 갔다.
Swun.i ka cilum-kil *lo* hakkyo ey kassta.
'Suni went to school *by* a shortcut.'

As we can see from these examples, *lo* has a greater variety of usage than any other particle. Moreover, besides the above kinds of usages, it also functions to change a noun into an adverbial phrase; for example, *cwu lo* 'mainly', *taytay lo* 'generation after generation', *ttayttay lo* 'occasionally', *cin-sil lo* 'truly', *nal lo* 'daily', and so on. However, in these cases it is perhaps better to consider *lo* a derivational suffix rather than a particle.

5.1.1.6 Comitative Case Particles

The basic comitative case marker is *wa/kwa*. The form of this particle after a vowel is *wa*, and after a consonant *kwa* (in the following discussion *kwa* stands for both forms). One function of *kwa* is simply to link nouns together, and in this usage it is usually translated as 'and'. Because of this linking function, the particle is sometimes called a "connective marker" (e.g., Sohn 1994:225). When used as a connector in this way, *kwa* ties two or more noun phrases together into a larger construct that then functions as a single element. Case particles that attach to the last noun phrase govern the entire, larger construction linked by *kwa*.

(1) 순이와 영희가 커피를 마신다.
Swun.i *wa* Yenghuy ka khephi lul masinta.
'Suni *and* Yŏnghŭi drink coffee.'

(2) 영희는 장미와 백합을 좋아한다.
Yenghuy nun cangmi *wa* payk.hap ul coh.a hanta.
'Yŏnghŭi likes roses *and* lilies.'

But simple linking is not the only function of *kwa*. It is also used as a "comitative marker" (공동격조사) to show nouns interacting on, harmonizing with, or accompanying each other. These nouns can be linked together directly by *kwa*, as in the following examples, where the English translation 'each other' shows the semantic effect of the comitative marking:

(3) 순이와 영희가 닮았다.
Swun.i *wa* Yenghuy ka talm.ass.ta.
'Suni *and* Yŏnghŭi resemble *each other.*'

(4) 순이와 영희가 싸웠다.
Swun.i *wa* Yenghuy ka ssawess.ta.
'Suni *and* Yŏnghŭi fought *with each other.*'

In a related comitative construction, one of the interacting nouns is expressed as the subject of the sentence, while the other noun is marked by *kwa* and stands by itself as an independent phrase. In this kind of construction *kwa* is often translated as 'with'.

(5) a. 순이가 영희와 싸웠다.
Swun.i *ka* Yenghuy *wa* sasswess.ta.
'Suni [*subject*] fought *with* Yŏnghŭi.'

b. 영희가 순이와 싸웠다
Yenghuy *ka* Swun.i *wa* ssawess.ta.
'Yŏnghŭi [*subject*] fought *with* Suni.'

(6) a. 순이가 영희와 커피를 마신다.
Swun.i *ka* Yenghuy *wa* kephi lul masinta.
'Suni [*subject*] drinks coffee *with* Yŏnghŭi.'

b. 영희가 순이와 커피를 마신다.
Yenghuy *ka* Swun.i *wa* kephi lul masinta.
'Yŏnghŭi [*subject*] drinks coffee *with* Suni.'

Notice how the comitative meaning of (6), in which the two girls necessarily drink coffee together, differs from the simple connective meaning expressed by the particle in (1). In the comitative type of construction, the subject is often omitted if it is understandable from the context:

(7) 어머니와 시장에 갔다.
Emeni *wa* sicang ey kass.ta.
'(She) went to the market *with* (her) mother.'

(8) 그 사람과 사이가 나쁘다.
Ku salam *kwa* sai ka napputa.
'(He) is on bad terms *with* that person.'

When two nouns are linked together with a comitative interpretation, some Korean speakers sometimes use the comitative marker after both nouns:

(9) 난 밥과 나물과 섞어서 먹었다.
Na n pap *kwa* namul *kwa* sekk.ese mek.ess.ta.
'I ate rice mixed *together with* greens.'

Certain Korean verbs are paradigmatically used with a comitative marker. *Kyelhon-hata* 'to marry', for example, requires that an accompanying noun appear as a comitative phrase instead of as a direct object—as in English: *Tok.il-salam kwa kyelhon-hayss.ta* 독일사람과 결혼했다 '(He) married (with) a German'.[5] Other verbals requiring a comitative phrase include *kalla-seta* 갈라서다 'break off relations (with)', *kyelthwu-hata* 결투하다 'duel (with)', *kyep-chita* 겹치다 'overlap (one another)', *kyotay-hata* 교대하다 'alternate (with)', *talmta* 닮다 'resemble', *taylip-hata* 대립하다 'be opposed (to each other)', *mannata* 만나다 'meet (with)', *macwu-chita* 마주치다 'meet up (with)', *mac-seta* 맞서다 'confront', *putic-chita* 부딪치다 'run up (against)', *sakwita* 사귀다 'associate (with)', *salang-hata* 사랑하다 'love', *ssawuta* 싸우다 'fight (with)', *akswu-hata* 악수하다 'shake hands (with)', *ipyel-hata* 이별하다 'part (from)', *ihon-hata* 이혼하다 'divorce', *thonghwa-hata* 통화하다 'assimilate (with)', *hey.ecita* 헤어지다 'leave (someone)'.

In addition to *kwa*, the particles *hako* and *lang* are also used as comitative markers. These two particles have almost the same distributions and functions as *kwa*; the difference is one of style, because *hako* and *lang* are more colloquial. In fact, since the particle *lang* is informal to the point of being a nursery word, the situations in which it can be used are very restricted.

(10)a. 너는 누구(하고/랑) 놀래?
Ne nun nwukwu *(hako/ lang)* nollay?
'Who're you gonna play *with?*'

b. 엄마랑 같이 먹자.
Emma *lang* kath.i mek.ca.
'Let's eat together *with* Mama.'

5.1.1.7 *Vocative Case Particles*

The particle *a/ya* is used after someone's personal name in order to call that person. The form of the particle is *a* after a consonant, and *ya* after a vowel. The particle is not used with a surname.

(1) a. 영숙아, 전화 좀 받아라.
Yengswuk *a*, cenhwa com pat.ala.
'Yŏngsuk! Please answer the phone!'

b. 민호야, 지금 몇 시니?

Minho *ya*, cikum myech-si ni?

'Minho, what time is it now?'

This vocative particle is used freely in certain informal speech styles. It is certainly common enough in the intimate speech style known as *panmal*, but more often the particle is simply omitted entirely, and the person is called by his or her name alone. In such cases, it is usual to add the nominal suffix *-i* to a name ending in a consonant. In speech styles beyond these most informal levels, vocative forms are made by adding an appropriate title to the name or surname or by using the title alone. In other words, beyond the informal styles, vocative particles are not used. (Speech styles and their usage will be discussed more fully in chapter 7.)

(2) a. 영숙이, 전화 좀 받아 주겠어. [*panmal* form]

Yengswuk-*i*, cenhwa com pat.a cwukeyss.e.

'Yŏngsuk, would you answer the phone?'

b. 민호, 지금 몇 시지? [*panmal* form]

Minho, cikum myech-si 'ci?

'Minho, what time is it now?'

(3) a. 민호군, 전화 받게. [*kwun* is a title used with an equal or inferior]

Minho-*kwun*, cenhwa patkey.

'Minho, answer the phone.'

b. 영희씨, 전화 받아요. [*ssi* is a courtesy title]

Yenghuy-*ssi*, cenhwa pat.a yo.

'Yŏnghŭi, please answer the phone.'

(4) a. 김 과장님, 전화 왔습니다.

Kim *Kwacang-nim*, cenhwa wass.supnita.

'*Director* Kim, there's a telephone call for you.'

b. 어머니, 전화 받으세요.

Emeni, cenhwa pat.usey yo.

'*Mother*, you have a telephone call.'

Besides *a/ya*, *ye/iye* also serves as a vocative particle. However, this particle is a specialized form found mainly in poetry and the language of the Bible; it is not used in ordinary conversation. It is considered to be an elegant usage, an expression with a poetic flavor.

(5) a. 님이여, 내 드디어 그대 앞에 왔노라.

Nim *iye*, nay tutie kutay aph ey wass.nola. ,

'My love, I have at last come before thee.'

b. 주여, 이들의 간절한 기도를 들어 주소서.
Cwu *ye*, i-tul uy kancel-han kito lul tul.e cwusose.
'Lord, please hear these fervent prayers.'

5.1.2 Special Particles

As we have said, special particles are unlike case particles. Case particles are the postpositional elements used to express case relationships, while special particles add to the semantic content. Special particles also have syntactic distributions different from those of case particles. A special particle can be added to certain noun phrases already marked by a case particle; it can also be combined with an adverb or an inflected form. For example, the particle *man* appears in a variety of different places in (1), below; in each case, it functions to add the meaning of 'only'.

(1) a. 이 소나무는 산에서만 잘 자란다. [follows the locative particle *eyse*]
I sonamu nun san eyse *man* cal calanta.
'This pine grows well *only* in the mountains.'

b. 그곳 사람들은 고기를 낚시로만 잡았다. [follows the instrumental *lo*]
Ku kos salam-tul un koki lul nakksi lo *man* cap.assta.
'The people there caught fish *only* with a fishing line.'

c. 나는 지금 울고만 싶다. [follows the gerund ending of the verb]
Na nun cikum wulko *man* siph.ta.
'I *just* want to cry now.'

d. 빈 손으로 와도 좋으니 일찍만 오세요. [follows the adverb 'early']
Pin son ulo wato coh.uni ilccik *man* osey yo.
'It's all right to come empty-handed, so *just* come early.'

However, when one of these special particles is used with a subject or a direct object, the case particle (*i/ka* or *ul/lul*) is usually omitted. In these constructions it might appear that the special particle is serving to mark the case, but that is not so. As we have seen, when there is no case particle, case is determined solely by word order; and here, just as it does following other kinds of words, the special particle functions only for what it adds semantically.

(2) a. 이 산에서는 소나무만 잘 자란다. [used after a subject]
I san eyse nun sonamu *man* cal calanta.
'In these mountains *only* pines grow well.'

b. 저 화가는 소나무만 즐겨 그린다. [used after a direct object]
Ce hwaka nun sonamu *man* culkye kulinta.
'That painter *only* enjoys painting pines.'

A fairly exhaustive list of these so-called special particles is given below in (3). There are a few other forms that some grammarians, depending on their analysis, would add to the list; but those other forms are in any event not central to our discussion. Here we will focus only on the meanings and usages of the most commonly used particles.

(3) *un/nun*   subdued focus, marks a theme; 'as for'
     to   highlighting focus, emphasis; 'also'
     man   restrictive; 'only, just'
     cocha   'even, too, in addition'
     kkaci   extent, emphasis; 'until, up to, so far as'
     mace   'also, even, going to the limit of'
     mata   'each, every, all'
     (i)na   'and/or, either . . . or'
     (i)nama   'at least, even'
     (i)yamallo emphatic; 'this very (thing), this indeed'
     (i)ya   'if it be, even, indeed'
     khenyeng   'to say nothing of, let alone, not only'

Let us now examine the usage of each of these particles.

5.1.2.1 *to*

The particle *to* expresses the meaning of inclusiveness, that something shares some quality or description with something else. The adverb 'also' is usually given as the best English equivalent of its meaning.

(4) a. 민호도 사과를 좋아한다.
        Minho *to* sakwa lul coh.a hanta.
        'Minho *also* likes apples.'

     b. 민호가 사과도 좋아한다.
        Minho ka sakwa *to* coh.a hanta.
        'Minho likes apples *also*.'

Sentence (4a) has as its precondition that some other person besides Minho likes apples; the precondition of (4b) is that Minho likes some other fruit besides apples—grapes, say, or pears. The syntactic location of the particle *to* makes it clear which of these interpretations is intended. Note, by way of comparison, that the English translation of (4a) is ambiguous in its printed form, because what "also" refers to in this sentence depends more upon context and intonation than syntactic ordering.[6]

But *to* does not have to mean 'also'; it is sometimes used simply to emphasize. Take the sentence in (5), for example. The particle *to* does not have the meaning 'also' here. It is true that the sentence is at least potentially ambiguous because in the right context, it can certainly mean that there are also a lot of people (in addition to something else). But unless that "something else" that is numerous has been talked about or understood, the sentence simply means that there are really a lot of people—in other words, in this sentence *to* is being used for emphasis only.

(5) 해수욕장에 갔더니 사람도 많더라. [follows a noun ('people')]
Hayswuyok-cang ey kass.teni salam *to* manh.tela.
'When I went to the beach, there were *really* a lot of people there.'

The use of *to* for emphasis is especially common when the particle attaches to an adverb, such as in (6). Of course, depending upon context, an occurrence of *to* following an adverb can still have the meaning 'also', as it does in (7), for example. But the emphatic meaning of *to* is the more general one after an adverb.

(6) a. 사람이 많이도 모였구나. [follows an adverb ('much')]
Salam i manh.i *to* mo.yess.kwuna.
'An *awful* lot of people have gathered, I see.'

b. 지난 겨울은 몹시도 추웠다. [follows an adverb ('very')]
Cinan kyewul un mopsi *to* chwuwess.ta.
'Last winter was *really* very cold.'

(7) 조련사가 원숭이에게 바나나를 많이도 주어 보고 조금도 주어 보고 하며 훈련을 시킨다. [follows adverbs ('much' and 'little')]
Colyensa ka wenswungi eykey panana lul manh.i *to* cwue poko cokum *to* cwue poko ha.mye hwunlyen ul sikhinta.
'The trainer tried training the monkeys *both* by giving them a lot of bananas and *also* by giving them just a few bananas.'

5.1.2.2 *man*

The particle *man* means 'only, the only choice'. That is, the noun phrase to which *man* attaches has a value opposite that of the possible candidates for comparison. Thus, the meaning of (8a) is that all the people in question besides Minho do not like apples; an expression such as (8b) means that Minho does not like anything besides apples.

(8) a. 민호만 사과를 좋아한다.
Minho *man* sakwa lul coh.a hanta.
'*Only* Minho likes apples.'

b. 민호가 사과만 좋아한다.
Minho ka sakwa *man* coh.a hanta.
'Minho *only* likes apples.'

This restrictive meaning of *man* also holds true when the particle follows an adverb or some other part of speech:

(9) 빨리만 하면 되니? 잘 해야지. [follows an adverb ('fast')]
Ppali *man* ha.myen toyni? Cal hayyaci.
'You think it's okay *just* to do it fast? You have to do it well.'

5.1.2.3 *nun*

The special particle *un/nun* (which will be referred to as *nun* in the following discussion) has the form *un* after a consonant, *nun* after a vowel.

Of all the special particles, *nun* has the meaning that is the most complex and difficult to analyze and explain; it is the special particle that is the most truly "special." This is particularly true when *nun* is used after a noun in the subject position; in this kind of construction it is difficult to describe consistently how the meaning differs from that of a sentence with the nominative particle *i/ka*. The contribution of *nun* to the meaning in such cases, as well as in a variety of other usages, is usually a subtle one depending upon the larger context in which the utterance appears. For example, the sentence in (9a), below, might be the answer to a question about *who* likes apples: 'Who likes apples?' 'Minho. Minho [marked by *ka*] likes apples'. In this situation, *nun* would be quite ungrammatical. But, in a discussion of the fruits various people prefer, (9b) would imply that other people besides Minho like other things besides apples: 'Minho likes apples (but that's not necessarily true of the other people)'. Here the use of *ka* would be odd. In these cases, and in perhaps the majority of situations, it is the context beyond the sentence itself that determines which of the two particles[7] is to be used.

(9) a. 민호가 사과를 좋아한다. [*ka* following the subject]
Minho *ka* sakwa lul coh.a hanta.
'Minho likes apples.'

b. 민호는 사과를 좋아한다. [*nun* following the subject]
Minho *nun* sakwa lul coh.a hanta.
'Minho likes apples.'

(10)a. 워싱톤이 미국의 수도다. [*i* following the subject]
Wesingthon *i* Mikwuk uy swuto 'ta.
'Washington is America's capital.'

b. 워싱톤은 미국의 수도다. [*un* following the subject]
Wesingthon *un* Mikwuk uy swuto 'ta.
'Washington is America's capital.'

The basic function of *nun* is to subdue the focus on the word to which it attaches and draw the listener's attention to the rest of the sentence.[8] It is as if the speaker is saying: 'Washington—now here's what I'm going to tell you about that city — it's America's capital.' There are a variety of reasons why a speaker would use *nun* in this way. One is that the person or item has actually been mentioned before. Or it might be something generic—like *salam* 'man' in (11). When a noun of this kind is used in a conversation, it is put into the background of the sentence with *nun*.

(11) 사람은 이성적 동물이다.
> Salam un iseng-cek tongmul ita.
> 'Man [marked by *nun*] is a thinking animal.'

This latter kind of usage, which is also seen in the sentences of (12), is one in which *nun* sets off something to be defined or established as a rule. When used as a marker for a generic noun of this type, *nun* cannot be replaced by *ka* without the sentence seeming quite unnatural—or, in the case of (11), were *salam* 'man' to be followed by *ka,* it would mean something like: 'Not something else, but just *man* (is a thinking animal)', and the meaning of the sentence would of course no longer be one of definition.

(12) a. 할아버지는 아버지의 아버지다.
> Hal.apeci *nun* apeci uy apeci 'ta.
> 'A grandfather [marked by *nun*] is one's father's father.'

b. 한국은 삼면이 바다로 둘러쌓인 반도다.
> Hankwuk *un* sammyen i pata lo twulle ssah.in panto 'ta.
> 'Korea [marked by *nun*] is a peninsula surrounded on three sides by seas.'

In (13a), below, *nun* is used after the direct object of the verb, and in (13b), after a locative phrase. In both of these examples, the phrases marked by *nun* have been displaced to the front of the sentence, where they serve as the topic of that sentence. They are what the sentences are about. Because *nun* is found so often after the topic of a sentence in this way, it is commonly known as the "topic marker."

(13) a. 돈과 명예는 누구나 좋아한다.
> Ton kwa myengyey *nun* nwukwu na coh.a hanta.
> 'Money and fame [marked by *nun*], everyone likes them.'

b. 로마에서는 로마법을 따라야 한다.
> Loma eyse *nun* Loma-pep ul ttalaya hanta.
> 'In Rome [marked by *nun*], one has to follow Roman law.'
> (I.e., 'When in Rome do as the Romans.')

But *nun* is not found exclusively after topics. Let us look at some other common usages of this very special particle.

One clear-cut function of *nun* is to show contrast. If two items are to be contrasted, they will both be marked by *nun*. The effect of this contrastive marking with *nun* is to draw attention away from the two items and focus it onto the ways in which they contrast: *Minho nun sakwa lul coh.a haci man, na nun coh.a haci anh.a* 민호는 사과를 좋아하지만, 나는 좋아하지 않아 'Minho likes apples, but I don't.' When only one of the items is mentioned, a contrast is still implied by the use of *nun*.

The use of *nun* to show contrast is clearest when the particle appears in a place other than the subject position. In (11), below, the implication is that Minho may like apples, but he is probably not too fond of other fruits. Notice that nothing in the sentence is overtly said about any other fruits; the idea of other fruits arises naturally because the use of *nun* here strongly implies a contrast.

(11) 민호가 사과는 좋아한다.
Minho ka sakwa *nun* coh.a hanta.
'Apples [marked by *nun*], Minho likes.'

In fact, a *nun*-marked phrase anywhere but the initial position in the sentence is highly marked for this kind of contrastive interpretation. Anyone hearing (12) gets the strong impression that Yŏnghŭi's eyes might be pretty, but her other facial features are not:

(12) 영희가 눈은 예쁘다.
Yenghuy ka nwun *un* yeypputa.
'Yŏnghŭi, as far as her eyes are concerned, they're pretty.'

Often, an element of a sentence—particularly a long one—is selected as the least novel, or the least necessary, and then put at the beginning of the sentence and marked by *nun*.[9] By doing so, attention is drawn away from the element and shifted onto the rest of the sentence. In (13), for example, 'I' could just as easily be omitted from the sentence; instead, it is said first and marked by *nun*. Although this position is customarily called the "topic" position, there is really no helpful reason to think of 'I' here as the topic of the statement. The pronoun is simply background information, and the focus on it is therefore subdued. Backgrounding the word is the function of *nun* in this sentence.

(13) 나는 지난 토요일밤에 공원에서 친구를 만났다.
Na *nun* cinan thoyoil-pam ey kongwen eyse chinkwu lul mannass.ta.
'Me, I met a friend last Saturday night in the park.'

Because of its use to put information into the background, *nun* is not compatible with a subject that is newly introduced information. In example (14), *makwi halmeni* 'witch' is new information. It is the subject of the sentence and the focus of attention, and as such, it cannot be followed by *nun*. The sentence would be ungrammatical if *nun* were substituted for *ka* after this word.

(14) 옛날 옛날 옛적에 아주 마음씨 고약한 마귀 할머니가 있었답니다.
     Yeys-nal yeys-nal yeys-cek ey acwu maum-ssi koyak-han makwi-halmeni *ka*
     iss.ess.tapnita.
     'Once upon a time, long ago, there was a very evil witch [marked by *ka*].'

For the same reason, the answer to the question of who? (or what, etc.) cannot be followed by the particle *nun*. By its very nature, the answer to a question-word question is new information, after all. Thus, in (15), *nun* cannot be used in place of *ka*.

(15) (누가 이겼니?) 민호가 이겼어요.
     (Nwuka i.kyess.ni?) Minho *ka* i.kyess.e yo.
     '(Who won?) Minho [marked by *ka*] won.'

We can see from these examples that the nominative case marker *ka* has the function of conveying *new* information, while the special particle *nun* is used for *old* information. In (12), above, 'a grandfather' and 'Korea' are not newly introduced items of information; no matter when one uses *hankwuk* 'Korea' in the conversation, the information that there is a country called "Korea" is shared knowledge. For this reason, the word 'Korea' is *old* information and can be used as a topic even if it has never once been mentioned before. The particle *nun* can follow a word like this that is shared information the first time it is brought up in the conversation.

To summarize, the special particle *nun* backgrounds a word or phrase in order to draw attention to what is about to be said. The backgrounded word must be old information, and that can be either because it has actually been mentioned before or because it is generic information. In either case, if a word is the topic of what is about to be said, it is marked by *nun*. A word is also marked by *nun* when it is being contrasted with something else; showing contrast is another major function of this particle.

The three special particles we have looked at so far—*nun*, *to*, and *man*—share the characteristic that they bring into question one of the possible candidates for comparison. But they differ in the value they have for the remaining possible candidates for comparison: *nun* is isolating (or reserving); *to* is inclusive; and *man* is exclusive. Since most special particles strongly reflect the speaker's subjectivity, they have the restriction that they are not often used in objective contexts. In contrast, since *nun*, *to*, and *man* appear freely in subjective contexts or objective contexts, their range of usage is broad.

5.1.2.4 *iya*

Next, let us examine a few of the other special particles. The first we will look at is *iya*. The particle has the shape *iya* after a noun ending in a consonant but is abbreviated to *ya* after a noun ending in a vowel.[10]

It is easier to understand the meaning of *iya* by comparing it to the particle *nun*, since, like *nun*, *iya* functions to show contrast. But *iya* has a much more restricted distribution and usage than *nun*. In most contexts, *nun* can be substituted for *iya*, but it is only under very special conditions that *iya* can stand in place of *nun*. One important restriction on the use of *iya* is that it can only be used in a declarative sentence where it implies a contrastive interpretation. And so, for example, a sentence like *Minho ya sewul ey kaci* 'Minho is going to Seoul' may end in a sentence-ending, finite suffix, but the use of *iya* to mark the noun *Minho* raises the expectation that something contrastive like 'however . . . (somebody poor like me can't go)' will follow; if it does not, it is at least implied.

(16)a. 민호야 서울에 {가지, 가겠지, 가지만}
   Minho *ya* Sewul ey (kaci, kakeyss.ci, kaci man)
   'Minho (marked by *iya*) is going to Seoul.' (with verbal endings that permit, or require, a following, contrastive clause)

b. ?민호야 서울에 간다.
   ?Minho *ya* Sewul ey kanta.
   '(id.)' [the verbal ending is finite and conclusive]

What is most interesting is that *iya* has this contrastive implication in a declarative sentence but cannot be used at all in interrogative, imperative, or comitative sentences. Note that the particle *nun* is used quite naturally in these latter sentence types, and always with a strong contrastive interpretation.

(17)a. 민호는 서울에 가라.
   Minho *nun* Sewul ey kala.
   'Minho, (you) go to Seoul [unlike others, who are not to go].'

b. 민호는 서울에 가자.
   Minho *nun* Sewul ey kaca
   'Minho, let's go to Seoul [others are not to go].'

c. 민호는 서울에 가니?
   Minho *nun* Sewul ey kani?
   'Minho, are you going to Seoul? [unlike the others]'

d. ×민호야 서울에 {가라, 가자, 가니?}
   ×Minho *ya* Sewul ey {kala, kaca, kani?}[11]

In the above examples, the implicational meaning of the particle *nun* requires elaborate English paraphrases.

In the following example, *iya* is used naturally in the first clause, but in the conclusive, main clause, *nun* is the particle of choice:

(18) 돈이야 김씨가 더 많지만, 자식은 이씨가 더 잘 두었지.

    Ton *iya* Kim-ssi te manh.ciman, casik *un* I-ssi ka te cal twuess.ci.

    'As for money [followed by *iya*], Mr. Kim has more, but as for children [followed by *nun*], Mr. Yi has done better.'

The particle *iya* encompasses the adverbial meaning 'naturally, of course'. Therefore, it is often used together with the adverbs *tangyen.hi* 'naturally' and *mullon* 'of course', which reinforce the interpretation. In other words, even though *iya* has the contrastive meaning of *nun*, it cannot be used in completely objective contexts, but only those in which the speaker acknowledges that the statement is naturally implied.

(19) 돈이야 {물론, 당연히} 김씨가 많지.

    Ton *iya* {mullon, tangyen.hi} Kim-ssi ka manh.ci.

    'As for money, {of course, naturally} Mr. Kim has more.'

5.1.2.5 *ina*

Like the particle *man*, the basic meaning of the particle *ina* is 'the only choice'. However, while *man* is used to express a positive choice that eliminates all other possibilities, *ina* indicates a passive choice that shows the speaker has chosen what remains after other possibilities have been eliminated; in other words, *ina* indicates that the best choice is not possible and that the speaker is opting for what is next best.

(20) a. 양복을 살 돈이 모자라니 넥타이나 사자.

    Yangpok ul salq ton i mocalani neykthai *na* saca.

    'Since we don't have enough money to buy a suit, let's buy *just* a tie.'

  b. 도움을 못 주겠으면 욕이나 하지 말지.

    Towum ul mos cwukeyss.umyen yok *ina* haci malci.

    'If you can't help, *at least* don't criticize.'

5.1.2.6 *inama*

A particle with a usage very similar to that of *ina* is *inama*. Both of these particles can be used to express a choice; the difference is that *ina* is used when the speaker is dissatisfied and thinks of the choice negatively, while *inama* is used when the speaker is happy with the choice and thinks of it positively.

(21) 겨우 넥타이나 사니 {ˣ다행이다, 한심하다}.

　　　Kyewu neykthai *na* sani {ˣtahayng ita, hansim-hata}.

　　　'{ˣIt's lucky, It's pitiful} that I could *just* barely buy a tie,'

(22) 넥타이나마 사니 {다행이다, ˣ한심하다}.

　　　Neykthai *nama* sani {tahayng ita, ˣhansim-hata}.

　　　'{It's lucky, ˣIt's pitiful} that I could *at least* buy a tie.'

The usages in the following examples are similar. In (23), since it is difficult to think of being an entrepeneur as something less desirable than being a salaried worker, *inama* is unnatural. And in (24), it is hard to realistically consider a house with a garden as less desirable than one without—after all, a house with a garden represents the dream of the ordinary person. Therefore, *inama* cannot be used in this context, either.

(23) 월급장이 그만두고 사업 {이나 ˣ이나마} 할까?

　　　Welkup-cangi kuman twuko saep {ina ˣinama} halkka?

　　　'Shall I quit my job and go into business for myself?'

(24) 정원 딸린 집 {이나, ˣ이나마} 한 채 있었으면!

　　　Cengwen ttallin cip {ina, ˣinama} han-chay iss.ess.umyen!

　　　'If I only had a house with a garden!'

When linked to an adverb or a quantity expression, however, the particle *ina* can also be used for emphasis with no implication of choice—as in (25), for example. The particle *inama* cannot be used in this kind of context because it does not have the function of emphasis.

(25) a. 사과가 너무 {나, ˣ나마} 비싸다. (emphasis)

　　　　Sakwa ka nemu {na, ˣnama} pissata.

　　　　'Apples are *too expensive.*'

　　　b. 사과 한 개에 천원 {이나, ˣ이나마} 해요? (emphasis)

　　　　Sakwa han-kay ey chen-wen {ina, ˣinama} hay yo?

　　　　'One apple costs a *thousand wŏn* [that much]?'

Of course, *ina* does not have to be used just for emphasis after a quantity expression. In (26a), even though the particle is linked to the quantity expression 'many, much', the context is one of choice. The reason the particle *inama* is not idiomatic in this example is because *manh.i* 'many, much' represents a desirable situation. In (26b), the context is also one of choice, but because 'used clothing' can represent something unfortunate, *inama* as well as *ina* is possible here.

(26) a. 깎아 주지 않으려면 많이 {나, ˣ나마} 주세요. (choice)

Kkakk.a cwuci anh.ulyemyen manh.i {na, ˣnama} cwusey yo.
'If you don't want to reduce the price, then at least give me some more
[of the items than the previously discussed quantity].'

b. 정 없으시면 그 헌옷{이나, 이나마} 주세요. (choice)
Ceng eps.usimyen ku hen-os {ina, inama} cwusey yo.
'If you really don't have anything, then [at least] give me those old
clothes.'

5.1.2.7 *kkaci, cocha, mace*

The special particles *kkaci, cocha,* and *mace* express meanings that are
very similar; their basic meaning of 'in addition' and 'also' is very close to
that of the particle *to.* However, in contrast with *to,* which is used without
contextual restrictions, the particles *kkaci, cocha,* and *mace* have semantic restrictions on their use, as can be seen in (28b), where the context is one in
which the results follow as a natural consequence of the situation.

(27) 너{도, 까지, 조차, 마저} 나를 이해해 주지 않는구나.
Ne {to, kkaci, cocha, mace} na lul ihay-hay cwuci anh.nunkwuna.
'*Even* you don't understand me!'

(28)a. 우등생인 민호{도, 까지, 조차, 마저} 시험에 떨어졌다.
Wutungsayng in Minho {to, kkaci, cocha, mace} sihem ey ttel.ecyess.ta
'*Even* Minho, who is an honor-roll student, failed the exam.'

b. 우리 반 꼴지인 민호{도, ˣ까지, ˣ조차, ˣ마저} 시험에 떨어졌다.
Wuli pan kkolci in Minho {to, ˣkkaci, ˣcocha, ˣmace} sihem ey
ttel.ecyessta.
'Minho, who is at the bottom of our class, failed the exam, *too.*'

As can be seen in these examples, *kkaci, cocha,* and *mace* have similar
meanings and can be used in similar situations, but there are subtle semantic distinctions between them. *Kkaci* and *cocha* express the extreme case,
when the outcome is something the speaker did not expect, while *mace* indicates that the outcome is an extreme, even outlandish, possibility. In addition, when the phrase appears in positions besides that of the subject, it is
natural to use *kkaci* in an affirmative construction and *cocha* is more natural
in a negative construction. That is another difference between the two particles. In (29), the phrase *cip kkaci* is used in the meaning 'something as important as the house, too,' implying that even though the speaker might lose
the house, there could also be other property left. However, the use of *cip
mace* shows that "everything was lost, including the last thing to remain, the
house"; in other words, *cip mace nallyessta* means that the person was cleaned

out, with no remaining property at all. In (30), since not greeting neighbors is something unexpected, both *kkaci* and *cocha* should be possible, but since the sentence has a negative connotation, *kkaci* is unnatural here. As for *mace*, since a failure to greet the neighbor is surprising but not unimaginably outrageous, its use would be awkward. In (31), one would not normally expect a present from a miser, but, again, it is certainly not beyond the realm of possibility, and so the use of *mace* is awkward here, too. The use of *cocha* is unnatural because the sentence is an affirmative one.

(29) 그는 도박으로 집{까지, ?조차, 마저} 날렸다.

Ku nun topak ulo cip {kkaci, ?cocha, mace} nallyess.ta.

'Through gambling he *even* lost the house.'

(30) 그는 이웃과 인사{?까지, 조차, ?마저} 안 한다.

Ku nun iwus kwa insa {?kkaci, cocha, ?mace} an hanta.

'He doesn't *even* greet the neighbors.'

(31) 그 구두쇠가 선물{까지, ?조차, ?마저} 사 올 줄은 몰랐다.

Ku kwukwusoy ka senmul {kkaci, ?cocha, ?mace} sa olq cwul mollass.ta.

'I didn't know that miser was *even* going to bring a present.'

By attaching the particle *to* to *kkaci, cocha,* or *mace,* the meaning is emphasized more strongly, as is the case in (32):

(32) 우등생인 민호{까지도, 조차도, 마저도} 시험에 떨어졌다.

Wutungsayng in Minho {kkaci to, cocha to, mace to} sihem ey ttel.ecyessta.

'Even *Minho, who is an honor student,* failed the exam.'

Besides these usages, *kkaci* is also used in the construction '__*puthe* __*kkaci*', where it has the meaning of the final endpoint. In this construction *kkaci* cannot be replaced by *to*. Here the usage is distinguished from that of special particles.

(33) 서울부터 부산{까지, ˣ도} 기차로 몇 시간 걸리지?

Sewul puthe Pusan {kkaci, ˣto} kicha lo myech-sikan kellici?

'[I wonder] How many hours by train it is from Seoul to Pusan?'

5.1.2.8 *mata*

The special particle *mata* means 'each'. For those familiar with the usage of this particle, its meaning might appear to be similar to that of the plural suffix *tul*, but it is not. The particle is distinct from *tul*, which only marks plurality; *mata*, in contrast, functions as a universal quantifier. In addition,

tul is only used with unreduplicated nouns (for example, *cip-tul* 'houses', not
ˣ*cip-cip-tul*), while *mata*, as in (34) and (35), can be used with both reduplicated and unreduplicated nouns. Also, *mata* and *tul* can be combined and
used together, as in (35), and the meaning is not significantly different from
that of *mata* alone.

(34) 개천절이 되어 집집마다 태극기를 달았다.
    Kaychen-cel i toy.e cip-cip *mata* thaykukki lul tal.ass.ta.
    'On Foundation Day, [people] hung a *taegŭk* flag on *each* house.'

(35) 사람{마다, 들마다} 제각기 장점과 단점이 있는 법이다.
    Salam {mata, -tul mata} ceykakki cangqcem kwa tanqcem i iss.nun pep ita.
    '*Each* person has his or her own good points and bad points.'

5.1.2.9 *iyamallo*

The particle *iyamallo* means 'really, indeed, precisely that'. Its distribution is limited because it generally only appears in subject position.

(36) a. 노력이야말로 성공의 지름길이다.
    Nolyek *iyamallo* sengkong uy cilum-kil ita.
    'It is *precisely* effort that is the shortcut to success.'

   b. 모차르트야말로 천재 중의 천재다.
    Mochaluthu *yamallo* chencay cwung uy chencay 'ta.
    'Mozart is *truly* a genius among geniuses.'

5.1.2.10 *khenyeng*

The special particle *khenyeng* attaches to a noun or a nominalized verb
or adjective; it means 'anything but, far from, on the contrary, not only, contrary to expectations'. It is often used in the pattern "A *nun khenyeng* B *to*
. . .", and when it attaches to *nun*, it emphasizes the meaning of that particle.
When *khenyeng* attaches to the nominalizing suffix *-ki*, it is especially natural
for *khenyeng* to be preceded by *nun*. Moreover, "A *nun khenyeng* B *to*. . ." is
generally followed by a negative expression.

(37) a. 우승은커녕 예선에도 못들겠다.
    Wusung *un khenyeng* yeysen ey to mos tulkeyss.ta.
    '*Far from* winning, [we/they] won't even make the preliminary round.'

   b. 뛰기는커녕 걷지도 못하겠다.
    Ttwiki *nun khenyeng* ketci to mos hakeyss.ta.
    'I can't even walk, *much less* run.'

5.2 Verb Endings

As was pointed out in the introduction, Korean verb endings are complex, both in their structure and in how they are used. They carry much of the functional load of the grammar. An extremely large number of grammatical phenomena, including the sentence type, mode, speech level, tense, conjunction, and so on, as well as various subtler semantic connotations, are expressed through verb endings. There is disagreement as to how many verb endings there are; the number varies according to which grammatical analysis is being used. Still, at the very least, there are more than forty, and perhaps more than seventy, different inflectional morphemes.[12] All of these endings differ in function and meaning.

Verb endings can be subdivided into a number of subclasses (cf. 4.2.4). First, by their distributional position, they are divided into *prefinal endings* (선어말어미) and *final endings* (어말어미). Final endings end the word—that is, they are the last element in the conjugational ending. Prefinal endings, by necessity, combine with a following final ending; in other words, they are inflectional elements that come between the stem and the final ending.

Prefinal endings are few in number, and their functions are simple; they are not divided into subclasses. However, final endings include a number of different subtypes. First, they are divided according to whether they end the sentence or not into *sentence-final endings* (문말어미) and *nonsentence final endings* (비문말어미). Then, nonsentence final endings are further subdivided into *conjunctive endings* (접속어미) and *function-converting endings* (전성어미). *Conjunctive endings* link clauses; they do not cause changes in the original forms of the verbs or adjectives linked by these endings. Function-converting endings cause the inflected word to function as some other part of speech, such as a noun or an adnominal. Therefore, function-converting endings are subdivided into *nominalizing endings* (명사화어미) and *adnominalizing endings* (관형사화어미), depending upon which part of speech the inflecting word is converted into. These various classes and subclasses are shown in Figure 8.

In this section, we will examine the inflectional endings of Korean categorized by these classes. Rather than attempt to treat all the endings, we will focus attention instead on representative inflectional endings that have important grammatical functions.

5.2.1 Prefinal Endings

Prefinal endings function to show *tense, aspect, modality,* and *subject honorification.* The prefinal ending *-si-,* which is used for subject honorification, will be treated in detail in chapter 7. Here we will look only at the prefinal endings *-ess-, -ess.ess-, -keyss-,* and *-te-.* Since these endings are all in a general

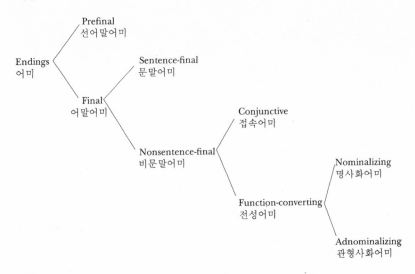

Figure 8

way related to tense, the discussion in this section can also be considered a treatment of the concept of tense in Korean.

5.2.1.1 *-ess-*

The phonological shape of this morpheme is in most cases *-ess-*, but it becomes *-ass-* when the last vowel of the stem is *o* or *a*.[13] For example, *po-assta* (보 았다) 'saw', *cwu-essta* (주었다) 'gave'. Following the verb stem *ha-* 'to do', the shape of the ending is uniquely *-yess-*; and, in colloquial usage, the resulting combined form *hayess-* becomes *hayss-*: *ha-yessta* (하였다) → *hayssta* (했다) 'did'.

The main function of *-ess-* is to express past tense. As can be seen in (1) and (2), it is used to show either a past action or past situation. It is used with a verb stem, or an adjective stem, or the copula.

(1) 영희는 어제 부산에 갔다.
    Yenghuy nun ecey Pusan ey k*ass*.ta.
    'Yŏnghŭi *went* to Pusan yesterday.'

(2) 김여사는 젊었을 때 미인이었다.
    Kim-yesa nun celm.*ess*.ulq ttay miin i*ess*.ta.
    'When Mrs. Kim *was* young, she *was* a beauty.'

However, *-ess-* is also used in environments where it cannot be considered simply past tense. In cases such as the following, *-ess-* expresses not some past action, but rather an existing situation.

(3) a. 겨울이 가고, 봄이 왔다.
   Kyewul i kako, pom i w*ass*.ta.
   'Winter has gone, and spring *is here*.' (Lit., 'came', 'has come')

   b. 신랑이 너무 늙었다.
   Sinlang i nemu nulk.*ess*.ta.
   'The bridegroom *is* too *old*.' (Lit., 'has aged')

   c. 너는 오늘도 그 빨간 조끼를 입었구나.
   Ne nun onul to ku ppalkan cokki lul ip.*ess*.kwuna.
   'I see you'*re wearing* that red vest today, too.' (Lit., 'have put on.')

In the case of (3a), it is difficult to pinpoint concretely when 'spring coming' actually happened (compare, for example, the sentence *Pom i ecey wassta* 'Spring arrived yesterday'); the meaning that is expressed here is only that the season now is spring. In (3b) the verb *nulkta* 'grow old, be old' has a special usage. Since this inflecting form cannot be used to describe a concrete event or action, *nulk-essta*, with the ending *-ess-*, expresses not a past action or event but always a situation in the present. The statement in (3c), as well, describes a present situation in which someone is wearing—now has on—a red vest.

In the kinds of usages that we see in (3), the meaning of *-ess-* bears a strong resemblance to a past participle in English. Like the English past participle, *-ess-* expresses in these cases not the past, but a situation that now exists as a result of something that has happened or changed before the present time. The question has often arisen among Korean linguists as to how, in a unified way, to account for these two different meanings of *-ess-*. The problem, however, is not one of the semantics of *-ess-*. The interpretation of *-ess-* as past or past participle depends, rather, upon context and the lexical items with which it is used, particularly the verb.

Let us look at a few concrete examples. The forms *cwuk-* 'die', *(pul ul) khye-* 'turn on (the light)', *kyelhon ha-* 'marry', and *(kong ul) cha-* 'hit, kick (the ball)' are punctual verbs that cannot be inflected for the present tense. But when these verbs are combined with *-ess-*, the interpretation of the resulting form varies depending upon which verb is being used. For example, the statement *Swun.i nun kyelhon hayss.ta* (순이는 결혼했다) means that Suni completed the act of marriage at some unspecified time in the past, and also that she presently is married—that is, she now exists in the state that resulted from that marriage ceremony. Translation of the sentence into English is somewhat arbitrary, because English forces a choice between the meanings 'Suni got married' and 'Suni is married', and, without a supporting context, both meanings are encompassed by the Korean sentence. However, the sentence *Kong ul chass.ta* (공을 찼다) 'He hit the ball' can only be interpreted as the completion of an act and cannot refer to a resulting situation. In examples of noun + copula, such as in (2), above, the use of the morpheme *-ess-*

can only be interpreted as describing a past situation. If someone says *Hyeng un kwun.in iess.ta* (형은 군인이었다) '[older] Brother was a soldier', he is describing a past situation, and from the statement we cannot tell whether the brother is still a soldier or not. We can see from these examples that although the function of *-ess-* depends on the context in which it is used, the differences are principally determined by the type of predicate and that the basic function of *-ess-* is in any event the expression of past tense.

However, in examples such as the following, *-ess-* occurs in a context set in the future:

(4) a. 나는 결혼식 때 한복을 입었으면 좋겠다.
Na nun kyelhon-sik ttay hanpok ul ip.*ess*.umyen coh.keyss.ta.
'At my wedding ceremony I hope I'll be wearing Korean clothes.'
[Lit., 'it will be good if [I] have put on Korean clothes.']

b. 내일 소개받을 사람이 미남이었으면 좋겠다.
Nayil sokay pat.ulq salam i minam i*ess*.umyen coh.keyss.ta.
'I hope the man I meet tomorrow will be handsome.'
[Lit. 'it will be good if [he] was a handsome man.']

In (4), it seems difficult to consider *-ess-* a marker of past tense because it is being used in connection with an event that has still not happened. However, the act is only a future event from the perspective of the time when the speaker makes the utterance; thinking of the act this way fails to make a distinction between natural time and the expression of tense in language. If, on the other hand, tense is understood as tense relative to when the event occurs, then *ip.ess.umyen* 'if [I] have put on' and *minam iess.umyen* 'if [he] was a handsome man' will each be an event or condition taking place in the past compared to the following predicate, *coh.keyss.ta* 'it will be good'. In (4b), the condition whether or not the man is handsome is something that was already determined in the past, and only the time of the verification of the fact is in the future. Moreover, even though the verification is set in the future, it is only after that verification takes place that 'it will be good' has validity. Thus, *minam iess.umyen* is in the past relative to the predicate 'it will be good'. Note that the pattern *-ess.umyen coh.keyss.ta* is a set, idiomatic phrase used to express longing for a hypothetical situation. The time of this longing is the present, but the fulfillment of the conditions that make it good must occur before some future point in time when it is judged to be good. Thus, the analysis of *-ess-* as marker of past tense is semantically consistent in this case as well.

5.2.1.2 *-ess.ess-*

The phonological shape of *-ess.ess-* becomes *-ass.ess-* following a stem ending in *o* or *a*. Following the verb stem *ha-* 'to do', the shape of the ending is *-yess.ess-*, and in colloquial usage this combined form *hayess.ess-* becomes *hayss.ess-*: *ha-yessessta* (하였었다) → *hayssessta* (했었다) 'did'. The form *-ess.ess-* looks at first like a reduplication of the past morpheme *-ess-*. However, the vowel of the second *-ess-* is not subject to the same vowel alternation; in other words, there may be an etymological reason for identifying *-ess.ess-* as a reduplication, but in the modern language the form behaves as a single morphological unit, not two separate occurrences of the past morpheme. Moreover, when considered from a functional point of view, it is difficult to find a need to analyze *-ess.ess-* into two parts.

The ending *-ess.ess-* generally expresses a more remote past than something indicated by *-ess-*. This does not necessarily mean linearly farther back in time, however. Example (1b), below, describes an event that simply took place yesterday and is independent of subsequent developments. The friend being talked about could subsequently have gone home, or he could have stayed. In (1a), the event itself is not something that necessarily took place before what is being described in (1b); what is meant, rather, is that the event was first completed and then the situation changed. In other words, (1a) means that the friend came and then left, thus changing the situation. In other words, what is expressed by *-ess.ess-* is not a simple past but rather circumstances implying a juncture, a discontinuation of the situation.

(1) a. 어제 친구가 놀러 왔었다.
   Ecey chinkwu ka nolle w*ass.ess*.ta
   'A friend came yesterday (but left again).'

   b. 어제 친구가 놀러 왔다.
   Ecey chinkwu ka nolle w*ass*.ta.
   'A friend came yesterday.'

The functional difference between *-ess-* and *-ess.ess-* is perhaps best illustrated when the meanings of the two forms are least clearly distinguished. The meaning of a change of state is especially conspicuous when the predicate is an action verb and less so when it is descriptive of a situation. In cases such as (2), below, a change of state might be obvious, but because of practical considerations the meanings expressed by *-ess-* and *-ess.ess-* are not as clearly distinguished as they are in (1), where an action is involved. For example, there are certain adjectival and copular expressions that imply a change of state even without the use of *-ess.ess-*. The sentence in (2a) is like this. If the predicate were *yeyppess.ta* instead of *yeyppess.ess.ta*, there would be very little difference in meaning. Of course, the grammatical structure of *yeyppess.ta* may not overtly signal that the woman is no longer pretty, but because in the real world (and perhaps especially in Korean society) there is an association of feminine beauty with youth, the pragmatics of usage mean that both forms imply a change of state. Similarly, in (2b) *kolmok-taycang* 'neighborhood bully' is not an expression used to describe adults, and so the intepretation of a change of state would be much the same whether the speaker used *-ess-* or *-ess.ess-*.

(1) a. 김여사는 젊었을 때 예뻤었다.
Kim-yesa nun celm.ess.ulq ttay yeypp*ess.ess*.ta.
'Mrs. Kim was pretty when she was young.'

b. 김장군은 어렸을 때 골목대장이었었다.
Kim Cangkwun un elyess.ulq ttay kolmok-taycang i*ess.ess*.ta.
'General Kim was a neighborhood bully when he was a child.'

However, even in these cases the effect of *-ess.ess-* is to strengthen the feeling that there has been a change of state. Even here, the ending is used to give emphasis to the change. In other words, while *-ess-* simply marks the past tense, *-ess.ess-* signals that the event or situation is something in the past from which we are cut off and that no longer exerts influence in the present. For this reason, *-ess.ess-* is often called the "remote past tense" (대과거시제).

This "remote past tense" of Korean is different from the past perfect, or pluperfect, of English. In English, what transpires after the action marked by the past perfect is usually explicitly stated in the sentence, while in Korean, as we have seen in the preceding examples, this is not done. The Korean sentence contains only the implication of change; if what has changed were actually expressed, the sentence would break down into something less idiomatic. Koreans stylistically favor the implied over the explicit, and it is this cultural tendency that has perhaps helped shape syntactic usage here.

5.2.1.3 *-keyss-*

The prefinal ending *-keyss-* is often considered a marker of the future tense, and it is true that the ending is often used in reference to things that at the present time have not taken place:

(1) a. 나는 내일 설악산에 가겠다.
Na nun nayil Sel.aksan ey ka*keyss*.ta.
'I'll go to Sŏraksan tomorrow.'

b. 너는 뭘 먹겠니?
Ne nun mwel mek.*keyss*.ni
'What are you going to eat?'

(2) a. 오후에는 날씨가 개겠지요?
Ohwu ey nun nalssi ka kay.*keyss*.ci yo?
'Do you think the weather will clear up in the afternoon?'

b. 네가 떠나고 나면 나는 참 쓸쓸하겠다.
Ney ka ttenako namyen na nun cham ssulssul-ha*keyss*.ta.
'After you've left I'm going to be really lonely.'

However, as we see in the following examples, -*keyss*- is also often used for things existing or occurring at the present time or before the present time. In other words, -*keyss*- is also used for both the present and the past.

(3) a. 지금 서울은 무척 춥겠다.

   Cikum Sewul un muchek chwup*keyss*.ta.

   'Seoul must be extremely cold now.'

   b. 순이가 지금 울고 있겠지.

   Swun.i ka cikum wulko iss.*keyss*.ci.

   'Suni is probably crying now.'

(4) a. 김 선생은 학생 때에도 점잖았겠다.

   Kim-sensayng un haksayng ttay ey to cemcanh.ass.*keyss*.ta.

   'Dr. Kim was probably very genteel when he was a student, too.'

   b. 너는 어렸을 때에도 미인이었겠다.

   Ne nun elyess.ulq ttay ey to miin iess.*keyss*.ta.

   'You must have been beautiful when you were a child, too.'

We can see from these examples that -*keyss*- is not a morpheme that marks tense. In examples such as those of (1), -*keyss*- expresses instead the intent of the subject. In other words, (1a) is not a simple statement of what will happen in the future, for that would be expressed as *Na nun nayil Sel.aksan ey kanta* (나는 내일 설악산에 간다) 'I'm going to Sŏraksan tomorrow'. What sentence (1a) means is 'I intend to go to Sŏraksan tomorrow', it is my plan; I have every reason to believe that the trip will take place, but my statement is primarily an expression of intention. In the remaining examples, where the predicate is a verb whose meaning cannot be influenced by the intention of the speaker, -*keyss*- expresses the speaker's judgment. We can conclude that -*keyss*- is a prefinal ending that expresses the psychological attitude of the speaker, his volition or conjecture. That is, -*keyss*- is a morpheme that expresses modality. In Korean there is no marker for the future tense.

5.2.1.4 -*te*-

Often called the "retrospective", -*te*- has the most idiosyncratic and complex usage of all the prefinal endings. The basic function of the morpheme is to subjectify and transmit facts perceived and known by the speaker from outside the present locale. This feature could be called "remoteness"; that is, the morpheme is a grammatical element that cannot be used in connection with something occurring here and now. If that something is happening now, then it must be in another place; if it is here, then it must be at another time. Only when these conditions are satisfied can -*te*- be used.

The morpheme is written 더 (-*te*-), and that prounication is considered standard Korean. However, in colloquial, unselfconscious Seoul speech, the morpheme is also often pronounced 드 (-*tu*-).[14] Following this prefinal ending -*te*- (or -*tu*-), the final ending -*ta* changes to -*la*; -*e.yo* combined with -*te*- becomes -*teyyo*.

(1) 너 {ˣ지금, 어제} 입은 옷 참 예쁘더라.
   Ne {ˣcikum, ecey} ip.un os cham yeyppu*te*la.
   'The clothes [I saw] you wearing {ˣnow, yesterday} are really pretty.'

(2) 지금 {ˣ이곳, 부산}에는 비가 오더라.
   Cikum {ˣi kos, Pusan} ey nun pi ka o*te*la.
   '[I see] it's raining {ˣhere, in Pusan} now.'
   (said, for example, by a speaker in some place besides Pusan while watching the weather report on television)

Since -*te*- refers to facts that have already been perceived, it can only be used in declarative and interrogative sentences. It cannot be used for imperatives or requests and promises since these sentence types deal with situations that at present have not taken place.

(3) a. 민수가 학교에 가더라.
     Minswu ka hakkyo ey ka*te*la.
     'Minsu went to school [as I recall—I saw him go].'

   b. 민수가 학교에 가더냐?
     Minswu ka hakkyo ey ka*te*nya?
     'Did [you see] Minsu going to school?'

(4) a. ˣ선생님께서 학교에 가더십시오.
     ˣSensayng-nim kkeyse hakkyo ka*te*sipsio.
     ([to a respected teacher] ˣ'Please [I see] go to school.')

   b. ˣ운동회에서 우리 반이 우승을 하더자.
     ˣWuntong-hoy eyse wuli pan i wusung ul ha*te*la.
     (ˣ'let's our class [I see] win at the athletic competition.')

   c. ˣ방학 때는 제주도에 보내 주더마.
     ˣPanghak ttay nun Ceycwuto ey ponay cwu*te*ma.
     (ˣ'I'll send you to Chejudo during school vacation[, I see].')

By saying that -*te*- is only used for something in the past, we are referring not to when the event occurred, but rather to the time of perception. In this sense, -*te*- is a marker of relative tense. In (2), the discussion is about something occurring 'now', but the perception of what is occurring takes place before the time of the utterance. In (5a), below, the departure of the train will take place an hour from now, but the speaker uses -*te*- to indicate that he has already, in the past, become aware of that fact. In cases such as (5b) and (5c), we see that -*te*- can also be combined with -*ess*- or -*keyss*-. The past marker plus -*te*-, -*esste*-, is used to indicate that an event took place before the time of perception, and -*keysste*- is used for a conjecture about a situation that has still not taken place at the time of perception.

(5) a. 기차는 한 시간 후에 출발하더라.
  Kicha nun han-sikan hwu ey chwulpal-ha*te*la.
  '[I see] the train will leave an hour from now.'

 b. 기차는 한 시간 전에 출발하였더라.
  Kicha nun han-sikan cen ey chwulpal-ha.y*ess.te*la.
  '[I see] the train left an hour ago.'

 c. 순이는 이번 시험에 합격하겠더라.
  Swun.i nun i pen sihem ey hapkyek-ha*keys.te*la.
  '[I see that] this time Suni will pass the exam.'

Since -*te*- indicates the speaker has observed the fact at some remove, he cannot use it in connection with his own action. However, an action of his that took place in a dream or without his conscious awareness is exempted from this rule; in such cases, the use of -*te*- places the speaker in a separate, objective position, from which he has, in a sense, observed himself.

(6) ˣ내가 매일 도서관에 가더라.
  ˣNayka mayil tosekwan ey ka*te*la.
  ('ˣ[I see] I go to the library every day.')

(7) a. 어제 꿈 속에서 내가 도서관에 가더라.
  Ecey kkwum sok eyse nayka tosekwan ey ka*te*la.
  '[I notice that] in my dream last night I went to the library.'

 b. 졸업을 했는데도 무심코 학교 앞으로 가게 되더라.
  Col.ep ul hayssnuntey to musimkho hakkyo aph.ulo kakey toy*te*la.
  'Even though I've graduated, [I see] I inadvertently went to school.'

However, when the predicate expresses the feelings of the speaker, only the speaker can be the subject of that predicate. (Adjectives such as *chwupta* 'be cold', *musepta* 'be frightening', *kipputa* 'be happy', *cohta* 'be good', *silhta* 'be unpleasant', *maypta* 'be spicy', and *tepta* 'be hot' function as these kinds of predicates.) The reason is that such feelings cannot be observed at a remove by a third party.

(8) a. {나는, ^x너는, ^x그는} 드라큐라가 너무 무섭더라.

    {na nun, ^xne nun, ^xku nun} Tulakhyula ka nemu musep*te*la.

    '[I find] Dracula is awfully scary {for me, ^xfor you, ^xfor him}.'

b. {나는, ^x당신은, ^x민호는} 제2악장이 가장 좋더라.

    {Na nun, ^xtangsin un, ^xMinho nun} cey-2 akcang i kacang coh.*te*la.

    '{I, ^xyou, ^xMinho} [find] the second movement to be the best.'

Since *-te-* refers to facts the speaker has directly perceived, it is awkward to use the morpheme in contexts such as (9a) and (10a), where it is difficult for the speaker to directly perceive what is being stated or where the facts are historical ones that took place before the speaker existed. However, in (9b) and (10b) the use of *-te-* is natural because the contexts are ones where the speaker is able to perceive the facts.

(9) a. ?지구가 둥글더라.

    ?Cikwu ka twungkul*te*la.

    (?'[I see] the world is round.')

b. 위성 사진을 보니 지구가 정말로 둥글더라.

    Wiseng sacin ul poni cikwu ka cengmal lo twungkul*te*la.

    'Looking at satellite photographs, [I see] the world really is round.'

(10)a. ?거북선은 이순신 장군이 만들었더라.

    ?Kepuksen un I Swunsin Cangkwun i mantul.ess.*te*la.

    (?'[I see] General Yi Sunsin made the Turtle Boats.')

b. 역사책을 보니 거북선은 이순신 장군이 만들었더라.

    Yeksa-chayk ul poni kepuksen un I Swunsin Cangkwun i mantul.ess.*te*la.

    'Looking at the history book, [I see] General Yi Sunsin made the Turtle Boats.'

As we have seen above, *-te-* has the idiosyncratic function of relating things of the past from one step removed. On the basis of this function, *-te-* is often referred to as the "retrospective tense" (회상시제). However, it must be cautioned that *-te-* functions in rather complex ways that are difficult to describe simply as "tense."

So far, through prefinal endings, we have taken a general look at tense (as well as aspect and mood) in Korean. We have seen that there is no separate future tense, but there is a present and a past tense, as well as a remote past tense and a retrospective tense. However, in our discussion, we have not dealt with the question of how the overall system is structured. Do we consider the remote past tense and the retrospective tense to be on an equal footing with present and past tense, or do we treat them as secondary? An even more basic question is whether separate grammatical categories should be established in Korean for aspect and tense. These questions are important topics of controversy dealt with in various different ways in Korean grammars. A detailed treatment of these issues, however, is beyond the scope of our discussion here.

5.2.2 Final Endings

A number of final endings serve to end the sentence. These endings function first to divide the sentence into *declarative, interrogative, imperative,* and *propositive* sentence types, and, at the same time, they function in the honorific system to show a politeness level to the listener. (Cf. section 7.5.) In the following chart showing typical final endings, the verb *mak-* 'to block' and the adjective *cak-* 'to be small' are displayed according to sentence type and politeness level:

Style	Declarative	Interrogative	Imperative	Propositive
Formal	막습니다	막습니까	막으 십시오	막으십시다
(합쇼)	작습니다	작습니까	— — —	— — —
Polite	막아요	막아요	막아요/막으세요	막아요
(해요)	작아요	작아요	— — —	— — —
Semiformal	막으오	막으오	막으시오	막읍시다
(하오)	작으오	작으오	— — —	— — —
Familiar	막네	막아	막으오	막세
(하게)	작네	작아	— — —	— — —
Panmal	막아	막아	막아	막아
(반말)	작아	작아	— — —	— — —
Plain	막는다	막느냐	막아라	막자
(해라)	작다	작으냐	— — —	— — —

A few remarks should be added about the above chart. First, notice that adjectives do not inflect for imperative and propositive sentence types (and so English expressions such as "be happy!" or "let's be happy!" are equivalent to different kinds of constructions in Korean). Next, the *panmal* style (which literally means 'half-language')[15] does not have separate endings to differentiate among declarative, interrogative, imperative, and propositive sentences; the same forms are used for all of these sentence types. In the *panmal* style, a rising intonation at the end of the sentence is the only indicator of a question, and the only way to differentiate among declarative, imperative, and propositive is by context. In the polite and semiformal styles, declaratives and interrogatives are distinguished by intonation.

The propositive ('let's') has special constraints on its use. Since, by its nature, it includes the speaker as one of the participants in the action, a speaker who uses it in the formal and polite styles seems to be applying the same terms of honor to herself as to her listener. This can cause a certain sociolinguistic awkwardness, and as a result these verb forms are in practice only rarely used. However, the semiformal verb form in (1) is perfectly natural in most situations, while in (2a), where the listener commands high respect from the speaker, the semiformal verb form is not especially respectful. The situation here would seem to demand the use of the formal *mak.usipsita*, but in actual practice that form occurs rather infrequently. The reason is that the propositive construction itself seems too direct, and thus a bit abrupt and rude, when used with a person of much higher social rank. As a result, the kind of construction generally used in this type of situation is an indirect imperative such as *mak.usiciyo*, as seen in (2b). In the polite style, the use of an imperative such as *mak.ayo* instead of a separate, unique propositive form is also probably the result of this sociolinguistic constraint on the use of the propositive form.

(1) 여러분, 우리의 모든 힘을 합쳐 적의 침략 을 막읍시다.
      Yele-pun, wuli uy motun him ul hap-chye cek uy chimlyak ul mak.upsita.
      'People! Let us stop the invasion of the enemy by working together!'

(2) a. 선생님, 저희랑 여기를 막읍시다.
      Sensayng-nim, cehuy lang yeki lul mak.upsita.
      'Professor [Kim], let's stop up this place.' [not quite respectful enough]

    b. 선생님, 저희랑 여기를 막으시지요.
      Sensayng-nim, cehuy lang yeki lul mak.usici yo.
      'Professor [Kim], why don't we stop up this place.'

In the plain style, there is also an interrogative form *-ni* that is used with almost the same frequency as *-nunya* (or, with an adjective stem, *-(u)nya*), but *-nunya* has a wider distribution than *-ni*. For one thing, the form *-ni* is not used in the written language, while *-nunya/unya* is idiomatic in both written and spoken Korean; also, as can be seen in example (4), *-nunya* can function unchanged as the head of a noun phrase. For this reason, we have used *-nunya/unya* instead of *-ni* as the representative ending of the plain style interrogative.

(3) a. 순이야, 너 어디 가느냐/가니?
      Swun.i ya, ne eti kanunya/kani?
      'Suni, where are you going?'

    b. 어디가 더 넓으냐/넓니?
      Eti ka te nelq.unya/nelpni?
      'Which place is the widest?'

(4) 누가 고양이 목에 방울을 {다느냐, ˣ다니}가 문제다.
Nwuka koyangi mok ey pangwul ul {ˣtanunya, tani} ka muncey 'ta.
'The question is, who will hang the bell on the cat's neck?'
[Here the interrogative with *-nunya* functions as the subject]

As a rule, the plain style is used in most writing intended for general audiences, such as newspaper articles and books. However, in the case of questions, the familiar style is the style chosen. In (5) and (6), below, both forms shown are in each case possible in the spoken language, but the forms marked here as ungrammatical are not idiomatic in the formal written style of things such as textbooks.

(5) 한국의 수도는 {서울이다, ˣ서울이네}.
Hankwuk uy swuto nun {Sewul ita, ˣSewul iney}
'Seoul is the capital of Korea.'
[plain style]

(6) 한국의 수도는 {ˣ어디냐, 어디인가}?
Hankwuk uy swuto nun {ˣeti 'nya, eti inka}?
'What is the capital of Korea?'
[familiar style]

Besides the basic sentence types given in the above chart, other sentence types can also be set up for Korean, including the promissory, the exclamatory, and the permissive. These other kinds of sentences require special, separate endings in the plain style. However, in speech styles other than the plain style, these additional types of sentences are expressed through the use of the endings given in the above chart for the basic sentence types. Thus, in these other speech styles, the additional sentence types can be thought of as special uses of the declarative and imperative.

(7) a. 이번 휴가 때는 꼭 너희 집에 가마.
I pen hyuka ttay nun kkok nehuy cip ey ka*ma*.
'I'll definitely come to your house this vacation.'
[Promissory sentence in plain style using the verb ending *-ma*]

b. 이번 휴가에는 꼭 선생님 댁에 가겠어요.
I pen hyuka ey nun kkok Sensayng-nim tayk ey kakeyss.*e yo*.
'I will definitely come to your house [to pay my respects] this vacation.'
[Promissory sentence in polite style using the declarative ending]

(8) a. 기러기가 참 많이도 날아가는구나!
Kileki ka cham manh.i to nal.a ka*nunkwuna*!
'There are really a lot of wild geese flying by!'
[Exclamatory sentence in plain style using the verb ending *-nunkwuna*]

   b. 기러기가 참 많이도 날아갑니다!
      Kileki ka cham manh.i to nal.a ka*pnita.*
      'There are really a lot of wild geese flying by!'
      [Exclamatory sentence in formal style using the declarative ending]

(9) a. 가고 싶으면 가렴/가려무나.
       Kako siph.umyen ka*lyem*/ ka*lyemuna.*
       'If you want to go, please go.'
       [Permissive sentence in plain style using the verb ending *-(u)lyem(una)*]

   b. 가고 싶으면 가요.
      Kako siph.umyen *ka yo.*
      'If you want to go, please go.'
      [Permissive sentence in polite style using declarative/imperative ending]

   The diversity of Korean final endings goes well beyond what has been discussed here, particularly because of the deferential forms in the honorific system. These deferential forms and the honorific system will be discussed later in chapter 7.

5.2.3 Conjunctive Endings (접속어미)

   Conjunctive endings end the clause but not the sentence. They tie the clause to the clause that follows. This conjunction can be *coordinate* (등위접속) or *subordinate* (종속접속). Coordinate conjunction links two or more independent clauses of equal standing, while subordinate conjunction indicates that the first clause is subordinate to the second and has a meaning of cause, condition, or the like. It is the choice of conjunctive ending that ordinarily determines whether the conjunction is coordinate or subordinate.[16]
   Some endings have distinctive morphemic shapes. The vowel -*u*- at the beginning of certain endings is elided after a stem ending in a vowel. The infinitive ending -*e* has the shape /e/ after stems ending in *e, u,* or *wu* and the shape /a/ after stems ending in *a* or *o*; after the verb stem *ha*- 'to do', the infinitive has the shape -*ye* in more formal speech, while, in the colloquial language, *ha*- 'to do' plus the infinitive ending becomes, idiosyncratically, *hay.*
   The conjunctive endings are the most numerous type of endings found in Korean, and their functional meanings are the most varied and difficult to explain. Moreover, of these conjunctive endings, the subordinate conjunctives are the most complex.
   We will first look at some representative forms used for coordinate conjunction. In the following examples, the endings in (1) are used to enumerate a simple series; those in (2) to indicate contrast; and those in (3) to indicate choice.

(1) a. 산은 높고, 바다는 깊다.
       San un noph.*ko,* pata nun kiph.ta.
       'The mountains are high, *and* the sea is deep.'

b. 아버지는 엄하셨으며, 어머니는 인자하셨다.
   Apeci nun em-ha.syess.*umye*, emeni nun inca-ha.syess.ta.
   'Father was strict, *and* Mother was affectionate.'

(2) a. 형은 떠났으나, 동생은 남아 있다.
   Hyeng un ttenass.*una*, tongsayng un nam.a iss.ta.
   '[My] older brother has left, *but* [my] younger siblings are still at home.'

b. 몸은 떠났지만, 마음은 고향에 있다.
   Mom un ttenass.*ciman*, maum un kohyang ey iss.ta.
   'I may have physically left, *but* my heart is still in my old home place.'

(3) a. 술래는 노래를 부르거나, 춤을 추어라.
   Swullay nun nolay lul pulu*kena*, chwum ul chwuela.
   'The one who's 'it' has to either sing a song *or* do a dance.'

b. 민수가 가든지, 민호가 가든지 누구든 빨리 가거라.
   Minswu ka ka*tunci*, Minho ka katunci nwukwu tun ppalli kakela.
   'Minsu *or* Minho, somebody go quickly.'

Next, let us look at some examples of subordinate conjunction. As we have pointed out above, the endings of subordinate conjunction are varied and come in many different types. The examples that follow are divided into different semantic categories:

(4) time
   a. 조명이 꺼지고, 영화가 시작됐다.
   Comyeng i kkeci*ko*, yenghwa ka sicak-twayss.ta
   'The lighting was turned off, *and then* the movie started.'

b. 순이는 늘 음악을 들으며 공부를 한다.
   Swun.i nun nul um.ak ul tul.*umye* kongpu lul hanta.
   'Suni is always listening to music *while* she's studying.'

c. 갑자기 바람이 불면서 촛불이 꺼졌다.
   Kapcaki palam i pul*myense* chos-pul i kkecyess.ta.
   '*When* the wind suddenly blew, the candle went out.'

d. 종이배를 접어 시냇물에 띄웠다.
   Congi-pay lul cep.*e* sinays-mul ey ttuywess.ta.
   '[I] folded a paper boat, *and then* set it afloat on the stream.'

e. 비가 그치자 모두들 밖으로 뛰쳐나갔다.
   Pi ka kuchi*ca* motwu-tul pakk ulo ttwichye nakass.ta.
   '*As soon as* the rain stopped, everybody went outside.'

f. 나는 월급을 타자마자 컴퓨터 가게로 달려갔다.

 Na nun welkup ul tha*camaca* khemphyuthe-kakey lo tallye kass.ta.

 '*As soon as* I got my salary, I ran to the computer store.'

(5) reason, cause

a. 비가 와서 소풍을 못 갔다.

 Pi ka wa*se* sophung ul mos kass.ta.

 '*Because* it rained, [we] couldn't go on a picnic.'

b. 장마가 길어지니까 과일 값이 턱없이 오르는구나.

 Cangma ka kil.eci*nikka* kwailq-kaps i thek-eps.i olununkwuna.

 'Well, I see that *since* the rainy season was so long the price of fruit has gone up ridiculously.'

c. 이 학생은 다른 학생들의 모범이 되었으므로 이 상장을 줌.

 I haksayng un talun haksayng-tul uy mopem i toy.ess.*umulo* i sangcang ul cwum.

 '*As* this student has become an exemplar for other students, this certificate of merit is hereby presented [to him/her].'

d. 일요일에 등산을 가느라고 숙제를 못했습니다.

 Il.yoil ey tungsan ul ka*nulako* swukcey lul mos hayss.supnita.

 '*By* go*ing* hiking on Sunday, I couldn't do my homework.'

(6) concession

a. 아무리 바빠도 맡은 책임은 다 해야지.

 Amuli pa.ppa*to* math.un chayk.im un ta hayyaci.

 '*No matter* how busy one is, one has to do all one's assigned duties.'

b. 내가 어디에 간들 너를 잊을 수 있겠느냐?

 Nayka eti ey kan*tul* ne lul ic.ulq swu isskeyss.nunya?

 '*No matter* where I go, could I forget you?'

c. 우리가 몸은 비록 떨어져 있을지라도 마음만은 변하지 말자.

 Wuli ka mom un pilok ttel.ecye iss.u*lci lato* maum man un pyen-haci malca.

 'Even if our bodies will have deteriorated, let's at least don't let our feelings change.'

d. 내가 아무리 늙었을망정 너한테야 지겠니?

 Nayka amuli nulk.ess.*ulmangceng* ne hanthey ya cikeyss.ni?

 '*No matter* how old I may be, would I lose to YOU?'

(7) condition

  a. 내일 날씨가 맑으면 소풍을 가자.
     Nayil nalssi ka malk.*umyen* sophung ul kaca.
     '*If* the weather is clear tomorrow, let's go for an outing.'

  b. 순이를 만나거든 나한테 전화 좀 하라고 해 줘.
     Swun.i lul manna*ketun* na hanthey cenhwa com halako hay cwe.
     '*When* you see Suni, please tell her to give me a call.'

  c. 윗물이 맑아야 아랫물이 맑다.
     Wis-mul i malk.*aya* alays-mul i malk.ta.
     '*Only if* the water upstream is clear will the water downstream be clear.'
     [Proverb: 'The integrity of subordinates depends upon the integrity of
     their superiors.']

  d. 만약 코끼리가 없었던들 한니발이 알프스를 넘을 수 있었을까?
     Man.yak kho.kkili ka eps.ess.*tentul* Hannipal i Alphusu lul nem.ulq swu
     iss.ess.ulkka?
     '*If* he had had no elephants, could Hannibal have crossed the Alps?'

(8) situational indicator

  a. 내가 네 부탁을 들어 주었으니, 너도 약속을 지켜라.
     Nayka ney puthak ul tul.e cwuess.*uni*, ne to yaksok ul cikhyela.
     '*Since* I granted you your favor, you keep your promise, too.'

  b. 비가 오는데 왜 우산을 안가지고 가니?
     Pi ka onun*tey* way wusan ul an kaciko kani?
     '*Since* it's raining, why aren't you taking an umbrella?'

  c. 오늘도 이렇게 기다리건만 그 사람한테서는 소식 한 자 없구나.
     Onul to ileh.key kitali*kenman* ku salam hantheyse nun sosik han-ca
     epskwuna.
     '*Even though* [I]'ve waited like this today, too, [I] haven't heard a word
     from him/her.'

  d. 계획은 세웠거니와 실행할 예산은 어떻게 구할까?
     Kyeyhoyk un seywess.*keniwa* silhayng-hal yeysan un etteh.key kwu-
     halkka?
     'We've made a plan, *but even so*, how will we find the funds to carry it
     out?'

  e. 네가 알다시피 나는 모든 방법을 다 동원했다.
     Neyka al*tasiphi* na nun motun pangpep ul ta tongwen-hayssta.
     '*As* you must realize, I've tried every way there is.'

(9) objective

    a. 민수는 애인을 만나러 공원에 갔다.
       Minswu nun ayin ul manna*le* kongwen ey kass.ta.
       'Minsu went to the park *to* meet his girl friend.'

    b. 김 형사는 범인을 잡으려고 잠복 근무 중이다.
       Kim Hyengsa nun pem.in ul cap.*ulyeko* campok kunmu cwung ita.
       'Officer Kim is staked out *in order to* catch the culprit.'

    c. 우리들은 각자 맡은 일을 기일 안에 끝내고자 열심히 노력하였다.
       Wuli-tul un kakca math.un il ul kiil an ey kkuth-nay*koca* yelsim.hi
       nolyek-ha.yess.ta.
       'We're working hard *so that* we can finish the work each has been as-
       signed within the time limit.'

(10) result

    a. 자동차가 지나가게 조금만 비켜 주세요.
       Catongcha ka cinaka*key* cokum man pikhye cwusey yo.
       'Move out of the way just a little *so* the cars can go by.'

    b. 바람이 잘 통하도록 창문을 활짝 열어라.
       Palam i cal thong-ha*tolok* changmun ul hwalccak yel.ela.
       'Open the window up wide *so* we can get a lot of air.'

    c. 어머니는 자식들이 잘 되라고 매일 아침 기도를 한다.
       Emeni nun casik-tul i cal toy*lako* mayil achim kito lul hanta.
       'Mother prayed every morning *for* her children to do well.'

(11) other meanings

    a. 앞으로 곧장 가다가 오른쪽으로 꺾어들면 시청이 나옵니다.
       Aph ulo kotcang ka*taka* olun-ccok ulo kkekk.e tulmyen sicheng i naop-
       nita.
       'If you go straight ahead *and then* [shows a shift of action] turn right,
       city hall's right there.'

    b. 청소년들은 간섭이 심할수록 반항하려고 한다.
       Chensonyen-tul un kansep i sim-halq*swulok*[17] panhang-halyeko hanta.
       '*The more* severe the intervention with young people, *the more* they want
       to rebel.'

    The endings given above serve the function of conjoining one clause to
another, but there are also conjunctive endings that serve to link verbs to-

gether into verbal compounds. These are the endings *-a/e/ye, -key, -ci,* and *-ko.*
Verbs connected with these endings are not simply conjoined; the endings
connote various relationships depending on the context. For the time being,
these highly idiomatic and common endings will be classed as examples of
subordinate conjunction.

(12) 순이가 새 옷을 입어 보았다.
> Swun.i ka say os ul ip.*e* poass.ta.
> 'Suni tried on new clothes.' [= 'tried wearing'; (Lit.) 'put on . . . *and* saw.']

(13) 순이가 꽃다발을 들고 있다.
> Swun.i ka kkoch-tapal ul tul*ko* iss.ta.
> 'Suni is holding a bouquet.' [Lit., 'hold (in the hand) *and* is.']

(14) 나는 노래를 잘 부르지 못한다.
> Na nun nolay lul cal pulu*ci* mos hanta.
> 'I can't sing very well.' [the ending *-ci* is idiomatically used in negative
> constructions]

(15) 순이가 민수를 사랑하게 되었다.
> Swun.i ka Minswu lul salang-ha*key* toy.ess.ta.
> 'Suni came to love Minsu.' [the pattern *-key + toyta* 'become' indicates the
> result of this process of becoming]

We have looked at nonsentence final endings and, among them, a
number of types of conjunctive endings. Next, we will look at inflectional
endings that change the grammatical function of the word. Endings of this
type are used for *nominalization* and *adnominalization.*

5.2.4 Nominalizing Endings

Nominalization means making a sentence or predicate serve the function of a noun within another sentence. In *pi ka oki* 'the rain to come' in
(1a), below, the nominalizing ending *-ki* attaches to the stem of the verb *o-*
'come', and the phrase takes on the characteristics of a noun. Thus, *pi ka oki*
'rain to come' functions as the direct object of *kitalinta* 'waits', exactly like
chwuswu 'harvest' in (1b).

(1) a. 농부들이 비가 오기를 기다린다.
> Nongpu-tul i pi ka o*ki* lul kitalinta.
> 'The farmers are waiting for the rain to come.'

b. 농부들이 추수를 기다린다.
> Nongpu-tul i chwuswu lul kitalinta.
> 'The farmers are waiting for the harvest.'

There are two nominalizing endings in Korean, *-ki* and *-um*. These two endings are used in different environments, and they differ by which predicate they can be used with. Some predicates are only used with *-ki*, and some are only used with *-um*, as can be seen from the following examples.[18]

(2) 나는 영어 공부하{기, ˣ음}가 {쉽다, 어렵다, 좋다, 싫다, 괴롭다}.

Na nun yenge kongpu-ha{*ki*, ˣm} ka {swipta, e.lyepta, coh.ta, silh.ta, koy-lopta}.

'Study*ing* English is {easy, hard, pleasant, unpleasant, painful} for me.'

(3) 나는 영어를 잘 하{기, ˣ음}를 {바란다, 원한다, 기대한다, 희망한다}.

Na nun yenge lul cal ha{*ki*, ˣm} lul {palanta, wen-hanta, kitay-hanta, huy-mang-hanta}.

'I {wish, want, expect, hope} to do [= speak] English well.'

(4) 나는 영어를 잘 하{기, ˣ음}로 {작정했다, 결심했다, 약속했다, 마음먹었다, 소문났다}.

Na nun yenge lul cal ha{*ki*, ˣm} lo {cakceng-hayssta, kyelsim-hayss.ta, yak-sok-hayss.ta, maum-mek.essta, somun-nassta}.

'I have {planned, resolved, promised, made up my mind, been rumored} to do [= speak] English well.'

(5) 나는 내가 실수 했{음, ˣ기}을 {알았다, 몰랐다, 깨달았다, 발견했다, 느꼈다, 의식했다, 기억했다, 짐작했다, 발표했다}.

Na nun nayka silswu hayss{*um*, ˣki} ul {al.ass.ta, mollass.ta, kkaytal.ass.ta, palkyen-hayssta, nukkyess.ta, uysik-hayss.ta, kiek-hayss.ta, cimcak-hayss.ta, palphyo-hayss.ta}.

'I {knew, didn't know, realized, discovered, sensed, became aware, remembered, guessed, announced} that I had made a mistake.'

(6) 내가 실수를 했{음, ˣ기}이 {분명하다, 확실하다, 명백하다, 드러났다}.

Nayka silswu lul hayss{*um*, ˣki} i {punmyeng-hata, hwaksil-hata, myeng-payk-hata, tul.e nass.ta}.

'It's {clear, definite, obvious, been revealed} that I made a mistake.'

In modern Korean the nominalizer *ki* has a wider range of usage than *-um*. In the above examples, *-um* occurs in cases when the event has already occurred or been determined, while *-ki* is used when the outcome has not been decided. However, the ending *-ki* is not necessarily restricted to such indeterminate contexts. The following examples are fixed expressions where *-ki* appears in almost idiomatic usages and where the meanings are clearly not ones of indeterminacy.

(7) 세상살이에는 고생이 있기 마련이다.

Seysang-sal.i ey nun kosayng i iss.*ki* malyen ita.

'Life in this world inevitably has hardships.'

(8) 기차가 지나가기에 손을 흔들었다.
   Kicha ka cina ka*ki* ey son ul huntul.ess.ta.
   '[I] waved at the train going by.'

(9) 성경에 이르기를 원수를 사랑하라고 했다.
   Sengkyeng ey ilu*ki* lul wenswu lul salang-halako hayss.ta.
   'The Bible says to love your enemies.'
   [More lit., 'In the Bible it did the teaching, love enemies.']

(10) 영희는 마음씨가 곱기(가) 이를 데 없다.
   Yenghuy nun maum-ssi ka kop*ki* (ka) ilulq tey eps.ta.
   'Younghŭi has the sweetest disposition.'
   [More lit., 'Younghŭi being sweet has no place to arrive.']

There are also a variety of other set expressions, such as *-ki ttaymun ey* 'because of ___', *-ki wi-haye* 'for the sake of ___', and *-ki (ka) kuci epsta* '___ is boundless', in which *-ki* is used idiomatically.

5.2.5 Adnominal Endings

A sentence that is embedded in another sentence and is used as an element modifying a following noun phrase is an *adnominal*. An adnominal ending attaches to the predicate of the embedded sentence and serves the function of making the embedded sentence into an adnominal. In example (1a), *koksik i iknun* 'grain ripening' is an adnominal composed of the sentence *koksik i ik-* 'grain ripens' and the adnominal ending *-nun*. Here we can see that *koksik i iknun* function like the adnominal *senul han* 'cool' of (1b).

(1) a. 곡식이 익는 가을이 왔다.
      Koksik i ik*nun* kaul i wass.ta.
      'Autumn, when the grain ripens, has come.'
      [Lit., 'Grain-ripening autumn has come.']

   b. 서늘한 가을이 왔다.
      Senul-ha*n* kaul i wassta.
      'Cool, refreshing autumn has come.'

The adnominal endings of Korean are *-un, -nun, -ulq,* and *-ten.* The choice of these endings depends upon the tense of the embedded sentence and whether the predicate of the embedded sentence is a verb or an adjective.

When the predicate of the embedded sentence is a verb, the tense is differentiated as follows:

(2) 내가 지금 읽는 책은 춘향전이다.
   Nayka cikum ilk*nun* chayk un Chwunhyang-cen ita. (present)
   'The book I'm reading now is *The Tale of Ch'unhyang*.'

(3) 내가 어제 읽은 책은 심청전이다.
Nayka ecey ilk.*un* chayk un Simcheng-cen ita. (past)
'The book I read yesterday was *The Tale of Simch'ŏng*.'

(4) 내가 어제 읽던 책은 흥부전이다.
Nayka ecey ilk*ten* chayk un Hungpu-cen ita. (past)
'The book I was reading yesterday was *The Tale of Hŭngbu*.'

When the predicate of the embedded sentence is an adjective, the tense is as follows:

(5) 머리가 짧은 소녀가 순이야.
Meli ka ccalp.*un* so.nye ka Swun.i 'ya. (present)
'The girl whose hair is short is Suni.'

(6) 어제까지도 덥던 날씨가 오늘은 서늘하다.
Ecey kkaci to tep*ten* nalssi ka onul un senul-hata. (past)
'The weather, which until yesterday was hot, is cool today.'

These differences in the way adnominal endings are used to express tense constitute the principal structural difference between verbs and adjectives in Korean. As can be seen in the above examples, the present adnominal ending for verbs is -*nun*, while the present adnominal ending for adjectives is -*un*. Moreover, while there is only one ending each for present and past (-*un* and -*ten*) in the case of adjectives, there are two endings that express the past for verbs: -*un* and -*ten*. The choice between these two endings depends upon whether the action of the verb was completed or not: The ending -*un* is used to show that the act or situation was completed in the past, while -*ten* shows that the action was not completed, but only temporarily halted. Because of this characteristic, -*ten* is often called the "incomplete past" (과거미완). The difference between the two endings is therefore more one of aspect than tense.

(7) 이 사진 어제 찍은 거니?
I sacin ecey ccik.*un* ke 'ni?
'Is this photo one that was taken yesterday?'

(8) ×이 사진 어제 찍던 거니?
×I sacin ecey ccik*ten* ke 'ni?
×'Is this photo one that was being taken yesterday?'

(9) ?어제 먹은 사과가 어디 있지?
?Ecey mek.*un* sakwa ka eti iss.ci?
?'Now where is that apple that you ate yesterday?'

(10) 어제 먹던 사과가 어디 있지?

Ecey mek*ten* sakwa ka eti iss.ci?

'Now where is that apple that you were eating on yesterday?'

In (7) and (9), the ending *-un* shows that the action was completed. The result is natural in (7) but not in (9) since an apple eaten yesterday no longer exists. However, when the ending *-ten* is used here instead, the sentence becomes the perfectly ordinary one in (10) because *-ten* shows that the person started eating the apple but did not finish, leaving part of it uneaten. On the other hand, were *-ten* to be substituted for *-un* in (7), as it is in (8), the result would represent an impossible situation since the act of taking a photograph is instantaneous and cannot be halted in midstream.

In the case of adjectives, *-un* is used when some past situation has continued up to the present, and *-ten* is used in case that situation was interrupted and there has been a change of state. Since adjectives have no present continuative form, the present continuative marker *-nun* cannot be used with them; in addition, since adjectives cannot have a meaning of completion, there is no distinction between complete and incomplete for them, and *-ten* is therefore simply used to express past. As a result, what is expressed with the adnominal endings constitutes the principal semantic characteristics distinguishing adjectives from verbs.

Since the adnominal ending *-ulq* (-을) is mainly used when the narrative is about an event that has not yet taken place, the ending appears to mark future tense. However, since the ending is also used in cases of conjecture about present or past events, it is obviously something other than a future tense marker. A more accurate characterization of the ending *-ulq* is that it expresses conjecture or intent; it is used to indicate something that has still not taken place or facts that have not been verified.

(11) {지금쯤, 어제쯤} 도착했을 편지가 왜 아직 안 올까? (conjecture)

{Cikum ccum, ecey ccum} tochak-hayss.*ulq* phyenci ka way acik an olkka?

'Why has that letter that should have arrived {about now, about yesterday} still not come?'

(12) 다음 비행기로 도착할 승객 명단을 보여 주세요. (conjecture)

Taum pihayngki lo tochak-ha*lq* sungkayk myengtan ul po.ye cwusey yo.

'Please show me the list of passengers who will arrive on the next flight.'

(13) 나는 내일 떠날 예정이다. (intent)

Na nun nayil ttena*lq* yeyceng ita.

'I plan to leave tomorrow.'

The ending *-ulq* combines with the auxiliary noun *kes* 'the one that, the fact that' to form an adnominal clause that expresses conjecture or dependence. In this structure, the clause headed by *-ulq* modifies *kes*.

(14) 내일은 비가 올 것이다. (conjecture)
    Nayil un pi ka ol*q* kes ita.
    'It will probably rain tomorrow.'
    [literally, 'It is the case that tomorrow rain will probably come.']

(15) 나는 내일 떠날 것이다. (intent)
    Na nun nayil ttena*lq* kes ita.
    'I plan to leave tomorrow.'

However, there are instances where the meaning of *-ulq* is not so obviously one of conjecture or intent, or tense. We see this to be true, for example, in the formulaic usage of *-ulq* to gloss the readings of Chinese characters.[19] In such constructions as *kem.ul hyen* (玄) 'the *hyŏn* that means "black"' and *nwulul hwang* (黃) 'the *hwang* that means "yellow"' the usage of *-ul* is neutralized for case and aspect.

References

Ch'ae Wan 1976, 1977, 1986, 1990; Chang Kyŏnghŭi 1985; Ch'oe Hyŏnbae 1946; Greenberg 1963; Hong Chaesŏng 1987; Hong Saman 1983; Hong Yunp'yo 1978; Im Hongbin 1987; Kim Tongsik 1981; Kwŏn Chaeil 1992; Lee Chung Min (Yi Chŏngmin) 1977; Martin 1992; Nam Kisim (Nam Ki Shim) 1978, 1985; Nam Kisim (Nam Ki Shim) and Ko Yŏnggŭn 1985; Nam Mihye 1988; Pak Yanggyu 1978; Sanders 1977; Sŏ Chŏngsu (Suh Cheong-Soo) 1990, 1991; Sohn Ho-min (Son Homin) 1978, 1994; Song Seok-Choong (Song Sŏkchung) 1978, 1981; Yi Iksŏp (Lee Iksop) 1986; Yi Iksŏp (Lee Iksop) and Im Hongbin 1983; Yi Kwangho 1988; Yi Namsun 1988; Yu Tongsŏk 1981.

6

Syntax

6.1 Word Order

As was mentioned in the introduction (chapter 1), Korean is typologically an *SOV language*. That is to say, the basic word order is *subject-object-verb*. An SOV language such as Korean is characterized, first of all, by a predicate that comes at the end of the sentence. Another important characteristic of an SOV language is that modifiers always come before the word they modify. Thus, adverbs come before the verb, and relative clauses, genitive constructions, and demonstatives all come before the modified noun. In addition, in a typical SOV language like Korean, the main verb comes before auxiliary verbs and inflectional endings, and a noun is followed by particles (which are sometimes called "postpositions").

Korean sentences often diverge from the basic subject-object-verb order, however. That is because the use of case particles gives the language relative flexibility in how noun phrases are ordered. In Korean, since the grammatical function of a noun phrase is marked by one or more case particles, the relative position of the subject and the direct object can change (as long as they are not left unmarked) and the underlying interpretation will remain unaffected. In other words, case functions are determined primarily by case particles and only secondarily by word order. (Cf. 5.1) The one constant in this formulation of an SOV word order is that the verb always comes at the end of the sentence.[1]

(1) 민호가 순이를 사랑한다. (subject-object-verb)
    Minho ka Swun.i lul salang-hanta.
    'Minho loves Suni.'

(2) 순이를 민호가 사랑한다. (object-subject-verb)
    Swun.i lul Minho ka salang-hanta.
    '*Minho* loves Suni.'

When case particles are omitted, however, word order determines case relationships. We see, for example, that when two unmarked noun phrases appear before the verb, the structure of the sentence tends to be interpreted as subject-object-verb. So when Korean is called an "SOV language," what is meant is not that some other word order cannot occur but that this order is the neutral or unmarked one. In sentences where there are no case particles, such as those in examples (3) and (4), the natural interpretation is that the first noun phrase is the subject, and the second, the object. Since this interpretation is semantically difficult in the case of (4), the sentence is an awkward one.

(3) 민호 책 읽는다. (subject-object-verb)
     Minho chayk ilknunta
     'Minho is reading a book.'

(4) ?책 민호 읽는다. (subject-object-verb)
     ?Chayk Minho ilknunta.
     ?'The book Minho is reading.'

But the order "subject-object-verb" does not tell the whole story. To a certain extent, there is a natural, unmarked order for all the many elements of a Korean sentence. The basic word order for a number of the various cases is as given below:

	Nominative	Comitative	Instrumental	Locative	Accusative	Verb
Ex:	순이 가	민수와	물감으로	벽에	그림을	그렸다.
	Swun.i ka	Minswu wa	mulqkam ulo	pyek ey	kulim ul	ku.lyess.ta
	Suni	with Minsu	with colors	on the wall	painting	painted

'Suni and Minsu painted a painting on the wall with coloring materials.'

Note, however, that this is only the neutral or unmarked order. When a noun phrase is accompanied by a particle, or even in cases where there is no particle, the position of the noun phrase can change—and it often does. Ordinary spoken Korean is in fact replete with shifts in the unmarked word order. Why would a speaker move a noun phrase away from its usual, neutral place in the sentence? The reason can be found in how people ordinarily use language. Probably all languages use phonological and syntactic devices to focus attention on certain elements within the sentence. In English we use stress. We say a word louder and with greater force when we want to draw attention to it. In Korean, phonological stress plays a much smaller role. Saying a word louder in Korean does not have the effect that native speakers of English might expect—it can cause incomprehension or even in some cases signal rudeness, but not usually simple emphasis. In Korean, what are ordinarily used instead are (1) special particles and (2) changes in word order. In other words, the movement of elements within the sentence is an important stylistic device used in order to focus attention where the speaker wants it.

As a result, shifts in word order are so common in Korean, one seldom hears an idealized sentence like the one given above about Suni and Minsu painting. After all, a neutral or unmarked sentence is also a colorless sentence, and most speakers aim for more interesting ways of expressing themselves. In Korean, one method of doing that is with changes in word order.

A rule of thumb is that the closer a noun phrase is moved toward the verb, the more it becomes the focus of attention. That is to say, a Korean speaker tends to save new, important, or interesting information for last, a discourse strategy somewhat different from that of an English speaker, who would often simply give the important information additional stress.

A semantic factor working in the opposite direction is topicalization. As is well known, the topic comes at the beginning of the sentence, so when a noun phrase is made the topic, it moves to the front of the sentence. (In each of the following examples, the topic is given in italics.)

(5) a. 영이는 순이에게 인형을 주었다.
    Yeng.i nun Swun.i eykey inhyeng ul cwuess.ta.
    '*Yŏngi* gave Suni a doll.'

b. 순이 (에게)는 영이가 인형을 주었다.
    Swun.i (eykey) nun Yeng.i ka inhyeng ul cwuess.ta.
    '*(To) Suni,* Yŏngi gave a doll.'

c. 인형은 영이가 순이에게 주었다.
    Inhyeng un Yeng.i ka Swun.i eykey cwuess.ta.
    '*The doll,* Yŏngi gave to Suni.'

Thus, on the one hand, noun phrases within the sentence are relatively free to move. On the other hand, some aspects of Korean word order are highly constrained. For example, as we have already mentioned, certain kinds of word order related to modification are absolutely fixed. These include adnominal-noun, adverb-verb/adjective, genitive case-noun, and relative clause-noun.

Adnominal-noun:	예쁜 꽃이 피었다. 'Pretty flowers are blooming.'
	yey.ppun kkoch i phiess.ta.
	pretty-flowers
Adverb-verb:	민수는 축구를 잘 해서 인기가 좋다.
	Minswu nun chwukkwu lul *cal hayse* inqki ka coh.ta.
	well-plays
	'Minsu is popular because he plays soccer well.'
Adverb-adjective:	순이가 아주 예쁘게 화장을 했다.
	Swun.i ka *acwu yey.ppukey* hwacang ul hayss.ta.
	very-beautiful
	'Suni did her makeup very beautifully.'

Genitive case-noun: 코끼리의 코가 매우 길다.
                        Khokkili uy kho ka maywu kilta.
                        elephant's-nose
                        'The elephant's trunk is very long.'

Relative clause-noun: 코가 짧은 코끼리도 있을까?
                        Kho ka ccalp.un khokkili to issulkka?
                        nose being-short-elephants
                        'Are there any elephants that have short trunks?'

The order in these cases cannot be inverted. Another word order constant is, as we have said, the fact that the verb must come at the end of the clause or sentence.

Semantic interpretation also imposes certain constraints on word order. As in English, the movement of an adverb is constrained by its scope of application. In (6), the adverbial form *hwaksil.hi* 'clearly' can appear in any nonfinal position, even before the topic, and in each case with subtle differences in the intepretation of its scope. In (7), the adverb *cal* 'well, often' can only appear directly before the word it modifies.

(6) a. 확실히 민수는 범인이 아니다.
        Hwaksil.hi Minswu nun pem.in i anita.
        '*Clearly,* Minsu is not the culprit.'

     b. 민수는 확실히 범인이 아니다.
        Minswu nun *hwaksil.hi* pem.in i anita.
        'Minsu *clearly* is not the culprit.'

     c. 민수는 범인이 확실히 아니다.
        Minswu nun pem.in i *hwaksil.hi* anita.
        'Minsu is *clearly* not the culprit.'

(7) a. 순이가 그림을 잘 그린다.
        Swun.i ka kulim ul *cal* kulinta.
        'Suni paints paintings *well.*'[2]

     b. ˣ잘 순이가 그림을 그린다.
        ˣ*Cal* Swun.i ka kulim ul kulinta.
        [ˣ'Suni *well* paints paintings.']

     c. ˣ순이가 잘 그림을 그린다.
        ˣSwun.i ka *cal* kulim ul kulinta.
        [ˣ'Suni paints *well* paintings.']

When two (or more) noun phrases are linked together semantically in an inclusive relationship, the noun phrase that is larger in scope precedes.

That is the natural unmarked word order in Korean. The clearest examples of the way this word order works can be seen in how Koreans give locations in time and space. One says, or writes, the largest unit first. Thus, a letter might be dated: 2000-*nyen* 10-*wel* 9-*il*, and if the time of day were added, that time would follow the date. Similarly, a Korean address is usually given from the largest unit down: the country name first, followed by the province, the city, the district, the neighborhood, the street address or apartment name and number, and finally the name of the person to whom the letter is addressed. The order is exactly the opposite of the one used in English.

This syntactic order of large to small also has more general consequences for Korean sentences. In (6), below, *hyangki* 'fragrance' comes before *cangmi* 'roses', and so it has a generic meaning that refers to all fragrances, including the fragrance of roses. But in (7), since 'roses' comes before 'fragrance', 'fragrance' means only the fragrance of roses. Here 'roses' is the noun that is semantically larger in scope, and 'fragrance' is not generic but only one of the attributes of 'roses'.

(6) 향기는 장미가 좋다.
Hyangki nun cangmi ka coh.ta.
'The best fragrance is that of roses.'
[Lit,. 'Fragrances, roses are good.']

(7) 장미는 향기가 좋다.
Cangmi nun hyangki ka coh.ta.
'Roses have a good fragrance.'
[Lit., 'Roses, the fragrance is good.']

6.2 Sentence Expansion

A Korean sentence may consist of nothing but a predicate. For example: *Kapnita* '(I) am going'; *Alumtapta* '(It) is beautiful'; *Haksayng ita* '(She) is a student.' Sentences like these are idiomatic and quite common.

Thus, we can classify Korean sentence types by the kind of predicate they have. Korean linguists commonly classify simple Korean sentences along these lines into six basic types. Here are the six types, together with illustrative examples:

(1) Intransitive Verb
해가 뜬다.
Hay ka *ttunta.*
'The sun *is rising.*'

(2) Adjective
장미꽃이 아름답다.
Cangmi-kkoch i *alumtapta.*
'The roses *are beautiful.*'

(3) Transitive Verb
     민수가 책을 읽는다.
     Minswu ka chayk ul *ilk.nun.ta*
     'Minsu *is reading* a book.'

(4) Verb with Noun Complement
     민수가 군인이 되었다.
     Minswu ka *kwun.in i toy.ess.ta.*
     'Minsu *became a soldier.*'

(5) Ditransitive Verb (takes dative and accusative cases)
     엄마가 아기에게 인형을 주었다.
     Emma ka aki eykey inhyeng ul *cwuess.ta.*
     'The mother *gave* the baby a doll.'

(6) Copula
     순이가 학생이다.
     Swun.i ka haksayng *ita.*
     'Suni *is* a student.'

These sentence types can be expanded through modification of the basic elements, with adnominals modifying noun phrases and adverbs modifying verb phrases.

(7) 빨간 장미꽃이 매우 아름답다.
     Ppalkan cangmi-kkoch i *maywu* alumtapta.
     red   very
     (adnominal)   (adverb)
     'The red flowers are very beautiful.'

(8) 어머니가 귀여운 아기에게 예쁜 인형을 기꺼이 주었다.
     Emeni ka *kwiyewun* aki eykey *yey.ppun* inhyeng ul *ki.kke.i* cwuess.ta.
               cute   pretty   joyfully
               (adnominal)   (adnominal)   (adverb)
     'The mother joyfully gave a pretty doll to (her) cute baby.'

Two or more simple sentences can be combined to form compound sentences. These compound sentences may consist of simple sentences combined by *conjunction* (접속) or by *embedding* (내포) one into the other.

6.2.1. Conjunction

Korean sentences are conjoined by using *conjunctive endings*. There are many such endings, and each determines the semantic relationship between the sentences that are being combined. (Cf. 5.2.3)

(1) 바람이 불고 비가 온다.
Palam i pul*ko* pi ka onta.
'The wind is blowing, *and* rain is falling.'

(2) 민수는 학교에 가서 공부를 했다.
Minswu nun hakkyo ey ka*se* kongpu lul hayss.ta.
'Minsu went to school *and (then)* studied.'

What these conjunctive endings share is that they neutralize the marking for tense and aspect on the verb to which they attach. That is to say, for example, if the sentences conjoined in (1) were used independently, the first sentence would be *Palam i punta* 'The wind is blowing', with the verb overtly marked as nonpast. Similarly, the verb in the first sentence of (2) would carry the past tense marker *-ess-: Minswu nun hakkyo ey kassta* 'Minsu went to school'. As can be seen from these examples, when Korean sentences are conjoined, the verb taking the conjunctive ending loses its marking for tense. Tense is only indicated in the larger construction by the marking on the final verb.

6.2.2 Embedded Sentences

A sentence can be embedded into another sentence as a noun, an adnominal, or an adverb. An embedded sentence serving as an adverb is an example of the type of subordination discussed in section 4.2.5. In this section, we will briefly discuss *adnominalization* and *nominalization*.

The *adnominal endings* are *-un, -nun, -ulq*, and *-ten*. These were discussed in Section 5.2.5. As a grammatical process, adnominalization can in general be divided into *relativization* (관계화) and *complementation* (보문화).

(1) 내가 좋아하는 꽃은 장미다. - Relativization
Nayka coh.a ha.nun kkoch un cangmi 'ta.
'The flower *that I like* is the rose.'

(2) 내가 장미를 좋아하는 사실을 친구들은 다 안다. - Complementation
Nayka cangmi lul coh.a hanun sasil ul chinkwu-tul un ta anta.
'All of my friends know (the fact) *that I like roses.*'

The difference between relativization and complementation is in how the adnominal is formed. In (1), the head noun *kkoch* 'flower' is an element extruded out of the relative clause *nayka coha hanun* 'that I like'. In terms of both structure and semantics, the noun 'flower' can be interpreted as the direct object of the verb 'like'.

In contrast, the head noun *sasil* 'fact' in (2) is not an element from the embedded sentence. Rather, the noun explains and summarizes the content of the entire clause as a whole; 'that I like roses' is a fact, and all my friends know that fact. This kind of process is known as complementation.

There are two kinds of complementation: *direct* and *indirect*. The sentence in (2) is an example of direct complementation. In that construction, the adnominal ending simply replaces the final ending of the verb in the embedded clause. In (3) and (4), the final endings are not deleted, and the adnominal endings are added on after them. Sentences like these are examples of indirect complementation. They are called "indirect" because they incorporate indirect quotes. The ending of each embedded sentence shows that the speaker is reporting information he or she heard from someone else or otherwise learned or will learn, indirectly.

(3) 나는 민수가 장미를 좋아한다는 사실을 몰랐다.
     Na nun Minswu ka cangmi lul coh.a *hantanun* sasil ul mollass.ta.
     'I didn't know that Minsu *is said to* like roses.'

(4) 민수가 친구를 배신했다는 소문이 끈질기게 나돌았다.
     Minswu ka chinkwu lul paysin-*hayss.tanun* somun i kkun-cilkikey natol.assta.
     'There's a persistent rumor going around [*saying*] that Minsu betrayed his friends.'

Some nouns can serve as the head in both direct complementation and indirect complementation. The noun *sasil* 'fact' is one of these, as is the auxiliary noun *kes* 'the one, the person/thing'. Other nouns can be used with only one of these two types of complementation.

(5) 나는 민수가 장미를 {좋아하는, 좋아한다는} 사실을 몰랐다.
     Na nun Minswu ka cangmi lul {coh.a hanun, coh.a hantanun} *sasil* ul mollass.ta.
     'I didn't know (the *fact*) that Minsu {likes roses, is said to like roses}'

(6) 나는 기차가 6시에 {출발하는, 출발한다는} 것을 몰랐다.
     Na nun kicha ka 6-si ey {chwulpal-hanun, chwulpal-hantanun} *kes* ul mollass.ta.
     'I didn't know (the *one*) that the train {leaves at, is said to leave at} 6:00.'

(7) 민수가 친구를 {*배신한, 배신했다는} 소문이 끈질기게 나돌았다.
     Minswu ka chinkwu lul {*paysin-han, paysin-hayss.tanun} *somun* i kkun.cilkey notol.ass.ta.
     'There's a persistent *rumor* going around [saying] that Minsu betrayed his friends.' [ungrammatical as direct complementation]

(8) 만약 친구가 너를 {배신하는, *배신한다는} 경우에는 어떻게 하겠니?
     Man.yak chinkwu ka ne lul {paysin-hanun, *paysin-hantanun} kyengwu ey nun etteh.key hakeyss.ni?
     'What would you do if a friend betrayed you?'
     [Lit., 'in the *case* that a friend {betrays, *is said to betray} you?']
     [ungrammatical as indirect complementation]

(9) 네가 반드시 {×성공하는, 성공한다는} 보장이 있느냐?

 Neyka pantusi {×sengkong-hanun, sengkong-hantanun} *pocang*i iss.nu.nya

 'What *guarantee* do you have you'll necessarily succeed?'

 [Lit., 'guarantee that you {×will succeed, will be said to succeed}']

 [ungrammatical as direct complementation]

Head nouns that take direct complementation include the nouns *kyengwu* 'case', *kanungseng* 'possibility', and *kkatalk* 'reason, cause', and the auxiliary noun *cwul* 'the assumed fact', *pa* 'way, means to', *swu* 'ability to', *li* '(good) reason to', *tus* 'seems (to be)', *yang* 'appear (to be)', *chey* 'pretends to', *man* 'as much as', *pep* 'way to', *seng* 'quality, characteristic of'.

Head nouns that take indirect complementation include: the nouns *somun* 'rumor', *sosik* 'news', *mal* 'language, words', *cwucang* 'assertion, claim', *tan.en* 'declaration', *yaksok* 'promise', *poko* 'report', *poto* 'press report', *myenglyeng* 'order, command', *kopayk* 'confession', *yocheng* 'request', *sayngkak* 'thought', *nukkim* 'feeling, intuition', *kyenhay* 'opinion', and *ilon* 'theory'.

Nominalization is a process by which a sentence is embedded into another sentence where it functions as a noun or noun phrase. For example, *pom i oki* 'spring coming' is the nominalized form of the sentence *pom i onta* 'spring is coming', and in (10a) it has the same function that *pi* 'rain' does in (10b). Both serve as the direct object of the verb *kitalinta* 'are waiting'. In the same way, the italicized clause in (11a), which is headed by the nominalizing ending *-um*, has the same function as the italicized noun phrase in (11b).

(10)a. 새싹들이 봄이 오기를 기다린다.

 Say ssak-tul i *pom i oki* lul kitalinta.

 'The new shoots are waiting for the *coming of spring*.'

 b. 새싹들이 비를 기다린다.

 Say ssak-tul i *pi* lul kitalinta.

 'The new shoots are waiting for *the rain*.'

(11)a. 사람들은 세월이 그렇게 빨리 감을 깨닫지 못한다.

 Salam-tul un *seywel i kuleh.key ppalli kam* ul kkaytat.ci mos hanta.

 'People are not aware of *time passing so quickly*.'

 b. 사람들은 자기의 잘못을 깨닫지 못한다.

 Salam-tul un *caki uy cal-mos* ul kkaytat.ci mos hanta.

 'People are not aware of *their own mistakes*.'

A nominalization requires the ending *-ki* or the ending *-um*. These two nominalizing endings differ by the environments in which they are used, and certain predicates are used exclusively with only one of the two. (Cf. 5.2.4.)

However, sentences with one of the (plain-style) interrogative endings

-nu.nya/(u)nya, -nunka/(u)nka, -nunci/(u)nci/(u)lq.ci, or *-(u)lkka* can be used directly as noun phrases, without either of the nominalizing endings. These interrogative endings constitute an exception to the rules of nominalization, for no other endings can be used at the head of a noun phrase this way.

(12) 죽느냐 사느냐가 문제다.
　　　Cwuk.nu.nya sanu.nya ka muncey 'ta.
　　　'It is a question of life or death.'
　　　[Lit., '. . . of *does (one) live or die.*']

(13) 누가 먼저 갈지를 결정하자.
　　　Nwuka mence kalq.ci lul kyelceng-haca.
　　　'Let's decide *who goes first.*'

(14) 누가 정말 범인인가가 드러났다.
　　　Nwuka ceng-mal pem.in inka ka tule nass.ta.
　　　'*Who was really the culprit* came to light.'

(15) 누가 부산에 갈까를 생각해 보자.
　　　Nwuka Pusan ey kalkka lul sayngkak-hay poca.
　　　'Let's think about *who goes to Pusan.*'

6.3 Passives and Causatives

6.3.1 Passives

Passive verbs in Korean are formed by attaching one of the passive suffixes *-i-, -hi-, -li-,* or *-ki-* to the stem of a transitive verb. For example, *po-* 'see': *poi-* 'be seen, visible'; *tut/tul-* 'hear': *tulli-* 'be heard'; *cap-* 'catch': *caphi-* 'be caught'; *an-* 'embrace': *anki-* 'get embraced'; *noh-* 'put, place': *noh.i* 'be put, placed'; *mek-* 'eat': *mek.hi-* 'gets eaten up'. The conversion of a sentence from active to passive voice is as follows: the object of the active verb becomes the subject of the passive verb, and the subject of the active verb becomes a locative (marked by *ey, eykey, hanthey,* etc.) in the passive sentence.

(1) a. 대학생들이 이 소설을 많이 읽는다. (active)
　　　　Tayhaksayng-tul i sosel ul manh.i ilknunta.
　　　　　　　　subject　　object　　　　transitive verb
　　　　'College students read this novel a lot.'

　　 b. 이 소설이 대학생들에게 많이 읽힌다. (passive)
　　　　I sosel i tayhaksayng eykey manh.i ilk.*hi*n.ta.
　　　　　　subject　　locative　　　　　passive verb
　　　　'This novel is read a lot by college students.'

When the subject of the active verb is an inanimate noun, it will be marked with the particle *ey* in the passive sentence.

(2) a. 태풍이 도시를 휩쓸었다.
   Tayphung i tosi lul hwip.ssul.ess.ta.
   'The typhoon swept over the city.'

  b. 도시가 태풍에 휩쓸렸다.
   Tosi ka *tayphung ey* hwip.ssullyess.ta.
   'The city was swept over by the typhoon.'

When the subject of the active verb is a sentient being—that is, an animate noun—it is normally marked with *eykey* (or *hanthey*) in the passive sentence. However, the noun cannot be marked with *eykey* if the active sentence already contains a locative (*ey* or *eykey*) or an instrumental marked with *lo*. In such cases, the noun will be marked, instead, by *ey uy-hay(se)* 'through, by means of.' However, in sentences with so-called double objects, both *eykey* (or *hanthey*) and *ey uy-hay* are possible.

(3) a. 김씨가 박씨에게 집을 팔았다.
   Kim-ssi ka Pak-ssi *eykey* cip ul phal.ass.ta.
   'Mr. Kim sold the house *to* Mr. Pak.'

  b. 집이 {*김씨에게, 김씨에 의해} 박씨에게 팔렸다.
   Cip i {*Kim-ssi eykey, Kim-ssi ey uy-hay} Pak-ssi eykey phallyess.ta.
   'The house was sold by Mr. Kim to Mr. Pak.'

(4) a. 영이가 가위로 색종이를 잘랐다.
   Yengi ka kawi *lo* sayk-congi lul callass.ta.
   'Yŏngi cut the colored paper *with* scissors.'

  b. 색종이가 {*영이에게, 영이에 의해} 가위로 잘렸다.
   Sayk-congi ka {*Yeng.i eykey, Yeng.i ey uy-hay} kawi lo callyess.ta
   'The colored paper was cut by Yŏngi with scissors.'

(5) a. 영이가 어항에 금붕어를 담았다.
   Yengi ka ehang *ey* kumpunge lul tam.ass.ta.
   'Yŏngi put the goldfish *into* a goldfish bowl.'

  b. 금붕어가 {*영이에게, 영이에 의해} 어항에 담겼다.
   Kumpunge ka {*Yeng.i eykey, Yeng.i ey uy-hay} ehang ey tamkyess.ta.
   'The goldfish was put by Yŏngi into a goldfish bowl.'

(6) a. 경찰관이 도둑을 덜미를 잡았다.
   Kyengchalkwan i totwuk *ul* telmi lul cap.ass.ta.
   'The police officer grabbed the thief by the scruff of his neck.'
   [Both 'thief' and 'scruff' are marked as direct objects.]

b. 도둑이 {경찰관에게, 경찰관에 의해} 덜미를 잡혔다.

Totwuk i {kyengchalkwan eykey, kyengchalkwan ey uy-hay} telmi lul cap.hyess.ta.

'The thief was grabbed by the police officer by the scruff of his neck.'

['Scruff' remains marked as the direct object even with the passive verb.]

Not all verbs can be transformed into a passive since only a restricted set of verbs can take a passive suffix. Those that cannot be transformed into a passive include, first of all, the verb *hata* 'do' and all of the verbs derived with -*hata*. *Ditransitive verbs*[3], such as *cwuta* 'give', *patta* 'receive', *tulita* 'present', and *pachita* 'bestow', cannot be transformed into passives. Nor can *benefactive verbs* such as *etta* 'acquire', *ilh.ta* 'lose', *chacta* 'look for', *topta* 'help', *ipta* 'wear, put on', and *sata* 'buy'. Among the benefactives, only *phalta* 'sell' has a suffix-derived passive: *phallita* 'be sold'. *Experiential verbs* such as *alta* 'know', *paywuta* 'learn', *palata* 'hope', and *nukkita* 'feel', as well as symmetric verbs such as *mannata* 'meet', *talmta* 'resemble', and *ssawuta* 'fight' do not have corresponding passive verbs. In addition, verbs whose stems end in the vowel -*i*-, such as *tencita* 'throw', *cikhita* 'protect', *ttaylita* 'hit', and *mancita* 'rub', cannot form passives with one of the passive suffixes.

Another peculiarity of passive verbs is that some of them have idiomatic uses for which there is no active verb equivalent. Here are a few examples:

(7) a. 순이가 감기에 걸렸다.

   Swun.i ka kamki ey kellyess.ta.

   'Suni caught a cold.'

   [Lit., 'Suni was hung by (=on) a cold.']

   b. ˣ감기가 순이를 걸었다.

   ˣKamki ka Swun.i lul kel.ess.ta.

   [ˣ'A cold hung Suni.']

(8) a. 영이는 집안에 들어박혔다.

   Yengi nun cip-an ey tul.e pak.hyess.ta.

   'Yŏngi was confined to the house.'

   b. ˣ(X가) 영이를 집안에 들어박았다.

   (X ka) Yengi lul cip-an ey tul.e pak.ass.ta.

   [ˣ'(Someone) confined Yŏngi to the house.']

(9) 날씨가 풀렸다.

   'The weather moderated.'

   [Lit., '. . . came undone, untied.']

In these examples, we see that the meaning of the passive verb has drifted quite far from that of the corresponding active verb. In (7), for ex-

ample, the meaning of *kellita* has, in this idiomatic usage, very little semantically in common with the active verb *kelta* 'hang'. It is difficult here to
consider *kellita* derived synchronically from *kelta*. The same is true of *phullita*
in (9), because the noun *nalssi* 'weather' is never used—as subject, object, or
anything else—with the active verb *phulta* 'undo, untie'. In cases such as
these, it is clear that the relationship of the passive verbs to the corresponding active verbs has completely become a historical one.

In the modern language, passive verbs are simply learned as separate
words. Koreans do not normally create new passive forms. Passive verbs may
be obviously related, both semantically and morphologically, to the active
verbs from which they were once derived, but the process of derivation is no
longer a completely productive one.

There are a number of verbs in Korean with a causative form exactly
like that of the passive. For example, *pota* 'see': *poita* 'is visible (= is seen)/
shows (= causes to see)'; *capta* 'grab': *caphita* 'is caught/causes to hold'; *epta*
'carry (on the back)': *ephita* 'is carried (on the back)/puts (on the back)';
anta 'embrace': *ankita* 'is embraced/puts in (someone's) arms'; *multa* 'bite':
mullita 'is bitten/makes bite'; *ttutta* 'tear, pluck, bite off': *ttutkita* 'is torn, bitten off/have something bitten, torn off'. In these cases, the listener can only
tell whether the usage is causative or passive by the context.

(10)a. 서울 타워가 나에게 보인다.
　　　 Sewul Thawe ka na eykey *pointa.* (passive)
　　　 'Seoul Tower *is visible* to me.'

　　b. 어머니가 아기에게 그림책을 보인다.
　　　 Emeni ka aki eykey kulim-chayk ul *pointa.* (causative)
　　　 'The mother *is showing* the picture book to the baby.'

(11)a. 아기가 어머니에게 업혔다.
　　　 Aki ka emeni eykey *ep.hyess.ta.* (passive)
　　　 'The baby *was put on* its mother's back.'

　　b. 어머니가 순이에게 아기를 업혔다.
　　　 Emeni ka Swun.i eykey aki lul *ep.hyess.ta.* (causative)
　　　 'The mother *put the* baby *on* Suni's back.'

(12)a. 순이가 민호에게 안겼다.
　　　 Swun.i ka Minho eykey *ankyess.ta.* (passive)
　　　 'Suni *was embraced* by Minho.'

　　b. 순이가 민호에게 꽃다발을 안겼다.
　　　 Swun.i ka Minho eykey kkoch-tapal ul *ankyess.ta.* (causative)
　　　 'Suni *put* the bouquet *in* Minho's *arms.*'

From these examples, it can be seen that a passive cannot represent the intent or decision of the subject. When the subject is a sentient being, the passive can represent what is more or less a latent desire, but the subject's intention is not expressed overtly. This passivity is what characterizes a passive sentence. In the following examples, we see that even though a passive desire is fulfilled, the one who initiates and is responsible for the action is the other person. In situations such as these, the construction chosen is the passive.

(13) 아기가 엄마에게 달려가서 안겼다.
Aki ka emma eykey tallye kase ankyess.ta.
'The child ran to its mother and was taken into her arms.'

(14) 영이는 민수에게 못이기는 체하고 손목을 잡혔다.
Yengi nun Minswu eykey mos ikinun chey hako sonmok ul cap.hyess.ta.
'Pretending not to be won over by Minsu, Yŏngi was grabbed by him by the wrists.'

A passive sentence goes beyond simply transposing the subject; it shows that the circumstances or the action connected to the subject is not tied to the will or volition of that subject. The following are examples of expressions that idiomatically require the passive and where the active voice is syntactically impossible. These examples illustrate the type of meaning normally expressed by the passive.

(15) a. 그는 항상 죄의식에 쫓긴다.
Ku nun hangsang coy-uysik ey ccoch.kinta.
'He is always pursued by a feeling of guilt.'

b. ?ᵡ죄의식이 항상 그를 쫓는다.
?ᵡCoy-uysik i hangsang ku lul ccoch.nun.ta.
[?ᵡ'A feeling of guilt always pursues him.']

(16) a. 영이가 난처한 입장에 놓였다.
Yengi ka nanche-han ipcang ey noh.yess.ta.
'Yŏngi was put into a difficult situation.'

b. ?ᵡ(사람들이) 영이를 난처한 입장에 놓았다.
?ᵡ(salam-tul i) Yengi lul nanche-han ipcang ey noh.ass.ta.
['?ᵡ(People) put Yŏngi into a difficult situation.']

(17) a. 문이 바람에 닫혔다.
Mun i palam ey tat.hyess.ta.
'The door was (blown) shut by the wind.'

b. ?ᵡ바람이 문을 닫았다.
?ᵡPalam i mun ul tat.ass.ta.
['The wind shut the door.']

Passives are also formed with the auxiliary construction *-eci-* 'get to be, become'. For example: *mantul-* 'make', *mantuleci-* 'is made'; *nukki-* 'feel', *nukkyeci-* 'is felt'; *wumciki-* 'move', *wumcikyeci-* 'is moved'; *chac-* 'look for, find', *chacaci-* 'is found'. Composed of the infinite *-e/a* plus the intransitive verb *ci-* 'get, become characterized by', this auxiliary construction attaches to the stem of a verb, usually one that cannot take one of the passive suffixes. The result is that this very productive construction is used with a much wider range of verbs than are the passive suffixes.

(18)a. 순이가 영이에게 선물을 주었다.
　　　Swun.i ka Yengi eykey senmul ul cwuess.ta.
　　　'Suni gave Yŏngi a present.'

　　b. 선물이 순이에 의해 영이에게 주어졌다.
　　　Senmul i Swun.i ey uy-hay Yengi eykey cwue.cyess.ta.[4]
　　　'The present was given by Suni to Yŏngi.'
　　　[There is no corresponding passive verb for *cwuta* 'give', so the pas-
　　　sive must be expressed with the auxiliary *-ecita* (whose past form is
　　　-e.cyess.ta).]

But *-eci-* can also be used with verb stems that do take a passive suffix, and sometimes it is even combined with a passive verb. The result is that there are three kinds of passives: (1) passives using a passive verb; (2) passives made with the auxiliary *-eci-*; and (3) passives combining a passive verb with the auxiliary. Each of these three types of passives has a different meaning and different rules of usage. For the most part, a passive made with the auxiliary is used to express a passive intent in situations where the corresponding passive verb does not have this kind of interpretation. On the one hand, (19c), below, *an ilk.ecinta* '[literally] won't be read' refers to a situation in which the speaker cannot read even though trying to do so. On the other hand, in (19d), *ilk.hyecinta,* which combined the passive verb with the auxiliary, suggests a situation in which people actively look for the book and read it. In (20), *kelecyessta,* a passive formed with the auxiliary *-eci-*, is ungrammatical in this situation because the occurrence is a natural one intended by no one.

(19)a. 영이가 책을 읽는다.
　　　Yengi ka chayk ul ilknunta. (active)
　　　'Yŏngi is reading a book.'

　　b. 책이 영이에게 읽힌다.
　　　Chayk i Yengi eykey ilk.hinta. (passive using a passive verb)
　　　'The book can be read by Yŏngi.'

　　c. 나는 오후에는 책이 안 읽어진다.

Na nun ohwu ey nun chayk i an ilk.e.cinta. (passive using the auxiliary)
'I can't read books in the afternoon.'
[Lit., '(For) me, in the afternoon, books are not read.']

d. 좋은 책은 시대가 바뀌어도 여전히 읽혀진다.

Coh.un chayk un sitay ka pa.kkwieto yecen.hi ilk.hye.cinta. (passive
verb + aux.)
'Even when times change, good books are read as before.'

(20) 바람에 날려서 연이 대추나무에 {걸렸다, ˣ걸어졌다}.

Palam ey nallyese yen i taychwu-namu ey {kellyess.ta, ˣkel.e.cyess.ta}.
'Lifted by the wind, the kite was caught on a jujube tree.'

As we have seen, Korean passives are more often distinguished by their idiomatic semantic content than derived out of purely syntactic motivations. The fact that passive constructions come about through derivation instead of conjugation also speaks to the passive as a semantic issue.

6.3.2 Causatives

Causative verbs are formed by attaching the suffixes *-i-*, *-hi-*, *-li-*, *-ki-*, *-wu-*, *-kwu-*, and *-chwu-* to the stems of verbs and adjectives. Here are some examples: *mek-* 'eat': *mek.i-* 'feed'; *nelp-* 'be wide': *nelp.hi-* 'broaden'; *wul-* 'cry': *wulli-* 'make cry'; *wus-* 'laugh': *wuski-* 'make laugh'; *kki-* 'join in': *kkiwu-* 'put in, insert'; *tal-* 'become hot': *talkwu-* 'heat, make hot'; *mac-* 'fit': *macchwu-* 'make fit'. Just as is the case with the passive, the derivation of the causative is restricted to a given set of verbs and adjectives. Consequently, just as with the passive, the causative cannot be formed from ditransitive verbs, verb stems ending in the vowel *-i-*, symmetric verbs, or the verb *ha-* 'do'. However, the overlap with passives is not complete. For example, the transitive verb *al-* 'know' does not have a passive form, but it does have a commonly used causative form, *alli-* 'let know, inform'. In the same way, *ip-* 'put on, wear' has a corresponding causative form, *ip.hi-* 'dress, put on (someone else)'. It is difficult to formulate rules describing which verbs have a causative form, however, because the derivation of the causative is grammatically irregular.

For causatives derived from adjectives and intransitive verbs, what was originally the subject becomes the object; for causatives derived from transitive verbs, the original subject is expressed as the object or the locative. In other words, adjectives and intransitive verbs become transitive when they are transformed into causatives.

(1) a. 길이 좁다.

Kil i copta. (adjective)
'The road is narrow.'

b. 인부들이 길을 좁힌다.
   Inpu-tul i kil ul cop.hinta.
   'The workers narrow the road.'

(2) a. 아기가 잔다.
   Aki ka canta. (intransitive verb)
   'The baby is sleeping.'

b. 어머니가 아기를 재운다.
   Emeni ka aki lul caywunta.
   'The mother is putting the baby to sleep.'

(3) a. 아기가 우유를 먹는다.
   Aki ka wuyu lul meknunta. (transitive verb)
   'The baby is taking its bottle' [Lit., 'eating milk'].

b. 어머니가 아기에게 우유를 먹인다.
   Emeni ka aki eykey wuyu lul mek.inta.
   'The mother is feeding the baby its milk.'

Besides causative verbs formed with various causative suffixes, Korean also has causatives formed with the construction *-key hata*. This construction combines the adverbial ending *-key* with the generic verb *hata* 'do'. This particular construction is productive, and it has an extremely broad range of application; it can be used with verbs that take causative suffixes as well as with those that do not. In Korean linguistic usage, the type of causative derived with a suffix is often called "the short-form causative" (단형사동), and the causative derived with *-key hata* is called "the long-form causative" (장형사동).

For a long time, research on the Korean causative has focused attention on the semantic overlap between the short and long forms. Of course, the difference between the two could not become an issue for verbs that had no suffix-derived causative; but in cases where both kinds of causative were possible, the similarities and differences between the two have been closely scrutinized.

First of all, from the point of view of syntactic structure, the short form is a simple sentence, while the long form is a compound sentence. In other words, the long-form causative incorporates an embedded sentence adverbialized by *-key*. From the point of view of semantics, the long-form causative necessarily expresses an indirect causative, while the short-form causative can be ambiguous, the interpretation as direct or indirect depending on the type of verb and the context. The indirect causative is a causative in which the person who is the subject merely causes someone to do the act but does not himself participate in the action; in a direct causative, the subject is actively involved in the action. For example, the verb *cwuki-* 'kill', which is the short-form causative of the verb *cwuk-* 'die', is by necessity a direct causative.

In the sentence *Minswu ka ayngmusay lul cwukyessta* 'Minsu killed the parrot', Minsu did not just 'cause the parrot to die' (by neglect or the like), he killed the parrot by wounding it, feeding it poison, hitting it with his fist, or something else requiring a direct, overt action. It is a direct causative. But, the sentence *Minswu ka ayngmusay lul cwukkey hayssta*, which is formed with the construction *-key hata*, is a long-form, indirect passive meaning 'Minsu let the parrot die'. In this case, the parrot's death could have been caused by carelessness—leaving it near a cat or by leaving poison near its birdseed. It is an indirect causative. The interpretation as direct or indirect does not necessarily have to be controlled by objective circumstances. In actuality, even had Minsu not actually caused the parrot's death directly, he might feel responsible enough to say, *"Nayka ayngmusay lul cwukyesskwuna!"* 'I've killed the parrot!' Or some other person, blaming Minsu, might equally well say to him that he'd killed the parrot.

The difference between direct and indirect causatives can be seen in the following examples. In (4a), the short-form causative is direct, while in (4b) the same short-form causative is indirect, because the phrase *pissan os* 'expensive clothes' makes that interpretation the most natural one. Finally, the long-form causative in (4c) is indirect. As we can see, the causative in each of these three sentences has a very different interpretation.

(4) a. 엄마가 영이에게 옷을 입힌다.
   Emma ka Yengi eykey os ul ip.hinta. (short form, direct causative)
   'Her mother puts Yŏngi's clothes on (for) her.'

   b. 영이 엄마는 영이에게 언제나 비싼 옷만 입힌다. (short form, indirect)
   Yengi emma nun Yengi eykey encey-na pissan os man ip.hinta.
   'Yŏngi's mother always lets her wear expensive clothes.'

   c. 엄마가 영이에게 옷을 입게 한다.
   Emma ka Yengi eykey os ul ipkey hanta. (long form, indirect)
   'Yŏngi's mother lets her put (her own) clothes on.'

Depending on the verb, there are situations where direct participation of the subject in the action is impossible, and in such cases, even the short-form causative is interpreted as indirect. We see that to be the case with causative verbs such as *ilk.hita* 'get (a person) to read', *wuskita* 'make (a person) laugh', *wullita* 'make (a person) cry', and *nollita* 'let (a person) play'. With these verbs, no matter how closely involved the subject might be in the action, it is impossible for one to participate in the act the way one does, for example, with *mek.ita* 'feed (someone)', where one actually picks up the food and places it in the other person's mouth. For these kinds of verbs, even the short forms are interpreted as indirect causatives. Of course, these verbs can also have long-form causatives because this type of causative is productive: *ilk.key hata* 'let (a person) read', *wuskey hata* 'make (a person) laugh', *wulkey hata* 'make (a person) cry', *nolkey hata* 'let (a person) play'. In such cases, the long-form causative has a more passive meaning than does the short-form causative. For example, *ilk.hita* 'get (a person) to read' would be used in case a teacher, during classtime, was actively having a student read, while *ilk.key hata* 'let (a person) read' might be used in a more passive situation, when the teacher simply bought a book for the student without checking on whether the reading was actually done. Thus, we can see that even in cases where the short form is interpreted as an indirect causative, it still expresses an act that has more direct involvement than the corresponding long-form causative.

6.4 Negation

6.4.1 Types of Negative Constructions

Negative constructions in Korean are created in two ways: (1) with *an(i)* or *mos* added to the predicate; or (2) by using the negative auxiliary verb *mal-*. These two types of negatives are used with different types of sentences. The negatives *ani* and *mos* are used with declaratives, interrogatives, and exclamations, and the negative auxiliary *mal-* is used with propositives and imperatives: for example, *kaci mal.ca* 'Let's don't go', and *kaci mal.ala* 'Don't go'.

Korean has a *short form* and a *long form* of negation. The negatives *ani* and *mos* can be used in both types of negation, but the negative auxiliary *mal-* is only used in the long form. In the "short form" of negation, a negative adverb is placed in front of the verb or adjective. In this construction *ani* ordinarily is shortened to *an; an kata* 'not go', for example, is much more natural than the longer version of the negative, *ani kata.*

The "long form" of negation is structurally more complex than the short form. It is created by attaching the ending *-ci* to the predicate stem and then adding to that a negative auxiliary. For this type of negation, the negative adverbs *ani* and *mos* are transformed into auxiliaries by using the verb *hata* 'do': *ani hata* 'not do' and *mos hata* 'can't do'. In this usage, *ani hata* can be, and usually is, contracted to *anh.ta.*

The examples given below illustrate the various types of Korean negation. Note that when the predicate is a noun plus the copula, the only type of negation possible is the long form with *ani*. In this case, the construction takes the form *noun (+ i/ka) anita.*[5] The negative *mos* cannot be used with the copula; moreover, it is used only in restricted contexts with adjectives.

	Short Negative		Long Negative	
	ani	*mos*	*-ci anh.ta*	*-ci mos hata*
Copula:	—	—	*miin i anita,* 'is not a beauty'	—
Verb:	*an kanta,* 'not go',	*mos kanta* 'can't go'	*kaci anh.nunta,* 'not go',	*kaci mos hanta* 'can't go'
Adjective:	*an phuluta,* 'not be blue'	—	*phuluci anh.ta,* 'not be blue'	?x*phuluci mos hanta*
				-ci malta
(Copula:)				—
Verb:				*kaci mal.ala* 'don't go'
(Adjective:)				—

Besides these kinds of negation, Korean also has two words used for negation that are unique. One is *moluta* 'not know', and the other is *eps.ta* 'is not, does not exist, does not have'. Instead of using *ani* or *mos* with the verbs *alta* 'know' and *iss.ta* 'is, exists, has', Koreans habitually express these negative meanings with single verbs that have the negative fused into the word. These two negative verbs constitute a special characteristic of Korean.

6.4.2 Meanings and Constraints on Negation

The adverb *ani* (or the verbal *anh-*) means '(is/does) not'. It is the most general negative. But it can also refer to the subject's intent; for example, *an kanta* '(I'm) not going' expresses the speaker's decision or intention not to go. The adverb *mos*, on the other hand, refers to ability: *mos kanta* '(I) can't go'.

(1) 한국팀은 월드컵 대회 본선에 나가지 않았다.
   Hankwuk-thim un Weltu-khep tayhoy ponsen ey naka.ci anh.ass.ta
   'The Korean team didn't go into the final round of World Cup competition.'

(2) 한국팀은 월드컵 대회 본선에 나가지 못했다.
   Hankwuk-thim Weltu-khep tayhoy ponsen ey naka.ci mos hayss.ta.
   'The Korean team couldn't get into the final round of World Cup competition.'

The meaning of (1) is simply a neutral transmission of the fact that the team did not get into the competition, or that the team did not want to enter the competition so did not go. In (2), by contrast, the meaning is that the team made an effort to get into the competition, but was impeded by other intentions, or because the efforts of the team were inadequate, it was eliminated in the semifinal round. Therefore, as can be seen in the following examples, the use of *ani* would be odd if the team could not enter the competition in spite of its intentions; but, if the team members themselves make the decision not to enter, then the use of *mos* would be quite ungrammatical.

(3) 한국팀은 예선에서 탈락되어 본선에 나가지 {?않았다, 못했다}.

Hankwuk-thim un yeysen eyse thallak-toy.e ponsen ey naka.ci {?anh.ass.ta, mos hayss.ta.}

'Since the Korean team members were eliminated in the semifinal round, they {?didn't [want to], couldn't} get into the finals.'

(4) 한국팀은 편파적인 심판에 항의하기 위해 본선에 나가지 {않았다, ˣ못했다}.

Hankwuk-thim un phyenpha-cek.in simphan ey hanguy-haki wi-hay ponsen ey naka.ci {anh.ass.ta, ˣmos hayssta}.

'To protest the unfair refereeing, the Korean team {didn't, ˣcouldn't} enter the finals.'

The negative *ani* cannot be used to negate a verb such as *alta* 'know' that expresses the speaker's perception, and it is also not used together with verbs such as *kyentita* 'tolerate' and *chamta* 'endure' that incorporate the speaker's intent. With these kinds of verbs, however, the use of *mos* is quite natural.

(5) a. ˣ나는 그런 사실을 전혀 {안 알았다, 알지 않았다}.

ˣNa nun kulen sasil ul cenhye {*an* al.ass.ta, alci *anh*.ass.ta}.

[ˣ'I not knew at all those kinds of facts.']

b. 나는 그런 사실을 전혀 {몰랐다 (ˣ못 알았다)⁶ 알지 못했다}.

Na nun kulen sasil ul cenhye {mollassta (ˣ*mos* al.assta), al.ci *mos* hayss.ta}.

'I was completely ignorant of those facts.'

[Lit., 'I completely didn't know those facts.']

(6) a. ˣ어떻게 1년도 {안 견디고, 견디지 않고} 사표를 내?

ˣEtteh.kye 1-nyen to {*an* kyentiko, kyentici *anh*.ko} saphyo lul nay?

[ˣ'How can you submit your resignation after not wanting to endure even a year?']

b. 어떻게 1년도 {못 견디고, 견디지 못하고} 사표를 내?

Eteh.key 1-nyen to {*mos* kyentiko, kyentici *mos* hako} saphyo lul nay?

'How can you submit your resignation after not (being able to endure) even a year?'

Since *mos* indicates lack of ability, it cannot be used together with con-

structions used to show intent such as -*lyeko* 'intending to __', -*koca* 'prepared
to __', -*ko siphta* 'want to __'. In addition, verbs such as *mang-hata* 'fail, be
ruined', *yemlye-hata* 'be concerned', *komin-hata* 'agonize', *kekceng-hata*
'worry', *hwuhoy-hata* 'regret', *silphay-hata* 'fail', which represent situations
that could be avoided if one had the ability, do not occur with *mos*.

(7) a. ˣ나는 외국 여행을 {못 가려고, 가지 못하려고} 한다.
    ˣNa nun oykwuk yehayng ul {*mos* kalyeko, kaci *mos* halyeko} hanta.
    [ˣ'I don't intend to be able to go on a vacation abroad.']

   b. 나는 외국 여행을 {안 가려고, 가자 않으려고} 한다.
    Na nun oykwuk yehayng ul {*an* kalyeko, kaci *anh.ulyeko*} hanta.
    'I don't intend to go on a vacation abroad.'

(8) a. ˣ그는 사업에서 {못 망했다, 망하지 못했다}.
    ˣKu nun saep eyse {*mos* mang-hayss.ta., mang-haci *mos* hayss.ta}.
    [ˣ'He wasn't able to fail in his business.']

   b. 그는 사업에서 {안 망했다, 망하지 않았다}.
    Ku nun saep eyse {*an* mang-hayss.ta, mang-haci *anh.ass.ta*}
    'He didn't fail in his business.'

The rule is that *mos* is not generally used with most adjectives, but it can
be when they mean something desirable, such as *neknek-hata* 'be sufficient',
wuswu-hata 'be outstanding', *mancok-hata* 'be satisfied', *phungpu-hata* 'be
abundant', *nelp.ta* 'be wide, broad', *khuta* 'be big', *coh.ta* 'be good', In such
cases, *mos* expresses a meaning of disappointment that the ability or situation did not measure up to expectations. When *mos* is used with adjectives
this way, the only type of negative possible is the long form.

(9) 예산이 {풍부하지 못해서, ˣ못 풍부해서} 만족스럽게 일을 마치지 못했다.
    Yeysan i {phungpu-haci mos hayse, ˣmos phungpu-hayse} mancok-sulep-
    key il ul machici mos hayss.ta.
    'They didn't finish the job satisfactorily because the budget was not
    sufficient.'

As we have said, the negative auxiliary *mal-* is in general only used in
imperative and propositive sentences. However, it can also be used in declarative sentences when those sentences include constructions that express
the hope of the speaker; for example, -*ki palata* 'hope that __', -*ki kiwen-hata*
'pray that __', -*ki wen-hata* 'want __', -*ki lul!* 'if only __!' -*ass.umyen!* 'if just
__!' -*myen coh.keyssta* 'it would be good if __'.

(10) 날씨가 춥지 말았으면 좋겠다.
    Nalssi ka chwupci *mal.ass.umyen coh.keyss.ta.*
    'It'll be great if weather isn't cold.'

(11) 제발 죽지만 말았기를!
   Ceypal cwukci man *mal.ass.ki lul!*
   'If he just please doesn't die!'

The negative auxiliary *mal-* is also used with verbs in reduplicative constructions to form phrases such as *-tunci maltunci* 'whether (one) does or not', *-ta malta* 'does a while and stops', *-llak mallak* 'alternately does and does not', *-kena malkena* 'does or not indifferently', *-lqtus malqtus* 'does or not imperceptibly', *-nuntung manun twung* 'may or may not do', *-lkka malkka* '(hesitating) to do or not'.

(12) 그가 가든지 말든지 상관 없다.
   Ku ka ka*tunci maltunci* sangkwan eps.ta.
   'It doesn't matter whether he goes or not.'

(13) 저 멀리 보일 듯 말 듯한 집이 우리 집이야.
   Ce melli po*ilqtus malqtus* han cip i wuli cip iya.
   'That house you can barely see in the distance is our house.'

(14) 민수는 소풍을 갈까 말까 망설인다.
   Minswu nun sophung ul ka*lkka malkka* mangsel.inta.
   'Minsu is hesitating whether to go on the picnic or not.'

The negative *ani* is also used in constructions that are not negations, but rather expressions of confirmation or doubt. Confirmation with *ani* is a kind of tag question used to check on some presumed fact that the speaker assumes the listener ought to know. Example (15a) is this type of question; here the speaker is almost certain that Yŏngi ate the apple and is asking to get the listener to confirm the fact. A confirmation question like this differs from a negative question like (15b) by its intonation, and by the position where the prefinal ending showing tense is used. In a confirmation question, the end of the sentence has a falling intonation, while at the end of a negative question, the intonation rises. Also, in a negative question the prefinal ending of tense links up with *ani*, while in a confirmation question the tense ending links up with the stem of the main verb.

(15) a. 영이가 그 사과를 먹었지 않니?
   Yengi ka ku sakwa lul mek.*essci* anh.ni? (↘) (confirmation question)
   'Yŏngi ate the apple, didn't she?'

   b. 영이가 그 사과를 먹지 않았니?
   Yengi ka ku sakwa lul mekci anh.*ass*.ni? (↗) (negative question)
   'Didn't Yŏngi eat the apple?'

Constructions with *ani* showing doubt are governed by a higher verb that expresses doubt, fear, or worry, such as *uysim-sulepta* 'is doubtful', *twulyepta* 'is fearful', *musepta* 'is frightening', *kekceng-sulepta* 'is worrisome', or *yemlye-sulepta* 'is anxiety-causing'. In these constructions as well, *ani* does not have a meaning of negation. In other words, a sentence like (16a) with the negative element *ani* has the same basic meaning as a sentence like (16b), which does not have a negative; in both cases the meaning is one of worry or doubt that Yŏngi will go.

(16) a. 영이가 가지 않을까 {걱정스럽다, 두렵다, 의심스럽다}.
     Yengi ka kaci anh.ulkka {kekceng-sulepta, twu.lyepta, uysim-sulepta.}
     'I {worry, am afraid, doubt} that Yŏngi might go.'
     [Lit., '(I) {worry, am afraid, doubt}: Won't Yŏngi go?']

   b. 영이가 갈까 {걱정스럽다, 두렵다, 의심스럽다}.
     Yengi ka kalkka {kekceng-culepta, twu.lyepta, uysim-sulepta.}
     'I {worry, am afraid, doubt} that Yŏngi will go.'
     [Lit., '(I) {worry, am afraid, doubt}: Will Yŏngi go?']

On the face of it, this construction expressing doubt looks the same as the long form of negation. But in fact the position of juncture and stress is in each case different. (In the following illustrative examples, the symbol "∨" shows the major juncture, and the element with the major stress is italicized.)

(17) a. 영이가 가지 ∨ 않을까 걱정스럽다.
     Yengi ka kaci ∨ *anh*.ulkka kekceng-sulepta. (negation)
     'I worry that Yŏngi might not go.'

   b. 영이가 ∨ 가지 않을까 걱정스럽다.
     Yengi ka ∨ *ka*ci anh.ulkka kekceng-sulepta. (doubt)
     'I worry that Yŏngi might go.'

6.4.3 The Short Form and the Long Form of Negation

As was pointed out above, Korean has a short form and a long form of negation. These two types of negation differ according to the constraints of the predicate, and there are also instances where they have somewhat different meanings.

As far as the scope of negation is concerned, the short form and the long form are the same. Both can be ambiguous as to how far the negation extends. Both (1a) and (1b), for example, are ambiguous as to whether the negation refers to only some of the group or to the group as a whole.

(1) a. 손님이 다 {안, 못} 왔다.
     Son-nim i ta {an, mos} wass.ta.
     'The guests {didn't, couldn't} all come.'

or 'The guests all {didn't, couldn't} come.' [That is, none of the guests came.]

b. 손님이 다 오지 {않았다, 못했다}.
Son-nim i ta oci {anh.ass.ta, mos hayss.ta}.
['id.']

This ambiguity can to a certain extent be resolved by using special particles in the appropriate places. When the particle *nun* is used, as in (1c) and (1d), the interpretation is that the negation necessarily applies to only part of the whole.

(1) c. 손님은 다는 {안, 못} 왔다.
Son-nim un ta *nun* {an, mos} wass.ta.
'Not all the guests came.'

d. 손님이 {다 오지는 않았다, 다는 오지 않았다}.
Son-nim i {ta oci *nun* anh.ass.ta, ta *nun* oci anh.ass.ta}
'The guests didn't all come.'

In many cases the contexts in which the short form and the long form occur are different. In addition, the short form is more constrained by context than the long form is. When the predicate is a compound or a derivation, *ani* and *mos* cannot be used in the short form of negation.

(2) 그런 {×안 신사다운, 신사답지 않은; ×못 신사다운, 신사답지 못한} 행동을 하고도 부끄럽지 않니?
Kulen {×an sinsa-tawun, sinsa-tapci anh.un; ×mos sinsa-tawun, sinsa-tapci mos han) hayngtong ul hako to pu.kkulepci anh.ni? (predicate derived by -*tapta* 'is like __')
'Aren't you ashamed to do an ungentlemanly act like that?'

(3) 그 정보는 {×안 정확하다, 정확하지 않다; ×못 정확하다, 정확하지 못하다}.
Ku cengpo nun {×an cenghwak-hata, cenghwak-haci anh.ta; ×mos cenghwak-hata, cenghwak-haci mos hata}. (compound predicate)
'That information is not accurate.'

Moreover, it is ungrammatical to use *ani* in the short form of negation with the verbs *moluta* 'not know', *epsta* 'is not, not exist, have not', and *issta* 'is, exist, have'.

(4) 민수는 그 사실을 {×안 모른다, 모르지 않는다}.
Minswu nun ku sasil ul {×an molunta, moluci anh.nunta}.
'Minsu isn't unaware of that fact.'

(5) 민수에게도 잘못이 {ˣ안 없다, 없지 않다}.
Minswu eykey to cal-mos i {ˣan eps.ta, epsci anh.ta}.
'Minsu isn't without mistakes, either.'

There are instances where the short form of negation takes on a special, idiomatic meaning, and in those cases it is impossible to use the corresponding long form of negation. For example, *an twaystta* '(literally,) did not form' has the idiomatic meaning 'is unfortunate, regrettable'; *mos nan* ('can't become') means 'foolish'; *an tway* 'won't do, form' is used to put something off limits or ban; and *mos sayngita* ('can't grow') idiomatically means 'be ugly'.

(6) 홍수 피해를 당했다니 참 {안됐다, ˣ되지 않았다}.
Hongswu phihay lul tang-hayss.tani cham {*an twayss.ta*, ˣtoyci anh.ass.ta}.
'It's really *unfortunate* that they suffered damage by the flood.'

(7) 동생과 싸우다니 {못난, ˣ나지 못한} 녀석.
Tongsayng kwa ssawutani {*mos nan*, ˣnaci mos han} nyesek.
'*Foolish* fellow, to fight with your younger sibling.'

(8) 함부로 불장난 하면 {안돼, ˣ되지 않아}.
Hampulo pul-cangnan hamyen {*an tway*, ˣtoyci anh.a}.
'*Don't* recklessly play with fire.'
[Lit., 'If (one) recklessly does fire-tricks, it won't do.']

(9) 어제 소개받은 사람은 너무 {못생겼어요, ˣ생기지 못했어요}.
Ecey sokay pat.un salam un nemu {*mos sayngkyess.e yo*, ˣsayngkici mos hayss.e yo}.
'The person I was introduced to yesterday really *was ugly*.'

As we have seen, there are instances where the distribution and meaning of the long form and the short form are different, but for the most part speakers recognize both kinds of negations as the same. In most contexts both forms can be used, and there are many cases where there is virtually no difference in meaning. Speakers idiomatically use both variants for a sentence such as "Minsu didn't go to school" *(Minswu nun hakkyo ey an kassta/ kaci anh.assta)* with no difference at all in intent.

References

Ch'ae Wan 1976, 1977, 1986, 1990; Chang Kyŏnghŭi 1985; Ch'oe Hyŏnbae 1946; Greenberg 1963; Hong Chaesŏng 1987; Hong Saman 1983; Hong Yunp'yo 1978; Im Hongbin 1987; Kim Tongsik 1981; Kwŏn Chaeil 1992; Lee Chung Min (Yi Chŏngmin) 1977; Martin 1992; Nam Kisim (Nam Ki Shim) 1978, 1985; Nam Kisim

(Nam Ki Shim) and Ko Yŏnggŭn 1985; Nam Mihye 1988; Pak Yanggyu 1978; Sanders 1977; Sŏ Chŏngsu (Suh Cheong-Soo) 1990, 1991; Sohn Ho-min (Son Homin) 1978; Song Seok-Choong (Song Sŏkchung) 1978, 1981; Yi Iksŏp (Lee Iksop) 1986; Yi Iksŏp (Lee Iksop) and Im Hongbin 1983; Yi Kwangho 1988; Yi Namsun 1988; Yu Tongsŏk 1981.

7

Honorifics and Speech Styles

In any language, there are differences in speech that depend upon relative social rank. In English, choosing to call the other person by a first name instead of a title plus last name is a speech style decision of this kind. Telemarketers who use the first name of a potential customer are saying, "Now relax; I'm using an intimate style because there are no social barriers between us." Such people are using the linguistic rules of society for their own commercial purposes. But there is relatively little differentiation by social rank in America in any case. It often happens, for example, that one is on a first-name basis within a few hours of meeting, even when the other person is seven or eight years older or is even one's teacher.[1] Such a thing would be unimaginable in Korea. In Korea, one would never call someone five or six years older, or one's teacher, by their first name, nor would one ever address that person by the intimate-style pronoun, *ne* 'you'. (The meaning of this pronoun is roughly similar to that of French *tu* or German *du*.) For Korean students, among the most exotic experiences they have when studying abroad in American are the universal use of the pronoun "you" and calling one's professor by his or her first name. For them, the only form of address they have ever known for teachers is *sensayng-nim* (literally,) 'respected teacher'. It is not even permissible for the students to add the teacher's surname; to that title and use, for example, *Kim sensayng-nim* 'Professor Kim'[2]; nor can they use a second-person pronoun, even one that might otherwise be considered similar to French *vous* or German *Sie*. These interpersonal rules never change, even if the student himself later becomes president of the teacher's university or of the nation; the teacher from one's student days must always be *sensayng-nim*.

In this way, the Korean language strictly reflects the hierarchical order. Speech styles are divided according to a system of honorifics, and this system is complex and richly textured. In fact, it may well be that no language on earth has a more finely differentiated system of honorifics. Only Japanese is of a similar level of complexity. Even the famous honorific distinctions of Javanese appear to be of a much simpler dimension than those of Korean. Korean society accepts as a norm a complexity of honorific language mastered completely by few Koreans but to which the majority of its citizens aspire. This chapter is devoted to those norms and the extent to which they are used in everyday life.

7.1 Pronouns

In many languages, second-person pronouns are divided into a plain and an honorific form. In French there is *tu* and *vous,* in Italian, *tu* and *Lei*; in German, *du* and *Sie*; in Russian, *ty* and *vy*; these are typical of European languages. English is of course the exception, but in the past it, too, had a similar distinction between "thou" and "you". The use of different expressions depending on rank is commonly found in the pronouns of a language.

In the honorific system of Korean, *second-person pronouns* are also differentiated by rank, but the distinctions are not confined to a two-way one between plain and honorific. For example, if the sentence "Is this your book?" were a translation from Korean, various different words could be what is represented by "your". Which of the pronouns "your" represents would depend upon the speech style—and thus the relative rank of the person being addressed:

(1) a. 이거 너-의 책-이니?
       Ike *ne uy* chayk ini? (plain style)

     b. 이거 자네 책-인가?
       Ike *caney* chayk inka? (familiar)

     c. 이거 당신 책-이오?
       Ike *tangsin* chayk io? (semiformal)

     d. 이거 댁-의 책-입니까?
       Ike *tayk uy* chayk ipnikka? (polite or formal)

     e. 이거 어르신-의 책-입니까?
       Ike *elusin uy* chayk ipnikka? (formal)

In other words, depending on that other person's rank, "you" could correspond to *ne, caney, tangsin, tayk,* or—being extremely polite, as, for example, to an elderly patriarch—*elusin.* The pronoun *ne,* which is the most intimate, is used with one's friend or one's son or daughter or a child, and as one progresses through each of the other pronouns, the social rank of the other person rises correspondingly.

To a certain extent, focusing upon pronominal differences to examine the Korean honorific system reflects a bit of Western-language bias for the weight of the Korean honorific system does not rest solely, or even primarily, upon second-person pronouns. In fact, some sociolinguistic distinctions are not covered by pronoun use at all. In a great many cases it is not permissible to use a pronoun, and some other kind of appellation—a title or the like—must be used instead. There are many constraints on pronouns.

First, the pronoun *caney* is commonly used, for example, by university professors to address their students. This usage contrasts with that of elementary and secondary school teachers, who use the more intimate *ne*, and the shift to a different style at the university level is undoubtedly because the students are then considered to be no longer children. The fact that elementary school teachers address their former students in their thirties or forties as *caney* shows this generalization to be true. However, there must be a fairly great difference in age—say around twenty years or so—for the older person to use *caney*. The younger person cannot be as young as a middle or high school student, and even a senior professor has to be careful using *caney* with an unfamiliar person past his thirties. The reason is that, though it may be polite to use *caney* to a person of the right age, to a certain extent, the pronoun also signals that the other person has a social rank below that of the speaker. In short, the pronoun *caney* expresses an age difference, but it also implies that the speaker is in a position of authority, and for that reason it can offend the sensibilities of the other person if not used with care.

The pronoun *tangsin* is typically used by middle-aged and older married couples to address each other.[3] In addition, it is commonly used in advertising and in the titles of books to refer to an unspecified reader.

(2) a. 당신의 고민을 덜어드립니다. (a newspaper ad)
 Tangsin uy komin ul tel.e tulipnita.
 '(We) will eliminate *your* pain.'

 b. 당신의 우리말 실력은? (a book title)
 Tangsin uy wuli-mal sillyek un?
 '(How is) *your* Korean ability?'

However, *tangsin* must be used with great care when speaking to someone in ordinary, daily conversations. This pronoun may indicate a higher social rank than *ne* or *caney*, but the elevation is not of a particularly great degree, and the person hearing it might feel that he is not being treated with enough respect; therefore, *tangsin* can cause some feeling of discomfort. The kind of retort seen in (3a), below, is actually quite common, and in disputes like those in (3b, c) the pronoun *tangsin* is habitually used as a sign of some disrespect.

(3) a. 누구더러 '당신' 이라는 거야?
 Nwukwu tele 'tangsin' ilanun ke 'ya?
 'Who are you calling '*tangsin*'?'

 b. 당신 같은 사람은 처음 보겠어.
 Tangsin kath.un salam un cheum pokeyss.e.
 'I've never seen anyone like you (*tangsin*).'

c. 당신이 뭔데 이래라 저래라 하는 거야?

Tangsin i mwe 'ntey ilay la celay la hanun ke 'ya?

'Who do you think you are, doing whatever you want?'

[literally, 'What are you (*tangsin*), . . .']

One additional and particularly nettlesome complication is that *tangsin* is usually considered the nearest Korean equivalent to English "you". As a result, when confronted by a Korean-speaking foreigner, many Koreans habitually incorporate the pronoun into their speech in places where often no pronoun would be required at all. Since it is in any case difficult for Koreans to know where in the social hierarchy these outsiders belong, the social signals of the pronoun becomes garbled, to say the least.

In daily conversations *tangsin* has these restrictions. It has some special uses—for example, police officers often use it when making inquiries—but except between married couples, it is not a particularly easy pronoun to employ, regardless whether the other person is an acquaintance or a stranger.

The pronouns *tayk* and *elusin* are greatly constrained in their usage. The specialized word *elusin* is a term showing high respect, but it is not used for any public social relationship. It can be highly appropriate when addressed to someone in their seventies or eighties from the rural countryside, or one might use it as in (4), below, when one meets an older person respectably dressed in traditional Korean clothing on the subway. But it would not be natural to use this pronoun to address a school principal or a cabinet minister, or the president of the Republic of Korea. In other words, *elusin* is used in a traditional Korean setting, but it is not a word that is actively used even in those kinds of circumstances. The pronoun *tayk* is even more constrained than *elusin*; in fact, the existence of this pronoun is barely maintained in the modern language. Together with *elusin*, *tayk* is a pronoun that is difficult to use for anyone not steeped in Korean tradition. Also, while *elusin* can be used regardless whether one has a personal relationship with the other person, the same is not true of *tayk*, which can only be addressed to someone with whom one has no such relationship. Since *tayk* is a more respectful term of address than *tangsin*, there is no worry that it could cause the trouble or discomfort that *tangsin* might; still, the situations in which a sentence such as (5) can be used are extremely limited.

(4) 여기가 어르신의 자리입니다.

Yeki ka *elusin uy* cali ipnita. (to an elderly person on the subway)

'This is *your* seat, Sir.'

(5) 이 개가 댁의 개인가요?

I kay ka *tayk uy* kay inka yo?

'Is this *your* dog, Sir (*or* Ma'am)?'

Pronouns are used far less in Korean than they are in Western languages. *Third-person pronouns,* in particular, play a very minor role in the language. There is no rule in Korean, for example, that a noun used in an earlier sentence has to be replaced by a pronoun. To illustrate this point, we can see that in (6), below, the word *nwuna* '(a male's older) sister' is simply repeated again and again rather than pronominalized.

(6) 누나는 부산에서 태어났다. 누나가 고향인 부산을 떠난 것은 고등학교를 졸업하고서였다. 그 후 누나는 다시는 부산에 가지 못하였다. 그러나 고향을 향한 누나의 애정은 한 시도 식은 적이 없다.

Nwuna nun Pusan eyse thay.e nass.ta. *Nwuna* ka kohyang in Pusan ul ttenan kes un kotung-hakkyo lul col.ep-hakose 'yess.ta. Ku hwu *nwuna* nun tasi nun Pusan ey kaci mos ha.yess.ta. Kulena kohyang ul hyang-han *nwuna* uy ayceng un han-si to sik.un cek i eps.ta.

'*Sister* was born in Pusan. *She* left her home in Pusan after (she) had graduated from high school. After that, *she* never went back to Pusan. However, *her* love for her old home has never diminished one bit.'

In this short narrative, the noun *nwuna* is translated into English with a pronoun after the first occurrence, but in the Korean original it remains the same noun, unchanged. The usages of second-person pronouns such as those discussed above—*tangsin, tayk,* and *elusin*—are related to this characteristic. In addressing a person to whom the polite referents *tayk* or *elusin* would be appropriate, it is usual to refer to that person instead with a noun, such as *sensayng-nim* 'respected Teacher, Doctor', *son-nim* 'respected Guest', *acwumeni* 'Auntie', or the like.

First-person pronouns are also distinguished by speech level. For the singular, 'I/me', there is both a plain-form *na* and an humble-form *ce.* The corresponding plural forms are *wuli* and *cehuy.*[4]

(7) a. 누나, 나도 가겠어.
Nwuna, *na* to kakeyss.e.
'Sister, I'm going, too.'

b. 아버지, 저도 가겠어요.
Apeci, *ce* to kakeyss.e yo.
'Father, I'm going, too.'

(8) a. 누나, 우리가 이겼어.
Nwuna, *wuli* ka i.kyess.e.
'Sister, we won.'

b. 선생님, 저희들은 이만 물러가겠습니다.
Sensayng-nim, *cehuy-tul* un iman mulle kakeyss.supnita.
'Teacher, we'll take our leave now.'

The basic *third-person pronoun* is *ku*, 'he, she, it', a word that is also a demonstrative meaning 'that (one), those (things), the'. The use of this word as a pronoun is exceptional because, as a demonstrative, the element always occurs as the modifier of a noun. As a referent for people, *ku i* is more polite than *ku*, and *ku pun*, politer still. The other two Korean demonstratives, *i* 'this (one)' and *ce* 'that (one over there)' also appear in this latter usage as *i i* and *i pun* and *ce i* and *ce pun*. (All of these forms would be translated as 'he' or 'she'.) But, unlike *ku*, *i* and *ce* do not appear as independent pronouns. The pronoun *ku i* 'he' serves the role of elevating a bit above *ku* the person to whom it refers. It is mainly used by wives to refer to their husbands. Otherwise, it is not a commonly used word. When a Korean husband refers to his wife, he generally uses an expression such as *ku salam* 'that person', which signals a somewhat lower social rank. The pronominal reference *ku pun* (literally) 'that esteemed person' is the next level up from *ku i*. It functions to signal a relatively high social status for the other person. It is used much more widely that *ku i*.

There are a variety of idiosyncratic constraints on the use of these pronouns. As was pointed out above, successive occurrences of a noun are not normally pronominalized in Korean, so, for example, *ku pun* would not be used in a sentence as an anaphoric reference for *eme-nim* 'Mother'. But it is in any case extremely rare to refer to someone with whom one has a close relationship as *ku pun*. To refer to one's own mother as *ku pun* is something that would happen only in unusual circumstances, such as, for example, when looking at old photographs, as in (9).

(9) a. 그분은 우리 어머니셔.
   Ku pun un wuli emeni 'sye.
   'That person [pointing to her photograph] is my mother.'

b. 그분은 너희 5대조 할아버지시다.
   Ku pun un nehuy 5-tayco hal.apeci 'sita.
   'That person [pointing to his photograph] is your great-great grandfather.'

What we see in all of these third-person pronouns except *ku* is that structurally they are composed of a demonstrative plus a noun and mean 'that (or this) person'. And the use of *ku* itself as a pronoun is not particularly common — except of course in translations of pronouns in Western languages. Korean does not have a well-established category of words that could be called third-person pronouns.

7.2 Titles

The honorific system of Korean is reflected in great detail through the use of titles.[5] To illustrate, let us say that someone is being called, as in "Minho, where are you going?" Let us say further that the person is named Kim Minho, and he is a section chief in a Korean company. In this case he could be called by about fourteen different appellations, depending upon the rank and relationship of the person speaking. These fourteen appellations are arrayed, roughly in order of relative rank, as follows:

(1) 1. *Kwacang-nim* 2. *Kim Kwacang-nim* 3. *Kim Minho-ssi* 4. *Minho-ssi* 5. *Min-hyo-hyeng* 6. *Kim Kwacang* 7. *Kim-ssi* 8. *Kim-hyeng* 9. *Kim-kwun* 10. *Kim Minho-kwun* 11. *Minho-kwun* 12. *Kim Minho* 13. *Minho* 14. *Minho ya*

Let us look at each of these appellations and the characteristics of how they are used.

7.2.1 *Kwacang-nim* (과장님):

This title is the highest form of address that could be used for this person. Literally, it means 'Respected Section Chief' and consists of the honorific suffix *-nim* 'respected, esteemed' attached to Kim Minho's job title. This respectful appellation is a typical use of the honorific suffix *-nim*, one of the most widely used elements in the entire honorific system.

The suffix *-nim* is extremely productive because it functions to transform a plain appellation into an honorific one, as can be seen in the following, typical examples:

(2) a. 형/형님 *hyeng/hyeng-nim* '(a male's older) Brother', 누나/누님 *nwuna/nwu-nim* '(a male's older) Sister', 오빠/오라버님 *o.ppa/olape-nim* '(a female's older) Brother', 아버지 / 아버님 *apeci/ape-nim* 'Father', 어머니 / 어머님 *emeni/eme-nim* 'Mother', 아주머니 / 아주머님 *acwumeni/acwume-nim* 'Auntie', 할머니 / 할머님 *halmeni/halme-nim* 'Grandmother', 고모 / 고모님 *komo/komo-nim* 'Auntie' (father's sister), 이모 / 이모님 *imo/imo-nim* 'Auntie' (mother's sister)

b. 과장 / 과장님 *kwacang/kwacang-nim* 'Respected Section Chief', 국장 / 국장님 *kwukcang/kwukcang-nim* 'Respected Bureau Chief', 장관 / 장관님 *cangkwan/cangkwan-nim* 'Honorable Minister', 시장 / 시장님 *sicang/sicang-nim* 'Honorable Mayor', 소장 / 소장님 *socang/socang-nim* 'Respected Institute Director', 학장 /학장님 *hakcang/hakcang-nim* 'Respected College Dean', 선생 / 선생님 *sensayng/sensayng-nim* 'Respected Teacher', 박사 / 박사님 *paksa/paksa-nim* 'Respected Doctor' (Ph.D.), 소령 / 소령님 *solyeng/solyeng-nim* 'Respected Major', 하사 / 하사님 *hasa/hasa-nim* 'Respected Sergeant', *sencang/sencang-nim* 선장 / 선장님 'Respected Captain' (of a ship), 기사 / 기사님 *kisa/kisa-nim* 'Respected Engineer, Technician', 감독 / 감독님 *kamtok/kamtok-nim* 'Respected (film) Director, Foreman, Superintendent', 선배 / 선배님 *senpay/senpay-nim* 'Respected Senior' (earlier graduate of the same school)

The rules governing family terms are complex, and the role played by -*nim* in indicating these family relationships is an important one. One basic rule is that Koreans call younger siblings by their given names, but not generally older siblings. Korean males call their older siblings by the name *Hyeng* 'Older Brother' and *Nwuna* 'Older Sister', both when speaking to others and when addressing the siblings directly. The more polite terms for these brothers and sisters, *Hyeng-nim* '(Older) Brother' and *Nwu-nim* '(Older) Sister', are used when the siblings reach a fairly mature age (after about their thirties or forties). These polite terms are especially common when there is a relatively large difference in age; for if the speaker is much younger, the plain terms *Hyeng* and *Nwuna* cannot be used. These rules of reference apply no matter whether the "siblings" are actually members of the same household or are older cousins. Korean females call an older brother by the name *Oppa* and an older sister *Enni*. The corresponding polite term a woman uses for an older brother, *Olape-nim* 'Older Brother', has the same rules of usage that apply to *Hyeng-nim*, but the word has an extravagant feel about it and tends not to be used as often as *Hyeng-nim*. In addition, a Korean woman would never add the polite suffix -*nim* to the term she uses for her older sister, *Enni*. The polite terms *Ape-nim* 'Father' and *Eme-nim* 'Mother' are generally words a daughter-in-law uses when speaking to her husband's parents. However, they are also quite common when writing a letter to one's own parents, and, in addition, they can be used when addressing a friend's parents. The polite terms for grandparents, *Halape-nim* 'Grandfather' and *Halme-nim* 'Grandmother', serve as general terms of references for older persons. They are not often used, at least in everyday conversations, when speaking to one's own family members, but it is common practice to use them in correspondence or in formal compositions.

The honorific suffix -*nim* is more commonly added to job titles than to the terms for family relationships. The suffix cannot be combined with *taythonglyeng* 'president (of the country)', but this is an exception, for practically all other titles can.[6] Adding -*nim*, in fact, is the principal way to form appellations for people who hold those titles. With family terms, the use of the polite appellation is quite limited in scope, as can be seen in the case of *Ape-nim* 'Father', which is largely a daughter-in-law's word, or *Hyeng-nim* 'Older Brother', which is used only after the person is relatively old. But no such restrictions apply to the use of -*nim* with job titles. On the contrary, with job titles, it is the plain form of reference that is extremely limited in its range of application. While the plain forms are commonly used as ways to call one's family members, it would be unnatural to call professional people by their job titles without adding -*nim*.

In its usage with job titles, -*nim* is indispensable. Without -*nim*, it would often be practically impossible to call the people who hold those jobs; with it, an appellation of the politest kind can be formed quite naturally.

In Korean, the most idiomatic way to call people is simply to use the person's job title plus -*nim*: *Kwacang-nim* 'Respected Section Chief' — or whatever his position might be. These unpersonalized titles are much more common than titles such as that of 2, in which the person's surname is added. This Korean usage contrasts strongly with that of English, where it is unusual to refer to someone simply as "Professor", for example. An American teacher would feel somewhat estranged being called that instead of "Professor Smith"; just the opposite is true in Korea, where both student and teacher would feel a little uncomfortable if the name were added. The professor would probably feel insulted.

7.2.2 *Kim Kwacang-nim* (김과장님)

Adding the surname in front of the title lowers the level of politeness. The usual reason for adding a name this way is to avoid potential confusion when several people hold the same job title. In fact, this same reason may help explain why *Kim Kwacang-nim* as a title is lower in the esteem it shows than *Kwacang-nim.* When one says "*Kwacang-nim*" it gives the feeling to the other person that for me there is only you, whereas "*Kim Kwacang-nim*" conveys the feeling that you are one of several. In any event, it is discomfiting for a Korean professor, for example, to be greeted by one of his students, "*I Sensayng-nim, annyeng haseyyo?*" ('Professor Yi, how are you?'). An appellation such as *I Sensayng-nim* or *I Kyoswu-nim* is a title suitable only for use by one's younger colleagues at the same workplace or a few acquaintances from everyday life. Even parents of students have to say *Sensayng-nim* or *Kyoswu-nim.* The difference made by adding the surname or not adding the surname is surprisingly sharp.

7.2.3 *Kim Minho-ssi* (김민호씨)

This is a form made by adding the polite suffix *-ssi* to the person's full name. The suffix *-ssi* serves a function similar to that of *-nim,* but it is different in that it combines with personal names. It is also significantly lower on the scale of politeness. Its meaning is roughly that of English "Mr." or "Ms." "*Kim Minho-ssi*" is an appellation that would be heard most naturally in a bank, when a customer waiting to be served is called. In addition, it would be used in the same workplace to address a person not very different in age, in a similar job position, but of somewhat lower rank, with whom one is still not close enough to leave off all formalities. In any case, it is an appellation that shows respect to the other person, but not to the degree that Kim Kwacang-nim in 2. does. Including the given name, *Minho,* is already an element that lowers the degree of politeness; add to that the fact that *-ssi* does not show the deference that *-nim* does, and it becomes clear that *Kim Minho-ssi* is a level of politeness below that of *Kim Kwacang-nim.*

7.2.4 *Minho-ssi* (민호씨)

This is an appellation with the surname removed from the more polite form in 3. Since only the given name is used, the appellation is relatively informal; as a result, the level of politeness that it shows is lower than that of *Kim Minho-ssi. Minho-ssi* is a usage appropriate for a person within the same workplace with whom one is fairly close and who is about the same age, with a similar position but perhaps slightly lower in rank. However, it is not common for men to call female colleagues "*Kim Swunhuy-ssi*," "*Swunhuy-ssi*," or the like. Newly married wives frequently use this style when calling their husbands. However, one rarely hears a husband refer to his wife as *Swunhuy-ssi.*

7.2.5 *Minho-hyeng* (민호형)

The noun *hyeng* 'older brother' is of course originally a family term, but its use can be extended to those who are not family members; here it can be considered a kind of suffix serving a function like that of *-ssi* or *-kwun. Minho-hyeng,* like *Kim-hyeng* in 8., below, is not widely used, but it seems to be of a level of politeness above *Kim-hyeng.* It is an appropriate way to call juniors with whom one has had a close relationship from college.

7.2.6 *Kim Kwacang* (김과장)

In this form the honorific suffix *-nim* is removed from "*Kim Kwacang-nim*". By leaving off *-nim* this way, the level of politeness is lowered sharply; *Kim Kwacang* is an appellation used with colleagues and people of lower social rank.

7.2.7 *Kim-ssi* (김씨)

This is a form made by leaving the given name off *Kim Minho-ssi.* However, it should be carefully noted that this appellation runs counter to the way politeness is usually structured in Korean. As a rule, the surname alone represents the most formal way to refer to the other person, while using only the given name is the style freest of social barriers. Thus, if the order 7-3-4 is the norm, then one would expect 9-10-11 to be in descending order of politeness, but in fact that is not the case. *Kim-ssi* runs counter to the rule and is, on the contrary, of a lower level of politeness than *Minho-ssi.*

This violation of the usual hierarchical order may have come about because of another curious usage. Unlike *Minho-ssi* or *Kim Kwacang,* the appellation *Kim-ssi* is something that could never be used with an equal. *Kim-ssi* might be used in reference to a young or middle-aged man who had come to fix the plumbing. The appellation is certainly not used to put the other person down, but it is nevertheless used by a superior to someone inferior in rank, and since it presumes the listener occupies a lower social position than oneself, the politeness level of *Kim-ssi* is clearly not high.

7.2.8 *Kim-hyeng* (김형)

Just as is the case with 5. *Minho-hyeng,* above, this appellation is formed by using the familial term *hyeng* 'older brother' as a suffix. However, there is a significant difference between the two kinds of expressions. While forms such as *Minho-hyeng* also serve as actual family terms, a form made up of *hyeng* attached to a surname can never be used when addressing a family member. Another characteristic of *Kim-hyeng* is that, although it is sometimes used with a co-worker who is about the same age as the speaker, it is much more common to use it with a slightly younger, former schoolmate who was a couple of years behind the speaker in college. In this usage among former school-mates, *Kim-hyeng* implies that the person being addressed is from a lower grade than someone toward whom *Minho-hyeng* is used.

This distinction in usage between *Kim-hyeng* and *Minho-hyeng* resembles the case of *Kim-ssi,* which we have looked at, above. For again, we see an instance where the surname implies a lower level of address than the given name. However, it is important to keep in mind here that, unlike *Kim-ssi,* *Kim-hyeng* does not imply a lower social rank. Much more than is the case with *Kim-ssi,* *Kim-hyeng* implies that the speaker and the addressee are on fa-miliar terms with each other, and in this sense it is a higher form of address than *Kim-ssi.* Another point that should be made about *Kim-hyeng* is that it cannot be used toward a woman; in fact, there is no corresponding appella-tion in this case for females.

7.2.9-11 *Kim-kwun/Kim Minho-kwun/Minho-kwun* (김군/김민호군/민호군)

These appellations are formed by using the suffix *-kwun* instead of *-ssi.* They are arrayed in descending order of politeness. The suffix *-kwun* is mainly used with young men and implies a certain amount of familiarity. The conditions under which *-kwun* can be used are very much the same as those in which the pronoun *caney* is used. It is the most appropriate way for a college professor to call one of his students. It is like *Kim-hyeng* in that it is used with someone lower in rank, but *-kwun* indicates that there is a greater difference in age than *Kim-hyeng* does, and therefore it shows a lower level of deference. The suffix is seldom used with women but it is occasionally; a young female student might be called *Kim-kwun,* but seldom if ever would she be referred to as *Kim Swunhuy-kwun* or *Swunhuy-kwun.* Instead of *-kwun* it is possible to use *-yang* 'Miss', but the range of situations in which *-yang* can be used is extremely narrow. In an office, a young girl who takes care of mak-ing tea can be called *Kim-yang* or *Swunhuy-yang,* but it is much more com-mon in the office these days for a female worker to be known as *Misu Kim,* adopting the English title as a more neutral term of reference. As for the university setting, it would not be at all appropriate for a professor to call his young female students using the suffix *-yang.*

7.2.12 *Kim Minho* (김민호)

Calling a person by his or her full name without attaching a title is not particularly common in Korea. At the university, it is common practice for a teacher when calling students in a formal situation—as in a roll call. In addition, parents sometimes use this type of appellation when scolding their children because it has a somewhat formal-sounding flavor. It is this formal feeling of the full name that makes it a level of politeness above the given name alone.[7]

7.2.13 *Minho* (민호)

Calling someone by his or her given name is the most intimate style of address in Korean. However, as a person nears thirty or forty, the opportunities for using the name alone gradually decrease. Companions with whom one has been on a first-name basis since childhood, as well as one's favorite teacher from elementary school, then begin to use forms such as *Kim Kwacang* instead. Even parents begin to use names such as *Aypi* (or *Apem*) 'Daddy', meaning that he is their grandchildren's father. Only very close friends sometimes still call one by his name as he approaches middle age.

When a name is used as appellation, the vowel *i* is added at the end in case the name ends in a consonant. For example, the names *Changsik* and *Yengswun* regularly take *-i*, as shown in the exchanges, below. As can be seen in (5), if a phrase particle is attached, it follows the vowel.

(4) a. 창식-이 나 좀 봐.
Cangsik-i na com pwa.
'Changsik(i), come here a minute.'

b. 이거, 영순-이 아니니?
Ike, Yengswun-*i* anini?
'Isn't this—Yŏngsun(i)'s?'

(5) a. 오늘은 영식-이-가 제일 잘하는구나.
Onul un Yengsik-*i ka* ceyil cal hanunkwuna.
'Today Yŏngsik(i) is doing best, I see.'

b. 이 그림 영식-이-한테 줄까?
I kulim Yengsik-*i hanthey* cwulkka?
'Shall we give this painting *to* Yŏngsik(i)?'

7.2.14 *Minho-ya* (민호야)

In this appellation, the vocative particle *-a* is added to the name. The form of the particle is /a/ in case the name ends with a consonant, as in *Cangsik-a!* 'Changsik!'; but if the name ends in a vowel—as does *Minho*—the form of the particle is /ya/, as in *Minho-ya!* It is interesting that the addition of this vocative particle lowers the level of politeness below that of using the name alone (or with the vowel /i/ added at the end). An appellation such as *Minho-*

ya is used freely by close friends, parents, and older relatives until the person is about college age. But once the person is old enough to be married, or certainly around the age of forty or so, it becomes awkward to call him this way. From then on, the particle is omitted, and he is called by the names *Minho* or *Changsik-i*, for example. In this way, one shows a more respectful attitude and avoids giving the impression that the person is being treated like a child. The difference in the way these appellations feel is a delicate one, but the inescapable fact is that the addition of the vocative particle to the name places the appellation on the lowest level in the system of honorifics.

If the context is one in which the vocative particle cannot be used, then the difference between 13 and 14 disappears. If, for example, the name appears in a context such as *I ke Minho wusan ici?* 'Is this (your) umbrella, Minho?' the vocative particle cannot follow the name, and there is therefore no way to make the distinction between these two levels.

Here it is important to note that the vocative particle can only be used with the last level of appellations, number 14. All of the titles, or appellations, given in (1), above, are used as ways to call people—that is, as vocatives—but none of them except the last one can be used with the vocative particle. Otherwise, the various names and titles are used as vocatives alone, with no particle or other element added. That is because the vocative particle itself is representative of the lowest level in the Korean system of honorifics. In Middle Korean (during the fifteenth and sixteenth centuries) there was another, separate vocative particle used with names and titles at the higher levels. This particle, *-ha*, was used, for example, in the vocative *Nimkum-ha* 'O King!'; and it had an honorific function like that of the subject particle *-kkeyse* in modern Korean. In some modern dialects, also, there are vocative elements that are added only to titles of respect; for example, *Kwacang-nim yo* or *Sensayng-nim yey*. Since the vocative particle *a/ya* cannot be added to such titles, these dialect forms may represent the filling of a gap in the system. But, in any event, such a strategy does not exist in the modern standard language, where titles of respect can only be used as vocatives if they are not marked as such by a particle.

As we have seen, there are approximately fourteen levels of appellations in the Korean honorific system. Depending on how they are viewed, some of these levels can be merged. But several levels could also be added. One example of the latter is the use of only the last character in a name as a way to call that person. The shortening of the name works like this: A typical Korean name, such as *Minho* or *Cengswuk*, consists of two characters—that is, two syllables. A friend calling out to this person will usually say "*Minho-ya*" or "*Cengswuk-a*", but it also happens sometimes that the person may say simply "*Ho-ya*" or "*Swuk-a*". Leaving off the first syllable this way signals a closer relationship; in other words, the abbreviated form is like a nickname. Speaking of nicknames, Koreans make up and use these much as people in other societies do. Whether cruel or simply jocular, nicknames such as *Ccangkwu* (짱구) 'Pumpkin Head', *Ppayngkho* (뺑코)

'Needle Nose', and *Twayci* (돼지) 'Piggy, Chubby' are very much a part of Korean culture.

Another strategy used in a workplace for relatively high-ranking people is simply to call those people by the most honorific title, *Sensayng-nim* (*Kim Sensayng-nim, Kim Sensayng*), regardless what the person's actual job title might be. Among school compatriots, the title *Senpay-nim* (선배님) 'Respected Senior' is rather widely used without regard to whether the person is actually senior or not. A middle-school student living in the same neighborhood as Section Chief Kim would call him using a family term, *Acesi* 'Uncle' or, in case he were around seventy years old, *Halapeci* 'Grandfather'.

As these multilayered titles indicate, Koreans live in a complex web of social relations. Family relationships are particularly finely differentiated, and there are any number of different appellations Section Chief Kim's family and relations might use with him. Corresponding to what would be called an "uncle" in English, there are eight different Korean words. First, a father's unmarried younger brother would be *Samchon* (삼촌); once that uncle had married, the appellation would change and he would be called *Cak.un Apeci* (작은아버지 'Little Father'). An older brother of the father would be *Khun Samchon* (큰삼촌 'Big Samch'on') before marriage, and *Khun Apeci* ('Big Father') after marriage. If the "uncle" were one's father's first cousin, he would be known as *Tangswuk* (당숙). The husband of one's father's sister is *Komopu* (고모부), while the husband of one's mother's sister is *Imopu* (이모부). Mother's brother is *Oy samchon* (외삼촌 'Outside Samch'on'). And, finally, there is a general term for 'uncle', *Acessi* (아저씨), and that word can also be used.

When a woman marries, each of her in-laws must be called by the word appropriate for their relationship to her. This system is at least as complex as the one used within the family she has left. Whereas her husband calls his father and mother "*Apeci*" and "*Emeni*", she must use the more polite terms for them, *Ape-nim* (아버님) and *Eme-nim* (어머님). The daughter-in-law certainly cannot use the hyperchoristic words for father and mother her own children use, *Appa* 'Daddy' and *Emma* 'Mommy'. For her husband's older brother, she uses *Acwupe-nim* (아주버님); for her husband's younger brother, she uses *Tolyen-nim* (도련님) before he marries and *Sepang-nim* (서방님) afterward. For the husband's older sister, she does not use the expected female term *Enni* 'Older Sister', but, curiously, the male term *Hyengnim* (in other cases, 'Older Brother') instead. For her husband's younger sister, the wife is traditionally supposed to use *Akassi* (아가씨) before the sister marries and *Akissi* (아기씨) afterwards, but in recent years the situation has changed, and wives have begun to use *Komo* (고모) instead, a word which was originally the term used by a woman for her father's sister.

In Korean, the rules for using personal names are especially complex and restricted. If a sibling is only one year older, Koreans cannot call that sibling by name. If a relative is younger, but in the structure of the extended family is of an earlier generation (for example, a father's cousin), that person also cannot be called by name. Within the family, the only people one calls by name are one's younger brothers and sisters and one's children. However, even here there is a subrule. When a younger brother or sister grows older and has children, one cannot, without some reticence, call them by name anymore. Instead, one uses *Tongsayng* (동생) 'Younger sibling' or, borrowing the name of one of their children, 'So-and-so's Father' or 'So-and-so's Mother'. If, in the structure of the extended family, an older relative is of a younger generation, one again does not use a personal name but rather the familial term *Cokha* (조카) 'Nephew' or *Cokha-nim* (조카님) 'Respected Nephew'. The social constraints on name use are particularly strong in the cases where one is obliged to show great respect, toward one's teacher, for example, or toward one's father. In a situation where it becomes necessary to tell someone else what one's father's name is, one cannot simply say the name. Instead, Koreans use an indirect, convoluted method of conveying the information. For example, let's say the father's name is *Kim Minho*. In that case, the son or daughter would say '*Kim*, the character (字) *Min*, the character *Ho*'.

The American comic strip "Blondie" has been serialized for years in Korean newspapers. In a strip from 28 January 1994, we see a typical case of how the translation of names and family terms into Korean sometimes puts a somewhat different spin on their meaning—and the joke. In the first panel, "Mr. Bumstead" is rendered as 'Older Brother's (=your) Dad', which is the right thing to say. But in the last panel, where the little boy should call Mr. Bumstead "Uncle" (*Acessi*), he says instead "Uncle Bumstead", an extremely presumptuous thing to say and for which a Korean child would be severely scolded. It makes the deed that much more mischievous for a Korean audience—and the joke that much funnier. Using a person's name must be approached with great care in Korea; it is something that can be extremely rude.

Besides the rules for names and titles used in a family and at a workplace, there are also rules that apply when addressing strangers one meets on the street or encounters in shops. There are many situations in which Koreans feel great discomfort as they grope for the appropriate way to address the other person; there are sometimes even unpleasant scenes in which an adult is scolded for the misuse of these terms. The uncertainty Koreans themselves feel about such situations underlies the popularity of volumes on the Korean book market such as *Uri mal ŭi yeyjŏl* (우리말의 예절 'The polite forms of Korean' Chosŏn Ilbo-sa 1991), and the complexity of the subject is shown by the fact that a description of the terms and how they are used fills up the entire book. Part of the reason for the complexity of the system it describes can perhaps be placed upon the structure of the Korean family and the many terms that must be used for familial relations. But a more basic reason is surely the complexity of the Korean honorific system itself and the obligation Koreans feel to live by those rules and to use them with social grace and elegance.

7.3 Subject Honorification

Verbal inflection is the part of the Korean honorific system that is most
highly structured. This verbal inflection part of the honorific system is ordinarily divided into three categories: (1) subject honorification, (2) object exaltation, and (3) sentence style. The "style" expresses linguistically the
relative social rank of the person to whom the speaker is talking. For example,
Koreans choose a different style of verbal inflection when speaking to children than they do when speaking to a teacher. In other words, the sentence
style is determined by the relationship between the speaker and the listener;
it reflects sociological factors that are external to the utterance itself. This
part of the honorific system is not the same as subject honorification and object exaltation. For one thing, it is divided into more levels than these other
two categories of honorifics; its levels are related to the system of social categories reflected in the titles discussed above. Another difference is that subject honorification and object exaltation are not directly related to the rank
of the listener; instead, they express the degree of deference afforded to the
subject and the object of the verb in the utterance itself. These subjects and
objects of the verb can be, but certainly do not have to be, the person spoken
to. For example, the subject of a sentence said to a child could be someone
highly esteemed—such as a teacher. Subject honorification is divided into
two levels; it represents a decision to elevate or not to elevate the subject. Object exaltation likewise distinguishes two levels, in this case the degree of deference shown the person affected by the action of the verb. In other words,
subject honorification and object exaltation are both alike in that they are
determined by a referent within the sentence itself. In contrast, the sentence
style is something quite different from both because it is determined by
something outside the sentence, namely, the rank of the listener.[8]

All Korean nouns referring to people are divided into two types, according to whether or not the speaker must show deference. This distinction is somewhat similar to the grammatical category of gender in French, in
which all nouns are divided into masculine nouns and feminine nouns.
Thus, in Korean, once the speaker has determined that a given noun is
something toward which deference is necessary, he or she must then adopt
an appropriate form for it.

In the event that the noun toward which deference is necessary occurs
in the subject position, the speaker must incorporate the prefinal ending *-si-*
into the predicate. (The ending has the form *-usi-* after a consonant.) This
prefinal ending is often called the "honorific marker". In example (1a), *-si-*
expresses the speaker's respect toward his or her father, whereas in (1b),
since deference need not be shown to younger siblings, *-si-* is not used.

(1) a. 아버지가 오-시-ㄴ다/ 웃-으시-ㄴ다.
   Apeci ka o*si*nta/ wus.*usi*nta.
   'Father is coming/ laughing.'

b. 동생이 오-ㄴ다/ 웃-는다.
    Tongsayng i onta/ wusnunta.
    'Brother (or Sister) is coming/ laughing.'

However, this distinction in Korean between nouns toward which deference is necessary and those toward which it is not is quite different from gender in Indo-European languages. Linguistic gender is predetermined for each noun; it is unchanging and completely independent of the individual judgment of the speaker. In contrast, the honorific distinctions of Korean have to be determined on a case-by-case basis by the speaker. For example, the noun *apeci* 'father' is ordinarily one that requires an expression of deference, as it does in (1a); however, if the speaker is a friend or senior to the father, the honorific marker is not required, as can be seen in a sentence such as (2a). Since deference depends upon the relative positions of the persons involved, the person represented by 'father' in (2a) does not require a show of deference from the speaker. However, even in a situation like this one, Koreans also sometimes say things like (2b). In this case, the speaker makes a different decision about deference toward the subject. He adopts the position of the child and uses *-si-* anyway, thus projecting onto the child's father the respect that the child himself should show. The tone of the sentence then becomes somewhat gentler and friendlier.

(2) a. (너의) 아버지 언제 오-니?
       (Ne uy) apeci encey oni? (no honorific marker)
       'When is (your) father coming?'

    b. (너의) 아버지 언제 오-시-니?
       (Ne uy) apeci encey o*si*ni? (subject honorification)
       'When might (your) father be coming?'

The use of *-si-* is not strictly mechanical. There are also cases in which the relative positions of the subject and the speaker would seem to require *-si-*, yet it is not used. For example, Korean students demonstrating against school authorities often shout abuses like that of (3).

(3) 총장은 물러가라!
    Chongcang un mulle kala!
    'Resign, University President!'

However, the decision to accord deference to a personal noun is certainly not wholly an individual one—far from it. In most situations, the noun *apeci* 'father' takes deference because of the strictures and norms of society. We see something of how these rules work when a child, still in the process of learning to speak, says something like the following:

(4) a. 아빠 (아버지) 언제 와?

   Appa (apeci) encey wa? (using *wa* for 'come')

   'When is Daddy coming,(Mom)?'

At that point the child will often be corrected:

(4) b. '와'가 뭐야, '오셔' 라고 해야지.

   'Wa' ka mwe 'ya, 'osye' lako hayyaci.

   'What do you mean "*wa*"? You have to say "*osye*."'

The marking of a Korean noun for deference is an individual, case-by-case decision, but the decision is, to a very great extent, predetermined by social norms.

As we have said, nouns marked for deference normally must be words referring to people. One certainly would not accord deference to trees, rocks, wind, or even a country; the same is true of animals or birds. There is only one curious exception. Alongside the more general (5a), in some areas of Korea one also hears (5b), where deference seems to be shown to *pi* 'rain'. This expression is completely idiomatic. No one would use *-si-* in sentences such as *Pi ka kuchinta* 'The rain is (about to) stop' or *Pi ka siwen-hata* 'The rain is refreshing'; it is only in this one idiomatic expression, *Pi ka osinta* 'It's raining', that one hears the honorific marker *-si-* used for an inanimate object.

(5) a. 비가 오-ㄴ다.

   Pi ka onta.

   'It's raining.' (Lit., 'Rain is coming.')

   b. 비가 오-시-ㄴ다.

   Pi ka o*si*nta.

   'It's raining.'

Of course, the words *Hanu-nim* (or *Hana-nim*) 'God' and *sinlyeng-nim* '(respected) god, deity, spirit' also take subject honorification. These words are already marked with the suffix *-nim*, which is probably why they require *-si-* in the verbal inflection.

(6) a. 하느님은 다 아-시-ㄹ거야.

   Hanu-nim un ta a*si*lq ke 'ya.

   'God must know it all.'

   b. 신령님이 노하-시-었-나보다.

   Sinlyeng-nim i no-ha*si*ess.na pota.

   'The god must be angry.'

In order to show extreme deference toward an esteemed person, besides adding -*si*- to the verbal inflection, one must also replace the subject particle *i/ka* with *kkeyse*. For example, (7b) shows far greater deference toward father than (7a) because of the particle *kkeyse*.

(7) a. 아버지가 무슨 말씀 하셨니?
        Apeci ka musun malssum ha*sy*essni? (with only -*si*-)
        'What did (your) father say?'

    b. 아버지께서 무슨 말씀 하셨니?
        Apeci *kkeyse* musun malssum ha*sy*essni? (with *kkeyse* and -*si*-)
        'What did (your highly esteemed) father say?'

By rule, a person who merits the use of -*si*- should also take the subject particle *kkeyse*, and the use of *i/ka* instead should perhaps be thought of as exceptional. On a formal occasion, for example, such as that represented by the following, one cannot replace *kkeyse* by *i/ka* in the sentence.

(8) 대통령께서 입장하시겠습니다.
      Taythonglyeng kkeyse ipcang-hasikeyss.supnita.
      'The President will (now) make his entrance.'

However, in actuality, the particle *kkeyse* can often give the feeling of overdone honorification, and so in most situations *i/ka* seems more natural. Therefore, rather than thinking of -*si*- and *kkeyse* as linked together, it is probably closer to reality to consider occurrences of -*si*- as in (7) as compatible with any subject particle and *kkeyse* as serving the function of showing an extreme level of deference on the speaker's part. At the high level of deference that *kkeyse* shows, it is possible to add special particles following *kkeyse*. However, when these special particles are added, it is also quite common for *kkeyse* to be omitted—just as is invariably the case with the subject particle *i/ka*. But the high level of deference remains, nonetheless. In (9b) and (10b), below, the politeness level shows that it is *kkeyse* that has been deleted in these cases and not *i/ka*.

(9) a. 할머님께서는 이쪽으로 오세요.
        Halme-nim *kkeyse nun* i ccok ulo osey yo.
        'Grandmother, please come over here.'

    b. 할머님은 이쪽으로 오세요.
        Halme-nim *un* i ccok ulo osey yo.
        'Grandmother, please come over here.'

(10) a. 회장님께서도 오셨습니다.
        Hoycang-nim *kkeyse to* osyess.supnita.
        'The esteemed chairman has also come.'

b. 회장님도 오셨습니다.
Hoycang-nim *to* osyess.supnita.
'The esteemed chairman has also come.'

The honorific marker *-si-* can be used freely with virtually any verb stem. However, there are exceptions. In a polite context, a few common verbs are replaced by special polite verbs, which are always used with *-si-*. These special polite verbs include *capswusi-* 'respectfully eat, partake of food', *kyeysi-* 'respectfully reside, be at (a place)', *phyenchanh.usi-* 'be ill', and *tol.akasi-* 'pass away, die'. The verb *capswusi-*, for example, is used instead of the plain verb *mek-* 'eat' when deference is required. As a result, the verb *mek-* never occurs with *-si-*. Similarly, the verb *tol.akasi-* 'pass away' replaces *cwuk-* 'die', and therefore the expected honorific form, *ˣcwukusi-*, does not exist. The honorific marker has become an integral part of the stem, for if *-si-* were left off *tol.akasi-*, the form would mean 'return', not 'die'.

(11)a. 민호는 뭘 먹니?
Minho nun mwel *mek*ni?
'What is Minho eating?'

b. 할아버지는 뭘 잡수시니?
Hal.apeci nun mwel *capswusi*ni?
'What is Grandfather eating?'

(12)a. 저 집 아들이 죽었어요.
Ce cip atul i *cwuk*.ess.e yo.
'The son in that household died.'

b. 저 집 할아버지께서 돌아가셨어요.
Ce cip hal.apeci kkeyse *tol.aka.sy*ess.e yo.
'The grandfather in that household died.'

The special polite verbs *phyenchanh.usi-*[9] 'be ill' and *kyeysi-* 'reside, be at' are somewhat more complex. In the case of *phyenchanh.usi-* 'be ill', the polite verb does not replace the plain *aphu-* in all its polite uses. Rather, *phyenchanh.usi-* coexists alongside the regularly formed *aphusi-*, and each of the two has taken on a separate, specialized meaning. The special polite verb *phyenchanh.usi-* 'be ill' is used when the person is suffering from some illness in which the entire body is discomfited, while *aphusi-* 'be hurt' is used when only a part of the body is affected. In other words, the existence of *phyenchanh.usi-* 'be ill' has not replaced *aphu-* but only caused its range of meaning to narrow. As a plain verb, *aphu-* means both 'be sick' and 'hurt, be hurt'; however, as a polite verb, *aphusi-* means only 'hurt'.

(13)a. 할아버지, 편찮으세요?
Hal.apeci, *phyenchanh.use*y yo?
'Grandfather, are you *ill*?'

b. 할아버지, 어느쪽 이가 아프세요 (ˣ편찮으세요)?

Hal.apeci, enu ccok i ka *aphusey* yo (ˣphyenchanh.usey yo)?

'Grandfather, which tooth *hurts*?'

The situation with *kyeysi-* 'reside, be at' is quite similar. It coexists alongside the honorific form of *iss-*. As a plain verb, *iss-* has a broad range of meaning that includes both 'be at' and 'have, possess (something)'. But its polite form, *iss.usi-*, is used only in the latter sense because *kyeysi-* is used for the former.

(14)a. 너는 거기에 있어라.

Ne nun keki ey *iss*.ela.

'You stay [= be] there.'

b. 할아버지는 거기에 계세요.

Hal.apeci nun keki ey *kyeysey* yo.

'Grandfather, please stay [= be] there.'

(15)a. 너는 돈이 있니?

Ne nun ton i *iss*ni?

'Do you *have* any money?'

b. 할아버지는 돈이 있으세요 (ˣ계세요)?

Hal.apeci nun ton i *issusey* yo (ˣkyeysey yo)?

'Grandfather, do you *have* any money?'

When speaking to or about an esteemed person, there are times when the noun used in the utterance has a special form. In a sentence like that of (11), above, a noun like 'noodles' or 'apple' is the same word in both a plain and a polite context. But the same is not true of *pap* 'rice'. When referring to what an esteemed person eats, *pap* must be replaced by the special polite word for 'rice', *cinci* (진지). (In the following examples, note that 'rice', in both of its Korean forms, is used when talking about the general act of eating.)

(16)a. 민호는 밥을 잘 먹니?

Minho nun *pap* ul cal mekni?

'Minho, are you eating (*rice*) well?'

b. 할아버지는 진지를 잘 잡수시니?

Hal.apeci nun *cinci* lul cal capswusini?

'Is (your) grandfather eating (*rice*) well?'

There are a number of word pairs like *pap/cinci* 'rice'. These include *mal/malssum* 'speech', *nai/yensey* 'age', *cip/tayk* 'house, home', *atul-ttal (ai-*

tul)/cacey-pun 'children', and the like. The following are typical examples of
how these words are used:

(17)a. 내 동생은 말을 참 재미있게 한다.
    Nay tongsayng un *mal* ul cham caymi-isskey hanta.
    'My younger brother/sister really has an interesting way of *talk*ing.'

  b. 우리 선생님은 말씀을 참 재미있게 하신다.
    Wuli sensayng-nim un *malssum* ul cham caymi-isskey hasinta.
    'Our teacher really has an interesting way of *talk*ing.'

(18)a. 순희는 보기보다 나이가 많아요.
    Swunhuy nun poki pota *nai* ka manh.a yo.
    'Sunhŭi is greater in *age* than she looks.'

  b. 김선생님은 보기보다 연세가 많으세요.
    Kim sensayng-nim un poki pota *yensey* ka manh.usey yo.
    'Professor Kim is greater in *age* than he looks.'

(19)a. 순희 지금 집에 있습니까?
    Swunhuy cikum *cip* ey iss.supnikka?
    'Is Sunhŭi at *home* now?'

  b. 선생님 지금 댁에 계십니까?
    Sensayng-nim cikum tayk ey kyeysipnikka?
    'Is Teacher at *home* now?'

(20)a. 저 사람은 아이가(자식이) 많아.
    Ce salam un *ai* ka (*casik* i) manh.a.
    'That person over there has a lot of *children*.'

  b. 김 과장님은 자제분이 많으셔.
    Kim Kwacang-nim un *cacey-pun* i manh.usye.
    'Section Chief Kim has a lot of *children*.'

7.4 Object Exaltation

Object exaltation is the expression of deference toward the person affected
by the action of the verb. In older stages of Korean (in particular, Middle Korean), the verbal suffix *-sop-* (-ㅅ-) was used in this function; it formed an opposing pair with the honorific marker for the subject, *-si-*. If one wanted to
say that the king was coming — that is, the noun 'king' was the subject of the
sentence — one used *-si-* with the verb to show him respect. But in a sentence
that said that the populace caught a glimpse of the king or were listening to

his words, *-sop-* was used instead of *-si-* as a way of exalting him. (Cf. chapter 7.) In later stages of Korean, the traces of *-sop-* as a separate form were lost. As a result, there is no suffix used to show object exaltation in modern Korean; rather, object exaltation is now shown through special methods used in highly circumscribed contexts.

The element that shows object exaltation most clearly is the locative particle *kkey*. As the honorific form of *eykey* or *hanthey,* this particle has a function resembling that of the nominative particle *kkeyse*, which is used as a respect form in place of *i/ka*. In (1a), below, *kkey* is the only element showing that respect is being given to 'Grandmother'.

(1) a. 저 아이를 할머님께 보냅시다.
   Ce ai lul halme-nim *kkey* ponaypsita.
   'Let's send that child to (his) grandmother.'

   b. 저 아이를 제 형에게(형한테) 보냅니다.
   Ce ai lul cey hyeng *eykey* (hyeng *hanthey*) ponaypnita.
   'We're sending that child to his older brother.'

Along with *kkey,* there are a number of other vocabulary items that show object exaltation. Just as there are special polite words such as *cwumusita* 'sleep' and *capswusita* 'eat, partake of food' that show subject honorification, there are a number of words used for the special purpose of expressing object exaltation. These special words used for object exaltation are shown below along with their plain equivalents.

	Polite	*Plain*
'give'	드리다	주다
	tulita	*cwuta*
'ask, say'	여쭙다	묻다, 말하다
	yeccwupta	*mutta* ('ask'), *mal-hata* ('say')
'see, meet, visit'	뵙다	보다
	poypta	*pota*
'take with, accompany'	모시다	데리다
	mosita	*teylita*

Here are some examples of how these words are used:

(2) a. 이 만년필은 선생님께 드려라.
   I mannyenphil un sensayng-nim kkey *tu.lyela.*
   '*Give* this fountain pen to (your) esteemed teacher.'

   b. 이 장난감은 민호한테 주어라.
   I cangnanqkam un Minho hanthey *cwuela.*
   '*Give* this toy to Minho.'

(3) a. 그런 일은 할아버지께 여쭈어 보아라.

   Kulen il un hal.apeci kkey *yeccwue* poala.

   '*Ask* Grandfather things like that.'

   b. 그런 일은 나한테 물어 보아라.

   Kulen il un na hanthey *mul.e* poala.

   '*Ask* me things like that.'

(4) a. 우리 언제 선생님 한번 뵈러 가자.

   Wuli encey sensayng-nim han-pen *poyle* kaca.

   'Sometime let's go *see* (our old) teacher.'

   b. 우리 언제 순희 한번 보러 가자.

   Wuli encey Swunhuy han-pen *pole* kaca.

   'Sometime let's go *see* Sunhŭi.'

(5) a. 이 동물원에는 노부모님을 모시고 온 사람들이 많구나.

   I tongmulwen ey nun nopumo-nim ul *mosiko* on salam-tul i manh.kwuna.

   'I see there are a lot of people at this zoo who've *brought* their elderly parents.'

   b. 이 동물원에는 아이들을 데리고 온 사람들이 많구나.

   I tongmulwen ey nun ai-tul ul *teyliko* on salam-tul i manh.kwuna.

   'I see there are a lot of people at this zoo who've *brought* (their) children.'

Just as is the case with subject honorification, object exaltation entails using several other, incidental ways to show respect. Related to both subject honorification and object exaltation is of course the suffix *-nim*, as well as special polite nouns such as *cinci* 'rice', *malssum* 'speech', and *tayk* 'house, home'.

(6) a. 할아버지께서 진지를 잘 잡수셨구나.

   Hal.apeci kkeyse *cinci* lul cal capswu.syess.kwuna.

   'I see Grandfather has eaten [*rice*] quite well.' ('Grandfather' is the subject.)

   b. 할아버지께 진지를 때 맞추어 드려라.

   Hal.apeci kkey *cinci* lul ttay mac.chwue tulyela.

   'Serve Grandfather rice [= his food] in a timely way.' ('Grandfather' is the indirect object.)

(7) a. 선생님은 댁으로 가셨어요. ('Teacher' is the subject.)

   Sensayng-nim un *tayk* ulo kasyess.e yo.

   'Teacher has gone *home*.'

b. 네가 선생님을 댁으로 모셔 드려라. ('Teacher' is the direct object.)
Neyka sensayng-nim ul *tayk* ulo mosye tulyela.
'(You) accompany Teacher to his *home.*'

As can be seen from these examples, subject honorification and object exaltation differ only in where the noun is placed in the sentence to serve a particular function. They are alike in that the simple appearance in the sentence of the person to be esteemed obliges the speaker to use the various signals of respect. The rules for using the suffix -*nim* and special polite nouns such as *cinci* 'rice' and *tayk* 'home' are the same. However, the two phenomena cannot be brought together under the same classification because the other ways they require respect to be shown are strictly distinguished. Whereas verbs such as *cwusita* '(a superior) gives' and *posita* '(a superior) sees, looks' are chosen for subject honorification, the completely different verbs *tulita* 'give (to a superior)' and *poypta* 'see, meet (a superior)' are used for object exaltation. Here the directionality of the verbs shows that these two parts of the honorific system are completely different.

There is also a difference between subject honorification and subject exaltation in the reference point that gives rise to a show of deference. The question is: With whom is the esteemed person being compared? In the case of subject honorification, the person is being accorded respect as the speaker's superior. The speaker decides that he must show deference and use -*si*- because, in his judgment, the person who is the subject is of a higher social rank than he himself. In other words, subject honorification comes about as a measure against oneself. Object exaltation, however, is different from this. In the case of object exaltation, the comparison is not with oneself, but rather with the person performing the action of the verb. As an example, let us look at (5a), above, in which the people being esteemed are 'elderly parents'. The relative reference for according them esteem is not the speaker, but rather the 'people' *(salam-tul)* who have brought them. In other words, the 'elderly parents' are shown deference because their social position is higher than that of their children; object exaltation does not arise out of a comparison with the speaker, who remains outside the frame of reference. These relationships are displayed in the diagrams below. The sizes of the boxes in the diagrams illustrate the degree of social rank, and the lines connecting the boxes show the direction of deference.

Object exaltation does not have broad application in contemporary Korean; unquestionably, its range of use is unusual. In Middle Korean, during the fifteenth and sixteenth centuries, object exaltation had the same wide range of usage that subject honorification did. Perhaps the reason that the system has become as narrowly applicable as it is today is that the degree of active involvement by the speaker is not as great as it is with subject honorification. In subject honorification, the respect that is shown to the subject arises out of a comparison with oneself, while in object exaltation the respect takes as its standard a third person. The relative impor-

(8) Subject Honorification (주체경어법)

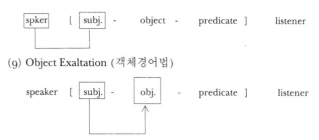

(9) Object Exaltation (객체경어법)

tance of this kind of respect is weaker, and that fact may well underlie the historical decline of this grammatical process. In any event, object exaltation today is a far less vital and much weaker part of the honorific system than subject honorification.

7.5 Style

The style is the part of the honorific system that depends upon the person listening to the sentence. It is completely independent of the personal nouns that appear in the sentence itself. In this sense, it is to be sharply distinguished from subject honorification and object exaltation, both of which express an attitude of respect toward persons mentioned in the sentence, who may or may not be present at the place the sentence is uttered. Also, unlike those two parts of the honorific system, which are only divided into two levels determined by whether someone is to be accorded deference or not, the style is finely differentiated according to the degree of respect to be given to the listener.

The element that bears the grammatical load of the style is the sentence-final ending of the predicate. This contrasts with the ending -*si*- used for subject honorification, which is prefinal. The ending used in Middle Korean for object exaltation was also prefinal. In addition, there is only one ending used for each of the other two processes, but there are an extremely large number of sentence-final endings that show style. For example, say there are six levels of style; then, if that is so, these six levels must be expressed not only for declarative sentences, but also for interrogatives, imperatives, and the like, producing a great variety of different endings. As a result, it is difficult to give a precise number when asked how many endings are used to express the style of a sentence.

Grammarians differ as to how many levels of style are distinguished in modern Korean. For the discussion here, we will assume that there are six. First, the endings used in declarative and interrogative sentences for each of the six levels are as follows:

Declarative	Interrogative	Examples
1. -nta.	-ni?	Pi ka onta. / oni?
2. -a.	-a?	Pi ka o-a(→wa). / o-a(→wa)?
3. -ney.	-na?	Pi ka oney. / ona?
4. -o.	-o?	Pi ka oo. / oo?
5. -ayo.	-ayo?	Pi ka o-ayo(→wayo). / o-ayo(→wayo)?
6. -pnita.	-pnikka?	Pi ka opnita. / opnikka?
		'It's raining. / Is it raining?'

Six levels are also distinguished for imperatives. However, a word of caution is in order when dealing with imperatives: Since the person listening to the command can also be the subject of the sentence, subject honorification must be applied in ways appropriate to the speech level.

Imperative	Examples
1. -ala.	I cali eynun Minho ka anc.ala.
2. -a.	I cali eynun Minho ka anc.a.
3. -key.	I cali eynun Minho-kwun i anc.key.
4. -uo.	I cali eynun Kim Kwacang i anc.uo.
5. -usi-eyyo (→useyyo).	I cali eynun Kim Kwacang-nim i anc.useyyo.
6. -usipsio.	I cali eynun Kwacang-nim i anc.usipsio.
	'(Please) sit here, Minho/Section Leader Kim/Sir.'

The Korean names for these six levels are shown below, along with the English terms that will be used here:[10]

Korean	English
1. *Hayla-chey* (해라체)	Plain Style
2. *Panmal-chey* (반말체 or 해체)	*Panmal* Style
3. *Hakey-chey* (하게체)	Familiar Style
4. *Hao-chey* (하오체)	Semiformal Style
5. *Hayyo-chey* (해요체)	Polite Style
6. *Hapsyo-chey* (합쇼체)	Formal Style

With the lone exception of (2) *panmal-chey,* which literally means 'half-speech style', these Korean names are taken from the imperative forms of the verb *hata* 'do', plus the Sino-Korean element *-chey* (體) 'body, -style'. These are not terms made up by linguists but are, rather, traditional ones that have long been used in Korea. They are based upon expressions such as *hayla-hanta* 'speaks in *hayla* style' and *hakey-hanta* 'speaks in *hakey* style', which are the ordinary words people use to talk about these speech levels in Korean. One might say, for example, "*Wuli nun selo hakey-hanun sai*" 'We (have) a *hakey-*speaking relationship with each other'. The designation *panmal* is particularly widely used in everyday Korean. One commonly hears such things as: *"Nwukwu hanthey panmal ul hanun ke ya?"* 'Who do you think you're speaking *panmal* to?' The colloquial nature of this word probably explains why the regularly formed term *hay-chey* 'hay style' is not as commonly used.

Today, when most people use the word *panmal,* they do not necessarily restrict its meaning to only this one style; they often use it, rather, as inclusive of the plain style, too. Moreover, the earlier idea that it was a style of speech used with the lower classes has disappeared. In fact, when Koreans talk about speech styles, the most common, and most general, contrast is between *panmal* 'informal, intimate speech' and *contayqmal* (존대말), which, roughly translated, means 'polite speech'. This is the contrast of which most Koreans are consciously aware.

Among the various Korean terms for speech style, the *hapsyo* of the *hapsyo-chey,* or 'formal style', is not quite the same as the actual form of the ending used. It seems to be, rather, a contraction of *hasipsio.* It is to be understood as etymologically an incomplete word. The name was attached to a way of speaking once used to express an ambiguous attitude toward people of the lower social classes, who were not assigned a definite level in the hierarchy.

Speech styles are also differentiated in propositive sentences—that is, in invitations for joint action ('let's'). Since propositives are a type of imperative, the listener can be represented as the subject of these sentences, just as in imperative sentences. Here are representative examples of propositives in the various styles, all with the general meaning of 'Let's go':

(1) a. 너도 우리랑 같이 가자.
   Ne to wuli lang kath.i kaca. (plain)
   'Go with us.'

   b. 너도 우리랑 같이 가 (←가아) / 가지.
   Ne to wuli lang kath.i ka (←kaa) / kaci. (*panmal*)
   'Go with us.'

   c. 자네도 우리랑 같이 가지.
   Caney to wuli lang kath.i kaci. (familiar)
   'Go with us.'

   d. (남편에게) 당신도 우리랑 같이 가요.
   (to husband) Tangsin to wuli lang kath.i ka yo. (polite)
   'Go with us, Dear.'

   e. 여러분, 어서 갑시다 / 가십시다.
   Yele-pun, ese kapsita / kasipsita. (formal)
   'Let us all go.'

However, the levels of speech style are not as clearly defined in propositives as they are in the previous three sentence types. For one thing, the use of the *panmal* style, as in (1b), above, is rather uncommon; the semiformal style is even more rarely used (and thus not represented above). In addition, the form *kapsita* seen in (1e) appears to represent the very highest level of speech since it is systematically related to *kapnita* (declarative formal) and *kapnikka* (interrogative formal), but that in fact is not the case. If, for example, one were to speak to one's former teacher as in (2a), the person hearing it would feel very uncomfortable. No one would consider an invitation worded this way appropriately respectful. It would be somewhat better to speak as in (2b), but that, too, is insufficient.

(2) a. 선생님, 저랑 함께 갑시다.
   Sensayng-nim, ce lang hamkkey kapsita.
   'Dear Teacher, go together with me.'

b. 선생님, 저랑 함께 가십시다.
   Sensayng-nim, ce lang hamkkey kasipsita.
   'Dear Teacher, please go together with me.'

No matter how respectfully one words a propositive, a sentence like this can make a superior feel uncomfortable. (To a certain extent, the same is true even in English—and perhaps in most other languages.) It might seem that the difficulty should be shared by imperatives, but in fact that is not the case. Absolutely no discomfort at all is caused by saying things such as *"Annyeng.hi kasipsio"* (literally) 'Go peacefully' and *"Manh.i capswusipsio"* (literally) 'Eat much'. Imperatives like these show the highest level of consideration and politeness. Perhaps the difference lies in the fact that imperatives involve the action of the listener alone, while propositives suggest that the speaker be included with the listener together in the action. The use of formal style signals such an enormous degree of difference between the levels of the speaker and the listener that suggesting to the person of high rank he be involved in some action with someone so far beneath him is bound to cause a certain amount of discomfort.

This explanation is supported by the following fact. As we have seen, word pairs such as *mekta/capswusita* 'eat' and *cata/cwumusita* 'sleep' are used to differentiate levels of deference in subject honorification. However, no matter which form we try to use with propositives, the result is awkward.

(3) a. ??선생님, 점심 먹읍시다.
   ??Sensayng-nim, cemsim mek.upsita.
   ['Teacher, let's eat lunch.']

b. ?선생님, 점심 잡수십시다.
   ?Sensayng-nim, cemsim capswusipsita.
   ['Teacher, let us eat lunch.']

(4) a. ?? 선생님, 이제 잡시다.

  ??Sensayng-nim, icey capsita

  ['Teacher, let's go to sleep now.']

b. ? 선생님, 이제 주무십시다.

  ?Sensayng-nim, icey cwumusipsita.

  ['Teacher, let us go to sleep now.']

In other words, if one speaks as in (3a) or (4a), the form used is terribly insulting to the teacher. On the other hand, if one speaks as in (3b) or (4b), there is less feeling of revulsion, but the result is unnatural because the speaker is elevating himself too much. This thicket of difficulties is the unavoidable consequence of binding the speaker and the listener together to create a curious structure as the subject of the action. It is surely the reason why forms such as *kapsita* 'let us go', which, from the point of view of structure, are of the highest degree of deference, from the point of view of meaning do not measure up to this level of politeness.

As a result, it can be concluded that it is difficult to establish the highest level of politeness for propositives. In actuality, if one wishes to direct a proposal to a person with whom one must use the formal style, one cannot use a propositive sentence at all; rather, one uses an interrogative as in (5) or some other, even more indirect expression. Note, especially, that in (5) both sentences are ambiguous as to whether the speaker is to be a participant in the action; it is only a context in which the speaker and the teacher had, say, arrived together that would imply the joint action of leaving together.

(5) a. 선생님, 그만 가실까요?

  Sensayng-nim, kuman kasilkka yo?

  'Teacher, shall (we) leave now?'

b. 선생님, 그만 가시지요.

  Sensayng-nim, kuman kasici yo.

  'Teacher, (you/we) should perhaps leave.'

Noting the special circumstances surrounding the use of propositives, we will nevertheless assume the general validity of the six different speech styles in Korean. Let us now look at the characteristics and usages of each of these levels.

Plain Style (해라체)

This style shows unceremonious familiarity. It is used with close friends, by parents to their children, or by a relatively older speaker to a child of up to high school age. Since it is the lowest speech level, it becomes awkward to use this speech style even among friends once they have reached middle age or older. Children and younger people of up to high school age use plain style with each other even when they are not particularly close or even when they first meet. In other words, the most important factor determining the use of this style is age: the listener must be young.

In written Korean, the plain style is ordinarily used when writing for a general audience. However, because spoken Korean and written Korean are not the same, the verb endings are different from those used in speech. For example, except when recording a colloquial conversation, the interrogative ending *-ni* is never used in writing. Instead, one writes *-nka* or *-nunka*, endings that are not used in speech. Here are some typical examples of written Korean:

(6) a. 우주는 과연 움직이는가?
    Wucwu nun kwayen wumcik.i*nunka?*
    'Does the universe ever move?'

   b. 인생이란 무엇인가?
    Insayng ilan mues i*nka?*
    'What is life?'

   c. 어느 문제가 더 중요한가?
    Enu muncey ka te cwungyo-ha*nka?*
    'Which problem is the more important?'

In addition, one writes simply *-la* for imperatives instead of the longer spoken form *-ala/ela*. The *-la* form is used, for example, in the written instructions for examinations:

(7) 다음 문제에 대해 상세히 서술하라.
    Taum muncey ey tay-hay sangsey.hi seswul-ha*la.*
    'Discuss in detail the following questions.'

Panmal Style (반말체 or 해체)

In most situations, this speech style alternates freely with the plain style. Varying one's speech between these two levels usually causes no problems whatsoever, and there is almost no difference in what is implied. Moreover, there is no corresponding ending in the plain style for some *panmal*-style endings (for example, the *-ci* in *kuleh.ci* '(that's) right'), so in the plain style there is no choice but to use *panmal* endings when they are called for by the context. Because of these facts, it would not be at all far-fetched to claim that the plain style and the *panmal* style actually represent a single level of speech.

However, the two speech styles do not always alternate freely with each other. For example, when college students first meet new friends in their department, it would be awkward for them to speak as in (8a). What happens is that they first begin by using *panmal*-style forms such as (8b) and (8c), then, when they have developed a bit closer relationship, they relax the relative formality and use plain style.

(8) a. 고향이 어디니?
     Kohyang i eti '*ni*? (plain style)
     'Where are you from?'

  b. 고향이 어디야?
     Kohyang i eti '*ya*? (*panmal* style)
     'Where are you from?'

  c. 고향이 어디지?
     Kohyang i eti '*ci*? (*panmal* style)
     'Where are you from?'

As another example, say a teacher at a girls' middle school meets some former students who have now married and have children of their own. In this case, the teacher has to be careful using the plain style he or she once used, but it is still perfectly natural to use the *panmal* style. An even clearer illustration of the difference between these two styles can be found in the way husbands and wives talk to each other. A husband may sometimes use polite language (존대말) with his wife, but he also quite frequently uses *panmal*, as in (9a). However, he could never drop his language use down to the plain-style form in (9b). A husband may treat his wife with great informality, but it would be offensive to treat her like a child, which is what using plain style would mean.

(9) a. 당신은 안 가겠어?
     Tangsin un an kakeyss.e? (*panmal* style)
     'Aren't you going?'

  b. 당신은 안 가겠니?
     Tangsin un an kakeyssni? (plain style)
     'Aren't you going?'

In ways such as these, the *panmal* style of speech signals a little more social distance between the speaker and the listener than does the plain style. It is used to show a little more reserve. Another difference is that the *panmal* style is not used in writing for the general reader. Once these facts are taken into consideration, we can see the basis for distinguishing *panmal* from plain style, and, by doing so, we can also begin to understand the nature of the Korean honorific system.

Familiar Style (하게체)

This style of speech is used when the listener is below the speaker in age or social rank, but not enough for the *panmal* or plain style to be appropriate. The style signals to the listener that the speaker will treat him with consideration and courtesy. Familiar style goes together with the pronoun *caney* 'you'; it is used almost exclusively by, and to, males.

(10)a. 이 일은 자네가 맡게.
     I il un caney ka math.key
     'You take this job.'

   b. 아까 자네 춘부장을 만났네.
     Akka caney chwunpucang ul mannassney.
     'I met your (respected) father a little while ago.'

As with the pronoun *caney* 'you', the greatest factor leading to the use of this style is age. The familiar style can never be used with anyone as young as an elementary school pupil, and until a person has graduated from high school, it would be difficult for him ever to have been addressed in this style. He must be of college age for others to make the determination that they should speak to him in this style instead of *panmal* or plain style. The speaker's age is also an important factor. The familiar style gives a feeling that the speaker is showing his authority; it also has the character of strong formality. For these reasons, the familiar style would cause embarrassment if the person who used it was not sufficiently mature. It would be difficult for a graduate student to use the style with the college students in his department. He must be at least in his thirties to begin using it.

These days, the age at which Koreans begin to use the familiar style seems to be gradually increasing. At one time, graduate students used it freely, but now they never do. The reason for the change is apparently related to the formality of the speech style. Nowadays, as Korean society moves away from authority and formality and tends toward freer, more unceremonious interaction, it has become difficult for people who are still young to adopt the formality of the familiar style. It is also significant that the familiar style is seldom used by women. Like much else in Korean society, the exclusionary use of the familiar style by males seems to be because women are farther removed from authority than men.

Semiformal Style (하오체)

Like the familiar style, the semiformal style is used with someone in an inferior position, but in this case the person is treated with a greater degree of reserve than is the case with the familiar style. It is a style a husband could use with his wife; an older man would use with a younger, former schoolmate *Kim-hyeng* or the like; a superior at a workplace with *Kim Kwacang*. It is the appropriate style for a former superior officer in the military to use when he sees again the men who were once under his command. It is also a style sometimes used with strangers whose social rank is clear but not considered particularly high. Letters written in this style are often used among friends to show reserve.

Some grammarians have maintained that the semiformal style is also used with superiors, but this is not true. Until the end of the nineteenth century, the semiformal style was used widely in the ways the polite style is used now; but with the emergence of the polite style, the range of the semiformal style narrowed, and it became a style used only with inferiors. It would be most out of place for a wife to use the (a) patterns in (11) through (13) when speaking to her husband, or a younger person to his older, former schoolmate. Unlike the polite style shown in the (b) patterns, which is the style used by the wife or younger person, the (a) patterns would be appropriate only if used by the husband or the older person.

(11)a. 당신은 안 가겠소?
      Tangsin un an kakeyss.so? (semiformal style)
      'Aren't you going?'

   b. 당신은 안 가겠어요?
      Tangsin un an kakeyss.e yo? (polite style)
      'Aren't you going?'

(12)a. 아까 전화한 사람이 누구요(←누구-이-오)?
      Akka cenhwa-han salam i nwukwu 'yo? (semiformal style)
      'Who was it that called a little while ago?'

   b. 아까 전화한 사람이 누구예요(←누구-이-어요)?
      Akka cenhwa-han salam i nwukwu 'yey yo? (polite style)
      'Who was it that called a little while ago?'

Moreover, if someone were to speak to a person of unknown background in the style shown in (14), below, the impression would not be that the person was a superior. The semiformal style may not be a form of address that carelessly degrades a person of unknown rank, but it is also most certainly not a style used for a person who could be above the social level of the speaker. If one were to subsequently learn that the person's social status was in fact above that of the speaker, the speaker would normally be conscience-stricken over her lack of respect.

(14)a. 거 누구요?
      Ke nwukwu yo? (semiformal style)
      'Who's there?'

   b. 거기 무슨 일이오?
      Keki musun il io? (semiformal style)
      'What do you want?'

In modern Korea, the semiformal style has almost fallen completely out of use. Only a small fraction of the population still uses it, and among the younger generation it continues to decline. In many cases the usual tendency is from the outset to use the polite style *(-eyo)* in places where the semiformal style would be appropriate. (As will be explained later, the polite style is used with people of lower social rank as well as superiors.) Overall, the complex system of Korean honorifics is becoming simpler, and the collapse of the semiformal and polite styles into a single level is a part of that process. As was mentioned above, the semiformal range has become extremely narrow under pressure from the expanding polite style. Since it is not easy to maintain this delicate distinction, modern Koreans may feel that it is less burdensome to simplify, and thus use the polite style in all of these situations instead.

Like the familiar style, the semiformal style is conspicuously formal. By attempting to treat an inferior with reserve, a superior naturally creates an air of authority, which also makes the formality that much more noticeable. This is even more true of the semiformal style than the familiar style. As with the familiar style, the semiformal style seems to be on the wane in this new age of less authority and formality.

Nevertheless, we must not overlook the fact that the semiformal style still occupies a unique niche in the system. It is perhaps surprising that the semiformal style is used a lot in Korean drama, but that is because in the theater its unique function is put to good use. In particular, when the speaker harbors a feeling of dissatisfaction toward the other person, as is the case in (14), then the semiformal style is appropriate, and it is difficult to substitute the polite style when this meaning is intended. In the following example, which is taken from the Korean edition of *Readers Digest* (January 1994), a forty-seven-year-old policeman is questioning a twenty-something year old stopped for a traffic violation and suspected of a drug offense. Here, the polite-style *toykeyss.eyo* in place of the semiformal *toykeyss.so* would not be the right thing to say. It would not fit the situation. Thus, the semiformal style is not especially friendly. In situations where one must keep the other person at arm's length, the semiformal style serves its most clearly defined function.

(15) 트렁크를 열어 봐도 되겠소?
    Thulengkhu lul yel.e pwato toykeyss.so? (semiformal style)
    'May I open the suitcase?'

Polite Style (해요체)

When the other person is a superior or, if not, someone one must treat with reserve, the polite style is the most widely used speech style. Unless the situation is very formal, the polite style is more often used than the formal style with a superior. With an equal or inferior, the formal style is not appropriate. As a result, the polite style is broadly used in virtually any situation where polite language is called for. It is the all-purpose style used with superiors and inferiors alike.

However, there are limitations on its use with inferiors. For example, it would be unnatural for a university student, trying to show courtesy, to speak in this style to elementary or middle school students. When someone in his twenties or thirties asks directions of a stranger on the street, that person being asked must be at least around college age for the polite style to be used. There are no restrictions on the age of the speaker when it comes to the polite style, but the age of the listener has a lower limit.

The classroom is an exception. Even in nursery school, the polite style is used when addressing the class as a whole. And though it is not always necessarily the case, a teacher generally uses the polite style when teaching. When directing a question to or teaching an individual student, it is common to use *panmal*, but for the class as a whole, the rule is to use polite style. This usage can perhaps be attributed simply to educational strategy, or perhaps the reason is that the group is viewed as more powerful than the individual and must therefore be treated more carefully and with more reserve. In any event, as in Japan, the classroom use of speech styles is divided between that used for the individual and that used for the group.

In ordinary Korean conversations, the polite style is clearly the most frequently heard style. It is the style most often used in stores between clerks and their customers; it is the way children speak to their parents or other adults in their household; it is how students speak to their teachers. Regardless whether he is in his thirties or in his fifties, if an adult foreigner stands on the streets of Seoul and asks directions in Korean, the answer he will hear, as in (16), will be in the polite style. The common greeting exchanged with a familiar person, *Annyeng-haseyyo* 'How are you?' is a polite style expression.

(16) 이쪽으로 곧장 가세요.
    I ccok ulo kot.cang kasey yo. (polite style)
    'Go straight in this direction.'

The polite-style ending *-ayo/eyo* is the element *-yo* added to the *panmal* ending *-a/e*. Also, when a noun is used by itself in the polite style, *-yo* is added to it directly. This is because a noun used by itself is a signal of the *panmal* style.

(17) a. 몇 층에 가? 3층?
    Myech chung ey ka? 3-chung? (*panmal* style)
    'What floor are you going to? Third?'

   b. 응, 3층.
    Ung, 3-chung. (*panmal* style)
    'Yeah, third floor.'

c. 예, 3층요.
   Yey, 3-chung yo. (polite style)
   'Yes, the third floor.'

Polite style and *panmal* style, two modes of speech that were not so commonly used in the past, have come to be the twin pillars of the speech-style system of modern Korean. This dynamic is surely not unrelated to the fact that the form of the polite style is derived from that of *panmal.* Adding *-yo* as a sign of politeness is a simple switching device that people today seem to find convenient. In any event, in ordinary conversations today, *panmal* represents intimacy and informality, while its opposite in almost all situations is the polite style, a mode of speech that represents general courtesy and the reserved use of language.

Formal Style (합쇼체)

Of all the six levels of speech in Korean, the formal style is clearly the highest. It is the speech style that is used to treat the listener with the most reserve and the most respect. As was pointed out above, since the degree of reserve is so high, the formal style is not suitable for use with social equals or inferiors; the style is usable only with persons of higher rank than oneself. In being appropriate only for superiors, the formal style is distinguished from the polite style, which is used much more broadly. And even though both styles can be used with superiors, the difference in the degree of reserve and formality differentiates the formal style from the polite style. As an example, we see that it would be awkward to use (18a) with an equal or inferior. With a superior, one could use either of the expressions in (18), but (18a) shows an attitude of greater respect and formality than (18b).

(18)a. 다녀오겠습니다.
      Tanye okeyss.supnita. (formal style)
      'I'll be back.'

   b. 다녀오겠어요.
      Tanye okeyss.e yo. (polite style)
      'I'll be back.'

The question that is raised here is, does one use formal style with some superiors, and the polite style with others? In other words, are the distributions of the two styles distinguished exclusively by rank? The answer is that they are not. In general, one would use polite-style expressions like (18b) with one's parents, but in strict households formal-style expressions like (18a) are also used. Moreover, people who would normally use polite-style with their parents will, on occasion, depending on the situation, switch to the formal style. In the same way, one ordinarily uses formal style with one's teacher, but, again, depending on the situation, or if one comes to be particularly close to the teacher, one might tend to use the polite style more frequently. Thus, the mixture of formal and polite style that one uses will depend upon the feel of the situation and the atmosphere that one wishes to convey.

However, because of its formality and higher level of reserve, the formal style does have a usage that is unique and distinctive. For example, when a company is conducting interviews of job applicants, the candidates exclusively use the formal style when addressing the president of the company. Also, when reporting to a superior in the military, it is not appropriate, nor is it permitted, to use the polite style as in (19b). Even within a family, a person using polite style with a much older relative would be scolded severely.

(19)a. 이상없습니다.
Isang eps.supnita. (formal style)
'Everything is in order.'

b. 이상없어요.
Isang eps.e yo. (polite style)
'Everything's in order.'

The formal style is widely used in speeches delivered to a large audience, as well as in reporting the news or weather in television and radio broadcasts.

(20) 여러분의 졸업식에 와서 축사를 하게 된 것을 큰 영광으로 생각합니다.
Yele-pun uy col.ep-sik ey wase chwuksa lul hakey toyn kes ul khun yeng-kwang ulo sayngkak-hapnita.
'I consider it a great honor to deliver the commencement address at your graduation.'

(21) 여러분 안녕하십니까? 지금부터 아홉시 뉴스를 말씀드리겠습니다.
Yele-pun annyeng-hasipnikka? Cikum puthe ahop-si nyusu lul malssum tulikeyss.supnita.
'Good evening, ladies and gentlemen. Now we bring you the nine o'clock news.'

This style used in formal speeches contrasts sharply with the style used in formal writing, which is normally the plain style. Just as the *panmal* and polite styles form the two great axes of informal Korean usage, in situations that require formality, the plain and formal styles are the two axes of use.

However, not all writing is done in the plain style. In advertising, or in government documents intended for general public information, the style conventionally used is, instead, the formal style. Other kinds of writing for a general audience are occasionally put into the formal style as well. Documents in this style may be written in form, but the effect that they give is like the spoken language. By deliberately choosing what is normally a spoken medium, a writer produces a feeling of more personal involvement with the reader, and, when that kind of touch is appropriate, it can often give the writing stronger appeal. In cases such as these, the speech style is selected for stylistic effect rather than to match the social status of the listener.

We have examined all six levels of speech style in Korean. The boundaries of some of these styles are not clearly distinguished from a neighboring level with which it alternates; others are moving along a path toward obsolescence. There are differences depending upon which generation is taken as the standard. However, each of the levels has its own unique domain of application and function, and each conveys information about the situation and the social attitudes and assumptions of the speaker using the style.

Finally, as we have pointed out before, the six levels are in general organized into sets of two-way oppositions. We suggest that this binary system is structured as follows: At the first stage, speech style is divided into the two polar opposites of plain and formal. At the second stage, at a reduced level of formality, *panmal* and polite form the contrasting pair. At the third, and last, stage are the styles for treating subordinates with a little more reserve, the most minor levels of all, the familiar and the semiformal. This structure is shown in the diagram given below:

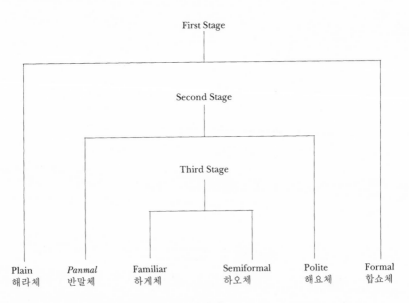

Figure 7 The Structure of Korean Speech Styles

7.6 Putting the Honorific System Together

Up until now, we have looked at the various dimensions of the Korean honorific system. On the one hand, the system is divided into the distinctions of pronouns and titles and, on the other hand, it is divided into distinctions in verbal inflection. Verbal inflection in turn is divided into prefinal endings and final endings. We have also noted the roles played by case particles and special honorific vocabulary. These various parts of the structure work in consort to form the honorific system used in the complex world of Korean society. These parts can on occasion be simply combined mechanically to form an overall structure; at other times, they clash and intertwine in a convoluted process that divides the honorific system into still subtler and more finely differentiated levels. Here we will examine the various ways these individual parts are put together and strategically used.

First let us look at some examples of how *subject honorification, object exaltation,* and the various *speech styles* interact. We will only use the plain and formal styles in these illustrations. In the following examples, *S* stands for subject, *O* for object, and *L* for listener. The + in parentheses indicates that the person is being elevated, and the - indicates that he is not.

(1) a. 민호가 동생에게 밥을 주었다.
   Minho ka tongsayng eykey pap ul cwuessta. (S -, O -, L -)
   'Minho gave his little brother/sister his/her meal.'

   b. 민호가 동생에게 밥을 주었습니다.
   Minho ka tongsayng eykey pap ul cwuess.supnita. (S -, O -, L +)
   'Minho gave his little brother/sister his/her meal.'

(2) a. 어머님께서 민호에게 밥을 주셨다.
   Eme-nim kkeyse Minho eykey pap ul cwusyessta. (S +, O -, L -)
   'Mother gave Minho his meal.'

   b. 어머님께서 민호에게 밥을 주셨습니다.
   Emen-nim kkeyse Minho eykey pap ul cwusyess.supnita. (S +, O -, L +)
   'Mother gave Minho his meal.'

(3) a. 민호가 어머님께 진지를 드렸다.
   Minho ka eme-nim kkey cinci lul tulyessta. (S -, O +, L -)
   'Minho gave Mother her meal.'

   b. 민호가 어머님께 진지를 드렸습니다.
   Minho ka eme-nim kkey cinci lul tulyess.supnita. (S -, O +, L +)
   'Minho gave Mother her meal.'

(4) a. 어머님께서 할머님께 진지를 드리셨다.
   Eme-nim kkeyse halme-nim kkey cinci lul tulisyessta. (S +, O +, L -)
   'Mother gave Grandmother her meal.'

b. 어머님께서 할머님께 진지를 드리셨습니다.

Eme-nim kkeyse halme-nim kkey cinci lul tulisyess.supnita. (S+, O+, L+)
'Mother gave Grandmother her meal.'

We can see that in these examples the three parts of the honorific sys-tem—subject honorification, object exaltation, and the speech style—are each used independently without influence from the other two. Each is used for its own reasons, and when two of them, or all three, are combined, a for-mula is chosen that accommodates each. The three structures can here be combined and used in ways that cause no conflict whatsoever.

However, a different kind of situation obtains when the subject of the sentence is also the listener. In this case, the rules for subject honorification and speech style are not independent of each other. For example, a highly esteemed person would, as subject, take the marker of subject honorifica-tion *-si-* and, as listener, the verbal endings of the formal style. The use of one requires the use of the other. Here, the rule is fairly simple and straight-forward. However, most situations are not this simple. The problem comes because in the real world the choices are not ordinarily restricted to the po-lar opposites of plain and formal styles. As can be seen in the following, the honorific marker *-si-* can be used, or not used, with polite style, semiformal style, familiar style, and, on occasion, even with *panmal.* All of the sentences in (5) through (10) can be translated as 'Where are you going?' But each implies different things about the relationship between the speaker and the listener, who is also the subject of the sentence.

(5) a. 어디 가십니까?
   Eti kasipnikka? (S+, formal style)

   b. ??어디 갑니까?
   ??Eti kapnikka? (S-, formal style)

(6) a. 어디 가세요?
   Eti kasey yo? (S+, polite style)

   b. 어디 가요?
   Eti ka yo? (S-, polite style)

(7) a. 어디 가시오?
   Eti kasio?   (S+, semiformal style)

   b. 어디 가오?
   Eti kao?   (S-, semiformal style)

(8) a. 어디 가시나?
   Eti kasina? (S+, familiar style)

b. 어디 가나?
Eti kana? (S -, familiar style)

(9) a. ?어디 가셔?
?Eti kasye? (S +, *panmal* style)

b. 어디 가?
Eti ka? (S -, *panmal* style)

(10)a. ×어디 가시니?
×Eti kasini? (S +, plain style)

b. 어디 가니?
Eti kani? (S -, plain style)

It seems theoretically inconsistent that -*si*- could be used with all of these speech styles. A person with whom the semiformal or familiar style is used should not be a person associated with the honorific marker. We see, for example, that when -*si*- is inserted in (11), where the subject is a person with whom the familiar style (11a) or the semiformal style (11b) would be used, the sentence becomes awkward. Thus, it seems curious that the examples with -*si*- in (7) and (8) are perfectly well-formed sentences.

(11)a. ??애들아, 김군이 어디 가시니?
??Yay-tul a, Kim-kwun i eti kasini? (-*kwun* is a familiar-style usage)
['Hey kids, where's Kim-*kwun* going?']

b. ??우리 집사람이 요즘 어디 좀 가셨어.
??Wuli cip-salam i yocum eti com kasyess.e.
['My wife is gone somewhere these days.']

The reason why the sentences work is another part of the complexity of the Korean honorific system. When the listener is also the subject of the sentence, six levels do not take care of the possible relationships to the speaker. There are instances where many more distinctions have to be made. For example, the familiar-style sentence in (8b), above, is a question a professor might ask a student who works as his assistant. But after some years had passed, and that student was now, say, a young professor himself, the professor might feel that adding -*si*-, as in (8a), would make the sentence more appropriate to the new situation. Of course, the old professor could also simply switch to the polite style. But the polite-style sentence in (6b) has a meaning that is yet again different from the nuances of (8a). Polite-style *Eti kayo?* 'Where are you going?' in (6a) is socially appropriate, but it is simply a bland, direct question, while the familiar-style *Eti kasina?* has a more indirect, gentler feel about it. The addition of the -*si*- to the old, paternalistic familiar style says to the young professor, "I still have warm, fatherly feelings toward you, but (by using *-si-*) I also have pride and respect for your newly won higher social position."

Related to this multifaceted use of *-si-* is another interesting complication in the honorific system. The process of subject honorification ordinarily entails a two-way choice between plain verbs such as *mekta* 'eat' and special polite verbs such as *capswusita* 'partake of food'; but, in addition, there are also vocabulary items such as *casita* 'eat' that occupy a middle level between plain and special polite. This third verb is used when the subject is someone to whom the speaker should show more reserve than with *mekta* but with whom it would be awkward to use a verb that showed as much deference as *capswusita*. Moreover, in addition to *casita*, a Korean speaker will also sometimes use a contracted form of *capswusita*, *capswusta*, which is slightly less respectful than the uncontracted form. All of these verb forms take the endings associated with different speech styles, and this produces a great variety of highly nuanced meanings.

(12)a. 이것 좀 자셔요.
   Ikes com casye yo. (S +, polite style)
   'Please have some of this [usually a woman to a man].'

   b. 이것 좀 자시게.
   Ikes com casikey. (S +, familiar style)
   'Have some of this.'

   c. 이 사람 그만 자셔.
   I salam kuman casye. (S +, *panmal* style)
   'Hey, you better stop eating.'

There are other ways besides these to put a finer point on the six levels of speech style. One can combine different appellations and titles for the people involved, as well as make various intermediate-level lexical forms. The titles that we have looked at could perhaps be expanded to make fifteen or sixteen levels. This number cannot be matched up on a one-to-one basis with the six levels of speech style. This means that any one of the six speech styles can go together with a number of different ways of calling people. For example, here are some possibilities with *panmal*:

(13)a. 김 과장, 나 좀 봐.
   Kim Kwacang, na com pwa.
   'Section Leader Kim, I'd like to see you for a minute.'

   b. 김군, 나 좀 봐.
   Kim-kwun, na com pwa.
   'Kim-*kwun*, I'd like to see you for a minute.'

c. 민호군, 나 좀 봐.
Minho-kwun, na com pwa.
'Minho-*kwun*, I'd like to see you a minute.'

d. 민호, 나 좀 봐.
Minho, na com pwa.
'Minho, I'd like to see you a minute.'

e. 민호야, 나 좀 봐.
Minho ya, na com pwa.
'Hey Minho, I'd like to see you a minute.'

Since these sentences are said in *panmal* style, it is certainly true that they all treat the listener with the lack of reserve that the next-to-lowest of the six levels implies. However, by using various different ways of calling out to the person, the speaker subdivides the utterance into still more finely graded distinctions. In none of the sentences in (13a) through (13e) does the speaker treat the listener the same.

Further differentiation of the honorific system is also created in other ways—for example, when a speaker makes a decision regarding the use of the respectful subject marker *kkeyse*. Each of the dimensions of the honorific system provides a set of distinctions that, when used by a sensitive native speaker, combine with the other parts of the structure to produce a delicate and minutely graded mode of expression. The complexity of the resulting system is surely on a scale found in few other languages in the world.

7.7 The Sociology of the Honorific System

In Korean, what is the basis for determining that a person is to be treated with respect, that he is of higher social rank? The standards for making this decision probably do not depart much from the categories of power and solidarity discussed by Brown and Gilman (1960). Nevertheless, the factors that influence this determination have a distinctly Korean character.

We have often mentioned age in the preceding discussion. It is the most important factor in determining how the honorific system is used. In Korea, age influences not only the language, but all aspects of life. Koreans have long taken the tenets of Neo-Confucianism most seriously, and, though it is often thought of as a cliché, the maxim *Cangyuyuse* (長幼有序) 'The old and the young know their place' still has widespread currency in Korean society. The young do not smoke in front of their elders; when a door is opened, the oldest person enters first; when the family eats, the young wait for the "adults" to pick up their spoons and chopsticks. Such rules of etiquette are surprisingly well kept. To a degree that can be embarrassing to Westerners, Koreans are interested in knowing a person's age. Koreans ask and freely reveal their ages, and they make a display of seniority; in a fight, a frequently used retort is *Myech sal intey, kenpang-cikey kwununya* 'How old are you, that you're acting like such a smart-aleck?' It is natural in a society where age plays such an important role that it occupy an important place in the language.

Among Americans, an age difference of about fifteen years seems to influence language use. In Korea, the difference is much smaller—at most, about three or four years. For example, how much older than oneself can a person be to still use *panmal?* The answer is, no more than three or four years. With an age difference of that degree, people from the same neighborhood who have been close since childhood, or, at a gathering where occupational position is unimportant, people who are very close friends can socialize using *panmal.* But even these examples push the boundary.

When age and occupational position are in conflict, an age difference of more than two or three years ordinarily cannot be ignored. According to one report, a superior officer in the military cannot treat the men under him without a measure of reserve when they are more than four years older than he is.[11] The situation in the military, where rank is more important than in any other place, shows just how great the role of age is in the social order.

Relationships formed at school also influence how the honorific system is used. Though related to age, this matter of who is senior and who is junior is not a question of age alone. At each level of schooling, the senior-junior relationship is always similar, but the rules are most strictly observed in middle school and high school, where a senior of only one year cannot be spoken to in *panmal.* At the college level, the rules are more strictly kept within the same department than with students from other departments. A student may sometimes use *panmal* with people one year senior if they are from the same department, but when speaking with students from other departments, *panmal* is fine even if they are two or three years' senior. Elementary school rules are a little less strict, but there is a boundary of about a year or two there, as well.

As we have suggested several times, the question of age is not only a matter of age difference; the absolute ages of the speaker and the listener also exert an important influence on language use. As both speaker and listener grow older, their titles and the way they are addressed change. People with whom one had once used *panmal*—for example, an older brother—must now be spoken to in polite style; both the familiar and the semiformal styles can only be employed once both speaker and listener have matured. Where approximately is the dividing line for this change? The time when Koreans take on these different linguistic roles seems to be around the age of marriage. These days, the age at which Koreans get married is gradually rising, a fact that may in part be explained by the more relaxed lifestyles of today. These social changes have brought about an overall delay in the age at which Koreans become more serious and formal.

The generational structure within a family is another important factor in the use of language. If a relative is of an earlier generation, unless he is extremely young, he cannot be spoken to in *panmal* even if he is more than ten years younger than oneself. Also, as we have already pointed out, he cannot be called by name but must instead be addressed with the appropriate family term. Still, what is important for language use is only whether the generation is higher or lower, not the degree of difference. The degree of reserve does not depend upon whether the relative is of one's grandfather's generation or one's uncle's generation.

An important concept in Korean language and society is the reckoning of the degree of kinship. This is done by counting what are known as *chon* (촌).[12] Brothers and sisters are two *chon* apart. Your father's brothers are called *sam-chon*; they are relatives of three *chon* distance. Their sons (your first cousins) are called *sa-chon* (four *chon*); your grandfather's brothers' sons are your father's *sa-chon* and your *o-chon* (five *chon*); and so on. In other words, for each generational difference, the kinship distance is increased one *chon*. Relatives up to ten *chon* apart are thought of as close kin, so, in other words, the fifth-generation descendants of a single ancestor are counted as close relatives in Korea.

The concept of degree of kinship is also incorporated into naming practices. A Korean given name, particularly that of a male, traditionally includes one character used as a generational name. This part of the name is the *hanglyel-ca* (항렬자) 'generational character', or the *tollim-ca* (돌림자) '(literally) turning character'. The generational character is shared not only by brothers within the same family, but also by distant relatives who belong to the same clan. One's father has another generational character, and one's grandfather has yet another, distinctive character. Therefore, all one needs do is to see a relative's name, and even if one has never laid eyes on that person before, one instantly knows where in the generational structure he belongs. One knows whether he is a collateral relative or, if not, how many generations up or down he may be.[13]

The concepts of kinship distance and generational structure cause the use of kinship-related honorific language to be strict. The generational structure exerts decisive influence upon power, and kinship distance decisively influences solidarity.

It goes without saying that at a workplace, occupational position is a deciding factor in the use of the honorific system. The rule is that to cadre, such as the company president, vice-president, and section chiefs, ordinary employees use polite, reserved language, and reserve is also shown toward employees one rank higher than oneself. However, depending upon the workplace, this boundary may not be strict. For example, in the academic world, professors do not have to show a particularly greater amount of deference toward the president of the university.

In the workplace, when there is conflict between age and occupational position, the occupational position seems to exert greater power. Superiors in a company will show appropriate reserve toward older people under them, but that deference is usually less than that shown by an employee to a boss who is older than himself.

Social class exerts surprisingly little influence. In the past, the strict division between *yangban* aristocracy and the *sangmin* under them had a clear influence on language use. As was mentioned above, *panmal* was at first an equivocating style the *yangban* used when speaking to older commoners, with whom they did not want to use polite language, but with whom they would have felt bad using plain style. The appellations of the social classes were of course different, and verbal endings and vocabulary had separate forms depending on social rank. Today, however, these differences have disappeared almost completely without a trace. In the modern age, there is no separate, particularly polite language that must be used if the listener is considered of high social class, nor, simply because the listener is lower class, is there especially condescending language that is used. What remains that is directly related to social class is only the treatment accorded to people of lower occupational status, such as one's housekeeper or the guard in front of the apartment building; the level of reserve shown in these cases is undeniably less. However, this distinction is of a different kind from that of the traditional social classes. In traditional Korea, social class was inherited, whereas the distinction used today is based upon occupational status, which is another aspect of the ranks used in the modern workplace.

Gender clearly influences language use. In general, one uses less deferential language to one's mother than to one's father, to a grandmother than to a grandfather. In some dialect-speaking regions, there are areas where people always use *panmal* with mothers and grandmothers. Even in Seoul, *panmal* such as in (1) is heard fairly often. A variant of the semiformal style *(hao-chey)*, which is illustrated in (2), is also quite widely used. This *hawu* style is slightly more respectful than the *hao* style. Also, though not always true, formal style is sometimes used when speaking to a grandfather, while language above polite style (that is, formal style) is seldom if ever used with a mother or grandmother. There is no question that the social status of females in Korea is lower than that of males.

(1) 엄마, 밥 줘.
     Emma, pap cwe. (*panmal*)
     'Mom, gimme something to eat.'

(2) 어머니, 언니 안 왔우?
     Emeni, enni an wass.wu? (*hawu* style, said by a female)
     'Mother, isn't Big Sis here yet?'

The same is true of married couples. As we have said, a husband can speak to his wife in semiformal style (or *panmal*), but the wife cannot speak to her husband the same way. Instead, she is supposed to use the polite style, which is one level higher. With appellations and pronouns, husband and wife

reciprocate by both using *Yepo* 'Dear!' and *Tangsin* 'You', but when it comes
to verbal endings, women are spoken to in a style that is one level lower.

To a certain extent, this language use probably reflects the traditional
modes of thought in which women were treated as inferior to men. This is
at least the simple way to look at it. Yet, there are other explanations. One
alternative way to see it, in the case of mothers and grandmothers, is that the
imbalance is more a difference in "solidarity" than a difference in "power."
That is, one uses less reserved language when speaking to one's mother and
grandmother because the relationships with them are closer. Most Koreans
feel warmer toward mothers and grandmothers than toward the men in the
household. In addition, in the relationship between a husband and wife, we
must remember that the husband is usually several years older than his wife,
and the all-important factor of age must come into play here. Even so, in the
rare case that the wife is older, the rules still do not change, showing that the
most important principle is that the husband is the head of the household.
These days, among the younger generation, the spread of the use of *panmal*
by both husband and wife (as well as the use of *caki* as the second-person pronoun instead of *tangsin*) can perhaps be seen as a step toward the correction
of the inequality between men and women.

There are also instances where women are treated with more reserve.
Traditionally, a man can use *panmal* with his wife's brother but not with her
sister. In addition, one treats someone else's daughter with more reserve
than that person's son. Male professors tend to be more constrained in their
language use with female students than with male students. In any event,
gender differences can be found in many aspects of the honorific system.

Solidarity is an important factor in the Korean honorific system as well.
People who have used polite language with each other switch to panmal
when they become close, a *Mal ul noh.nunta* 'putting down the language' or
Ne-na hanun sai ka toynta 'getting on *ne-na* (you-me) terms'. A feeling of solidarity regulates the level of language this way. However, if the factors that
we have discussed above are together called "power," then the influence
that that power exerts in Korea is greater than that exerted by solidarity. In
this sense, Korea is different from Western societies. In Korea, no matter
how close one may be, there are many barriers that cannot be crossed. As we
mentioned in the introduction, no matter how close one may be to one's
teacher, one can never use *panmal* with him or call him by name. The same
is true of the language used with a superior in a workplace, as well as how
one must treat a school acquaintance three or four years older. The
influence of power far surpasses that of solidarity.

In Korean, as we have suggested above, the influence of solidarity can
also have the opposite effect. If one becomes distant from someone with
whom one had previously been close, then one switches from *panmal* to more
polite language. When brothers and sisters mature, they change how they
call each other into a more reserved level of language. When children who
once used *panmal* with each other grow up and marry, they switch to polite

language. It has been claimed that in English, once social barriers have been reduced through solidarity, the previous vertical relationships are as a matter of principle never reinstated.[14] Whatever the extent to which this is true in English-speaking countries, the rule is certainly not kept in Korea.

There are other factors besides those we have mentioned that affect how the honorific system is used. It goes without saying, for example, that language use depends upon whether the setting is public or private. For instance, the person in charge of a meeting must be addressed as *Uycang* 'Mr. Chairman' because he cannot be called by name. Differences in formality of this kind are widespread and not unique to Korea.

References

An Pyŏnghŭi 1992; Brown and Ford 1961; Brown and Gilman 1960; Cho Chunhak 1982; Ch'oe Hyŏnbae 1937, 1959; Dredge 1977; Hŏ Ung 1963, 1975; Howell 1967; Hwang Chŏngnyun 1975; Kim Chugwan 1989; Lee Maeng-Sung (Yi Maengsŏng) 1973; Martin 1964, 1992; Park Young-Soon (Pak Yŏngsun) 1978; Sŏ Chŏngsu (Suh Cheong-Soo) 1984; Sohn Ho-min (Son Homin) 1983; Sŏng Kich'ŏl 1985; Wang Hansŏk 1984; Yi Iksŏp (Lee Iksop) 1994.

8

History

In the introduction, we put forward the idea that Korean had either branched off from Altaic or from some proto language ancestral to both Korean and Altaic. As we said then, the "Altaic" family of languages is a hypothetical reconstruction used to explain the systematic resemblances between Turkic, Mongolian, and Tungus. The Altaic hypothesis represents the belief that those three well-established language families are related to each other and that the resemblances between them have resulted from the fact that they are descended from the same ancestral language. A still bolder version of this Altaic hypothesis—sometimes called "Macro-Altaic"—would include Korean and Japanese as part of the family. According to this version of the hypothesis, Korean is related to Turkic, Mongolian, and Tungus, on the one hand, and to Japanese, on the other. That at least is the origin hypothesis generally accepted in Korea and much of the rest of the world.

The original Korean language—that is, the form of the language that branched off from the ancestral family—is known as *proto-Korean*. As yet, very little is known for sure about proto-Korean, either about its origins or what it sounded like or what processes it underwent as it developed into the later stages of the language attested in historical records.

Korean is often treated as if it has always been a unified, single language that has come down to us without fundamental change. However, it has been persuasively argued[1] that at one time there were two groups of languages spoken on the Korean peninsula, the Puyŏ group centered on the kingdoms of Koguryŏ and Puyŏ in the north, and the Han group centered on the Samhan tribes in the south. (The Samhan later became the kingdoms of Paekche and Silla.) These languages north and south were related but still quite distinctly different.

The earliest written records on the Korean peninsula date from the "Three Kingdoms" period—that is, the period during which the three kingdoms of Koguryŏ, Paekche, and Silla coexisted on the Korean peninsula. Beginning with the time those records were written and proceeding down to the present day, there are four historical stages of the Korean language:

Old Korean:	This stage (고대국어) extends from the Three Kingdoms period until the end of Unified Silla in the tenth century, a period of time lasting about one

thousand years. What is often spoken of as "Old Korean" refers to three languages spoken on the Korean peninsula, Koguryŏan, Paekchean, and Sillan, of which Sillan is thought to be the immediate ancestor of Middle Korean. The kingdom of Koguryŏ is said to have lasted from 37 B.C. to A.D. 668; Paekche from 18 B.C. to A.D. 660; and Silla from 57 B.C. to A.D. 935.

Middle Korean: This stage (중세국어) extends from the tenth century to the end of the sixteenth century. It lasted from the beginning of the Koryŏ period (918–1392) until the Imjin Wars (the Japanese invasion) of 1592. Middle Korean is further divided into Early Middle Korean and Late Middle Korean. Early Middle Korean lasted from the beginning of Koryŏ until around the founding of the Chosŏn dynasty. Late Middle Korean was the language represented in the earliest alphabetic texts in Korea, those of the fifteenth and sixteenth centuries.

Modern Korean: What is called "Modern Korean" (근대국어) could perhaps better be termed "Pre-Contemporary" Korean. It dates from the beginning of the seventeenth century until the end of the nineteenth; in other words, from the end of Middle Korean until the establishment of Contemporary Korean.

Contemporary Korean: This is the Korean of our own day (현대국어). The beginning of this stage is generally said to coincide with the early years of the twentieth century.

These four historical stages represent the periodization of the Korean language most widely used in Korea. However, it can be somewhat deceptive to think of the history of Korean in these terms. The four stages of development are not equally known or of equal significance. In considering the history of the language, the most important stage by far is Middle Korean. Before it—actually, before Late Middle Korean—there are few written records, and what these writings reveal is extremely limited. It is only with the invention of the Korean alphabet in the fifteenth century that we can see clearly and in detail what the Korean language looked like. Middle Korean is the foundation of what we know about the history of the language, as well as how the modern dialects, including the standard language, formed and developed.

8.1 Old Korean

Fragmentary records exist from Koguryŏ, Paekche, and Silla, but the bulk of these fragments are from Silla, the kingdom that unified the peninsula.

There are almost no written materials that remain from the languages of Koguryŏ and Paekche. The information we have about those two languages comes principally from place names that are transcribed in Chinese characters in the twelfth-century text the *Samguk sagi* ('Historical Records of the Three Kingdoms'). Some of these Koguryŏ and Paekche place names can be roughly deciphered because they are written in phonograms as well as in *hun* transcriptions of their meanings. (See 2.6.1, above.) A few forms that have been tentatively reconstructed for the Paekche language are given below:

Paekche word	Meaning	Phonograms
*pŭri	'fire'	夫里
*turak	stone'	珍惡 [2]
*sa	'new'	沙
*murke	'clear'	勿居
*muraŋ	'high'	毛良

The lexical items that have been preserved from Koguryŏ are slightly greater in number, but, like all linguistic evidence from the Three Kingdoms period, the evidence is thin and difficult to interpret. Altogether, about eighty different Koguryŏ words are found in the historical records, of which around twenty can be deciphered with any confidence. Around fifty of the elements that make up these words have been tentatively reconstructed.[3] Here are some of these suggested reconstructions:

Koguryŏ word	Meaning	Phonograms
*mai/mie	'water'	買
*nua	'earth'	內, 邢, 奴, 惱
*pai	'boulder, crag'	巴衣, 波衣
*tan/tuan	'valley'	旦, 呑, 頓
*tar	'mountain'	達
*hor	'fort'	忽
*mir	'three'	密
*ŭc	'five'	于次
*nanən	'seven'	難隱
*tək	'ten'	德

It is difficult to draw definite conclusions from such fragmentary and unsystematic evidence, but it appears that many, if not most, words preserved from the Paekche language have correspondences in Middle Korean (as well as in Contemporary Korean) vocabulary. However, many of the Koguryŏ words are quite unlike anything known from later stages of Korean. The words for numbers in particular are entirely different from those found in Sillan or in Middle Korean. These number words are, rather, strikingly similar to Old Japanese *mi* 'three', *itu* 'five', *nana* 'seven', and *towo* 'ten', as well as to Tungusic *nadan* 'seven'. Other lexical resemblances to Japanese have also not escaped notice. For example, in the short vocabulary list given above, **mai/mie* 'water' and *nua 'earth' quite obviously resemble Old Japanese *midu* 'water' and *na* 'earth'.

In Korea, opinion is divided as to whether the difference between Koguryŏan and Sillan was one of dialect or something more. The question has become a political matter, and scholars who point to the obvious dissimilarities as evidence that they were separate languages are often accused by ultranationalists of trying to "divide the homeland." In any event, there are certainly enough resemblances to ascertain that Koguryŏan, Paekchean, and Sillan were all related, however distant or close those relationships might have been. Of the eighty or so Koguryŏ words that have been preserved, about thirty—that is, around one third—correspond to words in Middle Korean. If, as is commonly believed, Middle Korean is the direct descendant of the language of Silla, then it is highly likely Koguryŏ and Silla shared an even greater percentage of their respective vocabularies. The significance of the Koguryŏ language is that it seems to share vocabulary not only with Silla, on the one hand, but with Japanese, on the other hand. Because of the Japanese-like vocabulary of Koguryŏan, some foreign scholars have thought it likely to be a close relative or ancestor of Japanese, but that idea ignores the fact that much of the vocabulary is clearly Korean. The relationship that Koguryŏan had with Japanese lies tantalizingly beyond our grasp.

Sillan is believed to be the direct ancestor of Middle Korean and thus of the language spoken in Korea today. It is "Old Korean" in the truest sense of the words. Since Silla was the kingdom that unified the peninsula, relatively more records of its language have been preserved than of Paekchean and Koguryŏan. There are seven kinds of data used for reconstructing the Silla language:[4] (1) proper nouns preserved in historical documents; (2) *idu* transcriptions (cf. 2.6.1.3, above); (3) *hyangch'al* transcriptions (2.6.1.1); (4) vocabulary fragments preserved in Chinese documents; (5) loanwords into Japanese; (6) the traditional readings of Chinese characters, which were standardized in the Silla period; and (7) internal reconstruction from Middle Korean and other later forms of the language.

The principal historical sources for Sillan are the *Samguk sagi* (1145) and the *Samguk yusa* (1285), the two oldest Korean books that still exist. These two histories contain Silla proper names, place names, and the names of government offices. A scattering of supporting data for these names and titles are to be found in Chinese and Japanese histories, as well. The *Samguk yusa*, along with the biography of the priest Kyunyŏ (written in 1075 but preserved as an appendix to the Samguk yusa), also contains all the extant *hyangch'al* transcriptions of Silla poetry. A few examples of Silla-period *idu* can be found in engraved inscriptions, such as that of the Sinsŏng Stele (新城碑), carved in Kyŏngju in 591. The various methods used in this period for representing Korean words are discussed above, in chapter 2.

The materials preserved from the Silla period are not sufficient to reconstruct the phonological system with any certainty. However, they do reveal information about certain general characteristics. For one thing, Old Korean had none of the reinforced consonants *(pp, tt, kk, ss, cc)* found in Korean today. This series of consonants had still not developed. However, it appears that Old Korean did have at least some aspirated consonants. In the *Samguk sagi* the Silla place name 'wild mountain', for example, is transcribed as 居柴山, and the first two characters are phonograms representing a word corresponding to Middle Korean *kechul-* 'be wild'. The aspiration in the reading of the second Chinese character makes it probable that the Silla language had an aspirated consonant **ch* contrasting with plain **c*. Similarly, the word corresponding to Middle Korean *pwuthye* 'Buddha' was written 佛體, which means that Sillan also had the consonant **th*; the reasoning is that the second character was selected because it had a reading with an aspirated dental stop. The fact that the pronunciations of Chinese vocabulary were standardized during the Silla period provides another reference point. On the one hand, Sino-Korean *th* and *ch* (versus *t* and *c*) reflect well original Chinese distinctions in the dentals and dental affricates; *ph*, on the other hand, does not reflect the aspiration of Chinese; and *kh* is extremely rare in Sino-Korean, being found in the readings of only four characters. On the basis of this and other evidence, it seems probable that Old Korean (the language of Silla) had regular aspiration distinctions only in the dental stops and affricates. In a few words, the labial aspirate *ph* may have been distinct from *p*; but the velar aspirate *kh* had a marginal existence, if it existed at all, in Old Korean. Comparative evidence from Altaic suggests that such contrasts developed some time after the proto-Korean stage, and internal evidence from Middle Korean shows that many of the aspirated consonants developed out of the reduction of consonant clusters.

One of the biggest questions in reconstructing the Old Korean consonant system is whether it had distinctively voiced consonants or not. Later, at the Middle Korean stage, the language had voiced fricatives *β* and *z* (written with the symbols ㅸ and △),[5] but these consonants are suspiciously found only in medial position — they never occur at the beginning or end of the word. The question is, where did these Middle Korean consonants come from, and did they contrast with **p* and **s* in Old Korean? Also, were there once additional voicing distinctions at the beginning of words? These questions are of particularly great consequence to historical linguists trying to establish Korean correspondences for voiced-voiceless distinctions in Altaic. At this point in time opinion is divided on the issue.[6]

Today, before a pause, Koreans pronounce the consonants written *t, s, c,* and *ch* (ㄷ, ㅅ, ㅈ, ㅊ) all alike, as [t]. But in the Old Korean period **t, *s,* and **c* were clearly distinguished from each other in that position; we know that to be true because all three were consistently transcribed with separate characters. However, there is no clear evidence that **ch* was pronounced differently from **c* at the end of a word. The same character was used to transcribe both.

Unlike later stages of the language, Old Korean seems to have had a distinction between **l* and **r*. The reasoning for this assumption is that what was later written as " ㄹ " in Middle Korean was consistently written in two different ways in Old Korean.[7]

The Old Korean vowels are even more difficult to reconstruct than the consonants. The best that can be done is to project back from the Late Middle Korean system using phonograms as approximate reference points. These phonograms give hints as to whether the vowel might have been rounded or not, or front or back, and so on, but little more. By reconstructing on the basis of the later, Middle Korean vowels and putting them together with this kind of evidence, a system of seven vowels has been proposed (the Korean letters in parentheses represent the vowels into which they later developed).

A Tentative Reconstruction of the Sillan Vowel System

i (ㅣ)	ü (ㅜ)	u (ㅗ)
ɔ̈ (ㅡ)		ɔ (·)
ä (ㅓ)	a (ㅏ)	

Other aspects of the Old Korean phonological system lie beyond our ability to recover from written records. These phonological puzzles include such things as whether or not earlier Korean had a system of vowel harmony and what kind of tone or accent distinctions it might have had. In such cases, as well as for more systematic information about consonants and vowels, we must rely upon internal reconstruction from Middle Korean, and (potentially at least) comparison with other, related languages when, and if, those relationships have been more fully established.

Some grammatical characteristics of Old Korean can be ascertained from *idu* and *hyangch'al*. Though such transcriptions in Chinese characters represent sounds extremely poorly and ineffectively, they do reflect word order fairly clearly. From them, we know that syntactic order in Korean was much the same then as it is today. Also, grammatical elements such as particles are represented in *idu* and *hyangch'al* more often than are other kinds of vocabulary. In Silla writings, we see the following representations of particles, for example:

Case markers	Middle Korean	Old Korean transcription
subject	*i* 이	伊, 是
genitive	*uy/oy* 의/인	矣, 衣
"genitive-*s*"	*oy/uy* 인/의	叱
object	*(l)ol/(l)ul* 올/을/를/를	乙, 肹
locative	*ay/ey/oy/yey* 애/에/인/예	中, 良中, 也中
instrumental	*lwo* 로	留
comitative	*kwa* 과	果

Special particles			
topic marker	(n)on/(n)un	온/은/ᄂ/는	隱
'also, too'	to	도	置

Some inflectional endings can also be identified. For example, Old Korean transcriptions reflect the following endings still found in Korean today:

Modern	Middle Korean	Old Korean
-(u)n	-(o/u)n -온/은/ㄴ	去隱春 'depart*ed* (=last) spring'
-(u)l	-(o/u)l -올/을/ㄹ	慕理尸心 'a long*ing* heart'
-i	-i -이	明期 'brightness' (불기)
-(u)le	-la -라	功德修叱如良來如 '(He) came *in order to* beg for food'
-mye	-mye -며	膝肹古召旀 'Correct*ing* her knee position,'
-taka	-taka -다가	夜入伊遊行如加 'Caroused into the night, *and then*'
-ko	-kwo -고	一等隱枝良出<u>古</u> 'Hav*ing* branched off from the same stem,'

Mysteries abound, of course. For example, the simple declarative ending, which today is *-ta,* was consistently transcribed in the Old Korean period with the character 如. Why in the world was that character chosen? The reading of the character is nothing like *-ta* (in Korean it is pronounced *ye,* and, in Chinese of the time, **ńio,* perhaps). Were the ancient Sillans transcribing some other ending that they used instead to express the declarative? Or, alternatively, has the declarative ending familiar to us today changed in pronunciation so completely over the centuries? More baffling still is the mystery surrounding the use of the character 薺. This character was used to transcribe some verbal ending, not only in Sillan poetry but in *idu,* as well. Yet, we simply have no idea what ending it was that the character might have represented.

Old Korean had an honorific system that seems to have been much like that of Middle Korean. To express subject honorification, Sillans used the prefinal ending *-si-,* which they transcribed with the character 賜. In Idu tradition, this transcriptional character is read *sya,* but in Old Korean, the pronunciation of the pre-final ending was perhaps something more like **si.* To express object exaltation (cf. 7.4 and 8.3.2), Sillan poets wrote the character 白 after the stem of the verb. Since the same character was used to transcribe the stem of the verb ancestral to modern *saloyta* '(humbly) tell, state, inform', it appears that at that time object exaltation was expressed by attaching that humble verb to the stems of other verbs. Later, in Middle Korean, the word would split into two separate morphemes. On the one hand, there would be the prefinal ending used for object exaltation, -ᅀᆞᆸ-, while, on the other hand, the form of the verb itself became ᄉᆞᆲ다 (to become, still later, modern *saloyta*).

It is difficult to say anything definitive about sentence styles in Old Korean. In the *hyangga* poem the "Song of the Presentation of Flowers" (獻花 歌), the character 音 (now read *um*) seems to have been used in a place appropriate for the Middle Korean polite marker *-ngi*. But since that character was customarily employed in Sillan verse to represent the sound *m*, it is not clear why it was chosen in this case.

As we have attempted to show, our understanding of Old Korean is still extremely fragmentary. Sillan—and even more so, its sister languages, Paekchean and Koguryŏan—remains beyond our ability to reconstruct in any deeply satisfying way. However, we can speak with some confidence about the general direction that the Korean language took after the Three Kingdoms period. The political unification of the peninsula must have also begun the process of linguistic unification; as a result, the modern language contains very few words that come directly from the speech of the other kingdoms besides Silla. Middle Korean, and thus the Korean spoken throughout Korea today, is the linguistic legacy of the Silla Unification. It is almost exclusively through Sillan that the origins of the language must be traced.

8.2 Early Middle Korean

The Middle Korean stage of the language began in the tenth century and lasted some seven hundred years, until the end of the sixteenth century. When the Koryŏ dynasty was established in A.D.. 918, the capital was moved from Kyŏngju, in the southeast, to Kaegyŏng (later to be renamed Kaesŏng) in the center of the peninsula. With this move, a new region became the political and cultural base of the nation and thus of the language. The central variety of the language has remained a kind of *de facto* standard ever since.

Middle Korean is further divided into Early Middle Korean and Late Middle Korean. Early Middle Korean is the language of the Koryŏ dynasty, and Late Middle Korean is the language of the first two hundred years of the Chosŏn dynasty. There does not appear to have been a significant change in the development of the language between these two stages. At the end of the Koryŏ period, in 1392, the founders of the Chosŏn dynasty built their capital at Seoul (then called "Hanyang"), on the northern side of the Han River. Unlike the move from Kyŏngju to Kaesŏng, this move from Kaesŏng to Seoul was a relatively short distance that is not believed to have much of an effect on how the language developed.

What did change profoundly, however, was writing. The written records from Koryŏ are all in Chinese characters, while materials from Chosŏn are in Hangŭl. For historians of the Korean language, this change in the writing system made all the difference in the world. While the written records from Koryŏ (and before) give at most broad hints about sounds and structures, the alphabetic writings of the fifteenth and sixteenth centuries show in astonishingly sophisticated detail what the Korean language was like. Thus, when discussing Early Middle Korean, we are in some senses still talking about prehistory, since many of the linguistic facts must be reconstructed.

There are two principal sources of information about the sounds of Early Middle Korean: the *Kyerim yusa* (鷄林類事) and the *Hyangyak kugŭppang* (鄕藥救急方). The *Kyerim yusa* was compiled in 1103 by a Chinese visitor to Korea named Sun Mu. It is, in essence, a vocabulary list of about 350 words and phrases from the "Koryŏ dialect." The *Hyangyak kugŭppang* is a pharmacological work from 1250 that lists the names of around 180 plants, animals, and minerals used in Korean herbal medicine. In addition to these two texts, there is a scattering of transcriptions of Early Middle Korean words to be found in various Korean, Japanese, and Chinese sources.

Until recently, these vocabulary lists were virtually the only known linguistic records from the Koryŏ period. Beginning in 1975, however, a new era in the study of Koryŏ-period language began. In that year, a Buddhist sutra annotated in the Koryŏ period with *kugyŏl* characters came to light, and soon, it was discovered that there were many other *kugyŏl* texts that had hitherto escaped notice. A society dedicated to the study and interpretation of these texts was established, and today the emergence of new linguistic materials from the Koryŏ continues unabated.[8] As was indicated in 2.6.1.2, above, *kugyŏl* are the most passive way of all of annotating a purely Chinese text. By their nature, they reveal little about Korean phonology. However, *kugyŏl* do give information about the use of grammatical markers. Through the skill of dedicated Korean philologists, these recent textual discoveries may yet reveal new and unsuspected information about the structure of earlier Korean.

As is the case with Old Korean, what is known about the sounds of Early Middle Korean is still limited. However, the extant transcriptions do show broadly some of the changes that were going on in the Korean language. For example, the reinforced consonants had still not developed into a distinct series, but the sources had in some cases become apparent. For example, 'daughter', which today is *ttal,* was transcribed by Sun Mu in the *Kyerim yusa* with two syllables, the first of which had an initial *p-. This means it was probably pronounced something like *$pɔtɔl$. Later, the vowel in the first syllable was lost, producing a form with an initial consonant cluster, *$ptol$. It was clusters of this kind that eventually became the reinforced consonants found in Korean today.

Among other things, it is clear that a *z existed in Early Middle Korean. For example, *aze 'younger brother', *$mazɔn$ 'forty', *$kɔzgai$ 'scissors'. In some cases, we can see how z developed through a weakening of *s and then was later lost; for example, the modern word *twue* 'a few' was originally a compound made up of *twul* 'two' and *se* 'three'. Thus: *$tül-se$ 'two-three' > *twuze* > *twue* 'a few'.

We also know that, unless it was followed by *i* or *y,* the consonant *c* (ㅈ) was pronounced [ts] or [dz] in Koryŏ times. This is a pronunciation now found only in P'yŏngan dialects in the northwest. Some words then had a medial [b] that was later lost; for example, *tübəl 'two' > twul; *sübəl 'wine' > swul; and *cebəl 'scale' > cewul. Some words ended in -h before a pause.

The vowel system can be tentatively reconstructed by examining the words Koreans borrowed from Mongolian during the time the Mongols were in Korea. By comparing the vowels of these loanwords with the Mongolian originals, we can get a good idea of how the Korean pronunciations must have changed since the time the words were borrowed. Here is what the basic vowels are thought to have sounded like:

A Reconstruction of the Thirteenth Century Korean Vowel System

i ( )	ü (ㅜ)	u (ㅗ)
e (ㅓ)	ə (ㅡ)	ɔ (·)
	a (ㅏ)	

As can be seen from the modern pronunciations of the Hangŭl letters, Korean is believed to have undergone a great Vowel Shift since the Koryŏ period. However, these changes in pronunciation are the subject of some controversy among Korean linguists. There is considerable disagreement about the Vowel Shift and when (or if) it is supposed to have taken place.

8.3. Late Middle Korean

Late Middle Korean is the language represented in the earliest Hangŭl works, the alphabetic texts of the fifteenth and sixteenth centuries. The period is defined by these texts. It begins with King Sejong's promulgation of the *Hunmin chŏngŭm* in 1446, and it ends with the Japanese invasion and the resulting Imjin Wars at the end of the sixteenth century. When publishing resumed after the wars, the orthography, spellings, and general written style had all changed significantly. By disrupting the written tradition, the Japanese invasion marked the close of the Middle Korean period.

In the strictest sense of the word, the history of the Korean language begins with Late Middle Korean.[9] Before that time, no systematic transcription of the Korean language existed; every sound value must be reconstructed. After the invention of the Korean alphabet, however, the phonological distinctions found in the language were all recorded in writing. It is a stark contrast. The Korean writing system may not be nearly as old as writing in some neighboring countries, but nothing in East Asia can match its quality. The Hangŭl texts of the fifteenth and sixteenth centuries are arguably the finest premodern records of a phonological system to be found anywhere in the world.

The Hangŭl texts from the Middle Korean period are not only of the highest phonological quality. The number and bulk of these richly varied works are also great.[10] In the year following the promulgation of the *Hunmin chŏngŭm* in 1446, the *Songs of the Dragons Flying to Heaven (Yongbi ŏch'ŏn ka)* was published. Since this collection of dynastic hymns had actually been composed in 1445, the *Songs of the Dragons* has the distinction of being the first work of Korean literature in which the language was systematically written down.[11] The 125 verses describe the deeds and exploits of the founders of the dynasty and Sejong's ancestors, "the Six Dragons from East of the Sea".

Some of the earliest and most important works of the period were Buddhist compilations. King Sejong was deeply interested in Buddhism, and following the untimely death of his queen in 1446, he encouraged his sons to compile Buddhist works in their mother's memory. One of them, Prince Suyang, led a group of writers who produced, in 1447, the multivolumed *Detailed Articles on the Record of Sakyamuni (Sŏkpo sangjŏl)*. Upon seeing his son's work of devotion, Sejong is said to have been so moved he himself wrote, in 1449, the hymns of praise known as the *Songs of the Moon's Imprint on a Thousand Rivers (Wŏrin ch'ŏn'gang chi kok)*. Later, following the death of his father, Prince Suyang (who was now King Sejo) combined these two great works into a third Buddhist compilation, the *Wŏrin sŏkpo*, which he had published in 1459. Altogether, at least seventeen works of Buddhist literature in Korean were published during the fifteenth century, many of which were voluminous and extensive.

King Sejong also initiated secular works intended for educational purposes. Among the most noteworthy of these publications was the Korean translation of the *Hunmin chŏngŭm*, which was included in the first volume of the *Wŏrin sŏkpo*. Another important work of a secular nature was the *Vernacular Interpretations of Du [Fu]'s poems (Tusi ŏnhae)*, which was compiled in 1481. Du Fu was (and is) one of the most beloved of the great Tang Chinese poets, and the appearance of these poems in fluent Korean translations was surely an event of broad general interest. The medical work *Kugŭp kani pang* was compiled in 1489. In order to broaden the base of public morality, a variety of Neo-Confucian works were translated into Korean. These include the illustrated collection of Confucian homilies *Sok Samgang haengsil to* (1514), and a translation of Zhu Xi's *Lesser Learning (Pŏnyŏk Sohak)* (1518).

One of the major uses of the alphabet was to rationalize and teach the pronunciation of Chinese characters. One of the first things Sejong did after the the alphabet was revealed to the world was to initiate a number of large-scale projects intended for research into Chinese lexicography and phonological theory and to create dictionaries of Sino-Korean pronunciations. These projects resulted, among other publications, in the *Correct Rhymes of the Eastern Country (Tongguk chŏngun)* in 1447.

In the sixteenth century, the most important works by far were those authored by Ch'oe Sejin, a professor of Chinese in the interpreters' school. Ch'oe was a prolific writer, who, among other things, produced dictionaries, textbooks, essays, and linguistic treatises. His *Sasŏng t'onghae* (1517) is considered by some to be the greatest lexical work compiled in Korea before modern times. His two Mandarin textbooks, *The Old Cathayan (Nogŭltae)* and *Interpreter Pak (Pak T'ongsa)*, are invaluable sources of information not only about Korean but also about colloquial Chinese; the Hangŭl transcriptions of Mandarin Chinese in these books are the best sources of information we have for northern Chinese pronunciations of the time. Choe's best-known work, however, is his Chinese-Korean glossary of 1527, the *Hunmong chahoe.* This pedagogical work is believed to be the earliest compilation of the actual Korean pronunciations of Chinese characters. Moreover, as was mentioned in 2.1, above, it was here that the modern names of the Hangŭl letters and their alphabetical order appeared for the first time. Ch'oe Sejin's alphabetic works are second in importance only to those of Sejong himself.

8.3.1 Phonology

Consonants

In Late Middle Korean, aspirated consonants systematically contrasted with plain consonants. This fact is obvious because Sejong created symbols for them (ㅍ, ㅌ, ㅊ, ㅋ) that were distinct from the corresponding plain consonants (ㅂ, ㄷ, ㅈ, ㄱ). But he did not create symbols for the reinforced consonants, which were still not a completely distinct series.

The consonant phonemes for which Sejong provided separate symbols are as follows:

Middle Korean Consonants					
Plain:	ㅂ p	ㄷ t	ㄱ k	ㅈ c	ㅅ s	ㅎ h
Aspirated:	ㅍ ph	ㅌ th	ㅋ kh	ㅊ ch		
Voiced:	ㅸ ß				ㅿ z	ㅇ Ø/γ
Nasal:	ㅁ m	ㄴ n	ㆁ ng			
Liquid:		ㄹ l				

But, in addition to unit consonants, Sejong also provided for some initial consonant clusters:

sp-	st-	sk-	(ss-	hh-)
pt-	pth-	ps-	pc-	
pst-	psk-			

In the section "Explanation of the Combining of the Letters" of the *Hunmin chŏngŭm haerye*, these initial clusters are introduced as follows: "With the initial sounds, two or three letters may be used together and written side by side. For example, in the colloquial language [i.e., Korean], *sta* (따) 'land', *pcak* (딱) 'one of a pair', and *pskum* (뿜) 'crack, opening'."

These clusters are strikingly unlike anything found in the language today, but they were unquestionably real. In fact, these clusters are where most of the modern reinforced consonants come from. For example, what Sejong wrote as *sta* (싸) 'land' is modern *ttang* (땅), and *pcak* (짜) 'one of a pair' is *ccak* (짝). Here are some additional examples: *psol* (쌀) 'rice' > *ssal; psi* (삐) 'seed' > *ssi; ptut* (쁟) 'meaning' > *ttus; psuta* (쁘다) 'use' > *ssuta; pstay* (때) 'time' > *ttay; pskwul* (쁠) 'honey' > *kkwul*. Thus, Sejong's transcriptions reveal for us the etymological sources of most reinforced consonants.

Sometimes, we can still see the traces of these consonant clusters today. For example, the word *ssal* 'uncooked rice' may no longer have an initial *p*- when it appears as a separate word. But certain older compounds reveal the consonant that has been lost. For example, *cop-ssal* 'hulled millet' (< *co* 'millet' + *ssal* 'rice'), *ip-ssal*[12] 'non-glutinous, white rice', *meyp-ssal* 'non-glutinous rice', *chap-ssal* 'glutinous rice' (*cha*- 'sticky'), *hayp-ssal* 'new rice' (< *hay* 'year'). The trace of an earlier *p*- can also be found in such things as *pyep-ssi* 'seed rice' (< *pye* 'rice seedling' + *ssi* 'seed') and *ip-ttay* 'this time' (*i* 'this' + *ttay* 'time') and *cep-ttay* 'that time' (< *ce* 'that' + *ttay* 'time'). Such compounds must have been made up when there was still a *p*- at the beginning of 'rice'.

This difference between Middle Korean and today's language does not mean that reinforced consonants did not exist in the fifteenth century, however. It has been shown fairly conclusively that, at least some of the time, some examples of the clusters *sk*- (ㅺ-), *st*- (ㅼ-), and *sp*- (ㅽ-) were pronounced like modern *kk*-, *tt*-, and *pp*-. In addition, there were other cases where reinforcement was simply written then as it is today, as doubled consonants. (This was certainly true of *ss*-, of course.) What we see is that, at the time Sejong created his alphabet, these sounds were still in the process of emerging as distinct consonants.

Another way in which the language has changed is that Middle Korean had distinctively voiced consonants. For two such consonants, Sejong created the letters △ and ㅸ. These symbols have long since been abandoned because the sound values they once represented are no longer found in the language. But in Sejong's day, the triangle △ represented the sound *z*, and the symbol ㅸ[13] was used to transcribe the consonant *β*, a voiced labial fricative.

The consonant *β* was the first to be lost. Beginning around 1450, transcriptional changes such as *kulβal* 'writing' > *kulwal*, *teβi* 'heat' > *tewi*, and *sukoβol* 'the countryside' > *sukowol* (> modern *sikol*) begin to appear, showing that *β* was changing to *w*. Today, a *w* still remains in many words as the trace of an earlier *β*; for example: Middle Korean *saβi* (사비) 'shrimp' has become *saywu*, *nwuβe* (누버) 'lying down' is now *nwuwe*.

The consonant *z* lasted at least a century longer. Since, for example, what was written as *sozi* (스시) 'interval' in Sejong's day was spelled *soi* (소이) in the *Tusi ŏnhae*, the compiler of that text, Cho Wi, probably did not have the consonant *z* in his own speech. We can conclude from the increase in spelling mistakes of this kind that the sound must have been lost some time in the late fifteenth century, or at least in the early sixteenth. The consonant *z* has of course now completely disappeared from the Korean language. But here are some examples of words in which it once could be found: *mozom* (무움) 'heart' > *maum; azo* (아우) 'younger brother' > *awu; kozol* (구울) 'autumn' > *kaul; kyezul* (겨슬) 'winter' > *kyewul; noyzil* (더윌) 'tomorrow'; *mozol* (무울) 'village' > *maul.*

Today, the Hangŭl letter ㅇ has two functions. At the end of a syllable, it represents the nasal sound *-ng,* and at the beginning of the syllable, it is used as a zero consonant. In Sejong's alphabet, however, there were two separate letters for these functions. The symbol ㆁ, with a "tail" added at the top, was used to write /ng/, while a simple circle without the tail was used as the "zero" consonant. However, there is another complication associated with this letter, because the tailless circle was also used to represent a voiced consonant, the velar fricative γ.[14] We have mentioned that the Early Middle Korean word for 'scissors' was **kɔzgai.* In Late Middle Korean this word was written ᄀ애 and pronounced *kozγay.* Today the word is pronounced *kawi* in the standard language, where both *z* and *γ* have been lost, but in certain outlying dialects, where /s/ and /k/ are reflexes of *z* and *γ*, the word for 'scissors' is *kasay* or *kasikay.* Other Middle Korean words with this voiced velar consonant include, for example: *mwolγay* (몰애) 'sand', *pelγey* (벌에) 'bug', *melγwuy* (멀위) 'wild grapes', *silγey* (실에) 'shelf', and *talγay-* (달애-) 'to placate'.

The consonant written ㅈ was pronounced [ts]. Unlike the modern language, the Middle Korean consonant had a palatal pronunciation [tʃ] only when it was followed by *i* or *y.* Thus, 장 [tsang] 'cupboard' contrasted in pronunciation with 쟝 [tʃyang] 'soy sauce', and 저 [tsə] 'oneself' was different from 져 [tʃyə] 'chopsticks'. Similarly, the pronunciation of 초 [tsʰo] 'vinegar' contrasted with that of 쵸 [tʃʰyo] 'candle'.

The letter ㅅ was pronounced much the same as it is today. However, in Middle Korean there were many words in which the consonant was followed by a *y* that has since been lost. For example, the word for 'island' was written 셤 and was therefore pronounced differently from 섬 'stone stairstep'. The word for 'cow, ox' was 쇼 [ʃyo], while 소 [so] meant 'swamp'.

The consonants *t* and *th* occurred freely before *i* or *y.* After the Middle Korean period (around the seventeenth or eighteenth century), however, such occurrences of *t* affricated and changed to *c.* For example: *tina* (디나) 'elapsing' > *cina; tyokhena* (됴커나) 'is good,' > *cohkena* (좋거나); *tye* (뎌) 'that over there' > *ce.* The consonant *th* likewise changed to *ch* before *i* or *y: thiketun* (티거든) 'strike,' > *chiketun; thyentong* (텬동) 'thunder' > *chentong.*

The consonant *n* was also found at the beginning of a word before *i* or *y,* but in this case, the consonant was later lost completely in that position. Here are some words that illustrate this change: *ni* (니) 'tooth' > *i; nima* (니마) 'forehead' > *ima; niph* (닢) 'leaf' > *iph; nyelum* (녀름) 'summer' > *yelum.*

The consonants distinguished at the end of a word were *-k, -ng, -t, -n, -p, -m, -s,* and *-l.* In other words, the situation was much the same in the fifteenth century as it is today, except that *-s* still contrasted with *-t* in that position.[15] Early spellings reflected this difference: 'writing brush' was 붇 [put], and 'sickle' was 낟 [nat], but 'pond' was 못 [mos], and 'taste' was 맛 [mas].

However, the consonant -*c* was not distinguished from -*s*: for example, before a pause or another consonant, 곶 'flower' was pronounced [kos] and 낮 'day-time' was [nas]. The loss of this distinction represented a change that had taken place after the thirteenth century.

Vowels

There were seven vowels in fifteenth-century Korean. Each of these vowels was written with a separate symbol, as is illustrated below:

	Late Middle Korean Vowels	
ㅣ i [i]	ㅡ u [ɨ]	ㅜ wu [u]
	ㅓ e [ə]	ㅗ wo [o]
	ㅏ a [a]	· o [ʌ]

The Middle Korean letter " · " has long been the focus of attention among Korean linguists, because the vowel it represented no longer exists in the standard language. That long-lost vowel is generally believed to have been [ʌ], primarily because that is the sound the vowel has in Cheju dialect, where it is still distinguished. In the standard language, the vowel was lost in the following way: In the first syllable of a word it became /a/, and in all subsequent syllables it became /u/. For example: *mol* (ᄆᆞᆯ) 'horse' > *mal; kolochi-* (ᄀᆞᄅᆞ치-) 'teach' > *kaluchi-; mozom* (ᄆᆞᅀᆞᆷ) 'heart' > *maum; talo-* (다ᄅᆞ-) 'be different' > *talu-*.

There were two semivowels, *w* and *y*. Just as is true today, both served as on-glides: *ya* (ㅑ), *ye* (ㅕ), *yo* (ㅛ), *yu* (ㅠ); *wa* (ㅘ), *we* (ㅝ). But, in addition, -*y* also functioned as an off-glide. In other words, what were written as ·ㅣ, ㅐ, ㅔ, ㅚ, ㅟ, and ㅢ were actually pronounced as such in the fifteenth century, with -*y* pronounced separately, as an off-glide. Today -*y* is an off-glide only in *uy* (ㅢ), and, as was mentioned in chapter 3, that form is widely considered to be a spelling pronunciation. Here are the changes that have taken place:

Vocalic element	Late MK		Contemporary Korean
·ㅣ	[ʌy]	>	[ɛ]
ㅐ	[ay]	>	[ɛ]
ㅔ	[əy]	>	[e]
ㅚ	[oy]	>	[ö]
ㅟ	[uy]	>	[ü]
ㅢ	[ɨy]	>	[ɨ]/[-i]/[e]/[ɨy]

This change from complex vowel to monophthong is one of the greatest differences between the Middle Korean vowel system and that of today's Korean.

A perhaps even greater structural difference, however, is represented

by Middle Korean vowel harmony. What is called "vowel harmony" is a phonological system in which the first vowel in a word affects the quality of the
vowels in subsequent syllables. In the Middle Korean system, the vowels were
arrayed into two groups of opposing pairs, um (陰) and yang (陽) vowels,
plus one "neutral" vowel:

yang:	·	ㅗ	ㅏ
um:	―	ㅜ	ㅓ
neutral:	ㅣ		

In the stem of a Middle Korean word, yang vowels occurred with yang
vowels, and um vowels occurred with um vowels. For example, both vowels of
panol (바놀) 'needle' were yang vowels, as they had to be; the modern form of
'needle', panul, could not have been a word in Middle Korean, because the
um vowel /u/ (―) would not then have occurred with the yang vowel /a/
(ㅏ). Similarly, salom (사룸) 'person' had only yang vowels, while yelum (여
름) 'fruit' had only um vowels. The neutral vowel /i/ was the only vowel that
freely occurred with either group; for example: tali (다리) 'leg', meli (머리)
'head'.

We can see the vowel harmony system at work in the behavior of particles and verb endings. For example, when the accusative case particle, -ol/
ul, was attached to a noun with yang vowels, such as salom (사룸) 'person', it
had a yang vowel: salom ol (사루몰). But if the same particle was attached to a
word with um vowels, it, too, had an um vowel: yelum ul (여르믈).[16] The locative particle -ay/ey worked the same way: palol ay (바루래) 'into the sea', nyelum ey (녀르메) 'in the summer'.

Here are some examples of verb endings. Note how the first vowel
changed shape to harmonize with the vowels in the stem:

	-oni/uni	-omyen/umyen	-a/e
yang-vowel stem: kaph- 'repay'	kaphoni 가프니	kaphomyen 가프면	kapha 가파
yin-vowel stem: et- 'receive'	etuni 어드니	etumyen 어드면	ete 어더

Tones

In addition to consonants and vowels, Middle Korean also had tones.
One of the most remarkable aspects of Sejong's writing system was that it
provided a way to record pitches. This marking convention for tones is explained at the end of the main text of the Hunmin chŏngŭm: "One dot added
to the left [of the syllable] indicates the Going Tone (去聲). Two indicate
the Rising Tone (上聲). If there are none, then it is the Even Tone (平聲)."[17]

What was called the "Going Tone" in this passage was a high pitch, and
the "Even Tone" was a low pitch. The "Rising Tone" was long and rising and,
in many cases, demonstrably a combination of a low tone plus a high tone.

Here are some examples of Middle Korean words that contrasted by tone:[18]

low	:	high		high	:	rising
손		·손		·발		:발
son 'guest'		SON 'hand'		PAL 'foot'		paAL 'bamboo blind'
비		·비		·솔		:솔
pi 'stele'		PI 'rain'		SOL 'pine'		soOL 'brush'

low-low	:	low-high	:	high-
가지		가·지		·가지
kaci 'eggplant'		kaCI 'type'		KACI 'branch'
		서·리		·서리
		seLI 'frost'		SELI 'midst'

Not all of the tones recorded in Middle Korean texts were necessarily distinctive. After the first high pitch in a verb stem or a noun, pitches seem to have been governed instead by automatic rules of prosody. Martin (1992:61) calls the typical string of nondistinctive pitches "an automatic 'sing-song' tune of alternating accents." But, regardless whether they were distinctive or not, the "tones" were marked consistently. The conventions for adding dots to record tones were followed rigorously, and apparently with very few mistakes, for the better part of a century and a half. It was a remarkable accomplishment. Few societies, even in modern times, have managed such strict orthographic standards, especially regarding the use of diacritics.

8.3.2 Grammar

The basic syntactic order of Korean has remained stable throughout the history of the language. Yet, within this basic framework, the Korean language has changed greatly over the past five hundred years. A speaker of Korean today cannot read a Middle Korean text without special training, and even among specialists, the interpretation of some Middle Korean structures is still open to question. In spite of the clarity of Late Middle Korean writings, and in spite of the reverence in which the texts are held in modern Korea, the language of King Sejong still contains many mysteries.

To illustrate the kind of language found in Late Middle Korean texts, here are the first two verses, or cantos, of the *Songs of the Dragons Flying to Heaven*:

1: 東 六龍·이 ᄂᆞᄅᆞ·샤·일:마다天福·이시·니 古聖·이 同符·ᄒᆞ시·니
Haedong 6-dragon SP fly-HON work each Heaven-favor is-HON old-sage SP same-token do-HON

"Haedong's six dragons rise in flight,

their every deed, heaven's gift,
the signs the same as the Ancient Worthies."

2: 불.휘기.픈ᄂᆞᆷ.ᄀᆞᆫᄇᆞᄅᆞ.매아.니:뮐.씨 곶:됴.코여.름.하ᄂᆞ.니
root deep tree TP wind-by not move-since flower good-and fruit is-great
:ᄉᆡ.미기.픈.므.른.ᄀᄆ.래아.니그.츨.씨 :내.히이.러바.ᄅᆞ.래.가ᄂᆞ.니
spring SP deep water TP drought-in not stop-since stream SP become sea-to goes

"The tree with deep roots does not tremble in winds;
  its flowers are perfect, its fruit abundant.
  Waters rising from a deep source do not end in drought,
  forming a river they flow to the sea."[19]

Let us look briefly at a few salient characteristics of Middle Korean grammar:[20]

Particles

Some Middle Korean particles were noticeably different from those found in the language today. For one thing, the nominative case particle did not have the alternate shape *ka* (cf. 5.1.1.1) in the fifteenth century; the "subject particle" was at that time *i* after both consonants and vowels.[21] However, after a vowel, *i* was orthographically incorporated into the last syllable of the noun,[22] indicating that there the pronunciation of the particle was *-y* instead of the full vowel sound [i]; for example:

(1) *pwuthye* (부텨) 'Buddha' + *i* → *pwuthyey* (부톄)
    pye (벼) 'rice plant' + *i* → *pyey* (볘);
    enu (어느) 'which thing' + *i* → *enuy* (어늬)

If a noun in the nominative case already ended in *-y*, the case particle was not transcribed at all—for example, *pwulhwuy* (불휘) 'root' in the second canto of the *Songs of the Dragons,* shown above.[23]

In Middle Korean, two different particles, *oy/uy* and *-s*, were used to mark the genitive case.[24] The particle *oy/uy* was used with nonhonorific, animate nouns, as can be seen in (2). The particle *-s* followed honorific nouns, as in (3a), or inanimate nouns, as in (3b). It is noteworthy that in Middle Korean a separate particle was used to show honorification, something that is not done in the language today.

(2) Nonhonorific animates + *oy/uy:*

사ᄅᆞᆷ익 ᄠᆮ들,	죵익 서리예,	거부븨 터리와
salo.m *oy* ptu.t ul,	cyong *oy* seli yey,	kepwu.p *uy* theli wa
people's wishes	servants' midst	turtle's hair

(3) a. Honorific noun + *s*:
世尊ㅅ 神力으로, 　　　　　부텻 道理
SEYSWON*s* SINLYEK ulo 　　pwuthye*s* TWOLI
Shakyamuni's divine power 　Buddha's truth

   b. Inanimate noun +*s*:
나랏 말쏘미, 　　　　　　　풍늣 소리니
nala*s* mal.sso.mi 　　　　　phwungnyu*s* swoli 'ni
country's language 　　　　　elegance-of sound (elegant sound)

In addition, as can be seen in (4), these genitive particles were often used to mark the subject of an adnominalized predicate:

(4) a. 네의 어미 그려호미
ney *uy* emi kulye ho.m i
you SM mother
'you long for [your] mother'

   b. 나는 부텨ㅅ ᄉ랑ᄒ시논 앗이라
na non pwutye *s* solang hosinwon az ila
　　　Buddha SM loves
'I am the younger brother whom the Buddha loves.'

There were two particles, *ay/ey/yey* and *oy/uy*, used to mark the locative case. The shape of the particle *ay/ey/yey*, from which the modern locative particle *ey* derives, was determined phonologically. The choice between the first two forms depended upon vowel harmony: *ay* occurred after *yang* vowels, for example: *stah ay* (짜 해) 'on the ground'; and *ey* occurred after *um* vowels: *nwun ey* (누네) 'in the eye'. The third shape, *yey*, occurred after an *i* or *y: kwuy yey* (귀예) 'in the ear'.

The particle *oy/uy* is somewhat problematic. The primary use of the particle, as we have seen, was to mark the genitive case after nonhonorific animate nouns. But it was also sometimes used to mark a locative case after certain inanimate nouns. Here are some examples:

(5) a. 새벼리 나진 도ᄃ니
say-pye.l i na.c *oy* twotoni
'The Morning Star appeared *at* noon.'

   b. 바믹 비취니
pa.m *oy* pichwini
'shone *at* night'

   c. 山 미틔 軍馬 두시고
SAN mi.th *uy* KWUNMA twusikwo
'*At* the foot of the mountain he left his troops and horses, and . . .'

The question is, why was *oy/uy* used instead of *ay/ey/yey* to mark a locative in cases like these? Why were certain inanimate nouns used with *oy/uy* while other nouns were used with *ay/ey/yey*? Moreover, there were also nouns in Middle Korean that were used with either particle. And why would a genitive marker be used as a locative marker anyway? These are examples of philological problems that have yet to be unraveled completely.[25]

In Middle Korean, the locative marker used with animates was a genitive marker plus a noun phrase meaning 'at that place'. For an honorific noun, the genitive marker *s* was used; for example: *wang s kungey* (王ㅅ그에) 'to the king'. As can easily be seen, the resulting phrase literally meant 'to the king's place'. In nonhonorific usage, the genitive marker was *oy/uy*, and this is where modern *eykey* comes from: *oy/uy kungey* > *oykey* > *eykey*.

The comitative marker *wa/kwa* was much the same in Middle Korean as it is today, except that the form *wa* was used after *-l* as well as after vowels; for example, *mol wa* (물와) 'horses and'; *ipsiwul wa* (입시울와) 'lips and'; *kwasil wa mul wa* (果實와 믈와) 'fruit and water'. Examples of *kwa* following *-l* begin to appear in texts from the early sixteenth century, and by the latter part of that century, the pattern became widespread: *mal kwa* (말과) 'speech and'; *sol kwa* 솔과 'pine and'.[26]

One interesting characteristic of *wa/kwa* found in Middle Korean is that, in linking nouns, it could also appear after the last noun in the series. We see this usage in the example (given above) *kwasil wa mul wa* (果實와 믈와) 'fruit and water'. In addition, that last occurrence of *wa/kwa* could be followed by another case particle:

(6) a. 부텨와 즁과를 請ᄒᆞᅀᆞᄫᅠᆯ려
    pwuthye *wa* cywung *kwa* lul chyeng-hozoWolye
    'called upon Buddha *and* the priests . . .'

   b. 비와 이슬왜
    pi *wa* isul *way* (wa + i)
    'rain and dew SP.'

Middle Korean had three particles used to mark a vocative, *ha, a,* and *ye*. The particle *ha* was used to call a superior. The particle *a* was used to call an equal or someone lower in rank. Thus, the distinctions of the Middle Korean honorific system extended to the vocative case. For example, if Shakyamuni called out to the king (who was of course his inferior), he would use the vocative particle *a: Taywang a* (大王아) 'King!'. But, if the king's subjects called out to him, they would use *ha* instead: *Taywang ha* (大王하) 'O King!'

The vocative particle *ye* is used today only as an elegant, poetic form (cf. 5.1.1.7). In Middle Korean it seems to have been used with an exclamatory effect.

In some cases, the Middle Korean forms show where the modern particles came from. We have already mentioned the source of the locative marker *eykey*. Another clear etymology is that of the particle *puthe* (브터) 'from, starting with . . .', which was the infinitive form of the verb *puth-* 'append, stick'. The Middle Korean form of *kkaci* 'until' was *skocang* (ᄭᅥ장) 'up to the limit'; it was a combination of the genitive particle *s* plus the noun *kocang* (ᄀ장), which in today's language has become *kacang* 'most, very'. The modern particle *cocha* 'even, too, in addition' comes from the verb *cwoch-* (좇-) 'pursue'.

Inflection

Middle Korean inflection was divided broadly into verbs and adjectives (sometimes called "descriptive verbs") plus the copula. In principle, these categories are the same as those of the modern language. Verbs were characterized, for example, by compatibility with the prefinal, continuative ending *-no-* (-ᄂᆞ-), an ending not used with adjectives. Since this ending has become *-n(u)-/-nun-* in the language today, we can see that in this respect the grammatical distinction between verbs and adjectives has not changed. However, these two inflectional categories have not remained completely the same. For example, in Contemporary Korean, both verbs of existence, *iss-* 'be, exist, have' and *eps-* 'not exist, not have', take the same inflectional endings. In Middle Korean, however, even though *is-* 'be, exist, have' occurred with *-no-*, its negative equivalent, *eps-* 'not exist, not have', did not. Thus, curiously, *eps-* behaved at that time as an adjective, not a verb.

The Middle Korean copula was highly irregular. The stem behaved phonologically exactly like the nominative case marker *i*; that is, it was /i/ after a consonant, and /y/ after a vowel, except after *-i* or *-y*, where it was omitted (see the discussion of the Middle Korean particle *i*, above).

The inflection of the copula differed from that of verbs and adjectives. The most conspicuous difference was that endings beginning with /t/ after verbs and adjectives began with /l/ after the copula; thus *-ta* was *-la*, *-tota* was *-lota*, *-teni* was *-leni*, and so on. Verbal and adjectival forms were, for example, *cwukta* (죽다) 'die', *hota* (ᄒᆞ다) 'do', and *huyta* (희다) 'be white', while the premodern form of the copula was *ila* (이라) 'is'. It is significant that the modern citation form of the copula, *ita*, is not found in texts earlier than the late nineteenth century. There were also various other phonological and inflectional peculiarities associated with the copula.

Inflectional Endings

The *prefinal inflectional endings* of Middle Korean indicated honorification, tense, aspect, or volition. Some were also emotives.

The prefinal ending used to show *volition* was *-wo/wu-* (-오/우-). This ending, which has not existed since the Middle Korean period, was used mainly with the first person and is believed to have functioned to show the speaker's intention.[27] The rules for the use of this morpheme were extremely complex; it occurred in a chameleonlike variety of shapes. After a stem ending in a consonant, the form of the morpheme was *-wo-* or *-wu-*, depending upon the rules of vowel harmony; after a vowel, there were several different pronunciations: the vowels *o* (˙) and *u* (ㅡ) dropped before this morpheme; *i* or *y* plus *-wo/wu-* became *-ywo/ywu-* (ㅡㅛ/ㅠㅡ); and after *a, e, wo,* or *wu,* the morpheme itself was usually deleted (but could sometimes be retained for clarity). When combined with the retrospective *-te-*, the morpheme became *-ta-*; put together with the honorific *-si-*, it became *-sya-;* the copula plus the volitive became *ilwo-* (이로ㅡ). Some examples of the volitive are given in (7), below:

(7) a. 내 이제 分明히 너ᄃ려 닐오리라
   Nay icey PWUNMYENG-hi ne tolye nil.*wo*lila
   'I will tell you clearly now.'

   b. 내 어저씌 다숫 가짓 ᄭ \ ᄆ ᆯ ᄭ\우니
   Nay ece.skuy tasos kacis skwu.m ul skwu*wu*ni
   'Last night I dreamed five dreams.'

   c. 五百 弟子ㅣ 각각 第一이로라 일ᄃ\ ᄂ 니
   WOPOYK TYEYCO i KAK.KAK TYEY-IL il*wo*la il.khot.noni
   'The five hundred disciples each said he was the best.'

   d. 가샴 겨샤매 오늘 다 ᄅ리잇가
   Kasyam kyes*ya*.m ay wonol taloli.ngiska.
   'Could staying or going make a difference today?'

The volitive morpheme had apparently already begun to fall into disuse in the fifteenth century. Then, for a time, it was used only with the nominalizer *-m* and the adverbial ending *-toy*. Finally, in the sixteenth century it disappeared completely.

   Three prefinal endings were used in the Middle Korean honorific system: *-si-* for subject honorification; *-sop-* for object exaltation; and *-ngi-*, the marker for polite style. The morpheme *-si-* was used in Middle Korean the same way it is today (cf. 7.3), except that when combined with the volitive morpheme *-wo/wu-* (see above) or the adverbial ending *-a*, its phonological shape was *-sya-*.[28] The morpheme *-sop-* had a number of different shapes. Its initial consonant was transcribed as *s* (ㅅ) after *k, p, s,* or *h*; as *z* (ㅿ) after *n, l, m,* or a vowel; as *c* (ㅈ) after *t, c,* or *ch*. Its final consonant was *p* (ㅂ) before a consonant, *β* (ㅸ) before a vowel.[29] The polite marker *-ngi-* only attached to a vowel. If the stem to which it attached ended in a consonant, a morpheme ending in a vowel would be inserted between the stem and *-ngi-*. Here are some examples of these three morphemes:

(8) *-si-*:

a. 안즈샤 오시 즈ㅁ 기우르시고 니르샤디
Ancosya wo.s i comokoy wulu*si*kwo nilus*ya*toy
'sat down and, letting his clothes settle, said in tears (as follows: . . .)'

b. 公이 닐그시논 거슨 엇던 마리잇고
KWONG oy nilku*si*nwon ke.s un esten ma.l i.ngiskwo
'What words are you reading, my Lord?'

(9) *-sop-*:

a. 仁義之兵을 遼在ㅣ 깃스텅니
ZINUY CI PYENG ul LYWOCAY i kis.so*ßo*ni
'Far and wide they rejoiced at [the deeds of] the Righteous Army.'

b. 내 如來 니르샨 經에 疑心을 아니 ㅎ습노니
Nay ZYELAY nilosyan KYENG ey UYSIM ol ani hozo*p*nwoni
'I do not doubt the scriptures spoken by the Enlightened One.'

c. 如來ㅅ일후ㅁ믈 듣즈텅면
ZYELAI s ilhwu.m ul tutc*oßo*myen
'if one hears the name of the Enlightened One, . . .'

d. 이 諸菩薩이 釋迦牟尼佛ㅅ 니르시논 音聲 듣즈오시고
I CEY-PWOSAL i SEK.KAMWUNI-PWUL s nilosinwon UMSENG tutc*o-wo*sikwo
'These assembled Boddhisatvas listened to the words spoken by Shakyamuni, and . . .'

(10) *-ngi-*:

a. 甚히 크이다 世尊하
SIM-hi khu.*ngi*ta SEYCWON ha
'It is extremely great, o Shakyamuni.'

b. 이 이리 엇데잇고
I i.l i estyey.*ngi*skwo
'How will this matter be?'

As was pointed out in chapter 7, the object exaltation morpheme *-sop-* was as productive and widely used in Middle Korean as *-si-* was. The two morphemes worked in tandem. Just as *-si-* functioned to elevate the subject of the sentence, *-sop-* functioned to express respect for the person affected by the action of the subject. Put another way, *-sop-* was a humbling form for the subject. For example, in (9c) *-sop-* expresses humility for the one hearing the name of the Enlightened One, and thus respect for the Enlightened One himself. In (9d) *-sop-* functions to show the humility of the Boddhisatvas and the respect they have for Shakyamuni.

The pre-final endings used for tense and aspect were the present (or continuative) *-no-*; the past (or perfective) *-ke-*, *-a/e-*[30]; the retrospective (imperfective) *-te-*; and the future (or conjectural) *-li-*. It is probably more accurate to consider these prefinal endings markers of aspect rather than tense. That is, *-no-* indicated that the action of the verb was continuing at the present time; *-ke-*, *-a/e-* showed that the action was completed in the past; *-te-* showed that the speaker was recalling an action that had taken place in the past but had not been completed; and *-li-* indicated a conjecture about something that had not yet taken place.

The emotive pre-final endings were *-two-* (-도-) and *-twos-* (-돗-). Here are examples:

(11)a. 이삭 모ᅀᆞ매 훤히 즐겁도다
    I za mozo.m ay hwen-hi culkep*two*ta
    'This very thing is a great delight to my heart.'

  b. 보니ᄂᆞᆷ의짓담 둘 다 믈어디돗더라
    Poni no.m oy ci[p] s tam tol ta mul.eti*twos*.tela
    'I see the walls of his house have all fallen down!'

The final endings of Middle Korean were classified into roughly the same categories of mood as those recognized for Contemporary Korean. The basic declarative ending was *-ta*, which, after the copula and certain prefinal endings, was realized as *-la*.

The interrogatives of Middle Korean were significantly different from those of today's language. First of all, instead of one, there were two basic question endings, *-kwo* and *-ka*. The ending *-kwo* (−고) was used only for question-word questions ('who', 'what', 'how', 'which', 'how many', etc.) and was never used with a yes-or-no question. The ending *-ka* was used mainly for yes-or-no questions (or choice questions), but, in rare cases, it was also used with question-word questions. (In today's language, *-ka* has completely displaced *-kwo* in all uses; it is thought that the Late Middle Korean situation was the beginning of this process.) Here are examples:

(12) question-word questions with *-kwo*:

  a. 이 엇던 光明고
    I esten KWANGMYENG '*kwo*
    'What kind of light is this?'

  b. 兩漢故事애 엇더 ᄒᆞ니잇고
    LYANG-HAN KWOSO ay este honi.ngis.*kwo*
    'How were [they], as far as the ancient matters of the Two Han are concerned?'

(13) yes-or-no questions with *-ka*:

a. 가샴 겨샤매 오늘 다ᄅ리잇<u>가</u>
   Kasyam kyesya.m ay wonol taloli.ngis*ka*
   'Could staying or going make a difference today?'

b. 이ᄂ 賞가 罰아
   I non SYANG *ka* PEL γ*a*
   'Is this a reward or a punishment?'

c. 이 두 사ᄅ미 眞實로 네 항것가
   I twu salo.m i CINSIL lo ney hangkes *ka*
   'Are these two people really your masters?'

These two interrogative endings also had other phonological shapes. For example, *-ka* was realized as *-γa* after /l/, as in (13b), above. Still greater phonological changes can be seen in the *hola* speech style (ᄒ라체, equivalent to plain style in Contemporary Korean). In that style, the prefinal endings *-ni-* and *-li-* combined with *-ka* to give *-nye* and *-lye*, and with *-kwo* to give *-nywo* and *-lywo*.

(14) a. 功德이 하녀 몯하녀
   KWONGTEK i ha*nye* mwot ha*nye*
   'Was his virtue great or not great?'

b. 이시려 업스려
   Isi*lye* epsu*lye*
   'Was there or was there not?'

(15) a. 어듸ᅀᅡ 시름 업슨디 잇<u>ᄂ뇨</u>
   Etuy za silum epsun toy isno*nywo*
   'Is there a place without trouble?'

b. 어드리 가료
   Etuli ka*lywo*
   'Where are you going?'

There were also various other forms and endings used in Middle Korean interrogatives.

The imperative endings *-sywosye* (–쇼셔), *-a.ssye* (–아쎠), and *-la* (–라) represented three different speech-style levels. The endings *-sywosye* and *-a.ssye* were used by subordinates when requesting action from a superior, and *-la* was the plain style imperative ending.

(16) a. 님금하 아ᄅ<u>쇼셔</u>
   Nimkum ha alo*sywosye*
   'Know this, O King.'

b. 내 보아져 ᄒᆞᄂᆞ다솔ᄫᅡ쎠
Nay pwoacye honota solßassye
'Please tell him I'd like to see him.'

c. 넷ᄠᅳ들 고티라
Neys ptu.t ul kothila
'Correct your thinking.'

The fifteenth-century exclamatory ending *-twota* (- 도 다) was com-
posed of the emotive *-two-* plus the declarative ending *-ta*. The present-day
ending *-kwuna* is derived from *-kwona* (- 고 나), an ending first found in
Ch'oe Sejin's midsixteenth century work, "Interpreter Pak."
The basic propositive ending was *-cye*, which, at the end of the Middle
Korean period, changed to *-cya* on its way to becoming the present-day propositive ending *-ca*. The polite ending used as a propositive in Middle
Korean was *-sa.ngita* (사이다), which is believed to be the source of the
present-day semiformal ending *-psita*.

(17)a. 우리 그저 뎨 가 자고 가져
Wuli kuce tyey ka cakwo ka*cye*
'Let's just go there and sleep and then go.'

b. 淨土애 ᄒᆞᆫ디 가 나사이다
CYENGTHWO ay hontoy ka na*sa.ngita*
'I would like to go to the Pure Land and be reborn there together [with
her].'

The promissory mood was expressed by *-ma*, which was always used together with the volitive *-wo/wu-*.

(18)내 너ᄃᆞ려 ᄀᆞᄅᆞ쵸마
Nay ne tulye kolochywo*ma*
'I will teach you.'

The conjunctive endings used in Middle Korean were extremely numerous. Here are some of them: *-kwo, -mye, -a/e, -ni, -may, -nol/nul, -lssoy, -kwan-
toy, -myen, -tun/ton, -ntay, -na, -wotoy/wutoy, -la, -lye, -kwocye, -acye, -kwatye, -kuyskwo,
-tolwok, -lsolwok, -tiwos, -kuy/koy, -key, -ti, -tol, -ntwong, -tulan, -tißi*. As can be
seen, many of these endings are still used today. But many are not.
The endings *-ni, -may, -kenol/kenul, -lssoy,* and *-kwantoy* are all used to indicate various types of causes. The ending *-may*, which in today's language is
a rather literary usage, is composed of the nominalizing ending *-om* plus the
case particle *ay*. The ending *-lssoy*, which was very commonly used in Middle
Korean, combines the adnominal ending *-ol/ul*, the nominal *so* 'thing; the
fact that', and the case particle *i*.

(19)브룸매 아니 뮐씬곳 됴코 여름 하ᄂ니

Polo.m ay ani mwilssoy koc tywokhwo yelum hanoni

'Since it does not move in the wind,'

The ending *-la* indicates the purpose of doing something. In today's language it has become *-le*.

(20)a. 나라해 빌머그라 오시니 다 몰라보ᅀᆞᆸ더니

Nala.h ay pilmeku*la* wosini ta mwolla pwozopteni

'He came [back] to his country to beg and no one recognized him.'

b. 道理 빅호라 나아가샤

TWOLI poyhwo*la* naa kasya

'He went out to learn the way.'

In Contemporary Korean, the ending used to form long negations is *-ci*. In Middle Korean on the other hand, there were at least four different endings used with one of the following negatives: *-ti, -tol, -ntwong, -tulan*. The most important and widely used of these by far was of course *-ti*, which is the ancestral form of today's *-ci*. The other four endings were used far less, *-ntwong* and *-tulan* being used only with *mwolo-* 'not know' or *mwot ho-* 'not be able to do'.

(21)a. 아디 몯ᄒ며

a*ti* mwot homye

'could not know, and . . .'

b. 아ᄆᆞ란 헌딘 동 몰래라

amolan hentuy*ntong* mwollayla

'did not know there was any sore whatsoever'

The ending *-tiβi* was used somewhat differently; it was used to affirm something by contrasting it with what was negated.

(22)부텨는 本來 變化ㅣ 다빈 사ᄅᆞ미 몯홀 이리라

Pwuthye nun PWONLAI PYENHWA i '*tiβi*

'The Buddha is in essence a mutation; it is not a work a person can do.'

The most commonly used nominalizing ending in Middle Korean was *-om/um*. The nominalizer *-ki* can also be found in some of the early texts, but such examples of its use are extremely rare.

The Middle Korean endings *-on/un* and *-ol/ul* were adnominal markers, just as they are today. But in Middle Korean they also served as nominalizers. For example, *el.wun* (얼운) 'adult' was derived from the verb *el-* 'marry' plus *-on/un*.

8.4 Modern Korean

As we have said, "Modern Korean" is really Pre-Contemporary Korean. It began immediately after the Imjin Wars, at the beginning of the seventeenth
century, when Korean writing suddenly and dramatically changed, and
lasted until the end of the ninteenth century. Books from that time are strikingly different from those of Middle Korean. For example, the dots used in
Middle Korean texts to mark tones are gone; the letter used to write z ($\triangle$)
had disappeared without a trace; the writing of consonant clusters had become inconsistent and confused, and many other spellings were confused as
well; grammatical structure and patterns are different. The differences are
so dramatic, in fact, scholars once thought that the wars with the Japanese
had fundamentally changed the way Koreans talked. Even today, one of the
popular myths still sometimes heard in Korea is that Hideyoshi's invasions
were so traumatic they caused Koreans to lose the ability to pronounce z's
and to distinguish tones.

The actual changes in the language, however, were not so sudden. The
long and exhausting years of war with the Japanese had been immensely de-
structive, not only of Korean lives and property, but also of Korean society
and institutions. During those seven years of war, writing conventions had
been thrown into chaos. The traditions of the Middle Korean period could
not be restored, and when Koreans began to write books again, the Hangŭl
that they wrote down reflected changes that had long since taken place in
the spoken language. Something else had changed, too. Unlike the printed
texts of the Middle Korean period, when there had been remarkable standardization of the orthography, writing in the three hundred years of the
Modern Korean period was marked by variation and inconsistency. Standardization of the kind seen in Middle Korean would have to wait until the
twentieth century.

The works that have been preserved from the Modern Korean period
are extensive and varied. What was particularly new about this Hangŭl writing was that not only did it have broader appeal beyond the *yangban* class,
but much of it was authored by people of lower social rank, a fact that may
help explain why there was more variation in spelling and grammar.
Though sometimes far from elegant, the style was freer than that of Middle
Korean and thus probably reflected more closely how people actually spoke.

When the wars with the Japanese ended, among the first works published were medical treatises. These were followed by reprintings of books
for which most copies had been destroyed in the wars. These reissued works
include second editions of such Middle Korean texts as *Songs of the Dragons
Flying to Heaven, Hunmong chahoe,* and *Vernacular Interpretations of Du [Fu]'s
Poems.* Didactic Neo-Confucian works were also reedited and made available
in new printings. In the seventeenth century, language textbooks of various
kinds came out in new editions, including *Interpreter Pak* and *The Old Cathayan,* as well as new lexical references for Chinese. One of the most inter-

esting of the foreign language works from this period was a Japanese-language textbook, the *Ch'ŏphae sinŏ*, ('A concise explanation of new expressions'), which was published in 1676 but had probably been written about fifty years before that. The author, Kang Usŏng, had been taken captive during the Imjin Wars and had subsequently spent ten years in Japan. When Kang returned to Korea, he wrote a textbook of colloquial, spoken Japanese that included a translation and line-by-line transliteration into Hangŭl. The result was a unique work that has been studied intensively both in Korea and in Japan. The eighteenth and nineteenth centuries saw a great number of new Korean translations of Chinese works, as well as reissues of older works and references of various kinds.

The most significant developments during the Modern Korean period were literary, however. For one thing, the seventeenth century marked the emergence of the Korean novel, and a very large number of popular novels were published in the Modern Korean period. The very first vernacular novel ever written in Korea is said to be Hŏ Kyun's *The Tale of Hong Kiltong*, which dates from around the second decade of the seventeenth century.[31] *The Tale of Hong Kiltong* was a bitter criticism of the unfairnesses of traditional society, and, in various forms, the story of Hong Kiltong, the romantic fighter for justice, is still popular today. Some of the other better-known Modern Korean novels include *The Tale of Hŭngbu*, *The Tale of Sim Ch'ŏng*, *A Record of the Imjin Wars (Imjin nok)*, *Dream of the Jade Chamber (Ongnu mong)*, and, the most famous and popular novel of all, *The Story of Ch'unhyang*, a morality tale of love and virtue transcending social class. Most editions of these and other Modern Korean works of fiction that have come down to us date from the nineteenth century.

Besides fiction, the Modern Korean period saw a flowering of new types of *sijo* poetry, diaries, travel journals, and personal correspondence in Hangŭl. As was the case with fiction, many of these works were written by people of social classes lower than the *yangban*; some were also written by women.

8.4.1 Phonology

Consonants

By the early seventeenth century, very few initial consonant clusters were left in the language. The *s*-clusters had been the first to go. This process had been well underway during the Middle Korean period, and writing *s*- in front of a consonant had become a conventional way to indicate that the pronunciation was reinforced. This convention continued throughout the Modern Korean period, when ㅽ-, ㅼ-, and ㅺ- were the usual ways in which *pp*-, *tt*-, and *kk*- were written. But that was not all. In texts from the beginning of the seventeenth century on, the clusters *psk*-, *sk*-, and *pk*- were all confused with each other, showing that the people who had written them down had

302   *History*

not been able to distinguish the pronunciations. Clearly, consonant clusters were being reduced to reinforced consonants, and by the middle of the seventeenth century, the process was almost certainly complete.

In addition, reinforced pronunciations were spreading more generally throughout the vocabulary. For example, Middle Korean *kwoskwoli* (곳고리) 'oriole' appears in Modern Korean texts in a variety of forms, such as 꾀고리, 쇠ㅅ고리, 쐬고리, showing that the actual pronunciation was already what it is today, *kkoykkoli* (꾀꼬리). The initial consonants of words such as *kkaykkus-ha-* 'be clean', *ttesttes-ha-* 'be honorable', and *ttattus-ha-* 'be warm' also developed their reinforcement in the eighteenth century. Reinforcement in a number of words is believed to have begun as an emphatic pronunciation.[32]

Modern Korean also had an unusual reinforced consonant that does not exist today. In Middle Korean, the word *hye-* 'pull, draw' had an alternate and probably emphatic pronunciation *hhye-*; in Modern Korean times, that same word was written 혀-, showing that the reinforcement was certainly genuine and still there. But the pronunciation was extremely rare; that one word was apparently the only place it ever occurred. Before the Modern Korean period ended, the pronunciation of the word changed to *khye-* and thus the reinforced *h* disappeared.

One of the most important changes in the Korean consonants was palatalization. That is, before *i* or *y*, the consonants *t*, *th*, and *tt* changed to *c*, *ch*, and *cc*; for example: *tisay* 'tile' > *cisay*, *thi-* 'strike' > *chi-*, (*tih->*) *ttih-* 'pound' > *ccih-*. In other words, not only were the consonants pronounced with palatal articulation, but they were also affricated. In Seoul and the central dialects, these changes took place around the seventeenth or eighteenth century.[33]

Related to palatalization is the loss of initial *n-* before *i* or *y*; for example: *ni* 'tooth' > *i*, *nimkum* 'king' > *imkum*, *nilu-* 'reach, attain' > *ilu-*. This change took place a little later than the palatalization of *t*, *th*, and *tt*; the forms without an initial *n-* are first found in texts from the latter half of the eighteenth century.

In Middle Korean, as was explained in 8.3.1, above, the consonants *-s* and *-t* contrasted in final position; for example, *nat* 'sickle', but *mas* 'taste'. But in the latter half of the sixteenth century, the contrast broke down, and in writings from the seventeenth century, the two consonants were badly confused. For example, 'taste' was then written both as *mat* and *mas*; the stem of the verb 'ask' appeared variously as *mut-* and *mus-* (묻고, 뭇디). These orthographic "mistakes" make clear that *-s* and *-t* were no longer distinct.

Spelling mistakes also show other changes in pronunciation. Among other things, *-ll-* and *-ln-* were no longer distinguished in the Modern Korean period; for example, the instrumental *-lo* was occasionally written as *-no* after *l*: for example, *cinsil no* (진실노) 'really'. Such mistakes were never made in the earlier, Middle Korean texts.

Vowels

The vowel system of late eighteenth-century Korean was almost the same as that of today's standard language. Virtually all of the changes in the vowels of Middle Korean had taken place by that time. For one thing, the Middle Korean vowel /o/ (·) had been lost. The general rule was that first-syllable occurrences of /o/ became /a/; occurrences of the vowel in non-initial syllables became /u/.

Monophthongization occurred in the late eighteenth century. Through this process, the complex vocalic element [ay] (written ㅐ) became pronounced as the unit vowel [ɛ]; [əy] (written ㅔ) became [e].[34]

The vowel system at the beginning of the nineteenth century was as follows:

The Nineteenth-Century Korean Vowel System

ㅣ i [i]	ㅡ u [ɨ]	ㅜ wu [u]
ㅔ ey [e]	ㅓ e [ə]	ㅗ o [o]
ㅐ ay [ɛ]	ㅏ a [a]	

Another systematic change that took place in the Modern Korean period was the rounding of the vowel /u/ (ㅡ) after a labial consonant, *m-, p-, ph-*, or *pp-*. After this change, the pronunciation of the word *mul* (믈) 'water', for example, was no longer distinct from *mwul* (물) 'group'. From the eighteenth century on, words such as *pul* 'fire', *spul* 'horn', and *phul* 'grass' (블, 쁠, 플) began to be written *pwul, spwul,* and *phwul* (불, 뿔, 풀). This process of rounding was probably complete by the end of the seventeenth century.

There were a number of other phonological changes as well. For example, around the beginning of the nineteenth century, the vowel *u* changed to *i* when it occurred after *s-, c-,* or *ch-*. Evidence of this change can be found in many words; such as *tasulinun* 'controlling' > *tasilinun, culkewun* 'pleasurable' > *cilkewun, ancutoy* 'though sitting' > *ancitoy*.

8.4.2 Grammar

The written language of the seventeenth century was sharply different from that seen in the Middle Korean books of only a decade or two earlier. For the most part, these transcriptional differences reflected changes that had been taking place over the past century but that had been masked by orthographic and stylistic standards. However, from the beginning of Modern Korean down to the nineteenth century, the written language was much less mistake-free and thus reflected more immediately the structural changes occurring in the language.

The most salient characteristic of Modern Korean grammar has been described as simplification. Writing during this period shows a clear tendency toward simpler structure. Earlier distinctions were lost. Here are just a few examples: The volitive *-wo/wu-*, a morpheme with subtly varied semantic distinctions, had fallen into complete disuse. The higher native numerals *won* (온) 'hundred' and *cumun* (즈믄) 'thousand' stopped being used as such, leaving only the Sino-Korean numbers *payk* 'hundred' and *chen* 'thousand'. The ordinal number *ches* 'first' was regularized and began to be used with the suffix *-cay* like the other ordinals. Causative derivations were simplified. Some of these causative constructions were no longer derived and, instead, were frozen as separate words. The causative of *ho-* (ᄒᆞ-) 'do', which in the fifteenth century had been *hoy-* (ᄒᆡ-), changed to *hoi-* (ᄒᆡ이-) in the sixteenth century, then was lost in Modern Korean and replaced by *siki-*. The inflectional endings used to derive adjectives from nouns had complex alternations in Middle Korean: *-loβ/loβoy-, -toβ/toβoy-*. In Modern Korean, however, these were first simplified to *-low-* and *-toy-*, and then, in the eighteenth century, the form *-sulew-* made its appearance. (For example, *elun-sulewun* 'grownuplike'.) The ending used to derive adjectives from verbs, *-βo/βu-*, completely stopped being productive (its trace is only found today frozen as parts of words such as *yeyppu-* 'pretty', *kippu-* 'happy', and *sulphu-* 'sad'). In details such as these, we can see the kinds of changes that were going on throughout the grammar of the language.

Particles

The particle *ka* was unmistakably used to mark a subject in the seventeenth century. It shows up prominently in the colloquial language of texts such as the idiosyncratic Japanese-language textbook *Ch'ŏphae sinŏ: poy ka wol ke.s ini* 'since the boats will be coming,'. But, curiously, at that time it seems to have only been used after nouns that ended in *-y*. From there, its use in the spoken language is believed to have spread gradually to nouns ending in vowels, but that fact cannot be verified in the written records. Interestingly enough, the particle *ka* was not used in written Korean during the eighteenth and nineteenth centuries, and its alternation with the particle *i* in the spoken language was first clearly noted by Western missionaries at the end of the nineteenth century.

The only *genitive* case marker used in Modern Korean was *uy*. By this time the Middle Korean genitive case marker *-s* was no longer productive; it continued to be written as a "medial *s*" (사이ㅅ) in various compound words (e.g., *hyes-kalay* 'rafter'), where it was generally pronounced as reinforcement of a following consonant. But it could no longer be used freely to mark genitives as it had been in Middle Korean.

The *comitative* case marker developed its present-day alternation, *wa* after vowels and *kwa* after consonants. In the sixteenth century, *kwa* had also been used after *-y*, but that usage disappeared soon after the seventeenth century. The honorific vocative, *ha*, was no longer used at all in Modern Korean.

The distinction between the two *locative* markers for animates, plain *uykey* and honorific *skey*, was lost in Modern Korean. However, around the same time, *skey* was combined with the suffix *-sye* to form a new honorific usage, the honorific subject marker *kkeyse*.

The Middle Korean *comparative* marker *twukwo* began to be replaced by *potaka* (a form derived from the verb *po-* 'see') in the eighteenth century. This latter form is still used in some nonstandard dialects, but in Seoul it has been shortened to *pota*.

Inflection

Many of the irregular verb and adjective stems had changed by the beginning of the Modern Korean period. The most obvious of these were stems with *-β-* or *-z-*. When the consonants *β* and *z* were lost, the alternations of these irregular stems naturally shifted; for example, *teβ-/tep- (teβun, tepkey)* 'hot' was now *tew-/tep- (tewun, tepkey)*, and *ciz-/cis- (cizul, cisnon)* 'make' was *ci-/cis- (ciul, ciskey)*. Now *s* and *p* no longer alternated with consonants. Phonological changes precipitated a number of other stem changes as well.

Another important stem change was that of the verb of existence ('is, exist, have'), which in Middle Korean had a variety of shapes: *isi-, is-, si-*. By the time of Modern Korean the stem only appeared as *is-*.

Inflectional endings also took on a different appearance. For one thing, the rules of vowel harmony weakened. Almost the only vowel harmony alternation that remained in the Modern Korean period was that of the ending *-a/e* (e.g., *kopa* 'bending', *kwupe* 'bending') — essentially the same as the system today.

Prefinal endings changed. First, as we have said, the volitive *-wo/wu-* disappeared. Another noteworthy change was that *-sop-*, the marker of object exaltation, metamorphosed into an integral part of the deferential ending used in the formal speech style. The Middle Korean inflectional ending *-zopnongita* (-ᅀᅟᆸᄂᆞᇰ잇다), which combined *-sop-* with the polite marker *-ngi-*, was written as *-opnoita* (-ᆸᄂᆞ잇다) in Modern Korean and used as a deferential speech style. This form is the ending out of which present-day *-(u)pnita* developed.

The *tense* and *aspect* system familiar to Koreans today began to emerge around this time. The Modern Korean marker of past tense was *-as/es-*, a form that had already been used to a much lesser extent in Middle Korean; it was a combination of *-a/e* and the verb of existence *is-*. The present-day prefinal ending *-keyss-* must also have developed in Modern Korean times even though it is not attested. It is generally assumed to be a melding of the adverbial ending *-key* with the verb of existence *-is*. In the sixteenth century, the Middle Korean continuative marker *-no-* (-ᄂᆞ-) combined with the declarative ending *-ta* as *-nta* after a vowel; in the seventeenth century, the form appeared as *-nunta* after a consonant.

In the *final endings*, the Middle Korean imperative *-assye* disappeared and was replaced by *-so*. The Modern Korean propositive *-upsay* combined the deferential *-up-* with *-say*, a contraction of Middle Korean *sai(ta)*.

Vocabulary

One of the most noticeable changes that took place in the Modern Korean period was the progressive loss of purely Korean vocabulary. For example, the Middle Korean words *mwoy* 'mountain', *kolom* 'river', *azom* 'relatives', and *wolay* 'door' were replaced by Sino-Korean *san, kang, chinchek*, and *mun*. Middle Korean verb and adjective forms like *woy-* 'drill (a hole)', *woypho-* 'engrave', and *hyek-* 'small' simply disappeared.

At the same time, the Middle Korean period brought in new Western as well as Chinese vocabulary. Before the seventeenth century, Koreans had had little contact with the outside world, but gradually, for the most part through China, material objects began to arrive from the West. We have already mentioned in chapter 4 (4.4.2) some of the new vocabulary that came with these things. Tobacco, *tampay,* arrived from Japan during this period.

A considerable amount of Sino-Korean vocabulary that existed in Modern Korean has since either disappeared or is now used with different meanings. In works of fiction from that time, we find that *inceng* (人情), for example, which now means (among other things) 'compassion', was used in the sense of 'bribe'. *Pangsong* (放送) 'broadcast' meant 'liberation', and *palmyeng* (發明) 'discovery' then meant 'excuse'. Moreover, as we have said in 4.1.2, there were also many words that were not, strictly speaking, Sino-Korean at all, but were rather borrowed directly from Chinese; for example, *mangken* 'a kind of horsehair headband' (網巾), *pitan* 'silk', *tahong* 'crimson', *mumyeng* 'cotton cloth'.

The meanings of native vocabulary also changed. In Middle Korean, *eyespu-* meant 'pitiful', but in Modern Korean it came to mean 'beautiful' (today's *yeyppu-*). At the same time, *eli-,* which had meant 'foolish', took on the meaning of 'young'. *Solang ho-* had meant both 'think' and 'love' in Middle Korean, but in Modern Korean it was used only in the meaning of 'love'.

References

An Pyŏnghŭi 1992; An Pyŏnghŭi and Yi Kwangho 1990; Hŏ Ung 1975; Ledyard 1966; Lee Ki-baik (Yi Kibaek) 1984; Lee Sang Oak (Yi Sangŏk) 1978; Martin 1992, 1996; Nam P'unghyŏn 1996; Ramsey 1978, 1991, 1994, 1996; Yi Iksŏp (Lee Iksop) 1986; Yi Kimun (Lee Ki-Moon) 1971, 1972a, 1972b, 1991a.

9

The Modern Dialects

Koreans speak a single, unified language. They have been held together by a central government for a very long period of time. The land that they live in is small. And yet, the Korean language, with its long history, possesses dialects of surprisingly great diversity. The speech in some areas of the country is so divergent, in fact, it is virtually incomprehensible to Koreans from other parts of the country. Were it not for the overarching and unifying web provided by the standard language, adequate communication between these various geographical regions would be impossible. In this chapter, we will look at how the dialects[1] of Korean differ from the standard language and into what dialect areas Korea is divided. We will also examine the process through which the standard language of Korean was established from the speech of a particular region.

9.1 Seoul Speech and the Standard Language

In modern South Korea, the language spoken in the city of Seoul is considered the standard. Seoul speech was first officially recognized as the standard language when the document "*Ŏnmun* Orthography for Use in Primary Schools" (普通學校用 諺文綴字法) was promulgated in 1912. The relevant passage is given in (1a), below. Seoul as the standard was established still more precisely in the "Unification Proposal for Hangŭl Spelling" (한글 맞춤법 통일안) of 1933, as shown in (1b). Then, in 1988, the "Rules of the Standard Language" (표준어 규정) changed somewhat the phrasing of the definition, as can be seen in (1c).

(1) a. "The language of Kyŏngsŏng [today's Seoul] shall be the standard." (1912)[2]
   b. "The standard language shall by and large be the speech used in middle class society in present-day Seoul." (1933)[3]
   c. "The standard language shall in principle be defined as the speech widely used by people with education in present-day Seoul." (1988)[4]

These three definitions share the concept that "Seoul speech" is to be considered the standard. But that is not the complete definition. The phrases "by and large" and "in principle" were in fact added as hedges against just that interpretation, because not all of Seoul speech as such represented standard usage. What the lower classes in Seoul spoke might be Seoul speech, but it was not to be included in the ranks of the standard. The conditions "in middle class society" and "people with education" make this point amply clear. The speech of the upper middle class was, and is, the form of the language most highly esteemed in Korean society.

Thus, even without an official definition by the government, the outcome would have been the same. There was never a possibility that the speech of any other region or group could have become standard. For some 600 years, Seoul had been the administrative, economic, and cultural center of Korea. Moreover, when the Chosŏn court moved the capital to Seoul (then Hanyang), Kaesŏng had already been the capital of Koryŏ for 475 years. Since Seoul and Kaesŏng are only separated by seventy-three kilometers, they probably belonged even then to the same dialect area; at the very least, the linguistic differences between them were certainly not as great as those that separated them from other areas of the country. The stabilization of Seoul speech as the standard language is something that took place long ago, in the remote past.

When Hangŭl was created in 1443, and it became necessary to analyze the language, the question of which variety of the language would be examined was not a matter of concern. To be sure, there was an awareness of regional dialects. This is certain because in the *Hunmin chŏngŭm* two special vowel letters were created to represent the sounds [yɨ] and [yʌ], which, it was explained, were used only in dialects. Nevertheless, this attention to dialects was apparently nothing more than an academic exercise, for these special symbols seem never to have been used in any text. There was no practical reason to write down any of these dialects. To that extent, Seoul speech had solidified from very early on its position as the standard language. Even though no particular standardization rule was ever stipulated—and it would have been highly anachronistic to have done so—Seoul's position as standard has to be considered to have been immovable.

As was pointed out above, not all of Seoul speech as such is accommodated into the modern standard language. This fact has practical implications when compiling dictionaries or establishing spelling rules. For in carrying out such tasks, those in charge must in actuality go through the procedure of examining each pronunciation, each word—everything—one by one. In this process, there are things that are in reality used in Seoul but not given the status of standard. To take one example, the vowel /oy/ (ㅚ) is generally not pronounced in Seoul as the monophthong [ö] but as the diphthong [we]; yet, it is the monophthong that has been chosen as standard. Or, to cite another well-known example, the phrase *ilk.ko ssuko* 'reading and writing' is often pronounced *ilkkwu ssukwu* (읽구쓰구) in Seoul; similarly, *ton* 'money' is frequently heard as *twun* (둔). Yet, only *ilk.ko ssuko* and *ton* have been accorded standard status. Similarly, as was pointed out in chapter 7, even though the *hawu* style of speech is widely used in Seoul (with connotations different from that of the *hao* style), it is not recognized as standard. But, there are also words not part of Seoul speech that are included in the standard language because the objects they refer to are not used in Seoul. The standard language may be based upon Seoul speech, but not everything in Seoul speech as it actually is qualifies as the standard language.

In assessing whether forms are to be recognized as standard or not, not only geographical region and social class are taken into consideration. There is also the question of whether new forms used by a new generation, or foreign words that have been newly imported from abroad, are to be adopted into the standard language. Often recognition must wait until the forms become more widely used in Korean society. But the criteria for making these decisions are not always objectively defined; instead, they often depend upon the personal judgment of the decision makers. For example, the word *caki* (자기) is now generally used as a term of endearment between younger couples instead of *yepo* (여보) 'Dear!' or *tangsin* (당신) 'you' and is used quite naturally in TV dramas, for example; yet this usage has still not received recognition as standard. Fashionable words such as "diskette" and "(computer) chip" became part of the standard language right away, while English words like "study" and "discount," though widely used, are the kind of vocabulary for which recognition as standard Korean is difficult to obtain.

There is also the matter of words that have long been included in dictionaries as standard but are now obsolete. For example, the word *mekwi-namu* (머귀나무) 'pawlonia' has now been displaced by the word *otong-namu* (오동나무) and is no longer used; similarly, *oyas* (오얏) '(damson) plum' has been replaced by *catwu* (자두). There are also cases where the pronunciation has changed and the spelling needs to be adjusted accordingly. Examples of such changes include *naphal-kkoch* 나팔꽃 (← *napal-kkoch*) 'morning glory', *kangnang-khong* 강낭콩 (← *kangnam-khong*) 'kidney beans', and *hyuci* 휴지 (← *swuci*) 'waste paper, toilet paper'. Adjustments in spelling such as these can be found in the "Rules of the Standard Language" issued in 1988. Korean is a living, changing language, and the linguistic standard periodically must be adjusted to keep pace.

In discussing standard Korean, some mention must also be made of the North Korean standard language. In 1966, North Korea adopted a new term for the standard language, *Munhwaŏ* (문화어) 'cultured language', and proclaimed that the speech of P'yŏngyang would be adopted as this new Munhwaŏ. In addition, it was announced that the speech of the working class would form the basis of the standard. The result of this policy was that a considerable number of words treated as dialect forms in South Korea, such as those shown in (2a), are used as standard forms in North Korea. Also, many Sino-Korean words were replaced by native words (2b), as were many foreign loanwords that are widely used in South Korea (2c). Perhaps there had to be two separate standard languages since the two countries are divided into polities with strikingly different social and political systems. Still, in spite of the North Korean proclamation that P'yŏngyang be adopted as standard, most of the new Munhwaŏ is still firmly rooted in the standard that had held sway for so many previous centuries, that is, the dialect of Seoul. Thus, in spite of numerous recent changes in vocabulary and usage, the North Korean standard is still easily and completely understood by all South Koreans.

(2) Differences Between Munhwaŏ and the South Korean Standard

	North	South
a.	(*P'yŏngyang*)	(*Seoul*)
'vegetable'	namsɛ 남새	tʃʰɛso 채소
'girl'	eminai 에미나이	kejibai 계집아이
'lettuce'	puru 부루	sangtʃʰu 상추
'much'	sutʰɛ 수태	ma:ni 많이
'very'	muduŋ 무둥	mutʃʰək 무척
'proud'	tsaraŋtsʰada 자랑차다	tʃaraŋsɨrəptʔa 자랑스럽다
'displease'	noyəpʰida 노엽히다	noyəpkʔe hada 노엽게 하다
'wilt'	ʃidɨlkʰida 시들키다	ʃidɨrəjida 시들어지다
b.	*Native*	*Sino-Korean*
'Korean clothing'	tsosənot 조선옷	hambok 한복
'toothpaste'	itʔakʔikʔaru 이딲이가루	tʃʰiyak 치약
'ink rubbing'	tʔənɛngirim 떠낸그림	tʰakpʔon 탁본
'ability'	ilbonsɛ 일본새	niŋnyək 능력
c.	*Native*	*Loan*
'ice cream'	ərimpʔosuŋi 어름보숭이	aisɨkʰirim 아이스크림
'knock'	songitsʰək 손기척	nokʰɨ 노크
'traffic circle'	to:ninnegəri 도는네거리	rotʰəri 로터리
'irony'	piyaŋ 비양	aironi 아이러니

9.2 Dialect Areas

The dialects of Korean are finely differentiated into a number of areas rather than two or three cohesive divisions. Korea does not have a clearly defined situation like that of France, where one country is divided primarily into two large and separate dialect areas, or that of Italy, whose dialects coalesce into three large areas.

There is, in other words, no obvious correlation between the modern dialects and the ancient historical divisions of Korea. Today's dialects are not divided according to the geography of Koguryŏ, Paekche, and Silla. Nor do they reflect differences between the territory of the Puyŏ versus the Han groups of languages. Far too much time has elapsed for these divisions to have left many modern traces. Moreover, since seventy percent of the country is mountainous, and travel is difficult, the language is quite naturally divided finely into numerous, different dialects.

Of course, if some particular dialect feature is taken as a single crite-rion, it is possible to set up larger dialect divisions. For example, if the cri-terion is whether or not tone functions as a distinctive feature, Korea is generally divided into an eastern and a western half. As can be seen in map 3, the territory with tones, though cut off at the waist, occupies the eastern half of the country and consists of Kyŏngsang, Hamgyŏng, and Kangwŏn, while the territory without tonal distinctions (but which for most part has vowel length instead) occupies the western half. If various other linguistic features are used as the metric, it is possible to divide the country into two different parts, a northern half and a southern half.

However, since each and every dialect has its own linguistic structure, one or two linguistic phenomena cannot be taken piecemeal as the charac-terizing linguistic features of a particular dialect. The comparison of one di-alect with another has to be a comparison of one linguistic structure with another, and all the isoglosses that separate the two have to be taken into consideration. For this purpose comprehensive data on the dialects must be collected, and detailed research, known as "dialectometry," must be con-ducted into the relative value assigned to each isogloss. However, dialecto-metry is a field that is still in the experimental stage worldwide. Moreover, the collection of comprehensive data remains a problem. Following the publication in 1944 of the extensive Korean dialect data collected by Ogura Shinpei earlier in the century, comprehensive work remained stalled for a while. Then, beginning in 1978, a ten-year plan of research was carried out in South Korea, which resulted in the publication of the nine-volume work *A Collection of Dialect Data* (方言資料集). But there was no way that the cor-responding data could be collected from North Korean dialects. A more sci-entific delineation of Korean dialect divisions must wait until these data are forthcoming.

To date, the most widely used dialect divisions are as shown below. (Cf. Map 1.) In general, these divisions follow Ogura Shinpei (1940, 1944). The criteria for demarcation are not especially precise, and, although the present delineations include some corrections, in general they follow Ogura's framework with only minor changes in terminology.

1. The Dialects of P'yŏngan (The Northwestern Dialects)
2. The Dialects of Hamgyŏng (The Northeastern Dialects)
3. The Central Dialects
4. The Dialects of Chŏlla (The Southwestern Dialects)
5. The Dialects of Kyŏngsang (The Southeastern Dialects)
6. Cheju Dialect

The names of these dialect areas are taken from the names of the po-litical divisions before provinces were subdivided into northern and south-ern units. The terms given in parentheses expand the terminology for the central dialects to the other dialects. Each dialect area is roughly cotermi-

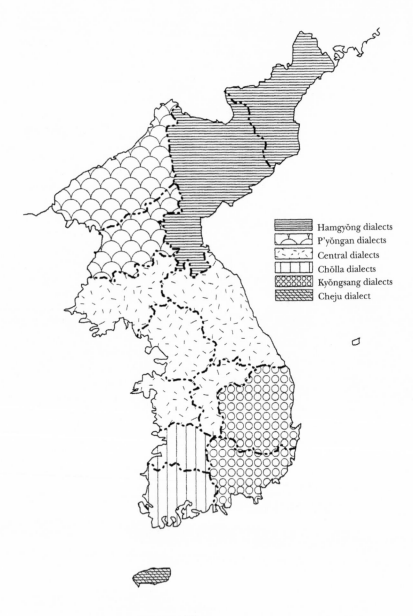

	Hamgyŏng dialects
	P'yŏngan dialects
	Central dialects
	Chŏlla dialects
	Kyŏngsang dialects
	Cheju dialect

Map 1 The Major Dialect Areas of Korea

nous with the political division for which it is named, but the two are not necessarily the same—for example, the area from Yŏnghŭng south within South Hamgyŏng Province belongs to the central dialect region. (Here we will not deal with a detailed demarcation of the borders between the dialect areas.) Terms of the form "northwestern dialects" or "southeastern dialects" have an aspect of greater objectivity. Such terminology is especially more useful when, as in North Korea, administrative units have been readjusted and, in some cases, names have also been changed. However, since terms that follow the names of administrative units are widely used and familiar to ordinary people, they are the terms we will use here.

Among the dialect areas given above, the Kyŏngsang dialects and the Chŏlla dialects are sometimes put together and called the "southern dialects." Accordingly, it should be possible to set up a northern dialect area, but that in fact is seldom done. The central dialects are often subdivided into smaller areas. This amounts to dividing the dialects contained within the central dialect area by province into the Kyŏnggi dialects, the Ch'ungch'ŏng dialects, the Hwanghae dialects, and the Kangwŏn dialects. Going one step farther, the Kangwŏn dialects are divided by the boundary line of the T'aebaek Mountain Range into the Yŏngdong dialects and Yŏngsŏ dialects (east and west of the mountains). In addition, the Kyŏngsang dialects and the Chŏlla dialects are each divided into north and south following the present provincial divisions, as are also the Ch'ungch'ŏng dialects.

These kinds of divisions have some basis in the characterizing features of the dialects, but they are also to a certain extent constructed simply for convenience of description. However, in the case of the Kangwŏn dialects, which are divided into the Yŏngdong dialects and the Yŏngsŏ dialects, the subdivision has special significance. Classifying the Kangwŏn dialects with the central dialects must be limited to the Yŏngsŏ dialects on the western side of the mountains, because the Yŏngdong dialects to the east have a distinctively different structure. As we have pointed out above in discussing tones, the Yŏngdong dialects belong to a different dialect area from the Central dialects. As can be seen from map 2, the Yŏngdong dialects show characteristics clearly dividing them from the Yŏngsŏ dialects, and the division is important enough to influence how the dialect areas of Korean as a whole are formulated.

In addition, attention should also be drawn to the need for a separate dialect area to be set up for the northern part of North Hamgyŏng province, in the ancient "Yukchin" area. As will be pointed out below (9.4 and 9.5), the Yukchin dialects are distinct from the Hamgyŏng dialects. In general, these dialects are more closely allied with the P'yŏngan dialects than with the Hamgyŏng dialects; moreover, there are vowel developments in these dialects that are found nowhere else. For the most part, putting the Yukchin dialects into a separate dialect division has more significance than dividing the Hamgyŏng dialects into North Hamgyŏng and South Hamgyŏng.

The more detailed dialect research becomes, the more natural it is to

314   *The Modern Dialects*

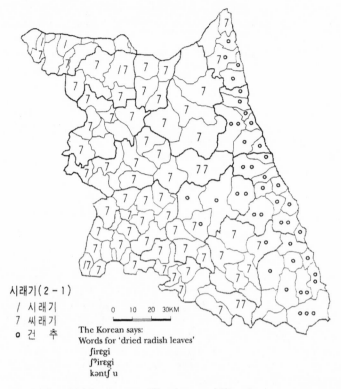

시래기(2 - 1)
/ 시래기
7 씨래기
ㅇ 건 추

0   10   20   30KM

The Korean says:
Words for 'dried radish leaves'
ʃirɛgi
ʃʔirɛgi
kəntʃ u

Map 2 The Dialect Division between Yŏngdong and Yŏngsŏ

subdivide dialect areas into smaller units. The subject matter of dialectology
has recently become more varied than before, and the size of the geographical units to be examined has grown ever finer, so that what used to be a general examination of the county (the *kun*) has now been replaced by an
examination of the township (the *myŏn*). As a result, the field is progressing
toward a delineation of increasingly smaller subdivisions of dialect areas.
For our purposes here, however, the six dialect areas shown above are
sufficient for a general overview. The only exceptions are that, for illustrative purposes, we will on occasion divide provinces into northern and southern parts; in addition, we will sometimes make separate reference to the
Yukchin dialects and the eastern and western divisions of Kangwŏn.

9.3 Phonology

In this section we will summarize some of the phonological features that differentiate the various Korean dialects. Note that, rather than treat each di-

alect area separately, we will discuss particular phonological features and how they are realized geographically. In subsequent sections, we will discuss grammar and vocabulary.

9.3.1 Tones

As we have seen in chapter 8, Middle Korean was a language in which tone functioned as a distinctive feature. In other words, the meanings of words were distinguished by differences in pitch. In the modern standard language, these tonal distinctions have been lost, and vowel length differences remain as their only trace.[5]

However, tone is still distinctive in certain other dialects. As was indicated above, the dialects of Korea can be classified into two large areas according to whether or not they have tonal distinctions. Dialects with tones are found in most of Hamgyŏng, all of Kyŏngsang, and in part of the Yŏngdong area of Kangwŏn (cf. map 3).[6] Thus, the territory where tones are distinctive occupies virtually the entire eastern half of the country. The only exception is in the middle of the country, where the toneless dialects found in the northern portion of Kangwŏn and the southern coastal area of Hamgyŏng cut off in the middle this region with tones. Otherwise, the existence or non-existence of distinctive tone roughly divides Korea into two parts.

Just as in Middle Korean, tone in the modern dialects consists of an opposition between high and low pitch.[7] However, the preservation of these distinctions does not mean that the dialects have preserved completely intact the earlier system. No modern dialect, for example, has the characteristic "sing-song tune of alternating accents" found in Middle Korean (cf. 8.3.1.); instead, once the pitch falls, it stays low to the end of the phrase. What is more important, the nature of these pitch distinctions is somewhat different. In a modern Korean dialect, a "tone" in isolation is not absolutely distinctive the way a tone is in Chinese or, presumably, one was in Middle Korean. For example, when pronounced in isolation, the Hamgyŏng syllable *pay* can mean either 'pear' or 'belly'. However, a following particle (or the copula) reveals the underlying tone of the noun: *pay NUN* (low-high) means 'pear', while *PAY nun* (high-low) means 'belly'. In other words, the perception of the tone of a syllable depends not on its absolute pitch height, but rather its pitch relative to that of a neighboring syllable.[8] Moreover, there is a clear difference between the tonal system of Hamgyŏng and that of Kyŏngsang. For example, in the Hamgyŏng dialects, 'head, hair' is pronounced *meLI* (low-high), while in Kyŏngsang the same word is pronounced *MELi* (high-low); Hamgyŏng *ciLUM* (LH) 'oil' corresponds to Kyŏngsang *CI-lum* (HL); Hamgyŏng *AYki* (HL) 'baby' corresponds to Kyŏngsang *AYKI* (HH). Thus, the pitches in individual words are often markedly, but consistently, different.

Nevertheless, the phonetic differences in how the tones are realized are relatively superficial.[9] Far more significant is the fact that both Hamgyŏng

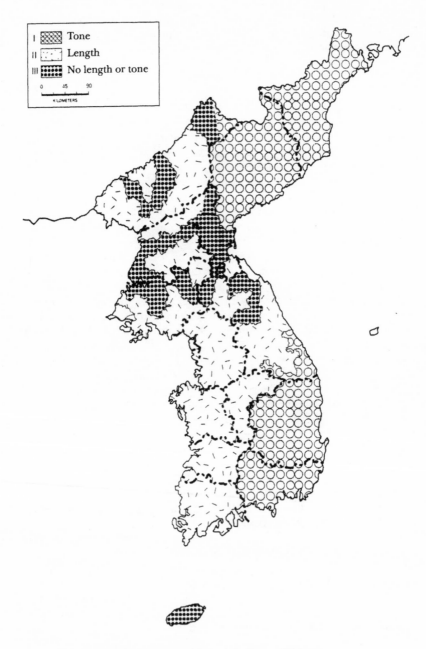

Map 3 The Distribution of Tone and Length in Korean Dialects

and Kyŏngsang have retained tone as a distinctive feature. Some examples of minimal pairs, where the meaning of the word depends upon a difference in tone, are given below. Though there is considerable complexity within each of the dialect areas, the examples in (1) generally represent the forms found in Hamgyŏng, while those in (2) generally represent (North) Kyŏngsang. (These examples are transcribed phonetically, with high pitch represented by capital letters; the nominative particle *i/ka* is attached, with close juncture, to the noun and enclosed in parentheses.)

(1) Hamgyŏng
    a. mar(I) 'horse' / MAR(i) 'language; quart'
    b. pɛ (GA) 'pear' / Pɛ (ga) 'belly'

(2) (North) Kyŏngsang
    a. MAR(i) 'horse' / MAR(I) 'quart' / MA:R(i) 'language'
    b. Pɛ (ga) 'pear' / Pɛ (GA) 'belly' / Pɛ :(ga) 'double'

A general characteristic of the tonal dialects is that many do not have vowel length.[10] At the same time, the dialects without tones generally have vowel length. In other words, tone and vowel length stand, to a certain extent, in a complementary relationship with each other. In spite of this general tendency, however, vowel length can also be found in some of the dialect areas with tones. Most of the dialects of North Kyŏngsang have both tone and vowel length. Another representative example where this is true is the southern portion of the Yŏngdong area of Kangwŏn (cf. map 3). As can be seen in (3) and (4), this dialect has both tone and vowel length functioning to distinguish the meanings of words. In (3a), *mal* 'quart' and *mal* 'horse' contrast by tone, and both form a contrast with *ma:l* 'language', which has a long vowel. In addition, as shown in (4b), words with vowel length can be further distinguished in meaning by tone, and in (4c), words with tones contrast further by vowel length. This suprasegmental structure, which is not found in other dialects, combines a system of tones with a separate system of vowel length.[11]

(3) a. mal 'quart' / MAL 'horse' / ma:l 'language'
    b. pɛ 'belly' / Pɛ 'pear' / pɛ: 'double'

(4) a. nun 'eye' / nu:n 'snow'
    b. tʃa: 'ruler' / TʃA: 'that child' (← tʃə ai)
    c. PO 'paper' (in game of "rock, scissors, paper") / PO: 'a wrapping cloth'

We have said that the question of whether a dialect has tones or not divides Korea into two parts. We have also said that the areas which do not have tones generally have vowel length instead. However, not all of the areas without tones have vowel length. There are parts of the country where the dialects have neither. Cheju Island is a representative area where this is true, and, scattered around North Korea, there are also other such areas. (Cf. map 3.) Moreover, in still other places, as we have just seen, both tone and vowel length exist. When such complexities are taken into consideration, it is possible to think of the suprasegmental structures found in the Korean dialects as existing in four types instead of two. Still, the presence or absence of tones is the most important criterion in this classification, and for this reason, we will continue to use a bipartite dialect division in describing suprasegmentals. The tendency among the younger generation of Koreans these days is toward a general weakening of length distinctions, a tendency that, if continued, may bring a time when tone is the only suprasegmental found in Korean. In that event, the Korean dialects will truly be divided by their suprasegmental structure into two distinct areas.

The fact that standard Korean does not have tones has made an impact on sociolinguistic judgments. To speakers of Korean dialects without tones, tones sound coarse and rude. When asked why, speakers of these toneless dialects respond by saying that tones make an ordinary conversation sound like an argument. By comparison, little is ever said about the presence or absence of vowel length in a dialect, showing that this phonological feature has not made a very strong impression on the average person. For a speaker of the standard language, tones are the linguistic feature probably most strongly associated with regional dialects.

9.3.2 The Vowel ʌ (' · ')

The letters representing the sounds ʌ, z, and β (· , △ , and ㅸ) are no longer used in modern Hangŭl writing. At the time the alphabet was invented, these symbols represented phonological distinctions in Korean, but, in the Seoul dialect, the phonemes were lost or merged with other phonemes after the Middle Korean period. Thus, the letters were no longer needed. In other parts of the country, however, the changes that the sounds underwent were different. Here we will examine how the dialects are separated from each other by these changes. We will begin with a discussion of the vowel ʌ.

The traces of this vowel have been largely lost in Contemporary Korean. In most of the dialects, it has developed into /a/, /u/, or /o/. However, there is also a place where it has been preserved, as /ʌ/, and that is in the dialect spoken on Cheju Island. Although Cheju dialect also has other unique features, it is, more than anything, the preservation of this one, "archaic" vowel for which it is best known. The existence of that vowel is the main reason why Cheju is accorded separate status as one of the six dialect areas of Korea. Let us look at some of the words in the Cheju dialect where this vowel can be seen:

	Cheju	Standard Korean	
'moon'	tʌl	tal	달
'bridge'	tʌri	tari	다리
'flesh, skin'	sʌl	sal	살
'village'	masʌl	mail	마을
'fly'	pʰʌri	pʰari	파리
'earth'	hʌk	hɨk	흙
'farming'	nongsʌ	noŋsa	농사
'feel'	mʌnjida	manjida	만지다
'teach'	kʌritʃʰida	karitʃʰida	가르치다
'do'	hʌda	hada	하다
'reach'	tadʌtta	tadarɨda	다다르다

The vowel ʌ in these Cheju words corresponds to the vowel represented by the letter ' ˙ ' in Middle Korean; thus, the Cheju vowel is clearly a preservation of that otherwise lost Middle Korean phoneme. The fact that Cheju is an island situated at some distance from the influence of the mainland is undoubtedly an important reason why the vowel has remained intact. No sound like it is found in the other Korean dialects.

One other important dialect division is linked to the development of the Middle Korean vowel ʌ. As we have seen in the above examples (as well as in the discussion in chapter 8), the Middle Korean vowel, when it occurred in initial syllables, generally developed into *a* in standard Korean. However, in some dialects the vowel has, in certain specific cases, become *o*. Typically, the development into *o* is found after labial consonants, as can be seen in the following examples:

	Yukchin	Middle Korean	Seoul
'horse'	mol	물	mal 말
'fly'	pʰori	풀/프리	pʰari 파리
'arm'	pʰol	풀	pʰal 팔
'redbean'	pʰotʃʰi	풋 ㄱ	pʰat 팥

	S. Chŏlla	Middle Korean	Seoul
'village'	mosil	ᄆᆞᄉᆞᆯ	mail 마을
'bright'	polktʔa	ᄇᆞᆰ다	palktʔa 밝다
'dry'	mollɨda	ᄆᆞᄅᆞ다	marɨda 마르다
'sell'	pʰolda	ᄑᆞᆯ다	pʰalda 팔다

But the change could also apparently occur *before* a labial consonant:

	S. Chŏlla	*Middle Korean*	*Seoul*
'other'	nom	ᄂᆞᆷ	nam 남
'greens'	nomul	ᄂᆞᄆᆞᆯ	namul 나물

This change of ʌ into *o* typically took place in the southern part of the peninsula, in South Chŏlla and South Kyŏngsang. But it is also often found in the Yukchin dialects in the extreme northern part of Hamgyŏng.

Thus, the development of the Middle Korean vowel ʌ roughly divides the dialects of Korea into three areas. One is the area where the vowel remains a distinct entity; another is where the vowel developed (in initial syllables) into *a;* and the third is where (in the presence of a labial) it developed into *o.*

9.3.3 The Consonants *z* (ᅀ) and *β* (ᄫ)

The Middle Korean consonant *z* (ᅀ) has completely disappeared, and the sound does not exist anywhere in Korean today. However, depending on the dialect, the consonant *s* is sometimes found in its place. These dialects with a corresponding *s* are believed by many to have preserved a form of the consonant more ancient than that of Middle Korean. Here are some examples of words with this consonant:

	N. Kyŏngsang	*Middle Korean*	*Seoul*	
'scissors'	kasɛ/kasigɛ	ᄀᆞᅀᅢ	kawi	가위
'autumn'	kasil	ᄀᆞᅀᆞᆯ	kaɨl	가을
'village'	masɨl	ᄆᆞᅀᆞᆯ	maɨl	마을
'fodder'	mosi	모ᅀᅵ	moi	모이
'fox'	yasi	여ᅀᆞ	yəu	여우
'radish'	musu/musi	무ᅀᅮ	mu:	무우
'kitchen'	pusək	브ᅀᅥᆨ	puək	부엌
'shepherd's purse'	nasɛŋi/nasi	나ᅀᅵ	nɛŋi	냉이

There are two broad areas where *s* (corresponding to Middle Korean *z*) has been preserved. In the south, it is found in Kyŏngsang, Chŏlla, and Ch'ungch'ŏng, and in the north, in Hamgyŏng.

There are also geographical areas where [b] (phonemically, /p/) is found corresponding to Middle Korean *β*. The Middle Korean consonant *β*, like *z*, was found only between voiced sounds and as a result weakened to *w* in the central dialects, including Seoul. However, in certain other dialects the process of weakening did not take place; there, [b] is preserved instead as what many consider a form of the consonant older than Middle Korean *β*. In general, these areas overlap with those where *s* is preserved in place of Middle Korean *z*. That is to say, the areas where [b] corresponds to Middle

Korean β include not only Kyŏngsang, Chŏlla, and part of Ch'ungch'ŏng in the south, but also, in the north, Hamgyŏng. From this geographical distribution it is clear that the development of z and β are dialect phenomena linked closely to each other. Some words where [b] has been preserved are given below:

	N. Kyŏngsang	Middle Korean	Seoul	
'shrimp'	sɛbi	사ᄫᅵ	sɛu	새우
'silkworm'	nube	누에	nue	누에
'mortar'	hobak	호왁	hwak	확
'hairpiece'	talbi	둘ᄫᅴ	tari	다리
'cold'	tʃʰubun	치ᄫᅳᆫ	tʃʰuːn	추운
'pretty'	kobun	고ᄫᆞᆯ	koun	고운

(In this list, note that some of the central-dialect words had already lost the consonant β by the Middle Korean stage of the language.)

Thus, the development of the Middle Korean consonants z and β divides the dialects of Korean into two areas. In one of the areas, which includes the standard language, the consonants are lost or replaced by w. In the other dialect area, the extreme south and the northeast, the two Middle Korean consonants correspond respectively to the consonants s and [b].

9.3.4 Palatalization

Using palatalization as the criterion for classification, the dialects of Korea are divided into three areas. In one area, the dialects underwent no palatalization whatsoever. In the second area, dental consonants (t, th, and tt) palatalized, but velar consonants (k, kh, kk, and h) did not. In the third dialect area, both of these two consonant types, velar as well as dental, palatalized. Since there was no palatalization of either kind in Middle Korean (cf. chapter 8), these three modern dialect areas each represents a separate stage of development that occurred after the Middle Korean stage of the language. Since the standard language represents the second type of dialect, the other two types of dialects are highly marked as regional, countrified speech.

The palatalization of t, th, and tt refers to the change of these dental stops to c, ch, and cc when the consonants occurred before i or y. This is called "t-palatalization" by Korean grammarians. Most of the dialects of Korea, including standard Seoul speech, underwent this change quite early after the Middle Korean period. (Cf. chapter 8.) However, the P'yŏngan dialects in the northeast have not. As a result, the unpalatalized forms are the most noticeable aspect of these North Korean dialects; they are their most typical characteristic.

(1)

	P'yŏngan	Seoul	
a.			
'station'	təŋgədaŋ	tʃəŋgəjaŋ	정거장 (停車場)
'lunch'	təmsim	tʃəmʃim	점심 (點心)
'midair'	tuŋtʰən	tʃuŋtʃʰən	중천 (中天)
b.			
'that side'	tekʰyən	tʃətʃʔok	저쪽
'temple'	təl	tʃəl	절
'It's good'	totʰiyo	tʃotʃʰiyo	좋지요
'write down'	təkta	tʃəktʔa	적다
'hit'	tʰida	tʃʰida	치다
'thrust'	ttirida	tʃʔirɨda	찌르다
'but,'	hədiman	hajiman	하지만
c.			
'together'	katʰi	kacʰi	같이
'firmly'	kudi	kuji	굳이
'harden'	kutʰida	kucʰida	굳히다

The examples given above under (1a) are Sino-Korean, while those under (1b) are native words. As can be seen, although the P'yŏngan dialects did not undergo *t*-palatalization, they have lost a *y*-glide that originally caused the palatalization in Seoul speech. For example, the Sino-Korean readings of the characters for 'station' were tyəŋgədyaŋ; in P'yŏngan the change was tyəŋgədyaŋ → təŋgədaŋ, while in Seoul it was tyəŋgədyaŋ → tʃəŋgəjaŋ. Similarly, the P'yŏngan form of the word for 'temple' changed from tyəl to təl. The examples given under (1c) are derived forms. Here, the standard Hangŭl spellings reveal that the forms from which the words are derived have an underlying t or th even in modern Seoul. From cases such as these, we can see that the process of *t*-palatalization did not, and does not, apply in the P'yŏngan dialects.

There is another structural fact related to *t*-palatalization that shows the conservatism of the P'yŏngan dialects in this regard. When *n* and *l* occur before [i] or [y], they are pronounced with a palatal articulation, as [ɲ] and [ʎ]. But since, in the standard language, palatal pronunciations of *n* and are not permitted at the beginning of a word (cf. chapter 3), the consonants drop in this position. The Seoul dialect underwent this phonological change quite early (cf. chapter 8). The P'yŏngan dialects however, and those dialects alone, did not undergo this change. In the case of initial *n*, as can be seen in (2), below, the consonant has been preserved. In the case of initial *l*,[12] the consonant has been replaced by *n*, as shown in (3). In both of these cases, however, occurrences of the semivowel *y* after the consonant have generally been lost.

(2) Initial *n-*

	P'yŏngan	Seoul	
'forehead'	nima	ima	이마
'leaf'	nipʰagu	ipsʔagwi	잎사귀
'tooth'	ni	i	이
'seven'	nilgup	ilgop	일곱
'woman'	nəja/nyəja	yəja	여자
'summer'	nərïm	yərïm	여름

(3) Initial *l-* (> *n-*)

	P'yŏngan	Seoul	
'haircut'	nibal	ibal	이발 (理髮)
'theory'	niron	iron	이론 (理論)
'conscience'	naŋsim	yaŋʃim	양심 (良心)
'*Yangban*'	naŋban/nyaŋban	yaŋban	양반 (兩班)
'cooking'	nori	yori	요리 (料理)
'June'	nuwəl	yuil	유월 (六月)
'fad, fashion'	nuhɛŋ	yuhɛŋ	유행 (流行)

The preservation of initial *n-* in (2) coincides with the phonological shapes found in Middle Korean. Just as was the case with *t-* in (1), the P'yŏngan forms have, in these words, retained the ancient shapes unchanged. And, since the word shapes in (3) also have to be viewed as older than those of the standard language (where the *l-* has completely been lost), the P'yŏngan dialects can be characterized as conservative with respect to palatalization.

However, the characteristics of the P'yŏngan dialects shown above can also be found in a place far removed from P'yŏngan Province, the Yukchin area of North Hamgyŏng. Yukchin forms such as [tyotʰa] 'good', [təgət] 'that (thing)', [nibujari] 'bedding', and [nyuksip] 'sixty' have the same initial consonants as the P'yŏngan forms. The Yukchin dialects form a kind of dialect island, where speech appears to have been relatively isolated from the dialects around them, and for that reason, some of the changes that took place in the other Hamgyŏng dialects did not occur there.

In the preceding, we have focused on the dialects where *t*-palatalization did not occur. We will now turn to the dialects where *k*-palatalization took place. The term "*k*-palatalization" refers to the change of the velars *k*, *kh*, *kk* to *c*, *ch*, *cc* when the consonants occur before *i* or *y*. Some representative examples of *k*-palatalization are as follows:

(4)

	North Kyŏngsang	Seoul	
'road'	tʃil	kil	길
'oil'	tʃirɨm	kirɨm	기름
'pillar'	tʃidong	kiduŋ	기둥
'Mr. Kim'	tʃim səbang	kim səbang	김서방
'chaff'	tʃe/tʃə	kyə	겨
'barely'	tʃeu	kyəu	겨우
'side'	tʃət	kyət	곁
'orange'	tʃul	kyul	귤
'long'	tʃilda	kilda	길다
'take aim'	tʃənuda	kyənuda	겨누다
'winnower'	tʃʰi/tʃʰeŋi	kʰi	키
'insert'	tʃʔiuda	kʔiuda	끼우다

The geographical area where *k*-palatalization occurred is quite extensive. It can be found widely distributed over Kyŏngsang, Chŏlla, Ch'ungch'ŏng, and Cheju in the south, Hamgyŏng in the north, as well as the eastern part of Kangwŏn (Yŏngdong). It should be pointed out that in this process, the velar fricative *h* also palatalized, as can be seen in example (5).

(5)

	North Kyŏngsang	Seoul	
'strength'	sim	him	힘
'older brother'	sə	hyəŋ	형
'tongue'	se	hyə	혀
'filial son'	soja	hyoja	효자
'bad crop year'	suŋnyən	hyuŋnyən	흉년

Thus, from the point of view of palatalization, the dialects of Korea are divided into three parts: the P'yŏngan dialects (and the Yukchin dialects); the central dialects (excluding Ch'ungch'ŏng and the eastern part of Kangwŏn); and the remaining dialects (Kyŏngsang, Chŏlla, Ch'ungch'ŏng, Cheju, eastern Kangwŏn, and Hamgyŏng). The P'yŏngan dialects are the most conservative, while all the other dialects have undergone many changes.

9.3.5 Inflection of *t*-irregular Verbs

In standard Korean, certain verb stems end in -*t*- before a consonant but -*l*- (phonetically [r]) before a vowel; for example, *tutko* 'hear and . . .', *tul̲.umyen* 'if (you) hear'. These are called "*t*-irregular verbs" by Korean grammarians. They include such common words as *tut-* (듣다) 'hear', *sit-* (싣다) 'load', and *ket-* (걷다) 'walk'. To illustrate how the inflection of these verbs works, some inflectional forms of *tut-* 'hear' are contrasted, below, with the corresponding forms of the regular verb *mit-* 'believe':

    (1) a. 'hear':   tu*t*ko, tu*t*nunta; tul̲.uni, tul̲.umyen, tul̲.ela, tul̲.essta
                    [tïkko] [tïnnïnda] [tïrïni] [tïrïmyən] [tïrəra] [tïrət²a]

       b. 'believe': mi*t*ko, mi*t*nunta; mi*t*.uni, mi*t*.umyen, mi*t*.ela, mi*t*.essta
                   [mikko] [minnïnda] [midïni] [midïmyən] [midəra] [midət²a]

However, in certain dialects, a *t*-irregular verb like 'hear' can occasionally have the regular inflection of verbs like 'believe' in (1b). One such case can be found in the P'yŏngan dialects. Although most *t*-irregular verbs have the same irregularities as the standard language, the one verb *tut-* 'hear' is regularly inflected like *mit-* 'believe'.

    (2) a. Amuri tïd̲əd̲o morïgasio.
         'No matter how many times I hear it, I don't understand.'

       b. Ki mal tïd̲ïni kïrəlt²ït hamme.
         'Now that I hear what you've said, it seems possible.'

There are also dialects with an inflection different from both of these two possibilities. In Kyŏngsang, Hamgyŏng, and the eastern part of Kangwŏn, the verbs in this class always have an *-l-* at the end of the stem. In other words, the final consonant of *t*-irregular verbs is never realized as *-t-*, even before a consonant. Here are examples of the inflection in these dialects:

    (3) a. 'hear': tïl̲k²o, tïl̲tʃ²i, tïl̲l nda, tïr̲ïni, tïr̲əra
       b. 'load': sïl̲k²o, sïl̲tʃ²i, sïl̲l̲inda, sïr̲ïni, sïr̲əra

Note that the final consonant is not a simple /l/, however. Since any obstruent that follows it is always reinforced — [tïl̲k²o], for example, instead of [tïlgo] — it can be inferred that the stems actually end in l². The glottal stop after the *l* causes a following obstruent to be reinforced but is dropped before a vowel. The situation contrasts with that of verbs such as *al-* (알다) 'know' and *mel-* (멀다) 'far', which do not cause reinforcement: [algo], [məlda]. In any event, the *t*-irregular verbs are regular in these dialects.

9.3.6 Phoneme Inventory

In the preceding section we looked at how the Korean dialects are divided according to whether or not they have tones, or according to whether they have the vowel ʌ. These factors naturally affect the inventory of phonemes in each dialect.

However, there are also many other differences to be found in each dialect's system of phonemes. For the most part, the differences are not in the consonants, where almost every dialect has an identical set of phonemes. The lone exception to this generalization is that in Kyŏngsang there is no contrast between *s* and *ss*; so, in that part of the deep south, the words *sal* 'flesh, meat' and *ssal* '(uncooked) rice' cannot be distinguished in pronunciation, nor can *sata* 'buy' and *ssata* 'cheap'. With this one salient exception, the differences in phonemic inventory are generally to be found in the vowels. Let us look first at monophthongs.

In the Kyŏngsang dialects there is no contrast between *e* and *u*. Thus, the (standard) words *kul* (글) 'writing' and *kel* (걸) 'third position (in the game of *yut*)' are both pronounced the same in these dialects. To the ears of people who speak other dialects, the Kyŏngsang vowel used in these words sounds like neither *e* ([ə]) nor *u* ([ɨ]), but, impressionistically, it seems somewhat closer to (Seoul) *e* than it does to *u*. Thus, the Kyŏngsang pronunciation of *cungke* (증거) 'proof' is heard by the Seoulite as *cengke* [cəŋgə] rather than *cengku* [cəŋgɨ]. In any event, because speakers of Kyŏngsang dialects have merged *e* and *u* into one phoneme, the phonemic inventory has one less vowel than other dialects.

Many dialects do not distinguish *ay* ([ɛ]) from *ey* ([e]). The center of this merger is, again, Kyŏngsang. Over almost this entire southeastern part of the country there is no contrast between the two vowels. In the dialects spoken in this area, the vowel that has resulted from the merger is usually neither [ɛ] nor [e] but rather something pronounced more like [ᴇ], a value somewhere between the two sounds. Speakers of the Kyŏngsang dialects do not distinguish between *kay* (개) 'dog' and *key* (게) 'crab' or between *nay* (내) 'my' and *ney* (네) 'your'. (The communication difficulties that arise in these particular cases has been relieved by changing the pronunciation of 'crab' to *ki* and 'your' to *ni*.) In addition to Kyŏngsang, the vowels have merged in many parts of South Chŏlla, and in parts of eastern North Chŏlla as well. Moreover, in recent years, younger generation speakers from Seoul and Ch'ungch'ŏng tend more and more not to be able to distinguish *ay* and *ey*, either. This tendency can be interpreted as the spread of innovation into Seoul and environs from the countryside, and from the south in particular.

In many dialects, the vowels *oy* ([ö]) and *wi* ([ü]) are not pronounced as monophthongs. The most significant area where [ö] and [ü] are not pronounced as such is in Seoul itself. The standard pronunciation of *oy* may be fixed as [ö], but the actual pronunciation of the vowel in Seoul tends to be the diphthong [we] rather than a monophthong. The usual Seoul pronunciation of *wi* is also a diphthong, a front-rounded semivowel (the glide equivalent of *ü*) plus the vowel [i]. Nevertheless, the area where the vowels *oy* and *wi* are pronounced as the monophthongs [ö] and [ü] still extends broadly over Ch'ungch'ŏng, Chŏlla, Hwanghae, and eastern Kangwŏn.

In areas where *oy* is not a monophthong, it is generally pronounced as the diphthong [wε] or [we] or perhaps [wε]. In P'yŏngan one generally hears [wε]. In some other dialect areas, the [w] in these forms has subsequently dropped, leaving the pronunciation [e] and merging the phoneme with *ey*. In a similar way, the monophthong [ü] is frequently pronounced, as in Seoul, as the diphthong [wi]; and in cases where the [w] has dropped, *wi* has merged with *i* and the phonemic distinction lost.

Many areas of Kyŏngsang have undergone these latter changes. There, dialects not only do not have the vowels [ö] and [ü], but speakers of those dialects cannot pronounce the diphthongs [we] and [wi], either. Thus, in Kyŏngsang, standard *oyka* (외 가 [öga]) 'one's mother's parents' home' is pronounced [ega], and *kwi* (귀 [kü]) 'ear' is pronounced [ki]. The result is a reduced set of vocalic distinctions.

Among the diphthongs, the dialect forms of *uy* are especially varied. In most dialects, the diphthong is realized only as a monophthong, either *u* or *i*. For example, (standard) *uysa* (의사) 'doctor' is pronounced, in various dialects, as [ɨsa] or [isa]; *uypok* (의복) 'apparel' is [ɨbok] or [ibok]. In Kyŏngsang, Chŏlla, P'yŏngan, and Hamgyŏng, the diphthong does not exist. Moreover, even in the central dialects represented by Seoul, virtually the only place where the diphthong is pronounced as such, as [ɨy], is at the beginning of a word, and only when it is not preceded by a consonant. When *uy* (morphophonemically) appears in any syllable after the first, it is generally pronounced [i], except in the case of the genitive particle *uy*, which is usually, and naturally, pronounced [e]. Nevertheless, in spite of these restrictions on its occurrence, the diphthong *uy* must, strictly speaking, be included in the phonological inventory of the central dialects.

In a number of dialects, the diphthongs *wa*, *we*, *way*, and *wey* ([wa], [wə], [wε], [we]) are not distinctive when preceded by a consonant. When this happens, the semivowel *w* drops. Thus, (standard) *kwaca* (과자) 'pastries' becomes [kaja]; *kkweng* (꿩) 'pheasant' is [kʼoŋ]; *twayci* (돼지) 'pig' is [teji]; and *kkweymayta* (꿰매다) 'sew' is [kʼimeda] or [kʼemeda]. When no consonant precedes, the diphthongs are pronounced as such in all but a small number of dialects. However, in parts of Kyŏngsang, two of these diphthongs have been completely lost. In those southeastern dialects, the diphthongs *way* and *wey* do not exist, and in their places, we find only the monophthong *e*.

In the cases we have examined so far, the regional dialects have fewer distinctions than the standard language. But there are cases where the opposite is true. In the Cheju dialect, we find not only the unique vowel ʌ; we also find the diphthong yʌ.

(1)

	Cheju	Seoul
'eight'	yʌd p	yədəl (여덟)
'many'	yʌrai	yərəʃi (여럿이)
'summer'	yʌrɨm	yərɨm (여름)
'side'	yʌp	yəp (옆)

This diphthong is almost certainly to be identified with the phonological value of 'ᅌᅵ', a Middle Korean letter created, according to the *Hunmin chŏngŭm haerye*, to transcribe "regional speech" (邊野之語). Although the letter was never actually used in any text, it is interesting that the sound it was meant to represent can still be found in these southernmost, isolated dialects.

In certain dialects, the vowel *u* ([ɨ]) can also be combined with the semivowel *y* to form the diphthong [yɨ]. This diphthong, generally pronounced with vowel length, characterizes the dialects spoken in the Yŏngdong area of eastern Kangwŏn.

(2)

	Kangwŏn	Seoul
'old gentleman'	yɨːŋgam	yəŋgam (영감)
'gallbladder'	yɨːl	sʔɨlgɛ (쓸개)
'key'	yɨːltʔɛ	yəlsʔwe (열쇠)
'pimple'	yɨːdɨrɨm	yədɨrɨm (여드름)
'soft'	yɨːrida	yərida (여리다)

Like [yʌ], this diphthong [yɨ] can also be identified with a Middle Korean letter, 'ᅴ', which, like 'ᅌᅵ', was described in the *Hunmin chŏngŭm* as intended for the transcription of dialects. In his 1905 work, *A New Revision of Korean Writing* (新訂國文), Chi Sŏgyŏng created the letter '미' specifically to be used to transcribe this same sound, a fact that suggests there must have been a rather broad awareness of the sound around the beginning of this century. Today, however, such is not the case, and the diphthong is found in only a few regional dialects.

An unusual vowel has been reported from the Yukchin dialects of North Hamgyŏng. It is said that in that border region the diphthong *uy* has been monophthongized into a vowel that is neither [ɨ] nor [i], but rather a phonological value somewhere between the two, [ï]. The vowel is further said to be found in the first syllable of the dialect words corresponding to standard *kikyey* (기계) 'machine', *uyhok* (의혹) 'suspicion', *huyta* (희다) 'white', and *sicip* (시집) 'marriage (for a woman)'. For the transcription of this vowel, North Korean linguists have created a special letter, ' + ', by combining ' — ' with ' ⎸ '. If it turns out that this Yukchin vowel is not an allophone of some other phoneme, then, as is the case with Cheju, the Yukchin dialects have a vowel phoneme that is found only there.

In the preceding we have looked at differences in the phoneme inventories, principally the vowels. To summarize, in the standard language, there are ten monophthongs and eleven diphthongs, which, at most, can be increased by one each, depending on the dialect. The minimal vowel systems to be found in Korean are in Kyŏngsang; these minimal vowel systems have six monophthongs and six diphthongs.

9.4 Grammatical Forms and Vocabulary

In demarcating the dialect areas of Korea, we have focused on phonological differences. But, needless to say, pronunciations are not the only ways in which dialects differ. There are also many other characteristics of regional speech, including ones stereotypically associated with dialects. The ones most easily and clearly recognized are differences in vocabulary. However, because differences in vocabulary are far too great in number to list in any comprehensive way here, we will look only at a few representative examples. We will take a similar approach to grammatical forms, looking selectively at particles and inflectional endings distinctive to each dialect. In determining the extent of dialect areas, these factors are not as important as, say, the phonological features of tone or palatalization, but they are certainly part of the features that characteristize each dialect area and must be included in the descriptions.

In the discussion that follows, we will examine in turn each dialect area and some of its characterizing vocabulary and grammar. The central dialects will be omitted from these descriptions, since they are linguistically close to the standard language.

P'yŏngan

Let us look first at the P'yŏngan dialects in the northwest. It is difficult to choose forms that are most representative of these dialects; nevertheless, let us begin with the example sentence given in (1), contrasting it with an equivalent expression in the standard language:

(1) nɛre kadirɛtʔiyo.   nɛga kasʔətʃʔiyo (내가 갔었지요.)
    'I went (but didn't stay).'

Any Korean hearing this sentence would immediately identify it as P'yŏngan dialect. The nominative particle [re] is a form peculiar to P'yŏngan. The verb ending [-dirɛt-] is the same; it marks the "remote past tense" ending and corresponds to -ess.ess- in standard Korean (cf. 5.2.1.2). Moreover, the fact that the final ending [-tiyo] begins with a *t* that did not undergo *t*-palatalization shows that, without a doubt, the speaker has to be from P'yŏngan.

In each dialect, there are forms such as these that allow the listener to determine instantly where in Korea the speaker is from. The examples given in (2) show other forms that uniquely characterize P'yŏngan. In the inflectional endings given there, there are many of these unique forms; in the endings [-mnekʔa] and [-ptʔeda], for example, the morphemes [-ne-] and [-te-] are peculiarly P'yŏngan forms. The P'yŏngan imperative ending is [-rayo]; the declarative is [-wayo]; the final ending *-iyo* following the prefinal ending [-as/əs-] or [-gas-] is distinctively P'yŏngan. The prefinal ending [-gas-] corresponding to standard *-keyss-* (-겠-) is also an important characteristic of P'yŏngan.

(2) a. ədɨme kaʃimnekʔa?   ədie kaʃimnikʔa (어디에 가십니까?)
         'Where are you going?'

     b. omanire kandaptʔeda.   əməniga kandaptʔida (어머니가 간답
                                      디다.)

         'Mother is going.'

     c. əsə kaʃirayo.   əsə kaseyo (어서 가세요.)
         'Please go quickly.'

     d. igə meniri kɛ on kaŋyəʃiwayo. igə myəniriga kajə on kəmun yəʃi yo
                                       (이거 며느리가 가져 온 검은엿이어요.)
         'This is black taffy my daughter-in-law brought.'

     e. karɛ taranaʃiyo.   kiɛnɨn taranasʔəyo (그애는 달아났어
                                     요.)

         'The child ran off.'

     f. onəl katʔa ogasʔuda.   onɨl katʔa ogesʔimnida (오늘 갔다오겠
                                     습니다.)

         'I'll go and come back today.'

The following examples also represent characteristics typical of P'yŏngan dialect. In particular, the form [ambulla], a special particle corresponding to standard *cocha* (조차) 'even; too', sounds as exotic as a foreign language to speakers from other parts of Korea. The verb form [əkʰagan], which is frequently heard in P'yŏngan, is a contraction of *ettehkey hakeyssnunya* (어떻게 하겠는야) 'what are you going to do?' Here, *ettehkey ha-* contracts to [əkʰa-], and the prefinal ending [-gas-] plus *-nunya* becomes [-gan]. There is also a rule that the marker of past tense [-as/əs-] plus *-nunya* contracts, in a similar way, to [-an/ən]. The form [-re] at the end of sentence (3b), which corresponds approximately to standard *-kwulye* 'so it is!' especially conveys the flavor of P'yŏngan dialect.

(3) a. na ambulla aŋgamun əkʰagan? najotʃʰa aŋgamyən ət ʔəkʰe hagenninya
                                      (나조차 안 가면 어떻게 하겠느냐?)
         'If even I don't go, what will you do?'

b. nimjane mani padas?udare.   taŋʃinnenin ma:ni padak?unyo (당신
                                네는 많이 받았군요.)
'You all got a lot, I see.'

As in any dialect, P'yŏngan vocabulary is richly differentiated. Here we
will look at just a few examples of forms unique to speech in that part of the
country. Although standard Korean forms are given for the sake of comparison, it should be cautioned that the words of one dialect do not always have
equivalents in another dialect. Also, it should be pointed out that the various
dialects within each dialect area are further differentiated among themselves, especially regarding vocabulary; however, this is a matter beyond the
scope of the present discussion.

(4)

	P'yŏngan	*Seoul*
'hail'	muru	우박
'distant relatives'	əlkʰəni	먼 일가
'children's winter footwear woven out of corn husks'	puntʰu	—
'active, lively'	pəltʃʰada	활발하다
'mother'	omani	əməni 어머니
'wife, woman'	emine	아내, 여자
'deliberately, on purpose'	udəŋ	일부러

Hamgyŏng

The Hamgyŏng dialects are spoken in the northeastern part of the
peninsula. The form that suggests these Hamgyŏng dialects most strongly to
other Koreans is probably the final ending [-tʃibi/jibi]. This ending corresponds to standard -ci (ㅡ지 a casual, *panmal* ending often used to elicit
confirmation or agreement from the listener); it is one of those dialect elements that typically, and stereotypically, mark regional speech.

(5) a. poribap?ogusa natʃ?ibi.   poribap?odaya natʃ?i (보리밥보다야
                                  낫지.)
     'It's better than barley rice.'
   b. iriru kamu hamhiŋ iro kajibi.   iriro kamyən hamhiŋ iro kaji (이리로
                                       가면 함흥으로 가지.)
     'If you go this way, you go to Hamhŭng.'

There are many other final endings unique to Hamgyŏng, among the
most typical of which are [-uda], [-m/sim], [-mme/simme], and [-ps?e/
ps?o].

(6) a. təbunde kɨrəŋgə ipʰiuji mauda.   təunde kərəŋgət ipʰiji maʃipʃʔio (더운
                                          데 그런 것 입히지 마십시오.)
        'It's hot, so please don't wear that.'
     b. hamhɨŋ sarɛm iuda.   hamhɨŋ saram imnida (함흥 사람입니
                                          다.)
        '(He) is a person from Hamhŏng.'

(7) a. oksʔukʔu sʔeu məgəsʔim.   oksʔusurɨl ma:ni məgəsʔimnida (옥수
                                          수를 많이 먹었습니다.)
        'I ate a lot of corn.'
     b. noŋsɛ cal tɛsʔimme.   noŋsaga cal twɛsʔimnida (농사가 잘 됐
                                          습니다.)
        'Farming has been good.'

(8) a. nallɛ kapsʔe.   əsə kase (어서 가세.)
        'Go quickly.'
     b. tʰŏkʔi hanmari caba opsʔo.   tʰokʔi hammari tʃaba oʃipʃʔio (토끼
                                          한마리 잡아 오십시오.)
        'Go catch a rabbit.'

A characteristic of Hamgyŏng speech is the use of [i/rɨ] as the accusative marker. Thus, standard *tok ul* (독을) 'jar (as verb object)' becomes [tog i], and *nongsa lul* (농사를) is [noŋsɛ rɨ]. Also, the special particle *un/nun* is realized as [ɨnɨ/nɨ] in most areas of Hamgyŏng. In both of these cases the final consonant of the particle has been elided.

A stereotypical feature of Hamgyŏng is the local pronunciation and usage of the negative morpheme *ani* (아니). One of the phonological characteristics of Hamgyŏng is the weakening of -*n*- and -*ŋ*- when these nasal consonants follow a vowel and precede *i* or *y*. When this weakening occurs, the preceding vowel is nasalized, and in place of the consonant -*n*- there is a constriction at the glottis.[13] The result is that the negative *ani* becomes [ãʔi], which people from outside Hamgyŏng hear as a particularly strong and forceful pronunciation. For this reason, the pronunciation of this negative immediately identifies the speaker as someone from the northeast. In addition, in Hamgyŏng usage the negative *ani* (as well as the negative *mos*) can come between the main verb and the auxiliary verb, and it can even be inserted into a compound verb. This syntax sounds strange to a speaker of the standard language and immediately marks the utterance as Hamgyŏng dialect.

(9) a. məgə ãʔi pasə.   məgəboji anasʔə (먹어 보지 않았어.)
        'I haven't tasted it.'
     b. mal ara mot tɨsʔo.   marɨl aradɨtʃʔi motʰɛyo (말을 알아듣
                                          지 못해요.)
        'I couldn't understand the language.'

Again, much of the vocabulary of these dialects differs greatly from that of the standard language. Moreover, the vocabulary used in the Yukchin area is often different from the rest of Hamgyŏng. The items in (10a) are examples of words common to much of Hamgyŏng, while (10b) consists of words unique to Yukchin.

(10)a.

	Hamgyŏng	*Seoul*	
'matches'	pijik²ɛ	səŋnyaŋ	성냥
'wife's parents' home'	əujip	ʧʰinʧʃəŋ	친정
'active, energetic woman'	p²əlʧʃ²uk²ə	hwalp²arhannyəja	활발한 여자
'dense fog'	ʧinɛ	—	
'muddled, dazed'	əlp²an hada	t²iŋhago məŋhada	띵하고 멍하다
'in want of, need'	ibapt²a/ibabuda	aʃwipt²a	아쉽다
'wife'	aŋk²an	anɛ	아내

b.

	Yukchin	*Seoul*	
'stable, cowshed'	moʃik²an	weyaŋk²an	외양깐
'bountiful harvest'	kosujegi	—	
'potato or millet powder'	kanbun	—	
'fingernail, toenail'	kʰwɛmadi	tʰop	톱
'gather firewood'	sanyaŋ hada[14]	namuhada	나무하다
'very'	polt²i	aju	아주

Kyŏngsang

The speech patterns of these southeastern dialects are perhaps the most widely and easily recognized of all the regional varieties of Korean. Speakers of Kyŏngsang dialects occupy conspicuous positions in the central government and South Korean society, and their speech has become intimately familiar to people in Seoul. The example in (11), below, shows a grammatical form typical of Kyŏngsang (especially the area around Taegu).

(11) mərakʰano?   mwərago haninnya
'What are you saying?'   (뭐라고 하느냐?)

In this sentence, there is first of all the characteristic Kyŏngsang final ending -no. It represents one of the most interesting grammatical features of the Kyŏngsang dialects, a distinction between two types of question, one indicated by -no or -ko, and the other by -na or -ka. In this distinction, a question-word question ('where', 'when', 'who', etc.) takes -*no* or -*ko* as the final ending (12a, 13a), while a yes-or-no question takes -*na* or -*ka* (12b, 13b). Since the distinction corresponds to an identical one found in Middle Korean (cf. 8.3.2), it appears that Kyŏngsang grammar has preserved this particular structure from earlier Korean.

> (12) a. ni ə*de* katˀə*no*? (question-word question)   nə ədi kasˀənni
>   '*Where* did you go?'   (너 어디 갔었니?)
>   b. pap muŋ*na*? (yes-or-no question)   pap məŋni
>   'Are you going to eat?'   (밥 먹니?)
>
> (13) a. igŏ *nu* tʃʰeg i*go*? (question-word question)
>   '*Whose* book is this?'
>   b. kigi ni tʃʰeg ai*ga*? (yes-or-no question)   kigət nəe tʃɛganinya
>   'Isn't this your book?'   (그것 너의 책 아니냐?)

But the element in example (11) that even more decisively signals Kyŏngsang is [-rakʰa]. This form consists of a contraction of the longer string [-rago ha-] that makes up the copular quotative and is a contraction that is found in no dialect outside Kyŏngsang. Similarly, in these dialects an intentive like *kallyeko ha-* (갈려고하다) 'intend to go' becomes [kallakʰa-]. Because of constructions such as these, the form [-rakʰa] has become an earmark of Kyŏngsang speech for most Koreans.

There are many endings characteristic of Kyŏngsang; among them, in the following examples, are the conjunctive ending [-nindoŋ] and the sentence-final endings [-də] and [-kˀyə]. In (14d) the ending [-ʃiiso] is the equivalent of standard -*sipsio* (-십시오); it is an example of the Formal Style in the Kyŏngsang system of speech styles. In (14e), the ending [-kˀo] corresponds to standard -*ko*; since such reinforcement of consonants in inflectional endings is common in these dialects, it is a feature used by people in Seoul when imitating or making fun of a Kyŏngsang accent. The repeated particle in the pattern [kʰaŋ ~ kʰaŋ] in (14f) corresponds to standard *lang* ~ *lang* (-랑-랑), and the particle [mentʃʰiro] is equivalent to standard *chelem* (처럼); both particles are characteristic of Kyŏngsang.

> (14) a. tʃibe innindoŋ əmnindoŋ molsˀieɛ.   tʃibe inninji morigesˀimnida (집
>   '   '   에 있는지 모르겠습니다.)
>   'I don't know if (he) is at home.'
>   b. yəgəga tʃonnidə.   yəgiga tʃosˀimnida (여기가 좋
>   습니다.)
>   'Here is good.'
>   c. halbe, əde kanikˀə?   harabəji ədi kaʃimnikˀa (할아버
>   지 어디 가십니까?)
>   'Grandfather, where are you going?'
>   d. pʰətˀək oʃiiso.   pˀalli oseyo (빨리 오세요.)
>   'come quickly.'

e. mə hallak?o?   mwə haryəgo (뭐 하려고?)
   'What do you want to do?'

f. ni kʰaŋ ne kʰaŋ talmətʃ?e?   nəraŋ naraŋ talmatʃ?i (너랑 나랑 닮
                                                                       았지?)
   'You and I are similar, aren't we?'

g. adəl mentʃʰiro wa kɨrano?   ɛdɨltʃʰərəm wɛ kɨrəni (애들처럼 왜
                                                                그러니?)
   'Why are (you) acting like children?'

Some of the vocabulary unique to Kyŏngsang is given below. The last example, [ənje], which in the standard language means 'when', is used as a kind of response to deny a compliment or invitation or to express the opposite meaning.

(15)

	Kyŏngsang	Seoul	
'cat'	k?wenegi/eŋgu	koyaŋi	고양이
'quietly, in earnest, with dignity'	kabundari	tʃindɨgi	진드기
'startled, surprised'	sik?əp het?a	nollat?a	놀랐다
'scold'	mərakʰunda	k?ujit?a	꾸짓다
'of course, right!'	hamo	am	암
'[polite response to a compliment]'	ənje	aniya	아니야

Chŏlla

Chŏlla lies in the southwestern part of the Korean peninsula. In the past, the region was known for political opposition and economic deprivation, and a Chŏlla accent is still, in some circles, the source of social prejudice. The sentence in (16), below, is an expression typical of the Chŏlla dialects—and one frequently imitated in Korean comedy routines when affecting a Chŏlla accent.

(16) hi poltʰimən hi poraŋk?e.
    'If you want to try it, go ahead.'

The final ending [-ŋk?e] is a form that can be thought of as the "face" of this dialect; it is distinctively Chŏlla dialect. It corresponds to standard *-ni-kka* 'because', which is used at the end of a dependent clause. However, even though [-ŋk?e] is not, at least in origin, a sentence-final form, it is often used that way, to end an utterance in colloquial Chŏlla speech. Depending on what precedes it, the ending can have various forms: [-raŋk?e], [-daŋk?e], [-ŋk?e], or [iŋk?e], and it can be followed by the form [-ro]. Moreover, [-k?e] can also be pronounced [-ge]. Here are some examples:

(17)

	Chŏlla	Seoul	
a. '(since) it's expensive'	pisaŋkʰeʔe	pisʔanikʔa	비싸니까
'(since) there aren't any'	əpsʔiŋkʰeʔe	əpsʔinikʔa	없으니까
b. '(since) (I say I'm) going'	kandaŋkʰeʔero	kandanikʔa	간다니까
c. '(since) it's our brother'	uri səŋ iraŋkʰeʔe	uri hyəŋ iranikʔa	우리 형이라니까
d. 'And so,'	kɨraŋkʰeʔe/kɨraŋkʰeʔe/kiŋkʰeʔe	kɨrənikʔa	그러니까

The word *hi* 'doing' in (16) is also a peculiarity of these dialects. It is
seldom heard in dialects outside Chŏlla. The form corresponds to standard
hay (해 [hɛ]) 'doing'; the only pronunciation difference is that the (standard) vowel [ɛ] has been raised to [i]. This same kind of raising can be seen
in the [tʰi] of [poltʰimən], which corresponds to the [tʰe] of standard [pol-
tʰemyən] (볼테면), and there are also numerous other forms showing standard [e/ɛ] pronounced [i] in Chŏlla; for example, the Chŏlla word
[kɨrəndi/kɨrandi] corresponds to Seoul [kɨrənde] (그런데) 'however,'. But
it is the word *hi* 'doing' that stands out and is recognized as a particularly distinctively Chŏlla form by most Koreans.

Other forms characteristic of Chŏlla dialects are shown in (18), below.
In some parts of Chŏlla, the form [tʔamsi] 'because of' in (18a) is pronounced [tʔamʃe]; there are still other areas where the completely different
forms [nanʃi], [tʃʔue], or [tʃʔiu] are used instead. In any event, it is the form
[tʔamsi] or [tʔamse] that most Koreans associate with these dialects. Another
Chŏlla characteristic is that [- rau] is used as a polite style ending instead of
standard [-əyo] (- 어요). Also, the prefinal ending [-ge/gyə] serves as the
honorific marker instead of -*si*- (- 시 -). In addition, the form [-iŋ], with question intonation, is often used at the end of a sentence as a confirmation
seeker ('. . . isn't that right?'); it is a usage peculiar to Chŏlla. Other dialects
have nothing that is quite equivalent. On the one hand, [-iŋ] corresponds in
form and meaning more or less to standard *ung* (응), but it differs from it in
a crucial way, because [-iŋ] can be used with polite or formal speech styles.
Since standard *ung* can only be used in plain or *panmal* conversational style,
the Chŏlla form [-iŋ] in more polite contexts is often misunderstood by people from Seoul as rude and impolite. Thus, this sentence-ending [-iŋ] not
only marks the speaker as being from Chŏlla, but it is viewed by other Koreans as a form revealing the true flavor of the Chŏlla dialects. When [-iŋ] is
added to the end of sentence (16), for example, the utterance becomes one
that, for other Koreans, is quintessentially Chŏlla dialect.

(18)a. mə tʔamsi   mwə tʔɛmune (뭐 때문에)
    'because of what'
   b. ibəsʔərau   ibəsʔəyo (입었어요)
    'have put on (clothing)'

tʃokʰuman irau   tʃokʰumanyo (좋구만요)
'It's good!'

c. kɨmsebo ogyərau?   pəlsʔə oseyo (벌써 오세요?)
'Are you here already?' [a polite greeting]

    kagyənnya?   kaʃyənninya (가셨느냐?)
'Has [some older person] gone?' [said to a child]

d. kɨraptʔida iŋ?
'You don't say?' [a polite response]

    ogyərau iŋ?
'Are you here?' [a polite greeting]

What follows are some words characteristic of the Chŏlla dialects. Although much the same can be said of other areas of the country, it should be noted that, in particular, there are many adjectives and adverbs in Chŏlla for which it is difficult to find equivalents in other dialects.

(19)

	Chŏlla	*Seoul*	
'smoke'	neŋgal	yəŋgi	연기
'pocket'	kŏbi	hojuməni	호주머니
'a future'	nijagu	tʃaŋnɛsəŋ	장래성
'meticulous'	ijənʃiraptʔa	kʔomʔkomhada	꼼꼼하다
'shakes amusingly' (?)	hosiptʔa	—	
'barely'	pʰodasi	kyəu	겨우
'on the contrary'	teptʔero	toriə	도리어

Cheju

Most mainlanders do not have many opportunities to hear the Cheju dialect. Since Cheju lies well off the southern tip of Korea, transportation to the island is relatively difficult, and the population of the island is small. But another reason the dialect is heard so infrequently is that the natives of the island almost always try to speak the standard language with people from outside. Since the Cheju dialect is so different from other varieties of the language, it is a strategy speakers have adopted to smooth communication difficulties. In any event, there have never been many forms that other Koreans associate with Cheju speech. Now, however, there is at least one exception; through indirect means such as mass communication, the expression [kamsuga] shown in (20) has become something like a billboard for the Cheju dialect. The word means 'Are you going?' and, because of the popularity of Cheju as a tourist destination, it has become widely known throughout South Korea.

(20) ədɨre kamsuga?
'Where are you going?'

The morpheme *-su-* in [kamsuga] is a prefinal ending used to indicate a deferential sentence style; it corresponds approximately to standard *-supni-* (- 습니 -). The form *-u-* seen in (21a) is an allomorph of this same morpheme. The [kʰ] that occurs before *-u-* in (21a) corresponds to the standard modal *-keyss-* (-겠- cf. 5.2.1.3), and the *-u-* that follows it is an element showing deference to the listener.

The morpheme *-m-* in [kamsuga] shows that the action is ongoing (or incomplete); it can also be seen in [saramjə] in (21b). The morpheme functions in opposition with the perfective [-at/ət-]/[-an/ən-], shown in (21c). The particle [yəŋ] in (21b) is unique to Cheju, and the conjunctive ending [-aŋ/əŋ] of (21a), and the final endings [-jə] of (21b) and [-masʔim] of (21c) are special endings for which there are no similar forms in any other dialect.

(21) a. kadaŋ murəŋ kakʰuda.   kadaga murəsə kagesʔimnida (가다가 물어서 가겠습니다.)

  'I'll ask directions on the way.'

 b. na yəŋ hʌndi saramjə.   naraŋ hamkʔe salgo itʔa (나랑 함께 살고 있다.)

  '(He) lives with me.'

 c. kɨ tʃʰek ta igənmasʔim?   kɨ tʃʰɛk ta: ilgəsʔimnikʔa (그 책 다 읽었습니까?)

  'Have you finished reading that book?'

  ta igətʃʔi   ta: ilgətʔa (다 읽었다.)

  'I've read it all.'

There are many words with forms unique to the Cheju dialect. A few of these are given in (22a), below. In addition, because of the island's geographical location, there are many words that were brought in from Japan; some examples of this Japanese vocabulary are shown in (22b). The words relating to horses in (22c) are from Mongolian; they represent what is a fairly significant amount of vocabulary introduced by the Mongols during their occupation of Korea.

(22) a.

	Cheju	Seoul	
'ant'	keyəmji	kɛ:mi	개미
'dragonfly'	paptʃʔuri/pamməri	tʃamjari	잠자리
'sparrow'	seŋi/tʃopsʔeŋi	tʃʰamsɛ	참새
'radish'	nʌmpʔi	mu:	무우
'garlic'	tɛsani/koptʔɛsani	manɨl	마늘
'marine products'	parɨt	hɛsammul	해산물 (海産物)
'rainbow'	hwaŋgoji	mujigɛ	무지개
'whirlwind'	tokʔöŋi	höoribaram	회오리바람

b.

	Japanese	Cheju	Seoul	
'sail'	ikari ('anchor')	ik'ari	tot	돛
'rice bowl'	chawan ('teabowl')	tʃawaŋ	papk'oŋgi	밥공기
'bathtub'	furo	huro	mogyokthaŋ	목욕탕(沐浴湯)

c.

	(Middle) Mongolian	Cheju	Seoul
'black horse'	qara ('black')	kara-mʌl	—
'red horse'	ʒe'erde	tʃəkt a-mʌl	—
'dappled horse'		wəlla-mʌl	—

We have surveyed broadly the characteristics of the Korean dialects and looked at their most important features. We have seen that the differences between these regional varieties are by no means small and that the more remote the area is from Seoul, the more unique features the dialect is likely to have. In some cases, the dialect has been conservative and has preserved older forms; in other cases, the dialect has, on the contrary, been the place where innovations have first begun. As transportation improves and the influence of mass communication and education grows, the contacts between dialects are becoming more frequent; and, in particular, as the standard language continues to spread, the barriers between dialects are gradually growing smaller. In the future, how each dialect will change, and into what form, is a separate topic about which we must wait to see how the situation unfolds.

References

Chambers and Trudgill 1980; Ch'oe Hakkŭn 1974; Ch'oe Myŏngok 1980; Han'guk Chŏngsin Munhwa Yŏn'gu-wŏn 1986-1994; Hwang Taehwa 1986; Hyŏn P'yŏnghyo 1962, 1985; Kim Ch'unghoe 1992; Kim Hyŏnggyu 1974; Kim Ihyŏp 1973; Kim Pyŏngjae 1959, 1965, 1975; Kim Yŏngbae 1992; Kim Yŏnghwang 1982; Kōno Rokurō 1945; Korean National Academy of Sciences 1993; Kwak Ch'unggu 1991; Martin 1992; Ogura Shinpei 1940, 1944; Ramsey 1974, 1978; Yi Iksŏp (Lee Iksŏp) 1981, 1984, 1986; Yi Kigap 1986; Yi Kimun (Lee Ki-moon) 1972a; Yi Sungnyŏng 1957, 1971.

NOTES

Introduction

1. This ranking is according to Donald Macdonald in a paper presented at the Korean Studies in the U.S. Conference at the Library of Congress (1992).

2. The reasons why are discussed in chapter 2.

3. Or 1444—see chapter 2.

4. Ramstedt is the best-known and most influential proponent of this theory, but he was by no means the first. H. J. Klaproth had already suggested over a hundred years earlier, in his *Asia Polyglotta* of 1823, that Korean was Altaic.

5. Cf. Yi Kimun 1972a.

6. Note that the modern Altaic languages do not preserve the original **p*; in Manchu, for example, the **p-* has changed into *f*, and in Mongolian it has been completely lost.

7. Martin 1992:244.

8. The subject of speech levels, honorifics, and protocol will be discussed in more detail in chapter 7. We owe Professor Young-Key Kim-Renaud thanks for sharing with us the term *speech protocol*.

Chapter 2

1. As originally conceived, it also had a marking convention for distinctive pitches.

2. Ch'oe was a public servant who among other things served as an official interpreter with Korean embassies to Peking and as the professor of Chinese in the interpreters' school. He was the compiler and author of many pedagogical linguistic works that are today primary sources not only for earlier Korean, but also for colloquial Chinese as it was then spoken in northern China.

3. The original order of the symbols, as found in the texts of King Sejong's day, was completely different. There, the order of the consonants had been based upon the conventions of Chinese rhyme tables; the order of the vowels had followed certain philosophical principles underlying their construction. The order that Ch'oe introduced was totally new.

4. Here Ch'oe was using the pronunciation of the word before a pause. In the sixteenth century, just as it does today, the word ended in *-th* when it was followed (in the same phrase) by a vowel, e.g., ...그테 *kuth ey* 'at the end (of) . . .'. The initial reinforced consonant of the modern form *kkuth* (끝) is a different matter. It resulted

historically from the incorporation of the so-called "genitive-*s*" (사이ㅅ); cf. p. 77–79, 290–93, below.

    5. In North Korean dictionaries a different alphabetical order is used. The letter names are also different.

    6. As originally conceived, the alphabet was provided with a separate, though similar, symbol for *ng:* ㆁ (note the longer vertical line on top of the circle). But in modern Hangŭl this symbol is no longer used, and only position now determines how ㅇ is to be interpreted.

    7. These units are called *ca*, a word that, depending on context, can mean 'letter' or 'character'. But originally the word *ca* (字) referred only to a Chinese character, and it is this legacy that we see in the meaning here. Since Chinese characters always represented syllables, the word *ca* also became associated with syllables.

    8. The two exceptions were the *Yongbi ŏch'ŏnka* (龍飛御天歌) and the *Wŏrin ch'ŏn'gang chi kok* (月印千江之曲), both of which were printed in 1447.

    9. That was the case in all early texts except the *Wŏrin ch'ŏn'gang chi kok* (月印千江之曲) of 1447.

    10. The suffixes are used to derive nouns from verbs or adjectives.

    11. Even North Korean officials, who generally use the pronunciations with some consistency, are reported to make mistakes in natural conversation. (Young-Key Kim-Renaud, personal communication).

    12. Lee Iksop 1977, 1992; Sampson 1985. The character simplifications adopted in the People's Republic of China are an example of script reform designed solely from the point of view of the writer. Fewer strokes make writing faster but not necessarily easier to learn; cf. Ramsey 1987:150–54.

    13. Cf. Vachek 1945–49, 1973; Chomsky and Halle 1968; Henderson 1982; Sampson 1985; Coulmas 1989.

    14. This translation is slightly adapted from Ledyard 1966:97–98.

    15. Details, and the reasoning about the identity of the inventor, can be found in a brilliant article recently published on the subject by Yi Kimun (Lee Ki-Moon) 1997.

    16. An approximation of the lunar calendar date of Chŏng Inji's postface to the *Hunmin chŏngŭm haerye* is 9 October.

    17. Translation adapted from Ledyard 1966:229.

    18. Translation adapted from Ledyard 1966:229.

    19. Ledyard 1966:233.

    20. These four vowels, [o], [a], [u], and [ə], were the only ones that, at least in the language of the capital, could be preceded by a y- onglide. The onglide could not precede one of the "basic" vowels, [ʌ], [ɨ], or [i], although, as reported in a later section of the *Haerye*, the "speech of children and the languages of the bordering regions sometimes have them." This phonological fact—that is, the "basic" vowels did not occur with an on-glide—may well underlie the decision to recognize these three vowels as basic in the first place.

    The treatment of the complex vowels also shows that the editors of the *Haerye*—and of course Sejong—were aware of the articulatory equivalence of the semivowel [y] and the vowel [i], as can be seen, for example, from the fact that they wrote explanations such as the following:

ㅛ與 ㅗ 同而起於 ㅣ
'ㅛ[yo] is the same as ㅗ[o], only it arises from ㅣ [i].'

21. This was a Sino-Korean rhyming dictionary, the *Tongguk chŏngun* ('The Correct Rhymes of the Eastern Country' 東國正韻) of 1447, Cf. Ledyard 1966:283-98.

22. Cf. the discussion in An Pyŏnghŭi 1997.

23. Cf., especially, the arguments for hP'ags-pa influence presented in Ledyard 1966 and 1997.

24. These questions are discussed in detail in An 1997 and, especially, in Ledyard 1966 and 1997.

25. The first character in the transcription (朝) means 'morning' only when it is read *zhāo*, in the first tone, in (modern) Chinese; but in the name for Korea the Chinese name is *cháo*, in the second tone, which means 'tide' or 'court'. The second character (鮮) usually means 'fresh meat' or 'fresh fish'; but it can never mean 'calm'. (Gari Ledyard was the first to point out these facts to me—SRR)

26. For the purpose of illustration, and to avoid the nettlesome problems of how Old Korean words were pronounced, the forms given are Contemporary Korean.

27. The textual source for the word is the preface that Ch'oe Haenggwi wrote to his Chinese translations of some of the *hyangga*. Ch'oe's preface and translations are both dated 967. In describing the *hyangga*, Ch'oe used the "name" *hyangch'al* 'local letters' as a phrase parallel to Tangmun (唐文) 'Tang script'—in other words, standard Chinese writing. For details, see Ledyard 1966:40ff. and the references cited there.

28. Cf. Ledyard 1966:47.

29. Ledyard 1966:49.

30. Cf. Ledyard 1966:53-55.

31. Cf. Yi Kimun (Lee Kimun) 1972a:50 and Lee Ki-baik (Yi Kibaek) 1984:84.

32. The first word in each of the two texts is interesting. The Japanese version of the instructions begins with the native word *toriatsukai* 'handling', which is written *kun*-style with Chinese characters, 取り扱い. The Korean instructions begin with the word 취급 *(chwikup)* 'handling', which happens to be the Sino-Korean reading of the same characters (取扱). The Korean word looks superficially to be a Literary Chinese loan, but it is not; it is a borrowing of the Japanese word, using the Chinese characters it is written with as the intermediary. In both Korean and Chinese, there are a surprisingly large number of Japanese loans like this. The Japanese source in such cases is almost completely hidden because the characters are read in a native way and thus pronounced totally unlike the original Japanese word. (See the discussion in 4.4.2, below.)

Chapter 3

1. The standard used in North Korea is a different matter, of course. However, in spite of public pronouncements over the years proclaiming the dialect of P'yŏngyang to be the official standard, the North Korean standard language is in actuality not greatly different from that of South Korea. It, too, had its beginnings in the dialect of the prewar capital, that is, in the speech of Seoul. The P'yŏngyang el-

ements in the modern standard are more like accretions to this earlier standard rather than the basis of a new standard. (Lee Ki-Moon, personal communication.)

2. Except, for some speakers in some environments, as a variant of the voiced version of /c/; cf. Martin 1992:29. But phonemic /z/, found in the capital dialect in the fifteenth and sixteenth centuries, has long since disappeared.

3. See Martin 1992:29.

4. In the original orthography designed for the alphabet by King Sejong, pitch and vowel length were indicated by "side dots" placed beside the syllable. This orthographic convention was abandoned after the sixteenth century, however.

5. Cf. Martin 1992:29-30.

6. The facts are spelled out, with an exhaustive list of lexical examples, in Martin 1992: 100-106. Our treatment here follows Martin's.

7. Cf. section 3.3.1, "Neutralization," on the change /ph/ → /p/.

8. Other such words, though considered nonstandard, can also be heard in Seoul; for example, *kwallyem* for *kwannyem* 'conception', *hallamtong* for *hannamtong* 'Hannam-dong [a section of Seoul]'. The replacement of etymological *-nn-* by *-ll-* occurs even in native words in some Korean dialects (cf. Ramsey 1978:57-58).

9. In some people's speech the second /n/ often has a slightly oral release; thus the name is pronounced [monn^{d}o], with a sound approximating the liquid in the original.

10. What is discussed here is only one aspect of the cross-cultural problem. Cf. Austerlitz, et al. 1980.

11. Cf. Martin 1954: 10.

12. Martin 1954: 10.

13. At normal speaking speed a *t* assimilates position to a *k*; and *kkk* is not phonemically distinct from *kk*.

14. The "side dots" indicating pitches in the original text are not reproduced here; cf. chapter 7. Our translation is taken from Martin 1992: 865.

15. Cf. Ramsey 1978: 205-207.

16. There are, however, a few lexicalized cases where the genitive *s* is realized phonetically as [d] (phonemically /t/); e.g., *wus-os* (웃옷) 'outer clothing', pronounced [udot].

17. The verb stem *ha-* 'do' is an exception, for the infinitive of the verb, with the ending -*a* (or -*e*), is an unexpected and irregular *hay*, a form that is usually short but is also sometimes pronounced long (cf. Martin 1992: 465).

18. The number of types of *l*-stem verbs doubles when vowel length and (in earlier Korean, as well as in some regional dialects) pitch distinctions are taken into consideration; cf. Ramsey 1978: 224ff and Ramsey 1992. The most concise description of the modern situation, along with lists and clear examples, can be found in Martin 1954: 32-33.

Chapter 4

1. That is, these words are nouns in the broader sense of the term, as will be explained below. Using narrower definitions of Korean word classes, *na* 'I' will be classed separately as a pronoun, and *tases* 'five' as a number.

2. See, for example, the parts of speech described in Martin 1992:88-89.

3. The Korean language makes use of a very large number of classifiers, which are also sometimes known as "counters." Martin (1992:179-85) gives a list of well over a hundred, which he says is "not quite exhaustive, but is fairly representative."

4. This particular expression, *nay cip malyen*, is especially to be treated with caution. Though now used in conversational Korean in the context of making preparations for buying a house, in origin, it is a term created by the Korean banking industry for advertising home loans. The expression is professional jargon that is not a productive part of the natural, colloquial language.

5. In literary writing, *ku* is used by itself in the meaning of 'he', and, depending on context, *ku* or *i* is even sometimes used in the sense of the pronoun 'it'; these uses are clearly translation influenced, however.

6. Even though *ani-* could be analyzed as the negative adverb *an* plus the copula *i-* (ˣ안 이-), Korean orthography treats it as a separate stem in its own right: 아니-.

7. This compound represents a modern restructuring of an older word. In Middle Korean, *olh* (올ㅎ) meant 'this year', but at some point in the history of the word, speakers must have taken it to mean, rather, the adnominal 'coming', then added *hay* 'year' to form the compound *ol hay*.

8. The language spoken in the fifteenth century, however, was markedly different. In those days there were many words that began with a complex consonant cluster; cf. chapter 8.

9. This example was pointed out to me by Professor Lee Sang Oak in personal communication. (SRR)

10. Yi Kimun (1991a:219-26) gives a list of these and other such loans attested in Middle Korean (and later) alphabetic documents.

11. *Paychwu* 'bok choy' is obviously from a form of the Chinese word represented by the characters 白菜. *Sangchwu* 'lettuce', however, is a bit more problematic. It seems to come from the readings of the characters 常菜, which mean 'ordinary greens', and that is how it is interpreted by Korean linguists. But since this compound word does not seem to have been used in Chinese, there is a good possibility that the compound was created in Korea.

12. This compound (沈菜), however, though it makes sense in Chinese, does not appear to have been a real Chinese word. More than likely, the compound was made up in Korea as a fancy word for a home-grown product. In any case, once the pronunciation changed and no longer represented standard Sino-Korean readings, the association with Chinese characters was lost.

13. This original meaning of *ci* was only recently discovered by Lee Ki-Moon (Cf. Yi Kimun 1991a:26-27.)

14. Kim Wanjin (1970) has proposed that the source of the borrowing was Old Chinese *tiər 'residence, lodge' (邸), which is not an unreasonable suggestion. Kim also makes a number of other suggestions for contact loans from Chinese into Korean that are worth noting. In any event, the (Middle) Korean word *tyel* 'Buddhist temple' was itself probably passed along to Japan, to become Japanese *tera* 'id.' (which phonetically may well have been [tyera]).

15. This etymology was first proposed by Kwŏn Tŏkkyu in 1928. [Cf. Yi Kimun 1991a: 108]

16. This word *pwuthye* 'Buddha' was almost surely around many centuries before it was attested in these fifteenth-century texts. One indication that it dates from the early days of Korean Buddhism is that it is probably the source through which the Old Japanese word for 'Buddha', *potoke,* was borrowed.

17. Cf. Yi Kimum, 1991b:35-44.

18. Cf. Yi Kimum 1991a:28.

19. Cf. Yi Kimum 1991a:211.

20. This etymology was suggested by Ch'oe Namsŏn in 1946.

21. This incident was described to me in personal communication by Professor Lee Iksop (SRR).

22. One of us (Lee Iksop) was in the first grade when the war ended. Even though his school was in a rural area of Kangwŏn Province, far removed from the capital and all political influence, he was known at the school only by his Japanese name, Hoshimura Keikō. All Korean words and names were strictly banned in all grade levels.

23. Cf. Miller, 1967:239.

24. Cf. Martin 1992:94.

25. This dictionary was compiled by the Han'gŭl Hakhoe and published by Ŏmun'gak, in four volumes, in 1991.

26. It is immaterial whether the compounds were originally created in China, Japan, or Korea; the point is that Koreans have assimilated and feel comfortable with the words and their morphology.

27. These two Sino-Korean words were especially prone to replacement because they represented the character readings of Japanese coinages (*deguchi* and *iriguchi*).

Chapter 5

1. Cf. Martin 1992: 316.

2. But cf. Martin 1992:192-216; Sohn Ho-min 1994:375ff.

3. The North Korean grammar *Chosŏn-ŏ munpŏp* (1:169-73) gives examples illustrating deletion of each and every particle (cited in Martin 1992:286-87). It might be questioned whether all of the examples given there represent actual cases of deletion of the particles claimed; and certainly, the position taken by South Korean linguists on particle ellipsis is far less extreme. But it is nevertheless true that omission of particles in colloquial situations is far more common than used to be believed.

4. Some grammarians reluctant to accept double-subject constructions at face value take a different approach and treat one of the two subjects as the surface realization of some other grammatical constituent. For example, using this approach, (6), (7), and (8) would probably be derived from structures such as the following:

(6) 목사에게 어떻게 재산이 많겠니?
Moksa *eykey* ettehkey caysan i manhkeyss.ni?
[Lit., 'A preacher *[locative]* how wealth *[-i]* be much?']

(7) 영회의 얼굴이 예쁘다.

Yenghuy *uy* elkwul i yeypputa.

[Lit., 'Yŏnghŭi *[genitive]* face is pretty.']

(8) 한강에 홍수가 났다.

Hankang *ey* hongswu ka nass.ta.

[Lit., 'The Han River [locative] a flood happened.']

The problem is, the paraphrases do not mean the same thing as the original sentences. 'Yŏnghŭi's face is pretty' is not the same as 'Yŏnghŭi is (face-)pretty'. It is not clear what would motivate such derivations other than the desire to be rid of the troublesome pattern.

5. The comitative construction associated with the Korean verb is of course why Koreans sometimes misuse the English verb *to marry* in ungrammatical constructions such as ˣ"He married with a German."

6. Primary stress on *Minho* forces interpretation (4a), while stress on *apples* turns the meaning into (4b). Yet another interpretation results from stressing the verb; if Minho were, say, an apple dealer, stress on *likes* would mean that not only does he *sell* apples, he also *likes* them.

7. Or no particle at all; cf. the discussion at the beginning of this chapter in 5.1, above.

8. This semantic interpretation is the one suggested by Martin (1992:896-97); Martin's analysis is an attempt to provide a unifying principle for all of the various usages of this ubiquitous particle.

9. This observation comes from Martin 1992:896; example (13) is also taken from that source.

10. The same phonological alternation is also found, for example, in the particles -*na/ina*, -*nama/inama*, and -*yamallo/iyamallo*. In all these cases, -*i*- is historically an occurrence of the copula and the particles etymologically derived from inflectional forms of the copula.

11. Note that these strings with *ya* could naturally be interpreted as occurrences of the homophonous vocative case particle (cf. above, 5.1.1.7) —but in that case the particle would be followed by a juncture.

12. Moreover, according to Martin (1992:244), the total number of "paradigmatic endings"—that is, the strings into which these inflectional morphemes are combined—"is well over 400."

13. In other words, this alternation depends on what are called "vowel harmony" relationships. (Cf. 4.3.4, above.) That is, the vowel in the ending must in some sense agree with the last vowel in the stem: /e/, which is considered a "yin" vowel, is used as the vowel of the ending in case the last vowel of the stem is also a yin vowel (/e, u, wu/) or /i/. The "yang" vowel /a/ is used in the ending in case the last vowel of the stem is a yang vowel (/a, o/). This vowel harmony relationship holds fairly consistently in most varieties of modern Seoul speech, though in older-generation usage, -*ess*- is the variant heard instead after the vowel /o/.

14. Though common enough in Seoul speech, -*tu*- is usually considered a dialect pronunciation.

15. This colloquial style is called the "intimate" style by Martin (1992:308).

16. There are a few cases where this is not true and where, depending on the ending, the interpretation of coordination or subordination is determined solely by the semantic relationship between the conjunctive clauses. However, such instances are not very numerous, and, for the most part, the indication of whether the conjunction is coordinate or subordinate is the function of the ending of the first clause.

17. In Yale Romanization the form in question here is written *halq swulok*, reflecting Martin's treatment as the prospective modifier *halq* plus postmodifier *swulok* (cf. Martin 1992:876-77). However, I have written the form solid to indicate that it is being treated as an inflectional ending, as the Hangŭl orthography suggests: 할 수록.

18. Martin (1992:323) makes the following generalization: "Verbs of perception and discovery are found to occur with *-um* but not *-ki*; verbs of beginning, continuing, or stopping occur with *-ki* but not *-um*; verbs of helping occur with either, but with differing connotations."

19. These reading formulae are used in, among other texts, the Korean version of the *Thousand Character Classic* (*Ch'ŏnja mun* 千字文), a textbook used in the traditional education of Chinese characters. But the reading formulae are also used in ordinary, everyday conversations among South Koreans to clarify for the listener which Chinese character is meant—as, for example, in someone's personal name.

Chapter 6

1. In colloquial speech, however, inversions commonly occur. For instance, in example (1) the speaker might save the subject and add it at the end: *Swun.i lul salang-hanta. —Minho ka* (순이를 사랑한다. 민호가) '(He) loves Suni.—Minho (does)'. Sometimes such inversions are used stylistically, to add or shift emphasis, and sometimes they simply represent an afterthought, something the speaker decides should have been said in the original sentence. In either case, these inversions do not constitute a violation of the rule that the verb comes at the end. The verb still has sentence-final intonation, and the added element is separated from the rest of the sentence by a juncture or a slight pause.

2. Since the adverb *cal* can have either the meaning 'well' or 'often', another interpretation this sentence might have is 'Suni paints a lot'. In a sentence such as *Swun.i ka cal kanta* (순이가 잘 간다) 'Suni goes a lot', however, the meaning is clearly 'often', because the verb 'go' does not ordinarily allow an interpretation of skill. But in a sentence about painting, the context would be the determining factor.

3. In Korean, 수여동사. These are verbs that take both an indirect object and a direct object.

4. As the translation indicates, the sentence would more likely be written than spoken.

5. In other words, the negated copula becomes *ani ta*, with the vowel of the copula elided. As Martin (1992:316) points out, however, Korean grammarians usually treat *anita* as an unanalyzed stem, the "negative copula," and the morphopho-

nemics of the construction do not give a clear indication which treatment is to be preferred.

6. Cf. the end of section 6.4.1, above. The negative verb *moluta* 'not know' is believed by some to be etymologically derived from *mos alta*.

Chapter 7

1. Cf. Brown and Ford 1961. This tendency of Americans to use first names has become even more pronounced since Brown and Ford's work was published. Today the use of a first name is rapidly becoming a badge of anonymity instead of a signal of friendliness. A clerk or telephone operator who reveals only her first name is keeping the customer at arm's length.

2. This particular sociolinguistic rule is not found in the otherwise similar honorific system of Japanese, where it is perfectly normal for a person to address his old college professor as *Tanaka sensei* or the like, using surname plus title.

3. These days younger wives have taken to using the reflexive pronoun *caki* '(your)self' with their husbands; young husbands, for their part, tend to simply use the more intimate *ne*.

4. As is illustrated in example (8b), these plural pronouns can also take what appears to be a pleonastic plural suffix, *-tul: wuli-tul, cehuy-tul.* In native Korean usage, the suffix *-tul* is not so much a plural marker as an indication that the noun to which it is attached is part of a group or is together with others. For a discussion of how this suffix works in Korean, see 4.2.3. But *-tul* is also frequently used to represent the plurals of English, and as a result its use in that sense has become more and more common. (Cf. Martin 1992:829-30.)

5. To the best of our knowledge, there has never been a serious study of the speech-level distinctions reflected in Korean titles, partly because of the complexity, but also because grammarians have been preoccupied with the honorific distinctions reflected in verb morphology.

6. With *taythonglyeng*, the honorific suffix added is *-kakha,* but *-kakha* is somewhat different from *-nim* because it is used only in more complex constructions, such as *Taythonglyeng-kakha-kkeyse osipnita* 'The Honorable President (of the Republic of Korea)' (announcing his entrance).

7. It should be noted that in Korean it is impossible to call someone by his or her surname only. In one of the episodes of the old Mash television series, a "Korean" mother, reunited with her child, called out to him: "Kim"—as if Kim was the child's given name!

8. Cf. Martin 1964 and Martin 1992: 299ff.

9. This verb is etymologically a contraction of the negation of *phyen-ha-* 'be comfortable': *phyen-haci anh-* 'not be comfortable' > *phyenchanh-*. This contracted negative form then takes the obligatory *-(u)si-* to give *phyenchanh.usi-.*

10. This English terminology follows Martin 1992: 300ff. but with one exception: Instead of using Martin's term "intimate style," we will use the everyday Korean word *panmal* in our discussion. Since the style is not the lowest level of speech in

Korean, it can sometimes be a bit confusing to say that it is "intimate" when in fact the "plain" style signals greater familiarity. For example, when college students become closer friends, they move from this style of speaking, which actually signals a certain amount of reserve, to the more relaxed plain style. Calling the style *"panmal"* is a way of avoiding the connotations of the English word "intimate".

11. Kim Chugwan 1989.

12. This term is written with a Chinese character (寸) but appears to be a native Korean word. At the very least, the usage here is uniquely Korean.

13. The generational character is graphically structured so that this information is immediately recognizable. Built into the character for each succeeding generation is the name of one of the five elements (五行) of Chinese cosmogony: water, fire, wood, metal, and earth (水火木金土). For example, the generational character 鎭 incorporates 金 'metal'; 漢 contains the element 水 'water' (the left part, or radical, of the character); and the character 東 has in its middle the element 木 'wood'. In many of Korea's clans, each of these generational characters is selected generations in advance and recorded in the clan's genealogical records (族譜).

14. Brown and Ford 1961.

Chapter 8

1. Yi Kimun 1972a. This classic work on the history of the Korean language is the source for much of the information given in this chapter.

2. The character 珍 is not used here as a phonogram; instead, it is a *hun* gloss of the meaning.

3. Yi Kimun (1971:78).

4. Cf. Yi Kimun 1972a: 59–62. To Lee's first six, I have added the seventh, which is implied in Lee's work and which I (SRR) feel is ultimately the most important of all.

5. There was also a voiced velar fricative that has been reconstructed from orthographic conventions (cf. Yi Kimun 1972b: 15-27). A related phenomenon is the alternation of /l/ with /t/ in certain lexical items; this alternation suggests the existence of yet another, earlier distinction in the dental obstruents.

6. Most Korean scholars believe that, whatever their phonetic value, the consonants must have been distinct from *$*p$ and *$*s$ in Old Korean. There are simply too many contrasts between the consonant pairs in Middle Korean that cannot be explained by phonological conditioning. Details of this reasoning are cogently explained in Yi Kimun 1972a: (68–69); still other arguments for the earlier contrasts are given in Ramsey 1991. However, Martin (1996) has put forward extensive and well-argued reasons for believing that the Middle Korean voiced consonants developed entirely through consonant lenition. It is also true that no convincing evidence has ever been found for an initial voicing contrast. The main problem with the lenition hypothesis is that, there still remains an intractable core of medial contrasts that cannot easily be explained.

7. Perhaps the clearest exposition of this evidence can be found in Yi Kimun 1972b: 95-96. Though both phonograms appear to have been used to transcribe consonants that correspond to Middle Korean occurrences of /l/, the two were not interchangeable. For one thing, only one of the two, 尸, was used to transcribe the verbal suffix used as the prospective modifier -*l(q)* (given here in the Middle Korean form). In contrast, the other phonogram, 乙, was always used for the object marker -*(u)l*. Lee suggests that 尸 represented -*r, while 乙 represented -*l. Thus, *r and *l were distinct in Old Korean, Lee says. He explains that the two consonants probably fell together after the Old Korean stage through the addition of a phonological rule of "implosion." Through implosion, syllable-final *r was no longer articulated with a release, phonetically becoming [l]; the result was that *r and *l fell together as /l/.

An obvious difficulty with this reconstruction, and something scholars continue to puzzle over, is that the (Middle) Chinese reading of the character 尸 is *si; no hint of an *r or a liquid of any other kind can be found in the reading. Lee is well aware of the problem (cf. Yi Kimun 1972a:63) but reconstructs *r anyway because of structural considerations.

There is in any case internal evidence within Middle Korean for an earlier distinction in the Korean liquids; cf. Ramsey 1996.

8. For a description of these recent events, see the introductory essay by Nam P'unghyŏn in the inaugural volume of *Kugyŏl yŏn'gu* (1996).

9. From this point on in our discussion, unless otherwise specified, the term "Middle Korean" should be taken as shorthand for "Late Middle Korean."

10. The best English-language description of these works can be found in Ledyard 1966: 261-330.

11. However, since the text was published with both a Korean and a Chinese version of the verses, there is a question as to which was composed first. Some philologists believe that Sejong conceived of the Chinese verses first and that the Korean verses represent later translations.

12. This compound is clearly derived from *i-* combined with *ssal*, but the meaning and etymology of *i* are obscure. Two things should be noted about this form. First, it is pronounced with a long vowel. Second, the form also appears in other compounds, such as *i-pap* 'plain white rice' and *i-phul* 'rice glue'. It is possible that *i* was once another word for 'white rice', but if so, it is not attested as such in earlier texts.

13. It is called 가벼운ㅂ (the "light *p*") by Korean linguists.

14. Cf. Yi Kimun 1972b: 17-27 for a detailed description of the philological evidence. Also cf. Ramsey 1978: 37-44; Martin 1992: 54-56.

15. The loss of this distinction between -*s* and -*t* began somewhat later in the Middle Korean period, in the sixteenth century.

16. Some particles (such as *to*) and endings (such as -*ke*-) that began with a consonant were exempt from this rule.

17. The categories of the analysis are Chinese, at least in form, as can be seen from this description. Chinese tones may not have been quite the same as the pitch distinctions of Korean, but since those were the terms of phonological science in Sejong's day, he had no choice but to use them. Yet, within the confining framework

of these Chinese categories, he was still able to represent Korean in a way that did not distort the data. His thinking rose above the limitations of theory.

18. In romanizing these forms, I have transcribed high pitches in upper-case letters.

19. These translations were suggested to me by David McCann (personal communication).

20. Most of the illustrative examples given in this section come from three sources: An Pyŏnghŭi and Yi Kwangho 1990, Yi Kimun 1972a, and Martin 1992.

21. It is not altogether clear where the shape *ka* came from. The earliest record of its use comes from a letter written in 1572 (cf. An Pyŏnghŭi and Yi Kwangho, 1990:164), but the particle generally escaped notice until recorded by foreign missionaries at the end of the nineteenth century (cf. Martin 1992:594).

22. If that noun ending in a vowel was written with a Chinese character, however, *i* was simply transcribed separately, next to the character, as ㅣ: for example, 字ㅣ *(coy)* 'character + SP'.

23. However, if the last syllable of the noun had a low tone, a trace of the particle would be left, because the low tone would change to a rising tone: *toli* (ㄷ리) 'bridge' + *i* → *to:li* (ㄷ:리).

24. The particle *oy/uy* is the Middle Korean form of the modern genitive particle *uy*; *-s* is the so-called "genetive *s*" or "medial *s*" *(sai-sios)*.

25. But see An and Yi 1990:177-78, where semantic criteria are proposed to describe the set of nouns used with *oy/uy*.

26. A curious development found in texts from around the same time is that *kwa* was also found after *-y*; e.g., *eskey kwa* (엇게과) 'shoulders and'. This pattern was also found later, in some texts from the Modern Korean period, but as time went on it gradually disappeared in favor of *-y wa*. (Cf. Yi Kimun 1972a:156.)

27. The morpheme clearly carries a volitional meaning in many of its occurrences, but in other cases its function is far from obvious. The interpretation of the morpheme as a marker of volition is the most widely accepted theory in Korea, but see Martin 1992:269-73 for other ideas about this very complex morpheme.

28. The morpheme *-si-* also had distinctive accentual, or tonal, characteristics, however; cf. Ramsey 1978:232.

29. From these mophophonemic alternations, it can be seen that the underlying shape was *-zoβ-*. The initial *c* (ㅈ) transcribed after dental stops and affricates is additional evidence that Middle Korean /c/ was phonetically [ts]; thus, what was transcribed, for example, as *tc*, as in *et.coβonywo* (얻ᄌᄫᅭ) must have phonetically been [tts].

30. The various forms of this morpheme were conditioned by morphemes with which it occurred (cf. An and Yi 1990:227).

31. Cf. Lee Ki-baik 1984:244.

32. Reinforced pronunciations are still growing this way today: reinforced *kkochwu* 'chili pepper' is displacing plain *kochwu*, probably because it feels spicier; *ccokkum* 'a little' is a tinier amount than *cokum; kkamta* 'wash' is more forceful and serious cleaning than *kamta;* and *sseyta* 'be strong' certainly has a stronger feel about it than *seyta* does.

33. In the nineteenth century, after the process of palatalization was complete, the vocalic sequence *-uy* changed to *-i* after *t*, *th*, and *tt*, producing new, unpalatalized occurrences of *ti*, *thi*, and *tti*; for example: *kyentuy-* (견듸-) 'endure' > *kyenti-*; *stuy* (쯰) 'belt' >*sti* (/tti/).

34. Since the written symbols remained the same, these changes are difficult to document. However, linguists believe evidence for the changes in pronunciation can be found in transcriptional changes such as 머기- 'feed' > 메기-. The argument they use is that the vowel [ə] (ㅓ) in the first syllable could only have changed to " ㅔ " if " ㅔ " was by this time pronounced [e]. In other words, the first-syllable vowel must have been pronounced farther front in the mouth in anticipation of the front vowel *i* in the second syllable. This kind of phonological change, called *umlaut*, is one that is common in Korean, especially in certain nonstandard dialects.

Chapter 9

1. In this chapter, our use of the word "dialect" refers only to regional variation. Omitted from discussion are what are sometimes called "social dialects"—that is, linguistic differences between social groups, including those related to age, gender, profession, social class, and the like.

2. 京城語를 표준으로 함.

3. 표준말은 대체로 현재 중류사회에서 쓰는 서울말로 한다.

4. 표준어는 교양 있는 사람들이 두루 쓰는 현대 서울말로 정함을 원칙으로 한 다.

5. Vowel length in the standard language preserves the length of Middle Korean syllables marked with rising tone—but only if the syllable occurs at the beginning of the word.

6. There is evidence that some residual pitch distinctions have also been preserved in parts of South Chŏlla. At the very least, the boundary between the tonal dialects of the southeast and the nontonal dialects of the southwest is unlikely to be a sharp one coinciding perfectly with the South Kyŏngsang provincial border.

7. Some of the southernmost dialects of South Kyŏngsang, however, have three pitch levels: high, mid, and low. (Cf. Martin 1992:60.) In these dialects, the low pitch corresponds to the long, rising tone (上聲) of Middle Korean, while the mid pitch is the low pitch of North Kyŏngsang dialects.

8. In part because of this fact, distinctive pitch in Korean has also been called "pitch accent" (cf. Martin 1992:60ff: Ramsey 1978:66 ff).

9. These phonetic and structural differences can be shown to have arisen historically in a fairly simple and straightforward way; cf. Ramsey 1974.

10. That is, there is no vowel length corresponding to Middle Korean rising tone. In Hamgyŏng, for example, where rising tone syllables are distinctively short, long syllables nevertheless exist, and, unlike long syllables in the standard language, they are not restricted to initial position. For example, in the Pukch'ŏng dialect of South Hamgyŏng, 'ant' is [kɛ:mi]; 'winter' is [cɔ:l]; 'lizard' is [tomabɛ:mi]; and 'it's light,' is [kabɛ:basə]. (Cf. Ramsey 1978:121-22.)

11. In Professor Lee's original Hangŭl transcriptions, a superscripted dot was used to indicate a high pitch. In romanizing the forms, I have assumed that, unless explicitly marked as high pitch, long syllables are phonetically low in pitch. These values need to be checked. [SRR]

12. The vocabulary items given as examples in (3) are all Sino-Korean. As far as is known, the liquid /l/ has never occurred initially in native words.

13. This glottal constriction is not found everywhere in Hamgyŏng, however. In some dialects of South Hamgyŏng the only trace of the consonant is the nasalization found on the preceding vowel; cf. Ramsey 1978:52-53.

14. The reflex of this word in the standard language, *sanyang hata* (사냥하다), means 'hunt'.

BIBLIOGRAPHY

An Pyŏnghŭi (Ahn Pyong-Hi). 1977. *Chungse kugŏ kugyŏl ŭi yŏn'gu* (A study of *kugyŏl* in Middle Korean). Seoul: Ilchi-sa.

———. 1992. *Kugŏ-sa yŏn'gu* (A study of the history of the Korean language). Seoul: Munhakkwa Chisŏng-sa.

———. 1997. "The Principles Underlying the Invention of the Korean Alphabet," in Kim-Renaud 1997.

An Pyŏnghŭi and Yi Kwangho. 1990. *Chungse kugŏ munpŏp-non* (The grammar of Middle Korean). Seoul: Hagyŏn-sa.

Austerlitz, et al. 1980. "Report of the workshop conference on Korean Romanization," Korean Studies 4.

Brown, R. and M. Ford. 1961. "Address in American English." *Journal of Abnormal and Social Psychology* 62.

Brown, R. and A. Gilman. 1960. "The Pronouns of Power and Solidarity," in T. A. Sebeok, ed. *Style in Language*. Cambridge, MA: The MIT Press.

Bryson, Bill. 1990. *The Mother Tongue: English & How It Got That Way*. New York: Avon.

Ch'ae Wan. 1976. "Chosa '-nŭn' ŭi ŭimi" (The meaning of the particle -*nŭn*). Kugŏhak 4.

———. 1977. "Hyŏndae kugŏ t'ŭksu chosa ŭi yŏn'gu" (A study of special particles in Contemporary Korean). *Kugŏ Yŏn'gu* 39.

———. 1983. "Kugŏ susa mit suryangsa-gu ŭi yuhyŏng-jŏk koch'al" (A typological investigation of numbers and quantifiers in Korean). Ŏhak Yŏn'gu 19.1.

———. 1986. *Kugŏ ŏsun ŭi yŏn'gu* (A study of word order in Korean). Seoul: T'ap Ch'ulp'an-sa.

———. 1990. "Kugŏ ŏsun ŭi kinŭng-jŏk koch'al" (A functional investigation of word order in Korean). *Tongdae Nonch'ong* 20. Tongdŏk Women's University.

Chambers, J. K. and P. Trudgill. 1980. *Dialectology*. Cambridge: Cambridge University Press.

Chang Kyŏnghŭi. 1985. *Hyŏndae kugŏ ŭi yangt'ae pŏmju yŏn'gu* (A study of modal categories in Contemporary Korean). Seoul: T'ap Ch'ulp'an-sa.

Chang Sŏkchin. 1993. *Chŏngbo kiban Han'gugŏ munpŏp* (Information based Korean grammar). Seoul: Hansin Munhwa-sa.

Chao, Y. R. 1968. *Language and Symbolic Systems*. Cambridge: Cambridge University Press.

Cho Chunhak. 1982. "A Study of Korean Pragmatics—Deixis and Politeness." University of Hawaii dissertation.

Ch'oe Hakkŭn. 1974. *Han'guk pangŏn sajŏn* (Korean dialect dictionary). Seoul: Hyŏnmun-sa.

Ch'oe Hyŏnbae. 1937. *Kŭlcha ŭi hyŏngmyŏng* (A writing revolution). Korean Ministry of Education.

———. 1946 (revised), 1959. *Uri mal pon* (The grammar of our language). Seoul: Chŏngŭm-sa.

Ch'oe Myŏngok. 1980. *Kyŏngbuk Tonghae-an pangŏn yŏn'gu* (A study of the North Kyŏngsang dialects along the shore of the Eastern Sea). Taegu: Yŏngnam-dae Minjok Munhwa Yŏn'gu-so.

Chomsky, Noam, and Morris Halle. 1968. *The Sound Pattern of English*. Cambridge, MA: MIT Press.

Comrie, Bernard. 1991. *The World's Major Languages*. Oxford: Oxford University Press.

Coulmas, Florian. 1989. *The Writing Systems of the World*. Oxford: Blackwell.

Crystal, D. 1987. *The Cambridge Encyclopedia of Language*. Cambridge: Cambridge University Press.

———. 1992. *Dictionary of Language and Languages*. London: Penguin Books.

Daniels, Peter T., and William Bright. 1996. *The World's Writing Systems*. Oxford: Oxford University Press.

DeFrancis, John. 1989. *Visible Speech: The Diverse Oneness of Writing Systems*. Honolulu: University of Hawaii Press.

Dredge, C. Paul. 1977. "Speech Variation and Social Organization in a Korean Village." Harvard University dissertation.

Gelb, I. J. 1963. *A Study of Writing*, 2nd ed. Chicago: University of Chicago Press.

Gerdts, D. 1985. "Surface Case and Grammatical Relations in Korean." *Harvard Studies in Korean Linguistics* 1.

Greenberg, J. H. 1963. "Some Universals of Grammar with Particular Reference to the Order of Meaningful Elements," in J. H. Greenberg, ed. *Universals of Language*. Cambridge, MA: The MIT Press.

Han'guk Chŏngsin Munhwa Yŏn'gu-wŏn. 1986-1994. *Han'guk pangŏn charyo-jip* (A collection of Korean dialect data).

Henderson, Leslie. 1982. *Orthography and Word Recognition in Reading*. London: Academic Press.

Hong Chaesŏng. 1987. *Hyŏndae Han'gugŏ tongsa kumun ŭi yŏn'gu* (A study of verbals in Contemporary Korean). Seoul: T'ap Ch'ulp'an-sa.

Hong Saman. 1983. *Kugŏ t'ŭksu chosa-ron* (A study of special particles in Korean). Seoul: Hangmun-sa.

Hong Yunp'yo. 1978. "Panghyang-sŏng p'yosi ŭi kyŏk" (Cases for marking directionality). *Kugŏhak* 6.

Hŏ Ung (Huh Woong). 1963. *Chungse kugŏ yŏn'gu* (A study of Middle Korean). Seoul: Chŏngŭm-sa.

———. 1965. *Kugŏ ŭmun-hak* (Korean phonology). Seoul: Chŏngŭm-sa.

———. 1975. *Uri yet mal pon* (A historical grammar of our language). Saem Munhwa-sa.

Howell, R.W. 1967. "Linguistic Choice as an Index to Social Change." University of California, Berkeley, dissertation.

Hwang Chŏngnyun. 1975. "Role of Sociolinguistics in Foreign Language Education with Reference to Korean and English Terms of Address and Level of Deference." University of Texas dissertation.

Hwang Taehwa. 1986. *Tonghae-an pangŏn yŏn'gu* (A study of dialects along the coast of the Eastern Sea). P'yŏngyang: Kim Ilsong University Press.

Hyŏn P'yŏnghyo. 1962. *Cheju-do pangŏn yŏn'gu, Charyo-p'yŏn* (A study of the Cheju dialect, Data volume). Seoul: Chŏngyŏn-sa (reprinted 1985, T'aehak-sa).

———. 1985. *Cheju-do pangŏn yŏn'gu, Non'go-p'yŏn* (A study of the Cheju dialect, Essay volume). Seoul: Iu Ch'ulp'an-sa.

Im Hongbin. 1987. "Kugŏ pujŏngmun ŭi t'ongsa wa ŭimi" (The syntax and meaning of Korean negatives). *Kugŏ Saenghwal* 10.

Iverson, Greg. 1982. "Korean *s.*" *Journal of Phonetics* 11.

Jones, Daniel. 1957. *An Outline of English Phonetics*. Cambridge: Heffer and Sons.

Kang Sinhang. 1985. "Kŭndae-hwa ihu ŭi oerae-ŏ yuip yangsang" (The influx of loanwords after modernization). *Kugŏ saenghwal* 2.

———. 1987. *Hunmin chŏngŭm yŏn'gu* (A study of the *Hunmin chŏngŭm*). Seoul: Sŏnggyun'gwan University Press.

———. 1991. *Hyŏndae kugŏ ŏhwi sayong ŭi yangsang* (Vocabulary usage in Contemporary Korean). Seoul: T'aehak-sa.

Kim Ch'angsŏp. 1981. "Hyŏndae kugŏ ŭi pokhap tongsa yŏn'gu" (A study of compound verbs in Contemporary Korean). *Kugŏ Yŏn'gu* 47.

———. 1996. *Kugŏ ŭi tanŏ hyŏngsŏng kwa tanŏ kujo yŏn'gu* (A study of the formation of words and the structure of words in Korean). Seoul: T'aehak-sa.

Kim Chinu. 1985. *Ŏnŏ* (Language). Seoul.

Kim Chin-W. (see Kim Chinu). 1965. "On the Autonomy of the Tensity Feature in Stop Classification." *Word* 21.

———. 1968. "The Vowel System of Korean." *Language* 44.

———. 1970. "A Theory of Aspiration." *Phonetica* 21.

Kim Chugwan. 1989. "Chondaemmal sayong ŭi isang-jŏk kyubŏm kwa silche-jŏk pyŏnisang" (The ideal model and actual variation in the usage of honorific language). Seoul National University Anthropology Department M.A. thesis.

Kim Ch'unghoe. 1992. *Ch'ungch'ŏng pukto ŭi ŏnŏ chiri-hak* (The linguistic geography of North Ch'ungch'ŏng Province). Inchŏn: Inha University Press.

Kim Han-Gon. 1975. "Conditions on Coordination and Structure Constraint." *Language Research* 11.2.

Kim Hyŏnggyu. 1974. *Han'guk pangŏn yŏn'gu* (A study of the Korean dialects). Seoul: Seoul University Press.

Kim Hyŏnok. 1985. "The Functions of Linear Order in Korean Syntax." *Harvard Studies in Korean Linguistics* 1.

Kim Ihyŏp. 1973. *P'yŏngbuk pangŏn sajŏn* (A dictionary of the North P'yŏngan dialect). Seoul: Han'guk Chŏngsin Munhwa Yŏn'gu-wŏn.

Kim Kwanghae. 1989. *Koyuŏ wa hanchaŏ ŭi taeŭng hyŏnsang* (The correspondences between native words and Sino-Korean words). Seoul: T'ap Ch'ulp'an-sa.

Kim Namgil. 1978. "*Tolok* Sentential Complements in Korean" in C. W. Kim, ed. *Papers in Korean Linguistics*. Hornbeam Press.

———. 1987. "Korean," in B. Comrie, ed., *The World's Major Languages*. Oxford: Oxford University Press.

Kim Pyŏngje. 1959, 1965, 1975. *Chosŏnŏ pangŏn-hak kaeyo* (A compendium of Korean dialectology), Volumes 1, 2, 3. P'yŏngyang: Sahoe kwahak-wŏn Ch'ulp'an-sa.

Kim-Renaud, Young-key (Kim Yŏnggi). 1974. "Korean Consonantal Phonology." University of Hawaii dissertation.

———, ed. 1997. *The Korean Alphabet: Its History and Structure.* Honolulu: University of Hawaii Press.

Kim Tongsik. 1981. "Pujŏng anin pujŏng" (Negatives that are not negatives). *Ŏnŏ* 6.2.

Kim Wanjin. 1970. "Irŭn sigi e issŏsŏ ŭi Han, Chung ŏnŏ chŏpch'ok ŭi ilban e tae hayŏ" (On a portion of the linguistic contact between Korea and China in early times). *Ŏhak yŏn'gu* 6.1.

———. 1980. *Hyangga haedok-pŏp yŏn'gu* (A study in the decipherment of Hyangga). Seoul: Seoul National University Press.

Kim Yŏngbae. 1992. *Nam-Puk Han ŭi pangŏn yŏn'gu* (A study of the dialects of North and South Korea). Seoul: Kyŏngun Ch'ulp'an-sa.

Kim Yŏnghwang. 1982. *Chosŏnŏ pangŏn-hak* (Korean dialectology). P'yŏngyang: Kim Ilsŏng University Press.

Kim Yŏngsŏk and Yi Sangŏk (Lee Sang Oak). 1992. *Hyŏndae hyŏngt'ae-ron* (Present-day morphology). Seoul: Hagyŏn-sa.

King, Ross. 1991. "Russian Sources on Korean Dialects," Harvard University dissertation.

———. 1996. "Korean Writing," in Daniels and Bright 1996, pp. 218–227.

Kōno Rokurō. 1945. *Chōsen hōgengaku shikō: 'Hasami' gokō* (A study in Korean dialectology: A study of the word for 'scissors'). Keijō (Seoul): Tōto Shoseki.

Korean National Academy of Sciences. 1993. *Han'guk ŏnŏ chido* (A linguistic atlas of Korea). Seoul: Sŏngji Munhwa-sa.

Ku Chasuk. 1995. "Politeness Theory: Universality and Specificity." Harvard University dissertation.

Kugŏ Yŏn'gu-hoe (*see* National Language Research Society).

Kungnip Kugŏ Yŏn'gu-wŏn (*see* National Language Research Institute).

Kuno, Susumu, and Young-Key Kim-Renaud (Kim Yŏnggi). 1987. "The Position of Quantifier-like Particles in Korean," *Harvard Studies in Korean Linguistics* 2.

Kwak Ch'unggu. 1991. "Hamgyŏng pukto Yukchin pangŏn ŭi ŭmun-non" (The phonology of the Yukchin dialect of North Hamgyŏng Province). Seoul National University dissertation.

Kwŏn Chaeil. 1992. *Han'gugŏ t'ongsa-ron* (Korean syntax). Seoul: Minŭm-sa.

Ledyard, Gari. 1966. "The Korean Language Reform of 1446: The Origin, Background, and Early History of the Korean Alphabet." University of California, Berkeley, dissertation.

———. 1997. "The International Linguistic Background of the Correct Sounds for the Instruction of the People," in Kim-Renaud 1997.

Lee Chung Min (Yi Chŏngmin). 1974. "Abstract Syntax of Korean with Reference to English." Indiana University dissertation.

———. 1977. "Pujŏng myŏngnyŏng ŭi punsŏk" (An analysis of negative imperatives). *Ŏhak Yŏn'gu* 13.2.

Lee Iksop (*see* Yi Iksŏp)

Lee Ki-baik (*see* Yi Kibaek). 1984. *A New History of Korea.* Cambridge, MA: Harvard University Press.

Lee Ki-Moon (*see* Yi Kimun)

Lee Maeng-Sung (Yi Maengsŏng). 1973. "Variation of Speech Levels and Interpersonal Social Relationships in Korean," in *Yi Chongsu paksa songsu kinyŏm non-mun-jip.* Seoul: Samhwa Ch'ulp'an-sa.

Lee Sang Oak (Yi Sangŏk). 1978. "Middle Korean Tonology." University of Illinois at Urbana dissertation.

———. 1986. "An Explanation of Syllable Structure Change in Korean." *Studies in the Linguistic Sciences* 16.2.

———. 1990. "Hyŏndae kugŏ ŭm-byŏnhwa kyuch'ik ŭi kinŭng pudam-nyang" (The functional load of sound change rules in Contemporary Korean). *Ŏhak Yŏn'gu* 26.3.

———. 1994. *Kugŏ p'yogi 4 pŏp nonŭi* (A discussion of Rule 4 of Korean orthography). Seoul: Seoul National University Press.

Lewin, Bruno. 1973. "Japanese and the Language of Koguryŏ," *Papers of the C.I.C. Far Eastern Language Institute* 4.

Lukoff, Fred. 1967. "Linguistics in the Republic of Korea," in Thomas A. Sebeok, ed., *Current Trends in Linguistics.* The Hague: Mouton.

Maling, J. and S. W. Kim. 1990. "The Inalienable Possession Construction and Case in Korean," *Papers from the Sixth International Conference on Korean Linguistics.* Toronto: University of Toronto Press.

Martin, Samuel E. 1954. *Korean Morphophonemics.* Baltimore: Linguistic Society of America.

———. 1964. "Speech Levels and Social Structure in Japanese and Korean," in Dell Hymes, ed., *Language in Culture and Society.* New York: Harper and Row.

———. 1992. *A Reference Grammar of Korean.* Tokyo: Tuttle.

———. 1996. *Consonant lenition in Korean and the Macro-Altaic question.* Center for Korean Studies Monograph 19. Honolulu: University of Hawaii Press.

Martin, Samuel E., Y. H. Lee, and S. U. Chang. *A Korean-English Dictionary.* New Haven: Yale University Press.

McCann, David R. 1997. "The Story of Ch'ŏyong." *Korean Studies* 21.

Miller, Roy Andrew. 1967. *The Japanese Language.* Chicago: Chicago University Press.

Morgan, J. 1988. "Some Grammatical Properties of -*ssik,*" *Papers from the Sixth International Conference on Korean Linguistics.* Toronto: University of Toronto Press.

Nam Kisim (Nam Ki Shim). 1978. *Kugŏ munpŏp ŭi sije munje e kwan-han yŏn'gu* (A study of the problems of tense in Korean grammar). Seoul: T'ap Ch'ulp'an-sa.

———. 1985. "Chuŏ wa chujeŏ " (Subject and topic). *Kugŏ saenghwal* 3.

Nam Kisim (Nam Ki Shim) and Ko Yŏnggŭn. 1985. *P'yojun kugŏ munpŏm-non* (A standard grammar of Korean). Seoul: T'ap Ch'ulp'an-sa.

Nam Mihye. 1988. "Kugŏ ŏsun yŏn'gu" (A study of word order in Korean). *Kugŏ Yŏn'gu* 86.

Nam P'unghyŏn. 1981. *Ch'aja p'yogi-pŏp yŏn'gu* (A study of the methods of transcription with borrowed characters). Seoul: Tan'guk University Press.

———. 1985. "Kugŏ sok ŭi ch'ayong—kodae kugŏ esŏ kŭndae kugŏ kkaji" (Loan-words in Korean—from Old Korean to Modern Korean). *Kugŏ Saenghwal* 2.

———. 1996. "Kugyŏl yŏn'gu ŭi ch'anggan e puch'ŏ" (Remarks on the inaugural volume of Kugyŏl yŏn'gu). *Kugyŏl yŏn'gu* 1.

National Language Research Institute (Kungnip Kugŏ Yŏn'gu-wŏn). 1991. *Uri mal ŭi yejŏl* (The polite forms of Korean). Seoul: Chosŏn Ilbo-sa.

National Language Research Society (Kugŏ Yŏn'gu-hoe). 1990. *Kugŏ yŏn'gu ŏdi kkaji wanna* (How far has research on Korean come?). Seoul: Tonga Ch'ulp'an-sa.

No Myŏnghŭi. 1990. "Hancha-ŏ ŭi ŏhwi hyŏngt'aeron-jŏk t'ŭksŏng e kwan-han yŏn'gu" (A study of the lexico-morphological characteristics of Sino-Korean). *Kugŏ Yŏn'gu* 95.

O'Grady, William. 1987. "Grammatical Relations and Korean Syntax," in *Linguistics in the Land of the Morning Calm II*. Hanshin Publishing Co.

Ogura Shinpei. 1940. *The Outline of Korean Dialects*. Tokyo: Tōyō Bunko.

———. 1944. *Chōsen hōgen no kenkyū* (A study of the Korean dialects). Tokyo: Iwa-nami Bunko.

Paik Ungjin (Paek Ŭngjin). 1986. "The Pause in Middle Korean." *Harvard Studies in Korean Linguistics* 2.

Pak Yanggyu. 1978. "Sadong kwa pidong" (Causative and passive). *Kugŏhak* 7.

Park Young-Soon (Pak Yŏngsun). 1978. "Aspect in the Development of Communicative Competence with Reference to the Korean Deference System." University of Illinois dissertation.

Poppe, Nicholas. 1960. *Vergleichende Grammatik der Altaischen Sprachen I: Vergleichende Lautlehre*. Wiesbaden: Otto Harrassowitz.

———. 1965. *Introduction to Altaic Linguistics*. Wiesbaden: Otto Harrassowitz.

Ramsey, S. Robert. 1974. "Hamgyŏng kwa Kyŏngsang yang-pangŏn ŭi aeksent'ŭ yŏn'gu" (A study of the accent in the two dialects, Hamgyŏng and Kyŏngsang) *Kugŏhak* 2.

———. 1978. *Accent and Morphology in Korean Dialects*. Seoul: T'ap Ch'ulp'an-sa.

———. 1987. *The Languages of China*. Princeton: Princeton University Press.

———. 1991. "Proto-Korean and the Origin of Korean Accent," in *Studies in the Historical Phonology of Asian Languages*, Michael J. Shapiro and William J. Boltz, eds. Philadelphia: John Benjamins, 1991.

———. 1994. "Some Remarks on Reconstructing Earlier Korean," *Language Research* 29.4.

———. 1996. "Some Preliminaries to Reconstructing Liquids in Earlier Korean," in Sim Chaegi et al., ed., *Yi Kimun Kyosu chŏngnyŏn t'oeim kinyŏm nonch'ong* (Theses in honor of the retirement of Professor Lee Ki-Moon). Seoul: Sin'gu Munhwa-sa.

———. 1997. "The Invention of the Korean Alphabet and the History of the Korean Language," in Kim-Renaud 1997.

Ramstedt, G. J. 1928. "Remarks on the Korean Language," *Mémoires de la société finno-ougrienne* 58.

———. 1939. "Über die Stellung des Koreanischen," *Journal de la société finno-ougrienne* 55.

———. 1949. *Studies in Korean Etymology*. Helsinki: Suomalais-Ugrilainen Seura.

———. 1952. *Einführung in die altaische Sprachwissenschaft II, Formenlehre*. Helsinki: Suomalais-Ugrilainen Seura.

———. 1957. *Einführung in die altaiche Sprachwissenschaft I, Lautlehre*. Suomalais-Ugrilainen Seura.

Ruhlen, M. 1987. *A Guide to the World's Languages 1*. Stanford: Stanford University Press.

Sampson, Geoffrey. 1985. *Writing Systems: A Linguistic Introduction*. Stanford: Stanford University Press.

Sanders, G. A. 1977. "A Functional Typology of Elliptical Coordination," in F. R. Eckman, ed., *Current Themes in Linguistics*. Washington: Hemisphere Publishing Corporation.

Sells, P. 1991. "Complex Verbs and Argument Structures in Korean," *Harvard Studies in Korean Linguistics 4*.

Shibatani, Matsuyoshi. 1990. *The Languages of Japan*. Cambridge: Cambridge University Press.

Sim Chaegi. 1982. *Kugŏ ŏhwi-ron* (A study of the Korean lexicon). Seoul: Chinmundang.

———. 1987. "Hancha-ŏ ŭi kujo wa kŭ choŏryŏk" (The structure of Sino-Korean and its morphological productivity). *Kugŏ Saenghwal 8*.

Sin Sŏngok. 1992. "Speaker-oriented and Event-oriented Causals." *Korean Linguistics 7*.

Sŏ Chaegŭk. 1970. "Kaehwagi oeraeŏ wa sinyongŏ" (Loanwords and new words in the enlightenment period). *Tongsŏ Munhwa 4* (Kaemyŏngdae Tongsŏ Munhwa Yŏn'gu-so).

Sŏ Chŏngsu (Suh Cheong-Soo). 1984. Chondae-pŏp ŭi yŏn'gu (A study of the honorific system). Seoul: Hansin Munhwa-sa.

———. 1990. *Kugŏ munpŏp ŭi yŏn'gu* (A study of Korean grammar), Volumes I and II. Seoul: Han'guk munhwa-sa.

———. 1991. *Hyŏndae Hangugŏ munpŏp yŏn'gu ŭi kaegwan* (A survey of the study of Contemporary Korean grammar), Volume I. Seoul: Han'guk munhwa-sa.

———. 1994. *Kugŏ munpŏp* (Korean grammar). Seoul: Ppuri Kip'un Namu.

Sohn Chong Young (Son Chongyŏng). 1973. "A Study of Grammatical Case of Korean, Japanese, and Other Major Altaic Languages." Indiana University dissertation.

Sohn Ho-min (Son Homin). 1978. "Kin hyŏng kwa tchalbun hyŏng" (The long form and the short form). *Ŏhak Yŏn'gu 14.2*.

———. 1983. "Power and Solidarity in Korean Language." *Korean Linguistics 3*.

———. 1994. *Korean*. London: Routledge.

Song Ch'ŏrŭi. 1992. *Kugŏ ŭi p'asaengŏ hyŏngsŏng yŏn'gu* (A study of derived forms in Korean). Seoul: T'aehak-sa.

Sŏng Kich'ŏl. 1985. *Hyŏndae kugŏ taeu-pŏp yŏn'gu* (A study of the honorific system of Contemporary Korean). Seoul: Kaemun-sa.

Song Seok-Choong (Song Sŏkchung). 1967. "Some Transformational Rules in Korean." Indiana University dissertation.

————. 1978. "Sadong-mun ŭi tu hyŏngsik" (Two forms of the causative). *Ŏnŏ* 3.2.

————. 1981. "Hanguk mal ŭi pujŏng ŭi pŏmwi" (The scope of negation in Korean). *Han'gŭl* 173.

Taehan Min'guk Haksul-wŏn (*see* Korean National Academy of Sciences).

Taylor, I. 1980. "The Korean Writing System: An Alphabet? A Syllabary? A Logography?" in P. A. Kolers, M. E. Wrolsted, and H. Boyma, eds., *Processing of Visible Language 2*. New York: Plenum Press.

Vachek, J. 1945-49. "Some Remarks on Writing and Phonetic Transcription," *Acta Linguistica* 5.

————. 1973. *Written Language: General Problems and Problems of English*. The Hague: Mouton.

————. 1976. *Selected Writings in English and General Linguistics*. The Hague: Mouton.

Wang Hansŏk. 1984. "Honorific Speech Behavior in a Rural Korean Village—Structure and Use." University of California at Los Angeles dissertation.

Whitman, John. 1984. "Korean Clusters," *Harvard Studies in Korean Linguistics* 1.

Yi Chiyang. 1993. "Kugŏ ŭi yunghap hyŏnsang kwa yunghap hyŏngsik" (Korean fusion phenomena and fusion forms). Seoul National University dissertation.

Yi Chŏngno. 1986. *Topics in Korean Syntax with Notes to Japanese*. Yonsei University Press.

Yi Hŭisŭng. 1955. *Kugŏ-hak kaesŏl* (An introduction to Korean linguistic studies). Seoul: Minjung Sŏgwan.

Yi Hŭisŭng and An Pyŏnghŭi. 1989. *Han'gŭl matchum-pŏp kangŭi* (Lectures on Korean orthography). Seoul: Sin'gu Munhwa-sa.

Yi Iksŏp (Lee Iksop). 1968. "Hanchaŏ choŏ-pŏp ŭi yuhyŏng" (Types of word formation in Sino-Korean). *Yi Sungnyŏng Paksa Songsu Kinyŏm Nonch'ong*. Seoul: Ŭryu Munhwa-sa.

————. 1981. *Yŏngdong Yŏngsŏ ŭi ŏnŏ punhwa* (The linguistic divergence between the Yŏngdong and Yŏngsŏ areas of Kangwŏn Province). Seoul: Seoul National University Press.

————. 1982. "Hyŏndae kugŏ ŭi panbok pokhabŏ ŭi yŏn'gu" (A study of reduplicated compounds in Contemporary Korean), *Chŏng Pyŏnguk Sŏnsaeng Hwan'gap Kinyŏm Nonch'ong*. Seoul: Sin'gu Munhwa-sa.

————. 1984. *Pangŏn-hak* (Dialectology). Seoul: Minŭm-sa.

————. 1986. *Kugŏ-hak kaesŏl* (An introduction to Korean linguistic studies). Hagyŏn-sa.

————. 1992. *Kugŏ p'yogi-pŏp yŏn'gu* (A study of Korean orthography). Seoul: Seoul National University Press.

————. 1994. *Sahoe ŏnŏ -hak* (Sociolinguistics). Seoul: Minŭm-sa.

Yi Iksŏp (Lee Iksop) and Im Hongbin. 1983. *Kugŏ munpŏm-non* (Korean grammar). Seoul: Hagyŏn-sa.

Yi Kibaek. 1967. *Han'guksa sillon* (A new history of Korea), Revised edition. Seoul: Ilcho-gak.

Yi Kigap. 1986. *Chŏlla Namdo ŭi ŏnŏ chiri* (The linguistic geography of South Chŏlla Province). Seoul: T'ap Ch'ulp'an-sa.

Yi Kimun (Lee Ki-Moon). 1963a. "A Genetic View of Japanese." *Chōsen Gakuhō* 27.

———. 1963b. *Kugŏ p'yogi-pŏp ŭi yŏksa-jŏk yŏn'gu* (A historical study of Korean orthography). Seoul: Han'guk Yŏn'gu-wŏn.

———. 1971. "Hangugŏ hyŏngsŏng sa" (The history of the formation of Korean), in *Hanguk munhwa sa taegye* V, Koryŏ Taehakkyo Minjok Munhwa Yŏn'gu-so.

———. 1972a. *Kugŏ-sa kaesŏl* (An introduction to the history of Korean), Revised edition. Seoul: Minjung Sŏgwan.

———. 1972b. *Kugŏ ŭmun-sa yŏn'gu* (A study of the phonological history of Korean). Seoul: Han'guk Munhwa Yŏn'gu-so.

———. 1991a. *Kugŏ ŏhwi-sa yŏn'gu* (A study of Korean lexical history). Seoul: Tonga Ch'ulp'an-sa.

———. 1991b. "Mongolian loan-words in Korean," *Alt'ai hakpo* 3.

———. 1997. "The Inventor of the Korean Alphabet," in Kim-Renaud 1997.

Yi Kimun (Lee Ki-Moon), Kim Chinu (Kim Chin-W.), and Yi Sangŏk (Lee Sang Oak). 1984. *Kugŏ ŭmun-non* (Korean phonology). Seoul: Hagyŏn-sa.

Yi Kwangho. 1988. *Kugŏ kyŏk-chosa 'ŭl/rŭl' ŭi yŏn'gu* (A study of the case particle *ŭl/ rŭl*). Seoul: T'ap Ch'ulp'an-sa.

Yi Namsun. 1988. *Kugŏ ŭi pujŏng-kyŏk kwa kyŏk-p'yoji saengnyak* (Indefinite reference in Korean and the deletion of case particles). Seoul: T'ap Ch'ulp'an-sa.

Yi P'iryŏng. 1993. *Kugŏ ŭi inyong kumun yŏn'gu* (A study of quotations in Korean). Seoul: T'ap Ch'ulp'an-sa.

Yi Pyŏnggŏn. 1979. *Ŭmun hyŏnsang e issŏsŏ ŭi cheyak* (Constraints on phonological phenomena). Seoul: T'ap Ch'ulp'an-sa.

Yi Sŏkchu. 1989. *Kugŏ hyŏngt'ae-ron* (Korean morphology). Seoul: Hansaem.

Yi Sungnyŏng (Lee Sung Nyong). 1957. "Cheju-do pangŏn ŭi hyŏngt'aeron-jŏk yŏn'gu" (A morphological study of the Cheju dialect). *Tongbang Hakchi* 3.

———. 1971. "Han'guk pangŏn-sa" (Korean dialect history). *Hanguk munhwa sa taegye* V, Koryŏ Taehakkyo Minjok Munhwa Yŏn'gu-so.

———. 1981. *Chungse kugŏ yŏn'gu* (A study of Middle Korean). Seoul: Ŭryu Munhwa-sa.

Yi Sŭngjae. 1992. *Koryŏ sidae ŭi idu* (*Idu* of the Koryŏ period). Seoul: T'aehak-sa.

Yi Tongjae (Lee Dong-Jae). 1988. "*l*-deletion Verbs in Korean." *Papers from the Sixth International conference on Korean Linguistics.* University of Toronto.

Yu Tongsŏk. 1981. "'*tŏ*' ŭi ŭimi e tae-han kwan'gyŏn" (A personal view regarding the meaning of '*tŏ*'). *Kwanak Ŏmun Yŏn'gu* 6.

Yu Yŏngmi. 1987. "Phrasal Phonology of Korean." *Harvard Studies in Korean Linguistics* II.

Yun Hyesŏk. 1987. "Some Queries Concerning the Syntax of Multiple Subject constructions in Korean." *Harvard Studies in Korean Linguistics* II.

INDEX